State, Faith, and Nation in Ottoman and Post-Ottoman Lands

Current standard narratives of Ottoman, Balkan, and Middle East history overemphasize the role of nationalism in the transformation of the region. Challenging these accounts, this book argues that religious affiliation was in fact the most influential shaper of communal identity in the Ottoman era, that religion molded the relationship between state and society, and that it continues to do so today in lands once occupied by the Ottomans. The book examines the major transformations of the past 250 years to illustrate this argument, traversing the nineteenth century, the early decades of post-Ottoman independence, and the recent past. In this way, the book affords unusual insights not only into the historical patterns of political development but also into the forces shaping contemporary crises, from the dissolution of Yugoslavia to the rise of political Islam.

Frederick F. Anscombe is a senior lecturer in contemporary history at Birkbeck, University of London. His publications include *The Ottoman Gulf: The Creation of Kuwait, Saudi Arabia, and Qatar* (1997); *The Ottoman Balkans, 1750–1830* (ed., 2006); and articles in *Past & Present*, *Journal of Modern History*, and *International History Review*.

State, Faith, and Nation in Ottoman and Post-Ottoman Lands

FREDERICK F. ANSCOMBE

University of London

CAMBRIDGE
UNIVERSITY PRESS

CAMBRIDGE
UNIVERSITY PRESS

32 Avenue of the Americas, New York NY 10013-2473, USA

Cambridge University Press is part of the University of Cambridge.

It furthers the University's mission by disseminating knowledge in the pursuit of education, learning, and research at the highest international levels of excellence.

www.cambridge.org
Information on this title: www.cambridge.org/9781107615236

First published 2014

Printed in the United States of America

A catalog record for this publication is available from the British Library.

Library of Congress Cataloging in Publication data
Anscombe, Frederick F.
State, faith, and nation in Ottoman and post-Ottoman lands / Frederick F. Anscombe.
pages   cm.
Includes bibliographical references and index.
ISBN 978-1-107-04216-2 (hardback) – ISBN 978-1-107-61523-6 (paperback)
1. Islam and state – Turkey – History.   2. Islam and state – Balkan Peninsula –
History.   3. Islam and state – Middle East – History.   4. Nationalism – Turkey –
Religious aspects – History.   5. Nationalism – Balkan Peninsula – Religious
aspects – History.   6. Nationalism – Middle East – Religious aspects –
History.   7. Turkey – History – Ottoman Empire, 1288–1918.   I. Title.
BP173.6.A575   2014
322'.10956–dc23   2013038166

ISBN 978-1-107-04216-2 Hardback
ISBN 978-1-107-61523-6 Paperback

For Márta, Lotti, Klára, and Frida
with love and thanks

Contents

Maps and Images

Acknowledgments

Various people and institutions have helped me on this and earlier, related projects. For funding the archival research that marked the starting point of the book, I thank the National Endowment for the Humanities, Washington, DC. Birkbeck, University of London, provided additional support, including travel funds for a conference in Montreal that clarified points in my views on the Selim III–Mahmud II era. For assistance enabling me to participate in two other conferences that proved similarly helpful, I thank Tolga Esmer of Central European University and Hakan Yavuz and Peter Sluglett of the University of Utah. Tolga and Joshua Landis kindly provided copies of their dissertations. For their help I am indebted also to the staffs of the Başbakanlık Archive in Istanbul, the National Archive in Kew, and Birkbeck Library.

I particularly wish to thank colleagues whose comments on some of my earlier work and whose perspectives on eighteenth- and nineteenth-century history have benefited me to an extent that they have probably never realized: Engin Akarlı, Virginia Aksan, Tolga Esmer, Benjamin Fortna, Colin Heywood, Michael Hickok, Mark Mazower, William Ochsenwald, Ayşe Ozil, Lucy Riall, Julian Swann, and Feroze Yasamee. Ayşe also provided helpful comments on much of the book manuscript, for which I am very grateful. Part of Chapter 3 first appeared in "Islam and the Age of Ottoman Reform," *Past & Present* 208 (Aug. 2010), 159–89, and parts of Chapters 2 and 3 first appeared in "The Balkan Revolutionary Age," *Journal of Modern History* 84 (2012), 572–606, and I thank the editors of both journals for permitting further use of the material. I wish that I could thank by name the anonymous reviewers of the articles and those commissioned by Cambridge to critique the book manuscript; I am very grateful for their suggestions for improvement.

Toward the end of my years in graduate school, I once marveled at the stack of correspondence in the hands of one of the scholars whose classes I had most enjoyed taking, the late Charles Issawi; with his usual good humor he complained that they were all letters demanding that he do something, and that he wished there were one saying simply that he was wonderful. I am still sorry that I never sent him such a note. This book presents my interpretation of Ottoman and post-Ottoman history, and I want to acknowledge with deepest thanks the debt I owe to those scholars who taught me (and thereby prepared me to think constructively) about the Ottoman empire and its effects upon successor countries: Carl Brown, Şükrü Hanioğlu, Halil İnalcık, Norman Itzkowitz, Cemal Kafadar, Heath Lowry, 'Abd al-Karim Rafiq – and yes, Charles Issawi. The experience of teaching, in turn, has had an enormous impact upon both my research interests and the views expressed in the book; I cannot acknowledge by name all of the students who have made teaching rewarding over the years, but I thank them for their interest, insights, and skepticism. By thanking scholars, students, and funders, I make no suggestion that any of them shares the views I present in the book; they have helped me, but all faults or errors are mine alone.

I wish to thank those at Cambridge University Press who have supported this project through the stages to publication: Marigold Acland, William Hammell, Sarika Narula, and Alison Daltroy. Their care has made the process enjoyable. I also thank Abidha Sulaiman and her team at Newgen Knowledge Works for their help with production of the book.

That Cambridge has published the book delights my mother, who is sure that my father would have been happy to see me somehow linked to the university at which he studied. To give such satisfaction is a slight token of thanks for all that they did to get me to this point. They, and the rest of my family in the United States, have my love and gratitude for all that they have done for me over the decades.

And the first shall be last: A gyönyörűségeim Márta, Lotti és Klára jól bírták a hangulatomat és a távollétemet, amíg írtam ezt a könyvet. Remélem, hogy a könyv megéri ezt az árat. To them I dedicate it.

Transliteration and Abbreviations

Transliteration of non-Latin-script terms follows Library of Congress conventions, subject to modest amendments, including use of English spellings that are widely recognized ("shaikh" rather than "shaykh"/"şeyh"). Diacriticals have been omitted from Arabic terms. Terms common to Arabic and Ottoman are problematic: for consistency they are given in Arabic form ("shari'a" rather than "şeriat," "milla" rather than "millet").

Abbreviations

BOA	Başbakanlık Osmanlı Arşivi, Istanbul
BriJMES	*British Journal of Middle Eastern Studies*
BSOAS	*Bulletin of the School of Oriental and African Studies*
Cev.Dah	Cevdet Dahiliye
CHT3	*Cambridge History of Turkey, volume 3: The Later Ottoman Empire, 1603–1839*, ed. Suraiya Faroqhi (Cambridge: Cambridge University Press, 2006)
CHT4	*Cambridge History of Turkey, volume 4: Turkey in the Modern World*, ed. Reşat Kasaba (Cambridge: Cambridge University Press, 2008)
EEQ	*East European Quarterly*
FO	Foreign Office
HH	Hatt-i Hümayun
IHR	*International History Review*
IJMES	*International Journal of Middle East Studies*
ILS	*Islamic Law and Society*

JMGS	*Journal of Modern Greek Studies*
JMH	*Journal of Modern History*
MES	*Middle Eastern Studies*
NA	National Archives, London
P&P	*Past & Present*
SH	*Scripta Hierolosymitana*

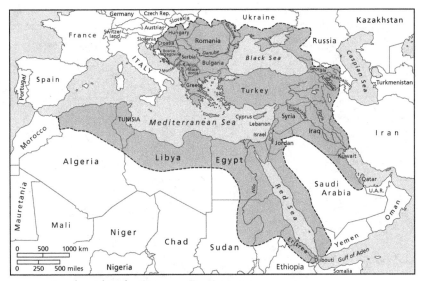

MAP 1. Lands within the Ottoman Empire

MAP 2. Lands Claimed for the Greek Nation (Early Twentieth Century)

MAP 3. Lands Claimed for the Serbian Nation (Early Twentieth Century)

MAP 4. Lands Claimed for the Bulgarian Nation (Early Twentieth Century)

MAP 5. Geographic Syria under British and French Mandates

Introduction

This book is about me. It may sound an alarming admission but is one that most authors could make, and I promise you that the book is no autobiography. It is about me in the sense that it reflects my personal and professional curiosity about the past and present of foreign lands, especially those of southeastern Europe and western Asia. Having lived in the Balkans, Turkey, and the Arab Middle East, I have been long fascinated by the politics of these areas. Much of that fascination has derived from the strength of feeling about ideas and identities that people with whom I had contact so clearly had: nationalism was always most evident, but other emotional attachments, from godless communism to God-fearing faith, were either more sporadically or more quietly shown. My basic reasons for being in those countries, however, were professional, and I should explain a little about my career in order to make my point of view easier to understand. I am a lecturer in contemporary history at Birkbeck, University of London. My teaching is weighted toward the post-1918 – and indeed contemporary – period, but my research interests lie in the history of the Ottoman empire (c. 1301–1922). Before coming to Birkbeck, I had some interesting years as a "Turkish nationalist" and sometime "agent working with the Turkish National Intelligence Service" (MIT).

Again, an alarming (and, I assure you, utterly misleading) statement requires explanation. In 1994 I began teaching at the American University in Bulgaria (AUBG) in Blagoevgrad (southwestern Bulgaria). I was hired because I had a plausible claim to expertise in Ottoman history (although to that point I had been interested primarily in the modern Middle East).

On the first day of my first course on the empire, all students attended, a practically unheard-of event. One later explained privately that everyone had wanted to see the "Turkish nationalist" whom the university had recruited. Another student comment overheard that term was "I know that his father is British [which was true] but I'm sure his mother is Turkish!" (an idea that will make my Anglo-Saxon Protestant mother say, "Gosh!", I am sure). I shrugged off such slightly surreal misperceptions as best I could, but I had a harder time keeping calm the following year, when I was named in Greek and Bulgarian newspapers as working with MIT to establish an independent greater Macedonia under Turkish domination. This (false!) report resulted only from my interest in Ottoman history (in the eyes of officials as well as students, a subject that could only interest Turkish nationalists) and the fact that I once traveled from Istanbul to Blagoevgrad via Greece. (For more on this episode, see Chapter 9.) Even if my two interests, that of the professional historian and that of the curious observer of the contemporary, were not closely linked in my own view, experience showed that there was no clear line separating them in other people's minds. Those interests shape this book, and I hope that my accounting of past and present and of the linkages between them will appeal to people who are similarly intrigued by both current events and the historical roots of the contemporary Balkans and Middle East.

Given the serious subject of the book, it may seem peculiar to pause for a joke, but perhaps I can sneak one in here. "A physicist, an engineer, and an economist are marooned on a desert island. A crate of canned food washes up. The physicist says, 'Great! I can calculate the force needed to open each can!' The engineer says, 'And I can make the tools to apply the force!' The economist says, 'Assume a can opener.'"

No, I didn't think it very funny, either – but my father loved it. When I gave up studying economics at university, he regaled me with it. He was a statistician, and in his view a discipline whose basic theorems tended to begin with unrealistic assumptions ("Assume a perfectly competitive market" being a good example) was truly a dismal science that I should not feel bad about dropping.[1] One of the reasons for writing this book is my sense that, despite recent changes in Ottoman, Balkan, and Middle Eastern history, basic assumptions of those fields survive with too

---

[1] One of his better-known contributions to statistics, incidentally, was "Anscombe's Quartet," which was a data set that could be graphed in four markedly different ways, depending upon the assumptions underpinning analysis of the data. F. J. Anscombe, "Graphs in Statistical Analysis," *American Statistician* 27 (1973), 17–21.

little questioning. "Assume the nation," in particular, seems ineradicable, despite its roots in the same Department of Wishful Thinking that also produces perfectly competitive markets and can openers.

Several examples illustrate why I feel ever less comfortable with that and other standard assumptions. The first was my experience teaching Ottoman history in the Balkans, where the nationalist creeds upon which the students' extant knowledge of history was based were utterly at variance not only with those supporting what I had been taught, but even with those absorbed by fellow students from other countries of the region. I challenged such beliefs vigorously, but from that it was a small step to questioning the assumptions of my own education. How far that questioning needed to go became clearer with my research into the turmoil besetting Ottoman Albania in the 1830s and then other "rebellions" seen elsewhere in the Balkans between 1792 and 1839.[2] The standard assumptions that unrest was driven by nationalism or by greedy provincial notables and closed-minded religious conservatives resisting the state's efforts to modernize and westernize became untenable. In most cases the violence seemed to be instigated by the state, and those who fought back had reasons for doing so that I – and other people – could understand. The harshness and apparent lack of concern for legal niceties shown by the imperial regime would have aroused opposition in practically any population subjected to arbitrary and oppressive rule. That opposition among Muslims was couched in the language of Islam, still in Western opinion an "uncivilized" religion, could not obscure the importance of justice as the regulator of state-society relations. The assumption that religion is inherently backward, violent, or merely a cloaking device for greed is as objectionable as the glorification of the nation, and is as commonly found in each of the fields of history addressed in this book.

My purpose is to work out the implications of questioning such assumptions in Ottoman, Balkan, and Middle Eastern history, arguing that an alternate view of late Ottoman history not only leads to fresh perspective on the empire but also makes clearer the flaws in assumptions framing our understanding of political shifts seen in post-Ottoman countries. Accounts of political history in each of these fields tend to be influenced by the views of the regimes governing the various countries, and especially regimes founded in the post-Ottoman period that have single-mindedly pushed the "assume the nation" approach. I do not start

---

[2] Frederick Anscombe, "Islam and the Age of Ottoman Reform," *P&P* 208 (Aug. 2010), 159–89, and "The Balkan Revolutionary Age," *JMH* 84 (2012), 572–606.

with the same assumptions that the regimes in question do (e.g., that an Ottomanist must be a Turkish nationalist) and to which many historians are schooled to be sympathetic, and my conclusions therefore differ even though drawn from similar evidence.

In bare outline, the main points of my narrative are that the Ottoman state retained an Islamic political identity from its beginning to its end, that the populations under its control similarly identified themselves primarily by religious criteria in affairs transcending the purely local, and that nationalism has been essentially an artificial, post-Ottoman construction that has had from its inception fundamental weaknesses as a basis for long-term political stability. In the Balkans and Turkey postimperial regimes designed and inculcated crude nationalism as a tool for legitimating the state: it was a repackaging of popular religious senses of community that had survived the withdrawal of Ottoman rule, a reformulation designed to make supralocal identity subservient to the young state. Arab nationalism shared in this redirection of religious identity but developed in even more dire circumstances, being required not only to legitimate new regimes but also to organize opposition to the influence of Christian powers in the post-Ottoman Middle East. Where contemporary nationalist regimes have obviously failed in some significant sense, the religious identities on which nationalism was built have regained some of the importance they had had in the Ottoman period. There may be variations in this pattern across the Middle East and the Balkans, but they are differences of degree, not fundamental nature.

EASTERN QUESTIONS

It is fair to ask whether any argument addressing contemporary politics needs to dwell much upon Ottoman history. When nonhistorians in western Europe or North America ask about my specialty, their reaction to my answer depends upon how I phrase it. If I say, "The Ottoman empire," most have no response other than "Oh." But if I say, "The Balkans" or "The Middle East," they often exclaim, "That must be fascinating! You must really be in demand! What do you think about what is going on today?" There is, of course, always something "going on today" in one or the other region: the drawn-out death of Yugoslavia made headlines throughout the 1990s; the attacks of 11 September 2001 shaped the international news of the following decade, to be succeeded by the tumult of the "Arab Spring"; and endlessly the Israel-Palestine problem clamors for attention by revving its engine and spinning its wheels farther into the sand. Virulent nationalism seems to epitomize the Balkans, as was true of the Middle East in the recent past; Islamic activism has given the most visible signs of political dynamism in numerous countries; and across Arab lands vigorous protest has confronted creaky regimes. Every one of these phenomena has riveted audiences in the West, taking observers by surprise and arousing all too regularly reactions of dread, anger, and contempt in the wider public. Their unrelatedness to each other helps to explain why each has triggered surprise: atavistic nationalism, religious obscurantism, and the thirst for democracy and development seemingly share little. Each deserves book-length treatment as a contemporary issue on its own – so why drag a long-dead empire into the picture?

One reason to discuss the Ottoman period is the fact that other observers of today speculate about old roots of contemporary problems.[3] All of the areas affected by the aforementioned turbulence of the past twenty years, as well as other unpredictable regions seemingly out of step with modernity such as the Caucasus, were formerly Ottoman territories. Such speculation usually refers to a belief that nationalism tore the empire apart, or that the Ottoman dynasty (the last rulers to combine the temporal authority of the sultanate with the religious role of caliph, leader of the Sunni Muslim community) must provide a model for Islamists, or that Turkey today is a "neo-Ottoman" regional power. Given the capacity of populations around the region to remember the past and its injustices, surely there must be Ottoman legacies still at work.

I see little, if any, specifically Ottoman political legacy in the countries of southeastern Europe and the Middle East, except to a degree in the Republic of Turkey. In ranging from the mid-eighteenth to early-twenty-first century and covering the Balkans, Anatolia, and the Arab Middle East, the interpretation of political history presented here traces patterns clarified by the unusual breadth of time frame and geographic spread, including parallels across and between regions that are too rarely recognized. Linking the histories of the late empire and the post-Ottoman states not only shows that there are practically no Ottoman roots to the politics of today, it also helps to identify causes and goals of the phenomena that have so surprised and alarmed Western observers in recent

---

[3] See, for example, Robert Kaplan, *Balkan Ghosts: A Journey through History* (New York: Vintage, 1994) and Niall Ferguson, "The Mideast's Next Dilemma," *Newsweek* June 19, 2011 (http://www.newsweek.com/2011/06/19/turkey-the-mideast-s-next-dilemma.html#).

decades. It is the political choices made in the early post-Ottoman period by newly independent regimes that still influence contemporary politics and problems. In order to understand why those choices were made, however, it is also necessary to recognize the nature of politics and the sources of political identity among the recently Ottoman populations over which the new regimes claimed authority. This is crucial because the transition between the Ottoman and post-Ottoman periods was too abrupt in most cases to permit a smooth segue between systems; knowledge of the "exit velocity" of lands and people escaping Ottoman control, and indeed the trajectory of their flight, produces a better understanding of the direction and speed with which new regimes moved.

Interpretation follows several main themes, which are those that usually generate the interest shown by people who ask about what I teach: nationalism and religion, and their relationship to the state as the nature of political authority has evolved in the modern period. It is the practical, mundane importance of religion and nationalism, especially in influencing group identity and giving ideological legitimacy to any regime claiming to rule or represent such groups, that receives greatest attention. This is self-evident for nationalism, an ideology (that of an "imagined community" of people, bound by common language, traditions, and history or political beliefs, who aspire for an independent country governed by and for members of the nation) of obvious political application. One assumption that I see no reason to question is that nationalism is indeed just a form of politics.[4] Religion, however, is more complex. All religions focus primarily on the relationship between the believer and God (or gods); this part of religion, including matters of basic theology and the practice of worship, is relevant to the subject of the book but is of less immediate importance. It is the social aspects of religion, which over centuries have shaped populations' senses of morality and ethics, of what is "right" and what is "wrong," that are of primary interest here. Religions contain much about the proper relationship between individuals and the ways in which individual and community should act, and such social power has made political authorities perennially interested in establishing strong relations with the institutions and hierarchies of religion. Religion, the frustrated Marx's "opium of the masses," made rule sustainable. It thus joins nationalism as

---

[4] John Breuilly, *Nationalism and the State* (Chicago: University of Chicago Press, 1994), 1–16. Breuilly sees nationalism primarily as a form of political opposition to the state, an interpretation that misses the dominant pattern in post-Ottoman lands of nationalism used by regimes to legitimate state power.

an ideology that has had great influence in legitimating (and sometimes delegitimating) state power across the region studied.

One advantage to the book's approach is that it breaks with entrenched conventions that have muddied interpretation of long-term trends, notably the pattern of writing about the modern history of the region from the perspective of the nation-state. Every post-Ottoman country exists under the principle of being a nation-state, and successive governments in each of them have consciously portrayed the Ottoman past in a self-serving, negative way, as a time of oppression or decay that was ended only with liberation (the creation of the nation-state). This message was drummed into students for decades, and, even at university level, little tolerance for overt questioning of the national version of history existed. The national view nurtured in "scientific" academic research in post-Ottoman countries clearly affected early generations of Western writers.[5] Historical accounts since then have tended to reflect the basic assumptions shaping those early works. Where histories of post-Ottoman countries address the preindependence period, they tend to discuss specifically the nation and its territories under Ottoman rule, which inserts a twentieth-century fact into an earlier time.

Historians whose main interest is the late empire have struggled to develop their own interpretations of imperial history independent of the post-Ottoman narratives. This is not reflected in meekly accepting the negative portrayals but rather in being driven to stress elements that refute the most antagonistic views. In this task the accounts of Western European observers of the empire and subsequent historians writing on Europe's "Eastern Question" (how to manage the dissolution of the empire without causing a wider European war) have proven even harder to ignore than the various post-Ottoman national narratives.[6] Ottomanist

[5] The most influential "assume the nation" work on the Balkans was Leften Stavrianos, *The Balkans since 1453* (Hinsdale, IL: Dryden Press, 1958). For "Kemalist" Turkish views of history, see Bernard Lewis, *The Emergence of Modern Turkey* (Oxford: Oxford University Press, 1961) and Niyazi Berkes, *The Development of Secularism in Turkey* (Montreal: McGill University Press, 1964). As in other ways, the Arab lands present an anomaly, in that George Antonius set the pattern with *The Arab Awakening: The Story of the Arab National Movement* (London: Hamish Hamilton, 1938) despite serving in an antinationalist colonial administration, but as countries gained independence from Anglo-French rule, the history that their regimes sponsored echoed the Antonius line.

[6] See, for example, M. S. Anderson, *The Eastern Question, 1774–1923: A Study in International Relations* (London: Macmillan, 1966) and David Fromkin, *A Peace to End All Peace: Creating the Modern Middle East, 1914–1922* (London: Deutsch, 1989), neither of which shows any comprehension of Ottoman affairs that would add a third dimension to the cardboard-cutout figure of the lazy, incompetent, venal, brutal Turk.

histories of the long nineteenth century (c. 1789–c. 1918) frequently seem most interested in highlighting the ways in which the empire was just as modern and advanced as the rest of Europe was.[7] They have stressed the rationalization of imperial government, in both structure and practical administration, which created a modern state matching the European model. The imperial regime instituted full equality for all citizens, and neither religious communities nor ethnic groups were subjected to oppressive or unfair treatment. Enveloping this narrative is the assumption that modernity entailed secularism for the Ottomans as much as for the rest of Europe. Insofar as religion gets attention, it is limited largely to its institutions and the Muslim *'ulama* (men learned in religious matters); Jewish and Christian religious figures receive even less attention than the wider non-Muslim populations. That institutions and religious authorities either fell under state control or, at the least, did not grow in line with the expanding institutions of administration has been taken as evidence that Ottoman state and society were secularizing, just as in Europe. And again as in Europe, nationalism grew in line with secularization. This picture thus melds with the Turkish nation-state narrative stressing the roots of westward-looking, secular republicanism in the empire.

Entrenched Turkish-Ottoman, Balkan, and Middle Eastern historiographic traditions have produced a grand narrative of political development in Ottoman and post-Ottoman lands over the last 250 years. Stripped to its essentials, it stresses a succession of themes that lead logically to a rosy view of the eve of the present as a progressive era, moving Europe's "near abroad" along a path of development reminiscent of the West's own. Each tradition tells a story of political westernization, a strengthening and rationalizing of the state, and the fostering of bonds between state and people; liberalism's battle against reactionary conservatism; the liberation of subject peoples who finally won control over their own destinies in independent nation-states; the struggle to overcome the unnatural, unjust restrictions of new borders and the economic and social backwardness inherited from the empire; and the political, social, and economic maturation of the nation in the second half of the twentieth century. Such themes' familiarity to Western audiences creates empathy by suggesting that peoples of the Balkans, Middle East, and

---

[7] Donald Quataert, "Ottoman History Writing and Changing Attitudes towards the Notion of 'Decline'" *History Compass* 1 (2003) ME 038, 1–9.

Turkey are "really just like us," going through struggles reminiscent of our own nations'. (The extent to which we remember how messy, mean, and often brutal national development in the West really was is a question I would love to address but cannot here.)

Empathy turns to dread, anger, and contempt when the atavistic irrationality of nationalism and religious politics, supposedly buried long ago in our own past, erupts in Europe's near abroad. Little in the standard narratives prepared its adherents for the major shifts seen in the late twentieth century. In the case of the Balkans, the picture of political maturation and concentration upon socioeconomic development offered no explanation for why the region should suddenly succumb to nationalist paranoia. Manic nationalism gripped not only the soon-to-disintegrate socialist Yugoslavia but other countries such as the Warsaw Pact stalwart Bulgaria, which carried out in the 1980s a bizarre campaign of forcing Bulgarian names on its Turkish minority and thus sparked a crisis of mass emigration, and the NATO- and EU-member Greece, which has embraced since Yugoslavia's dissolution the delusion that the Former Yugoslav Republic of Macedonia (FYROM) poses a serious threat to its territorial integrity. In seeking retrospective understanding of such unexpected atavism reminiscent of an earlier era in the rest of Europe, experts on the region either have focused upon the immediate details of individual cases of nationalist tensions to identify "the trigger" for turmoil or more broadly have fallen back on some form of Balkan exceptionalism, combining something close to pride in the strength of national determination to struggle against the odds with resentment that outsiders look down on southeastern Europe as feral and barbaric. Taken to a common conclusion, this view supports the notion that "the Balkans have too much history," or that "these people have been killing each other for centuries." At base, of course, is the idea that national passions are something born of the long experience of Ottoman oppression.[8]

As in the Balkans, so in the Middle East and Turkey. The ultimately Islamic revolution in Iran of 1979 took most Middle East watchers by surprise, but it was far from clear then that religious politics might spread from Persian, Shi'i Iran to Arab, Sunni countries, let alone to secular Turkey. No Middle Eastern country other than Syria identified with

---

[8] Andre Gerolymatos, *The Balkan Wars: Myth, Reality, and the Eternal Conflict* (Toronto: Stoddart, 2001).

Iran (although Israel and Libya supplied arms) in its long, brutal war with Iraq in 1980–8. Yet Islamist opposition groups gained clear political relevance in numerous countries, from Algeria to Egypt, Palestine, Lebanon, Jordan, and even Saudi Arabia. Perhaps most shocking was the rapid rise and then entry into government of "Islamist" parties in NATO-member Turkey. The revival of what seemed such a conservative, irrational, and frankly medieval ideology as religion represented a rejection of all the decades of progress that rationalist development efforts had promoted. Analysts again struggled to formulate explanations, with widely varying results: Islamism was a reaction against the dislocations associated with modernity, it appealed to the uneducated poor and rural migrants in cities who did not benefit from the social services provided by modernizing regimes, or it was a vehicle for protest because it was the only mode of thought that security services could not fully police. Most problematic has been the all-too-common judgment that there is something underdeveloped in Islam itself. Some commentary relies upon the notion that Islam recognizes no separation between the political and the religious, which thus explains the stubbornly unmodern and un-Western nature of politics in the Middle East. The figure who has attained the highest profile as an academic proponent of this latter view is Bernard Lewis – who, it may be noted with some irony, did more than any Westerner to promote the narrative of the nineteenth-century Ottoman empire as a story of westernization and secularization.[9] Such a view reflects Lewis's assumptions, not shallowness of learning or intellect, but the risk it carries becomes apparent when it is adopted by others who share his assumptions but are less learned about (or utterly ignorant of) the history of Muslim-inhabited regions.

Eventually, so many explanations of high-profile problems in the recent history of post-Ottoman lands somehow link back to what is thought to have happened in the imperial period. In order to understand the strength that both nationalism and religion have today, and therefore their perceived threat to the West and its view of how modern states and societies should comport themselves, it seems sensible to return to that bygone age when these two ideas and identities ushered modern politics into southeastern Europe and the Middle East.

[9] Bernard Lewis, *The Crisis of Islam: Holy War and Unholy Terror* (London: Phoenix, 2004), and *Modern Turkey*.

THE REPLACEMENT NARRATIVE

To replace the standard story lines of historical development across the region, the book offers a replacement narrative built on the themes of state, faith, and nation. It adopts a periodization mandated by trends in these issues. The first chapter gives a brief sketch of Ottoman political matters from the empire's foundation around 1300 to the mid-eighteenth century. It stresses the limited nature of the Ottoman state, which focused on the problems that preoccupied most premodern rulers: external defense, peacekeeping at home, upholding justice, and collecting revenue. This system survived until the rise of unprecedented military power in the hands of imperial neighbors and foes from the mid-eighteenth century, which necessitated improvements in the efficiency of the Ottoman military-administrative system.

Chapters 2 (mid-eighteenth century to 1808) and 3 (1808–39) examine the Ottoman imperial transition to political modernization, a chaotic period that almost destroyed the empire. The revised picture of this era underpins the altered view of subsequent periods. Rather than being an Ottoman "Age of Enlightenment" characterized by clear-sighted reform, the half-century 1789–1839 saw the veritable financial, military, political, and moral collapse of the venerable Ottoman state. Sultan Selim III (1789–1807) tried to strengthen the military by aping aspects of Christian European armed forces, arousing consternation among Muslims; because his measures were ineffective, Selim could not control opposition, causing unrest among non-Muslims as well. After Selim's deposition, Mahmud II revived his predecessor's flawed plans but ignored some of the legal restrictions that had hobbled Selim's efforts to overcome opposition. Mahmud relied on force to impose obedience on the population and to extract more resources out of the old imperial military-administrative system. His despotic mode of rule undercut his legitimacy as defender of the realm, protector of the peace, and upholder of justice; at his death, he faced overthrow by disaffected subjects. This period, usually portrayed as setting the empire irreversibly on the path of westernization and secularization, was the most extended existential crisis that the late empire faced. It raised fundamental questions about what the purpose of the state should be and what limits to its power it must accept.

These questions prompted the Tanzimat, a program of reform that marked a compromise between the state's desire to strengthen itself against foreign threats and the population's insistence that its rulers uphold justice. The perception of justice betrayed or suborned underpinned the opposition to Mahmud's despotic rule, and among Muslims the view had spread that the sultan's regime acted contrary to Islamic principles of the just society. Chapter 4 discusses the Tanzimat as a program designed to restore the state's identification with justice even as it required of its subjects greater contributions to imperial defense. The state did not seek westernization (Christian Europe being always the greatest threat to the empire's existence) or secularization. It sought to retain its identity as an Islamic state and to keep shari'a as the touchstone of the laws introduced to legitimate in the population's eyes all that the state sought to do. The Tanzimat program worked and was continued at least until 1908. The state faced no domestic threat to its legitimacy that ever rivaled the discontent seen in the half-century to 1839. It never became strong enough to eliminate threats from abroad, however, and dissatisfaction among army officers angered by the hesitancy of the regime in confronting security threats prompted the "constitutional revolution" of 1908.

Chapter 5 charts the collapse of the empire from the rise of the Committee of Union and Progress (CUP) to 1918. The elements of the CUP who controlled the state after 1908 had one urgent interest: strengthening the state and the military as rapidly as possible. They therefore weakened the Islamic principles regulating the state. As in most coups, men trained to be relatively junior army officers and bureaucrats turned out to be politically (and militarily) inept, and the empire collapsed a decade after they rose to power. Those few years marked a sharp, extremely painful end to six centuries of Ottoman continuity.

Chapters 6 and 7 examine the transition from Ottoman empire to post-Ottoman countries in the Balkans and Turkey. Every country of the Balkans was created by the great powers of Europe, and the states conjured into existence to administer them lacked any meaningful roots in the societies suddenly placed under their authority. Every state had two immediate goals: to become strong enough to compel the obedience of the population, and to transform that population into a nation to legitimate the existence of the country and the state. They remade religious institutions into "national churches," adopted revanchist programs aimed at liberating lands and people claimed for the nation, and built overlarge armed forces to give teeth to the program – and to give the government domestic authority. With minor exceptions, no regime prior to 1918 or even 1945 moved convincingly beyond these goals. Turkey faced a variation on the Balkan challenge, in that it was partially self-created and had inherited state structures and tradition. The republic nevertheless followed similar policies in order to intensify the CUP effort to strengthen the state, making it unchallengeable at home. With this goal in mind, the state embarked upon a nation-building program as intensive as any seen in the post-Ottoman Balkans. The need to acknowledge Islamic principles of law and justice had been the moral brake upon the Ottoman state, and Islam had been the vehicle for protest against perceived despotism. The early republic's vigorous efforts to transform Muslim into Turkish identity sought to loosen that moral brake and close an avenue of protest against state action. Turkey, like the Balkan states, succeeded in building national identity, but underneath that new identity still lived the earlier religious attachments.

Such a program of rapid remaking of identities to suit the needs of new states was more difficult to undertake in post-Ottoman Arab lands. The Arab countries, like those of the Balkans, were the products of Christian European intervention; unlike in the Balkans, however, European powers in the Middle East neither acted to create countries according to notions of national liberation nor proved willing to allow the countries the freedom to build their own states. Suspended for decades between the Ottoman past and the challenges of independent "nationhood," Europe's Middle Eastern creations became the seedbed of Arab nationalism. Chapter 8 explores the competition among local, religious, and Arab identities in the search for a new rallying point against foreign influence following the Ottoman collapse. Arab nationalism, the least natural choice, grew in strength as a result of the European mandate system's political and territorial arrangements and the consequent favor shown Arabism by the Hashimite monarchies of Iraq and Transjordan.

Chapters 9 through 11 take us to the contemporary period. In the Balkans, the demise of powerful stabilizing forces, most notably communism and the Warsaw Pact, did not reawaken nationalism (it had never gone to sleep) but rather raised fears in the major post-Ottoman countries (Serbia, Greece, Bulgaria, and Romania) that everything gained through the nineteenth-century revanchist programs was now again vulnerable in a period of fundamental unpredictability. The flash points were areas acquired late and containing populations not reliably assimilated by nation-building programs. It was symptomatic of post-Ottoman nations' origins in religious identities that religion became once again a significant factor in what has usually been portrayed as the revival of nationalism.

In Turkey, religion has had a more widely noted resurgence, although in fact the resurgence has been building since 1945. Part of this "revival" reflects the fact that Muslim identity had never been wholly subsumed within Turkishness, despite strongly authoritarian state attempts to make this happen; once one-party rule ended after 1945, elements of religion clearly reentered public life and competitive politics. Political groups that could be identified as committed to Islam's sense of social justice and morality were thus well positioned to thrive as their more avowedly secular competitors came to be seen as hopelessly venal, incompetent, and oppressive.

Venality, incompetence, and above all state despotism also explain much of the rising influence of Islam in public life in the Arab Middle East. Arabism suffered from its impracticality as anything more than an anti-European ideology; as a political program that has no remaining credibly achievable goal, and as a source of political legitimacy utterly mismatched to the legal realities of post-Ottoman borders, it has fostered state failure and political instability. Arab regimes have come to rely mainly upon coercion to ensure control over their populations, because they cannot adequately cast themselves as natural leaders of any supralocal community, be it national or religious. The sheer brutality of rule has stoked outrage and a growing willingness to challenge regimes across the region despite their formidable Praetorian Guards. As has happened repeatedly since the 1789–1839 period, Islam has become the vehicle of many of those wishing to see moral bounds restored to the powers of the state.

BALIK BAŞTAN KOKAR

The fish starts to smell at the head. (Turkish proverb)

Several key points run through this account of historical development. They concern the practice of politics and state policy making, the relationship between state and society, the nature and role of identity, and the influence of international affairs. The majority of these points are quite basic but often overlooked in broad considerations of historical development.

One of the fundamental facts of public affairs is that most of politics is reactive. Visionaries never thrive in their own lifetimes unless they address issues that a critical mass of potential followers recognizes as serious problems requiring action. This reactiveness of politics applies at both state and popular levels, but there is little doubt that the state has the greater ability to shape the problem to be addressed, be it by defining the target or by being itself the problem. When times grow troubled, looking at the role of the state often explains much; as the aphorism suggests, the bad smell usually originates in the leading organ. Throughout this history are examples of regimes that appeared to act shortsightedly or foolishly but in practically every case had comprehensible reasons for the choice of action: policy resulted from reaction to some real or perceived problem or threat. The population in turn reacted to state moves, with the response shaped by factors such as the extent to which the regime convinced people of the existence of the threat and the proper way of addressing it. This history has few angelic heroes or purely evil villains but rather people with varying abilities to perceive and analyze threats, as well as varying senses of proportionality in judging suitable responses to problems.

How populations respond to state action has always depended in part upon the nature of the long-term relationship between state and society. Pundits make too much of the dubious principle that "democracies do not make war on each other," but a development as catastrophic as the outbreak of conflict often results from great political-social instability or insecurity, which the absence of a strong relationship between state and society only makes more likely. Recognition of mutual responsibility or dependence strengthens such a relationship, and closely linked to that recognition is the principle of the legitimacy of power. Democracy is a good but not the only means of legitimating power and establishing a relationship of mutual responsibility. It has the advantage of being the most visible vindication of the principle of legitimacy that a state or government can enjoy, but in studying even openly democratic systems the actions of regime leaders cannot be simply assumed to reflect the electorate's opinion. It can be difficult but usually not impossible to gauge perspectives from the audiences to which heads of state played, the populations who were asked to support regime choices. Where it can be done plausibly in the course of this study, it does much to explain why state initiatives meant to resolve critical problems succeeded or failed – and why some policies were shaped by the need to strengthen a frail state-society relationship.

In building a durable state-society relationship, having an agreed set of rules that is observed by all parties involved is of tremendous importance. Law, in short, makes trust possible. It is particularly important that those who control the levers of power observe legal restrictions – "*Quis custodiet custodies?*" cannot remain unanswerable, especially in the modern era, when the power of the state has grown so overwhelming. Issues of law, both its formulation and its application, recur through the time covered in this book, and no ideology can obviate the need for a stable, effective system of justice.

Ideology has provided the base for building state-society relations most clearly in the modern period, but even earlier rulers needed identification with some kind of principle beyond "might makes right" to stabilize their authority over lands and people. For ideology to succeed in legitimating power, it must draw upon ideas with which the population can identify, which often necessitates an appeal to individual and group identities. Identity is learned: there is no genetic element, and only in very limited aspects can it be termed innate; even the sense of self takes time to develop in infants. Our most ingrained identities derive from what we learn while young, know most intimately, and to which we are most frequently exposed. Like so much else, identity is essentially reactive: The answer to the question "Who are you?" depends on the situation in which it is asked, with answers growing increasingly specific the closer to home and family that the questioner gets. Throughout most of history, society functioned at the local level, in that the identity question arose overwhelmingly in everyday circumstances: the identities that mattered were those of family (immediate and then extended), locale (neighborhood/village and then city/region), trade or profession, religion (specific congregation and then rite/sect), and perhaps patronage (those above and below who bestowed or received favored treatment). In the period covered in this book, the social cocoon of the local and familiar was pierced with increasing frequency by intrusions of the wider world – hard-fought wars, the settlement of refugees, and the growing presence and authority of representatives of the state. With each intrusion the circumstances of the identity question altered, forcing corresponding change in the answer. Lacking personal experience of much of that wider world, the answer to "Who are you?" was guided by what each person had been taught by people with the requisite knowledge – and sometimes in response to the assignment of identity by those very outside forces and the promotion or persecution that resulted therefrom.

As long as the Ottoman empire survived, religion was the primary guide to forming a sensible answer to the identity question asked in supralocal affairs. In part this was the result of the education about the supralocal world that Ottoman society had always received: the religious was the only element of local identity that produced regular exposure to the idea that the individual believer or congregation belonged to a larger "imagined community," that of the truly faithful to God. Religion, as the source or legitimator of the everyday practices that reflected communal norms of right and wrong, was also integrated into the sense of local community. The Ottoman state never saw an advantage to devising lasting policies based upon any principle other than religion; ethnicity was practically irrelevant to the needs of the state, most of whose subjects had little cause to use ethnicity as a meaningful element of their daily identities. It is worth noting that ethnic terms most commonly used in Ottoman sources prior to the nineteenth century referred to mainly Muslim nomadic or seminomadic groups (Arabs [meaning bedouin], Kurds, Albanians, Vlachs, Roma) that had the greatest propensity for stirring trouble with settled communities in lands into which they migrated or raided, creating unusual situations in which "ethnicity" could become a criterion of identity. It must be emphasized, however, that such supralocal identities, including the religious, were situational and far from the most important under everyday circumstances. Much the same must be said of nationalism, once ethnicity became the ideological principle adopted by post-Ottoman states in their quest for legitimacy and the strengthening of the state-society relationship. National regimes, lacking the preparatory and pastoral work carried out by religious leaders in Ottoman society and used to advantage by the Ottoman state, instituted intensive and prolonged campaigns to raise ethnonational identity to the level needed to make nationalism a viable ideology of state legitimation. Even where successful, they failed to make the national the main criterion of everyday identity.

One final point of recurring interest in the history set forth in the book: the influence of foreign powers, either as a model to be emulated or as a threat to be feared. Commentaries regularly make much noise about the lasting ill effects of Western imperialism in post-Ottoman (and other postimperial) lands, only to be rebutted by equally noisy dismissal of such charges as self-exculpatory "blame-the-West-first"-ism. Without siding wholly with either of these extreme positions, the interpretation of history presented here suggests that the Western record in the region is not one that should generate much pride in anyone who cares to claim it as heritage. Throughout the period, the Christian powers of Europe and, more recently, the United States have been seen primarily as threats, not as firm and faithful allies. Distrust of the West and dislike of foreign influence, let alone outright control, affected both Muslims and non-Muslims in the Balkans and the Middle East. Any "westernization" was driven less by unalloyed admiration than it was by the temptation to adopt whatever appeared to make the West strong, in order to keep the West at arm's length from the East. One way in which the West did serve as a model, however, was in nation building. Nationalism and the heavy-handed national state were introduced into the post-Ottoman countries of the Balkans primarily by natives or residents of Christian European powers. Nationalism was the ideology of carpetbaggers. The nation-states of Christian Europe also shaped the post-Ottoman countries of Turkey and the Middle East. As stated previously, this is not a history of heroes and devils, and the West cannot be blamed for all that may be or has been wrong in the region while the Ottoman and post-Ottoman states and societies escape blame. That said, the analysis presented here starts with the acknowledgment that the problems shaping the region, and the cycles of action and reaction, were influenced deeply by militarily dominant foreign powers.

In closing these introductory remarks, I want to note more explicitly this book's relationship to the standard historical narratives that anyone familiar with Ottoman, Middle Eastern, and Balkan history must recognize. I have no wish to see these narratives ignored: they have shaped the field, and my perspective has benefited from theirs. Like those narratives, mine is hardly the last word. I have had to cover much history in relatively little space, with a loss of nuance and without any claim to being all-encompassing in my account; I may go too far on some points (and probably not far enough on others). Rather than saying, "The king has no clothes!", I want to suggest that the king owns more than one outfit. I believe that the one that I sketch out suits him but cannot suggest that it makes the rest of his wardrobe unnecessary. I merely ask readers who wish to go further into the history of these regions to remember that multiple frameworks by which to interpret events and trends exist, and to keep an open mind in considering which seems to make most explanatory sense.

PART I

THE OTTOMAN EMPIRE

I

State, Faith, Nation, and the Ottoman Empire

This is a study in political history, and as such it is at root about the relationship between those with power and the populations under their formal control. The past several centuries have fascinated historians across many fields because in political terms "modernity" has meant the rapid increase in the scope and intensity of state authority, which in turn has placed state-society relations everywhere under tremendous pressure. This book covers the period from the eve of modernization in the Ottoman empire until the early twenty-first century in post-Ottoman countries, and the central question driving the analysis is that of how the state could legitimate itself to its subject population as its power grew. It argues that Ottoman rulers succeeded in maintaining a workable state-society dynamic as long as regimes took care to retain in practice the ruling dynasty's identification with religion. Leaving aside the powerful feeling of communal solidarity that shared belief can create (acceptance into which would tend to benefit any temporal ruler), Islam's strong moral content and attachment to the principle of justice gave promise of safeguards against arbitrary use of the state's growing power. This appealed to Muslims but also benefited non-Muslims, who remained loyal, or at least quiescent, as Ottoman citizens until the empire was broken apart. Nationalism held little appeal for Ottoman populations and in itself posed no real threat to Istanbul's rule: there never was any successful, or even serious, domestic nationalist uprising against Ottoman authority. Nationalism was fostered consciously by post-Ottoman regimes, which needed effective means under their exclusive control to build legitimacy for the existence of new states. Regimes promoted forms of nationalism that were (and still are) fundamentally state-serving, offering few benefits – and fewer safeguards against the arbitrariness of state power – to their subject populations. The weaknesses and failures of such nationalisms in fostering stable state-society relations have been exposed repeatedly, from the first post-Ottoman decades to recent years' experiences of violent instability in the Balkans, the rise of religion in public life across the post-Ottoman landscape, and the "Arab Spring" that began in 2011.

In order to make the rationale for such an argument about the trajectory of politics clear, this chapter discusses the path by which the Ottoman empire reached the "starting point" of the modern period. It offers a brief sketch of imperial development to the eighteenth century and of the relationship between state and population in the premodern period. In contrast to a common assumption, the empire and the ruling dynasty did not survive for some six centuries simply because of the sultanate's grandeur and absolute power. By any modern standard, Ottoman rulers were rather weak, having no well-developed machinery of state capable of coercing recalcitrant subjects. The rulers' limited responsibilities made such power unnecessary: the dynasty organized defense against foreign foes, the preservation of peace domestically, and the collection of revenue for these tasks and for the support of the ruling elite in appropriate comfort. No part of the Ottoman population suffered the full weight of serving any one of these sultanic interests without gaining enough from performance of the other two imperial duties to render active coercion unnecessary.

Ottoman dynastic authority survived also because the limited imperial administration suited the natural features of the sultan's domains very well. The strength and wealth of the empire resulted from its remarkable size: more than thirty countries of today contain formerly Ottoman land, from Hungary to Ukraine and the Caucasus in the north, and from Algeria to Yemen and Qatar in the south. In comparison to much of western and central Europe, however, most Ottoman land was neither densely populated nor rich in natural assets, including agricultural potential and basic minerals. This helps to explain the lack of significant cities across the empire that could possibly rival Istanbul, the capital situated in a relatively fertile area at the confluence of vital land and sea communication routes. Only Cairo, located in the exceptionally productive and densely populated Nile Valley and close to the Red Sea, could rival Istanbul. By no coincidence, Istanbul monitored Egypt more carefully than any other province, and with good reason, as it was a governor of Egypt, Mehmed (Muhammad) Ali Pasha, who in the 1830s mounted the greatest domestic threat ever posed to Ottoman dynastic authority. Other than Cairo, however, Istanbul faced no internal centers capable of challenging its rule, making it unnecessary for the imperial metropolis to be mobilized permanently to police its vast provincial expanse.

Istanbul's method of administration thus could rely safely upon intermediaries, to whom the sultanate devolved revocable authority. Devolution was eased in that the sultanate did not have to negotiate political matters with a hereditary landed aristocracy according to the various traditions in which the essentially feudal system of premodern politics was entangled in Christian Europe. It worked instead through a multitude of intermediary figures and groups (such as guilds and religious institutions), each of whom served as a fulcrum upon which the power of the sultanate could leverage the mass of land and people to fulfill the premodern state's limited tasks. The relative scarcity of good overland and even maritime transportation routes made commerce controllable, turning customs and excise into major sources of imperial revenue. By contrast, devolved authority and the sheer extent of the not tremendously productive provinces meant that Ottoman methods of taxation and military recruitment throughout the premodern period stressed extension – making sure that every area contributed something to the center's requirements – rather than intensity of exploitation. It is indeed possible to cast the theme of change in state-society relations during the modern period as the story of how the Ottoman state tried to shift from extensive to intensive exploitation, of its failures in the 1792–1839 period and successes after 1839, and of the weaknesses in successor regimes that took on the monumental challenge of building anew states capable of exploiting resource potential sufficiently to perform the core responsibilities of government.

Prior to the stresses of modernity, the system devised by Ottoman rulers was eminently sustainable, as long as the imperial center monitored its operation to soothe stresses whenever they appeared, and indeed the system promoted the stability of imperial administration that characterized the empire from its founding until the eighteenth century. One element that requires further note, however, as a result of its critical role in keeping the military-administrative framework functioning and in maintaining a healthy state-society relationship, is Islam, which provided the backbone for the Ottoman system of justice.

From the early days of the empire (arising c. 1301) the Ottoman dynasty and ruling elite maintained a close relationship between Islam and the state. This assertion does not suggest that Ottoman rule was unimaginative, inflexible, or relentlessly oppressive toward its non-Muslim population: Ottoman rule was highly practical, and had it relied upon systemic oppression, it would not have survived for six centuries. The assertion that the sultanic system developed in tight association with Islam suggests rather that for an imperial center of greater latent than mobilized strength, the religion served as a vital "amplifier" of the center's power. It gave the imperial regime an ideology that increased its legitimacy and encouraged submission to its moral authority. In a real sense, Islam gave the empire a strong state tradition in lands whose geography and recent past militated against tight control by a distant ruler; the Central Asian ancestral homeland of the Turks certainly had no strong state tradition, producing no noteworthy or durable institutions of administration and no notable dynasties except where, as in the case of the Mongols, ruling tribal elites adopted the religion and traditions of the lands they conquered.[1] Islam, through its emphasis on law, assured the population that a stable system of justice would prevent extremes of anarchy and oppression. With the aid of an effective and "objective" (might does not always make right) system of justice, the imperial center held the allegiance of not only the Muslim population that was to provide most of its military strength and a growing proportion of its tax revenues, but also non-Muslims who looked to the ruler's authority as the ultimate guarantor of justice, including protection against oppression by local wielders of power assigned by the sultan. The dynasty's identification with Islam also strengthened the loyalty of the local intermediary bodies (Muslim and non-Muslim learned hierarchies, guilds, etc.) and representatives to whom that generally loosely supervised authority was delegated (such as the holders of *timar* [see later discussion]), with those who executed the modest administration of the state expressing their sense of duty as service to the religion and the dynasty that served it (*din ü devlet*).

Ottoman principles and practices of government developed relatively rapidly, with a mere century and a half separating Osman's initial unsettled warrior band from Sultan Mehmed II's conquest of Constantinople (1453), the geographic key to the establishment of a durable empire. Although much remains unknown about the origins of Ottoman authority, it seems to have conformed to the usual developmental pattern of states, with power over communal affairs accruing to those proven effective in

---

[1] Byzantium retained a mere shadow of its power and reach in the fourteenth century, and Anatolia and the Balkans had been under no stable "imperial" authority for even longer.

military organization and leadership. Until the nuclear age, when war became too expensive and catastrophic for most states to wage, it was practically impossible to separate political authority from the state's military function, and in the Ottoman case, the founder of the dynasty, Osman, certainly appeared as a war leader. While his position may have originated in leading a tribe during conflict with Byzantium, the growth of his following before or after his initial recorded victory at Baphaeon (c. 1301) would have made the fiction of blood ties so important to tribal leadership impossible to maintain. Islam provided the supratribal legitimation for his leadership position: by all accounts, Osman's struggle against the Byzantines was *gaza*, or religiously legitimated raiding into the infidel Abode of War. That the religion in the early Islamic era was an effective tool in curbing Arab tribal practices and subsuming clan identity to membership in the community of believers presumably boosted its attraction in chaotic post-Selcuk Anatolia. Tribal custom would not be long accepted as law by followers not members of the tribe, but shari'a, no matter how rough-and-ready, was a recognizably authoritative and stable source of justice in adjudicating disputes. Islam thus aided the early growth of the leader's powers to command, expanding the martial function of Osman's war band to encompass effective mechanisms for keeping the peace, dispensing justice, and raising revenue. Osman and his descendants, and their followers, not only accepted Islam in name but took it to heart, and the state that they built conformed to Islamic principles.

Pragmatism and religion are not inherently irreconcilable, and the early Ottomans were quite pragmatic in constructing this limited state, drawing upon talent wherever found in the multiethnic (predominantly Christian) population and accepting local custom as the norm in administering various provinces. Such flexibility in itself did not contravene Islam, but over time Islamic identity did set some limit to pragmatism, in that the Ottoman army, a critical element of the state, may have included some Christians except for much of the nineteenth century but was essentially a Muslim institution. This institution shaped the state's categorization of society and its system of provincial administration into the eighteenth century. The durable term for the Ottoman elite was "military" (*'askari*); in return for serving the war leader's primary function, members of the military gained relief from taxation. Those who served the developing state's other main function, keeping the peace (notably men of religion), were accorded similar *'askari*, tax-exempt status. The prebendal cavalryman (*sipahi*) merged both functions, gaining temporary rights to revenues from specified lands (*timar*) to use to equip himself for campaign but also to assume routine local administration in much of the empire; if the sipahi failed to muster for campaign or shirked tasks such as providing local security around his timar, he forfeited the right to the specified revenues. The 'askari class, and the timar holders in particular, were overwhelmingly Muslim from the sixteenth century, when the majority of the empire's population was no longer Christian. At no point in Ottoman history does it seem that the military was equally ready to attack Muslim and non-Muslim enemies. The janissaries – a salaried standing force originally of the sultan's slaves – were unenthusiastic about campaigning against Iran in the east, at least in part because of reluctance to make war upon fellow Muslims, even the schismatic Shi'a. Religion regularly justified the targets of warfare, be they the unbelievers dwelling in the Abode of War or schismatics who promoted *fitna* (dissension or chaos) in the Abode of Islam.[2] The warrior dynasty perforce regularly maintained truces with ideological enemies, but its other duties, keeping the peace and promoting justice, were perennial and therefore ultimately exerted paramount influence upon the nature of the state. It was in the area of law that the empire most clearly demonstrated its nature as an Islamic state.

All students of the premodern empire become familiar with the "circle of equity/justice" that those giving advice to the Ottoman ruling class regularly cited: the world is a vineyard whose walls are the state; the state's regulator is the shari'a; the shari'a cannot take effect without the presence of land (the Abode of Islam, defined as territory under a Muslim ruler who can ensure freedom for shari'a); land cannot be seized without soldiers; soldiers cannot be recruited without property; property is accumulated by the subjects; the subjects pledge obedience to the world ruler whenever justice reigns; justice is the source of salvation of the world.[3] The trope of the circle's corruption nourished the now-discredited notion that the empire started to decline after the death of Süleyman I, the Magnificent, in 1566, but it is important not to dismiss the circle in the rush to discard the "long decline" thesis. It reflected an ideal taken seriously by all strata of Ottoman society and was constituted of the core concerns of any state: the military, the courts, and taxation, all regulated by the principle of justice. "Justice" has an obvious meaning

---

[2] John Guilmartin, "Ideology and Conflict: The Wars of the Ottoman Empire, 1453–1606," *Journal of Interdisciplinary History* 18 (1988), 721–47.

[3] Norman Itzkowitz, *Ottoman Empire and Islamic Tradition* (Chicago: University of Chicago Press, 1972), 88. On the tendency to cite the circle, see Bernard Lewis, "Ottoman Observers of Ottoman Decline," *Islamic Studies* 1 (1962), 71–87.

but also encompasses in affairs of state the broader concept of "good governance."[4] For the Ottoman world, shari'a was the source of law and the guarantor of justice, the force binding subjects to their ruler.

As a term that arouses abhorrence among so many in the West today, "shari'a" requires brief explanation. Shari'a, a word connoting "way," represents the basic precept of acting "in the path of God," or behaving in a way attuned to God's instructions for individuals and for the community of believers. It is not a law code or set of statutes: it is impossible to get a copy of "the shari'a" as it would be to find the text of the Code Napoléon, for example. It is rather a system of interpretation of sources (the core text of the Qur'an but also the *hadith*, the accounts of the actions of Muhammad and the members of the early Muslim community) to guide believers in living a "good" life and avoiding the wrong in everyday situations. The bulk of shari'a interpretation has addressed matters of faith and the permissibility of actions, not problems pertaining to social regulation through fields such as criminal law. Where it does address wrongs done to fellow humans rather than poor practice of faith, shari'a's main intent is to restore peace between Muslims and heal the moral order rather than to punish (a matter to be decided by God), except under very limited circumstances. As befits tort, crime is highly personal, with factors such as the moral and social standing of the parties involved and the intent of the perpetrator of wrong influencing the determination of guilt and the means chosen to make amends.[5] The Qur'an contains firm rules, to be sure, and the texts are not open to complete freedom of interpretation. There are nevertheless broadly accepted modes of varying interpretation, represented as "schools" (sg. *madhhab*) of Islamic jurisprudence.

Of the four Sunni schools, the Hanafi is the most inclined to pragmatic solutions to problems imperiling community peace. Hanafism (after Abu Hanifa [d. 767]) developed in southern Iraq, former borderland between the Byzantine and Sassanid (Persian) empires and the site of several major garrison-encampments populated by Muslim tribesmen from disparate regions of the Arabian Peninsula. The area also saw the most rapid rise

---

[4] Bernard Lewis, "Freedom and Justice in the Modern Middle East," *Foreign Affairs* 84/3 (May–June 2005), 38, citing Rifa'a Rafi' al-Tahtawi's explanation of (post)revolutionary France's "liberté" as the equivalent of Muslims' "justice."

[5] Lawrence Rosen, *The Anthropology of Justice: Law as Culture in Islamic Society* (Cambridge: Cambridge University Press, 1989); Rudolf Peters, *Crime and Punishment in Islamic Law: Theory and Practice from the Sixteenth to the Twenty-First Century* (Cambridge: Cambridge University Press, 2005).

in numbers of non-Arab converts to Islam. Its variegated population encouraged Hanafism's flexibility of approach to interpretation, including the greatest acceptance of popular custom (and not the custom of a specific place and time, as the Hijaz-centered Maliki madhhab did) as legitimate.[6] It is the school most given to interpreting on the basis of logic, "the common good," and "public interest." Because Hanafi interpretation is in many respects the least constricting of the schools, it was favored by numerous premodern regimes, including those with authority over extensive territories and variegated populations, from the Abbasid caliphate of Baghdad to Mughal India to the Ottoman empire.

Shariʿa in the Ottoman empire accepted custom into law, but it also accommodated sultanic decree (*kanun*). It is important to recognize that despite the large volume of royal directives, kanun supplemented rather than overshadowed shariʿa. Since shariʿa guides Muslims to act in accordance with God's wishes, matters of faith and proper comportment (e.g., ritual propriety, or the permissibility of wearing certain clothing or listening to music) far outweigh those of relations between believers. Guidance on interpersonal affairs, especially serious (*hadd*) crime, is also circumscribed by strong provisions, including testimony by multiple eyewitnesses of good character, admissibility of hard rather than circumstantial evidence, and consideration of intent; these provisions were meant to prevent miscarriages of justice that could lead to fitna among Muslims. Since shariʿa treats crime as essentially personal, moreover, no judge has a role until someone lodges a complaint or accusation. For a state that took seriously its responsibility to protect the society under its control, shariʿa's lack of detailed prescriptions for management of public affairs made supplementary regulation necessary. Shariʿa accepted this place for mundane authority in legal regulation under such terms as *siyasa*, the ruler's right to chastise his servants charged with imperial administration, and *taʿzir*, discretionary punishment in cases not punishable according to specified requirements of shariʿa. Ottoman imperial kanun developed in these areas to regulate and manage the empire's population more effectively.[7] Only in rare instances did kanun contradict an important sharʿi principle, as in the decree of Mehmed II that sultans could kill their brothers, or in application of the *devşirme*, by which children of

---

[6] Gideon Libson, "On the Development of Custom as a Source of Law in Islamic Law," *ILS* 4 (1997), 131–55.

[7] Muhammad Masud, Rudolph Peters, and David Powers, "Qadis and Their Courts: An Historical Survey," in *Dispensing Justice in Islam: Qadis and Their Judgments*, ed. Muhammad Masud et al. (Leiden: Brill, 2006), 12; Peters, *Crime and Punishment*, ch. 1.

Christian peasants could be made the sultan's slaves in contravention of the principle that non-Muslims who paid a head tax (*jizya*) are protected against such penalties. These contradictions discomfited the Ottoman ruling class, but they found justification in *istihsan* and *istislah* (seeking the greater good and, roughly, "public interest"), principles accepted in Hanafi jurisprudence.[8] As a body, therefore, Ottoman law was built upon an Islamic foundation and, in line with this basis, aimed at ensuring that justice was seen to prevail in both state and society.

Ottoman society had another obvious need for kanun law: until the addition to the empire of the Arab provinces in the sixteenth century, the population was majority Christian, and even thereafter it retained a large non-Muslim minority. Shari'a was Islamic, and under shari'a it was wrong to force people who refused to recognize the truth of the religion to apply its principles, except in issues affecting Muslims. Had law remained limited only to the shari'a, Ottoman rule probably would have been short-lived in the Balkans and even Anatolia. Greater flexibility existed in punishing by siyasa or ta'zir, however, the areas encompassing much of kanun, thereby creating a legal framework through which an otherwise ill-served part of the population could attain justice. The Ottoman supplementation of shari'a with kanun enabled the retention of non-Muslim acceptance of subservience to the Islamic state.

This contradicts the notion that non-Muslims accepted Ottoman overlordship because they were able to escape much of its control, as a result of the sultans' having granted autonomy to non-Muslim communities (*millas*/Ott. *millet*s). In the premodern period, when the state was concerned with matters of war, peace, and taxation, the non-Muslims had no unusual autonomy or exemption from state authority. After the fifteenth century, at least, they were in theory excluded (not exempted) from military service, and they paid the head tax that contributed crucial revenue to the central government's war chest. It was in collection of the head tax or other requirements such as the devşirme that could provoke unrest among non-Muslims where the state saw an interest in actively supporting the status of non-Muslim men of religion. This was not the granting of autonomy but rather the opposite, since support went with assignation of responsibility for ensuring acquiescence to the state's demands. In legal affairs the lack of autonomy was equally apparent. There was only one law of the land, and it was the Ottoman: kanun and shari'a, which, in Hanafi practice, made significant accommodation for custom

[8] Victor Ménage, "Some Notes on the 'Devshirme,'" *BSOAS* 29 (1966), 70–1.

or established practice (*'adat, 'urf*). Non-Muslim "courts" addressed only issues of comportment according to infidels' "misguided" notions of God's wishes that also made up the bulk of shari'a but not kanun: ritual and personal affairs, including marriage, divorce, and inheritance. The state simply did not care about these, as long as no Muslim was involved and no threat to communal peace arose. This freedom from interference in religious matters eased non-Muslim acceptance of Ottoman authority, but milla courts had no enforcement power or legal standing, explaining the lack of records left by such bodies.[9] Any non-Muslim dissatisfied with the opinion of the milla court was free to take the matter to the Ottoman judge to get another, and legally enforceable, decision, as many did. They could even appeal directly to the sultan in serious cases; for non-Muslims as well, "the religion and the dynasty" were the ultimate guardians of the population's spiritual and material well-being.

That some non-Muslims turned voluntarily to the Ottoman courts hints at the last important point to note regarding the nature of the state and its religiously shaped system of law: the premium placed upon achieving just resolutions to affairs unsettling local communities, rather than upon retributive punishment of lawbreakers. In comparison to a legal system such as premodern England's, with its notorious propensity to mete out the death penalty for a wide variety of seemingly minor crimes as a means of deterring offenders, the Ottoman legal system placed heavier emphasis upon protecting local communal peace. The premodern empire saw state-committed bloodshed, including executions of individuals and the attempted extermination of groups, but this tended to occur at times of high state stress and affected primarily the ruling class or, in the case of pro-Safavid *kızılbaş*, heretical "traitors" to the dynasty, not the general population. Sultans took seriously their responsibility for dispensing justice (*'adala*), and the main target of their justice rescripts (Ott. *adaletname*) was the state's officials, warning them against abuse of their authority over the taxpaying population.[10] The courts, by contrast, often sought reconciliation and arbitration of disputes; penalties levied when reconciliation was impossible or inappropriate inclined toward payment of restitution or compensation to the aggrieved; and punishment (fines,

---

[9] Jewish responsa, which bear a closer resemblance to Islamic fatwas than to court records, are the exception.

[10] Halil İnalcık, "State, Sovereignty and Law during the Reign of Süleyman," in *Süleyman the Second and His Time*, ed. Halil İnalcık and Cemal Kafadar (Istanbul: ISIS Press, 1993), 59–61; Boğaç Ergene, "On Ottoman Justice: Interpretations in Conflict (1600–1800)," *ILS* 8 (2001), 52–87.

imprisonment, or corporal injury) tended to be moderate to encourage reform or rehabilitation of the offender.[11] To illustrate this, consider a case involving a former provincial officer in the mid-eighteenth century.

One Ömer Bey of Ioannina (northwestern Greece) served as military commander of the district in the 1750s, when he was imprisoned in the citadel of Durrës (Albania) for reckless carriage of weapons and the presumably accidental but nevertheless wrongful killing of a Christian; having somehow secured release from prison, he then started to meddle in the management of timar lands. Having acted twice against the sultan's kanun, he lost his position and was imprisoned again in 1758, this time in the fortress of Limnos, so that he could repent and rehabilitate himself (*islah al-nafs*, implying moral improvement). He was released after a few months, on condition that he not engage again in such undesirable acts. Having lost his position, however, he became something of a confirmed rogue, perhaps out of necessity. He was imprisoned on another five occasions between 1760 and 1768, each time upon the petition of Muslim and non-Muslim subjects of good standing complaining of different illegal acts committed by Ömer and various partners. Each time he was to be imprisoned until he had reformed himself, a process that apparently always took months rather than years. Yet, in line with shar'i thinking, the state never deemed him beyond salvation and therefore neither locked him away permanently (or even for progressively lengthier periods as a recidivist) nor executed him.[12] Ömer's history indicates a relatively responsive, efficient, morally grounded, and humane legal system: an effective source of justice.

This chapter's discussion of themes as large as the development of the Ottoman state and of its close connection to Islam necessarily relies upon sweeping statements that belie variations, but it reflects the general characteristics of the topic. The stability of the link between Ottoman rule and Islam in the premodern period seems incontrovertible: the ethos and ultimate focus of public life, accepted by both rulers and ruled, was service to *din ü devlet* (the religion and the dynasty/state). This does not imply that religion supplied all the answers to all the questions posed by decision makers: the marriage between state and religion presented no bar to the Ottomans' noted practicality. Islam did place limits upon mundane authority, in that no sultan could claim to be truly an absolute

---

[11] See, for example, Engin Akarlı, "Law in the Marketplace: Istanbul, 1730–1840," in Masud, Peters, and Powers (eds.), *Dispensing Justice*, 247–51.

[12] BOA, Cev.Dah 3181, 11 June 1768.

ruler answerable to none, and acceptance of God's supremacy meant that no sultan or grand vizier could openly flout God's law or otherwise stray from service to God's wishes without running a rapidly escalating risk of popular disquiet. In return, however, Islam gave the dynasty a powerful ideological legitimacy, in effect providing a readily understood answer to the question "What is the state's purpose; what does it stand for?": protection and expansion of the Abode of Islam. This answer resonated particularly with the majority (from the sixteenth century) of the population, who also found in Islam the answer to the more personal question of "Why am I here?" and was at least acceptable to the significant minority who found their answer in other monotheistic faiths that had similar ethical principles. The stability of this system, however, would be tested from the late eighteenth century, when, under pressure from Christian European foes, the Ottoman state faced the need to strengthen itself at a pace more rapid than any seen since the early stages of building a state out of chaos in the fourteenth and early fifteenth centuries.

2

The Premodern Islamic State and Military Modernization

If the last, long century of the Ottoman empire's life was remarkable for its turbulence, there was no more critical period prior to the catastrophic 1911–22 years than the decades from 1768 to 1839. It determined in stark terms the primary goal that would challenge state and society for the remainder of the empire's existence: finding sustainable means to stave off the existential threat posed by a militarily dominant Christian Europe. Much of the turmoil seen in the reign of Sultan Selim III (1789–1807), culminating in his overthrow by a rebellion in Istanbul, was created by dissension over whether the ends justified the means that he chose. Following defeats by Russia and the Habsburgs, Selim's regime tried to unravel the secrets of their military supremacy and to copy the key elements, but the challenge of identifying such secrets proved impossible to solve. The regime fell because it lost the support of those who felt that preservation of the Abode of Islam would only be possible if the implicit and explicit understandings that bound state and society together under the old system were upheld, and the principles that made the empire the Abode of Islam were respected.

Much of that opposition resulted from the impression that the sultan was giving greater attention to adaptation of Christian ways than he had to supporting the Ottoman army while it suffered in trying to save the empire from the Russians and Habsburgs. Anger was magnified by Istanbul's perceived placement of blame for failures of the political-military system upon those who had shouldered the burden of defense. Ottoman defeats did not result from corruption but from basic lack of military competencies that Christian European armies had acquired by the end of the eighteenth century, courtesy of recent decades' experience

33

in butchering each other and the rise of absolutist governments capable of exploiting resources relatively intensively. Christian armies were better supplied, organized, commanded, trained, and disciplined. Above all, they were bigger and had better artillery, and more of it. Insofar as responsibility for not keeping pace fell on the Ottoman system, the fault lay in the slighting of military preparedness that became Istanbul's habit in the eighteenth century. The main weaknesses in the military-administrative system that caused this were the dominance of elite political households and the effective consolidation of much of the empire's revenue base in the hands of that elite through the institution of lifetime tax farming (*malikane*).

Defeat showed that something needed to be done to strengthen the state's defenses, but what measures might be necessary was less clear. Selim III's "reform" program represented a series of half-steps. He failed to address the systemic weaknesses crippling military preparedness, copying instead aspects of European armies that appeared most striking to Ottoman officers who had witnessed their strength in battle. He concentrated on creating a "European"-style army corps, the New Order (*Nizam-i Cedid*), and rebuilt the crippled Ottoman navy. The experiment ended unhappily, as the New Order proved little more effective than the old army, and it was dissolved when Selim was overthrown. After a brief, chaotic interlude under Sultan Mustafa IV, the first grand vizier under Mahmud II tried to restore order by drafting an agreed set of rules of politics (the Deed of Agreement) that all officeholders could follow to aid the state's recovery from crisis.

This chapter explains the path chosen by Selim III by considering the military-political system that he inherited, the military challenges confronting the empire on his succession, and the flaws in the New Order program. It concludes by explaining how the Deed of Agreement sought to resolve the tensions that had marred Selim's reign. Proper recognition of the problems facing the empire makes the decisions taken by him and his officers comprehensible and clarifies the reasons for the unrest that greeted his reforms.

THE EIGHTEENTH-CENTURY OTTOMAN STATE: POLITICS, MONEY, AND THE MILITARY

Complete stasis had never characterized the Ottoman political-military-taxation system since its inception in the fourteenth century, but over the course of the eighteenth century two important institutions rose in importance: the political household and the lifetime tax farm. Both of these developed for rational reasons, and the impetus for both originated in the imperial elite of Istanbul; each nevertheless contributed to the growing weakness of the empire in comparison to foes in Christian Europe.

Given its focus on making war, keeping peace, and raising revenue, the Ottoman state established from its earliest recorded years close connections among its political-administrative order, its military system, and its revenue-raising practices. As one of these three elements changed, the others faced alteration as well. The "classical" Ottoman empire of the late fourteenth through early seventeenth centuries rested upon the timar system, a relatively simple model of prebendalism. This created a larger, more dependable administrative and fighting force than the haphazard system of the initial Ottoman period, when the war leader depended upon booty, tribute, and vassals to organize both military campaigns and rudimentary administration. Prebendalism gradually faded in turn as cavalry-dominant armies lost their advantage to improved military fortification and firearm-bearing infantry from the late sixteenth century. This put a premium upon gathering cash to meet the growing janissary payroll, which meant that many timars gradually turned into tax farms or were assigned to infantry formations, such as citadel garrisons. The tax-farming system still struggled to raise revenues in line with growing military expenses through the seventeenth century and certainly made little contribution to administrative coherence, problems that were to aid the development of both malikane and the political household.

Weakening prebendalism, a strengthening standing army, and growing complexity of taxation added to the pressures upon the empire's authorities. With few exceptions, the sultans of the seventeenth century lacked the experience, intelligence, or simple interest needed to police an increasingly intricate system, and high officers under the sultan developed the "political household" as the unit capable of providing coherent administration. Mehmed Köprülü gave the household the greatest boost. He became grand vizier in the midst of a military crisis in 1656 and won from the young Sultan Mehmed IV (1648–87) the power to make other administrative appointments; occurring as it did after extended periods of political confusion, his perceived success in restoring competent rule, fiscal discipline, and military effectiveness ensured that the Köprülü family retained the grand vizierate for much of the rest of the century and continued to place their associates – their political household – elsewhere in the administrative hierarchy. Other pashas and viziers formed similar households. As their claim to authority rested on bureaucratic control, high officers who constructed political households made the bureaucracy the route to political power in the empire during the eighteenth century, pushing the once-dominant military leadership into the shadows.[1]

Mehmed IV "The Hunter" showed little ability or interest in restoring close sultanic control over government, and one of his successors who attempted to reassert royal command, Mustafa II (1695–1703), failed spectacularly. He was the last sultan to lead the army on campaign and thus bore responsibility for the last crushing Ottoman defeat in a long war against a "Holy League" of Habsburgs, Venice, Poland, and Russia (1683–99); his attempt to resurrect the devşirme and rebuild the timar system to create forces dependent directly upon him also failed; and his scheme to shunt most households aside by relying upon one headed by his trusted tutor, Feyzullah Efendi, led to his overthrow and death in 1703.[2] Mustafa's successor, Ahmed III, avoided directly challenging the multiplying political households but found other ways to limit their power and keep them tied to the monarchy, including fostering a free-spending court-based culture similar to Louis XIV's Versailles.[3] One significant act was the issuance of a decree in 1726 that provincial district governors must be locals, which limited Istanbul-based political leaders' ability to appoint their own clients to provincial posts. This move aided the rise of the "local notables" who later came to be vilified as forces of decentralization and instigators of chaos.

Malikane tax farms nevertheless provided links among the imperial center, the households, and the local notables. Beginning in 1695, Istanbul introduced long-term rights to collect tax revenues from large properties, farmed out by auction, in return for a big initial payment and then for the remainder of the auction winner's life the annual remittance of a set sum from the revenue legally collectable from the source. Malikane, devised by the wartime central authorities, was embraced by the political households of the capital for several reasons. The ascending bureaucratic class had an inevitable interest in grasping some of the economic resources

---

[1] Norman Itzkowitz, "Eighteenth Century Ottoman Realities," *Studia Islamica* 16 (1962), 73–94; Rifaat Ali Abou-el-Haj, "The Ottoman Vezir and Pasha Households 1683–1703: A Preliminary Report," *Journal of the American Oriental Society* 94 (1974), 438–47.

[2] Marc Baer, *Honored by the Glory of Islam: Conversion and Conquest in Ottoman Europe* (Oxford: Oxford University Press, 2008), only confirms Mehmed's reputation for mediocrity. On Mustafa II, see Rif'at Ali Abou-el-Haj, *The 1703 Rebellion and the Structure of Ottoman Politics* (Istanbul: Nederlands Historisch-Archaeologisch Institut, 1984).

[3] Donald Quataert, *The Ottoman Empire 1700–1922* (Cambridge: Cambridge University Press, 2005), 44.

previously available mainly to the sultan and the military. Evidence of this can be seen already in 1669 in the first land survey done of one of the last Ottoman conquests, Crete, in which the land tenure laws recognized private ownership rather than repeating the established principle that all land belonged to the sultan.[4] This worked to the advantage of the preeminent political household,. the Köprülüs, who gained landed wealth in every territory taken during their ascendancy.[5] Outside of new territories, however, the opportunities for acquiring land were modest; malikane promised access to the only fast-growing part of the Ottoman tax base, the cash duties on trade and commodities, as well as to large estates previously controlled by old elites or even properties set aside as charitable endowments. The very estates of the sultan were subjected to malikane auction, placing their revenue flows partially under vizierial control and thus adding further protection against sultanic efforts to undercut the household system.[6] The requirement of a large initial payment limited bidding mainly to the well-connected elite in the imperial capital, an edge reinforced by the holding of auctions for significant tax sources only in Istanbul, and the restriction of malikane proprietorship to the overwhelmingly Muslim ruling elite from 1718. The concentration of control over revenue collection in the hands of the households of the center indeed increased over the eighteenth century: the percentage of malikane farms held by people in Istanbul rose from 65 percent in 1734 to 87 percent in 1789.[7] When malikane tax farms became heritable in midcentury, collection of a significant proportion of state taxes had been essentially privatized into the hands of a well-connected Muslim elite.[8] To enable proper exploitation of tax farms, however, that Istanbul-based elite needed the help of agents or partners in the provinces: the local notables.

If rising political households and provincial notables profited from malikane, how did Ottoman leaders rationalize its retention? The state

---

[4] Molly Greene, "An Islamic Experiment: Ottoman Land Policy on Crete," *Mediterranean Historical Review* 11 (1996), 60–78.

[5] İ Metin Kunt, "The Waqf as an Instrument of Public Policy: Notes on the Köprülü Family Endowments," in *Studies in Ottoman History in Honour of Professor V. L. Ménage*, ed. Colin Heywood and Colin Imber (Istanbul: Isis, 1994), 189–98.

[6] Ariel Salzmann, *Tocqueville in the Ottoman Empire: Rival Paths to the Modern State* (Leiden: Brill, 2004), 88–9.

[7] Halil İnalcık et al., *An Economic and Social History of the Ottoman Empire* (Cambridge: Cambridge University Press, 1997), 713.

[8] Assessing the percentage of state income subject to malikane involves much guesswork, but the proportion might have reached 50% by the late eighteenth century.

gained financially: not only did the treasury receive more income from the larger initial payments from auction winners, but it also gained by furthering the trend away from taxes in kind to payments in cash. In theory, moreover, holders of malikane took better care of revenue sources than previous tax farmers with only short-term interests, thus lengthening the life of the empire's assets. Collection of state revenue was also concentrated in trusted hands at the capital, a fact not to be overlooked when considering the notion of decentralization. This tendency to consolidate authority in trusted hands politically and spatially close to the palace can be detected in other ways, including the rise of privileged families among the *'ulama*, with the post of shaikh al-islam (head of the religious hierarchy and chief mufti) held by members of a handful of families for much of the eighteenth century, and among the Phanariote Greeks of Istanbul, who monopolized the Orthodox patriarchates of Istanbul and other cities and the governorships of the Danubian principalities, Wallachia and Moldavia.[9] Christian authorities, incidentally, were treated akin to tax farmers but without lifetime tenure, with accession payments expected upon naming to any of these positions.

Such significant changes in tax and administration practices had less-desirable side effects, however, that took time to become apparent. The increased monetarization of both state and economy helped to stimulate "elite inflation," by which the remuneration expected by the upper levels of the state's administrators rose through the eighteenth century. One sign of this was the spread of *arpalık* (simony), with officers holding multiple positions, filling one but taking the pay due for all. The money not only supported the lifestyle expected of ranking notables but also eased the purchase of malikane. Absentee provincial governors and qadis could not perform their limited duties in monitoring the collection of nonmalikane taxes. Malikane supervision was primarily the responsibility of the center, but monitoring became increasingly difficult with the trend to formation of partnerships among multiple investors to collect the large sums needed to purchase malikane. The proliferation of parties pooled not only cash but also temptations to manipulate an increasingly complex system. Problems of malfeasance or disputes among partners could also result when tax collection was delegated or sublet to agents in the provinces. And given the central elite's own preponderance in

---

[9] Madeline Zilfi, *The Politics of Piety: The Ottoman Ulema in the Postclassical Age (1600–1800)* (Minneapolis: Bibliotheca Islamica, 1988).

malikane, those charged with regulating the system could be liable to police themselves as tax farmers.

It was the military that felt most deeply the side effects of the shift to malikane. The Ottomans are noted for having created the first standing army in post-Roman European history when they started the slave corps of janissaries and *sipahi*s of the Porte – but their perennial struggles to meet the payroll illustrate why no other state did it before. The Ottoman center had few means of meeting the standing military's cost, other than through booty and war indemnities: debasing the coinage (quickly self-defeating), paring janissary rolls, intensifying cash-based tax farming, and opening to the military nonsalary sources of income. Already in the sixteenth century, when the empire was at the zenith of relative power, prestige, and wealth, it gave the sultan's slave soldiers such avenues to supplementing their income, with sipahis of the porte involved in tax farming and janissaries entering trade and guild life. Malikane was introduced to improve the returns from tax farming, but at least in peacetime the political household system that dominated the eighteenth century neither automatically transferred such added revenue to the standing military nor had any interest in easing the military's access to this new form of tax farm.

In the late seventeenth and eighteenth centuries the state managed by the political households tried to keep military expenses in check, and the janissaries were the prime focus. That these households had their roots in administration rather than in the military presumably made them less attuned to the wishes of the standing army. In the long period of peace in the mid-eighteenth century, for example, the military supply system was permitted to wither, as the fact that soldiers marching to fight the Russians in 1768 were fed biscuit made from forty-year-old stores indicates.[10] During the long war with the Holy League in the late seventeenth century the janissary rolls were pruned sharply as a cost-cutting measure and did not grow again in an orderly fashion thereafter. The number of nominal janissaries rose in the eighteenth century, helped by Istanbul's own manipulation of the janissary pay ticket system. Ever short of money for salaries, the central government issued new pay tickets as a form of promissory note instead of disbursing cash; pay tickets inevitably became tradable, an item of commerce, a fact that the central authorities accepted from 1740. The multiplying pay tickets ultimately would enjoy longer

---

[10] Virginia Aksan, "The One-Eyed Fighting the Blind: Mobilization, Supply, and Command in the Russo-Turkish War of 1768–1774," *IHR* 15 (1993), 232.

lives than their original holders, often accumulating in the hands of high officials and wealthy civilians, and taxpaying Muslims in particular resorted to various subterfuges to win at least local recognition of being janissaries.[11] The state tried to control janissary growth bureaucratically but also retreated to concentrating on funding only those troops that it knew were necessary, particularly in the provinces, such as garrisons.[12] The revenue sources for these standing military units were progressively turned into malikane tax farms, however, and disputes with tax farmers or their agents posed a serious threat to the well-being and preparedness of fortresses and troops already under the pressure of fiscal restraint.[13]

For the standing military, the growth of a malikane-funded state thus had several long-term significant effects. The lack of assured, adequate funding led to a further melding of the corps with the commercial and trades sectors of the empire's cities, because most janissaries could not survive on a soldier's pay.[14] Although this damaged their efficacy as professional soldiers (which may not have been as great in previous eras as usually assumed),[15] the imperial center appeared untroubled by the trend, simply turning increasingly to hiring temporary soldiers paid only in wartime and only for the campaign season rather than the full year. Since the state took no responsibility for training these troops, its military system in the eighteenth century came to rely heavily on people from regions renowned for producing men who had to be good fighters to survive, meaning poor areas with rugged terrain and a history of conflict: Albanians, Bosnians, Kurds, North Africans, Arab tribesmen, and people from the Caucasus/eastern Black Sea, such as Georgians, Abkhaz, Laz, and Circassians. Such recruits were tougher and more skilled as both conventional and unconventional fighters than the semicivilian janissaries had become, and the state saw no reason to try seriously to reprofessionalize the military. The shortcomings of the

---

[11] İnalcık et al., *Economic and Social History*, 716; Yücel Özkaya, *XVIII. Yüzyılda Osmanlı Kurumları ve Osmanlı Toplum Yaşantısı* (Ankara: Kültür ve Turizm Bakanlığı, 1985), 27–38.

[12] By 1748, the state paid more to local units and garrisons than it did standing military forces such as the janissaries. Ahmet Tabakoğlu, *Gerileme Dönemine Girerken Osmanlı Maliyesi* (Istanbul: Dergah Yayınları, 1985), 186–7.

[13] Michael Hickok, *Ottoman Military Administration in Eighteenth-Century Bosnia* (Leiden: Brill, 1997), 98–112.

[14] See, for example, Amnon Cohen, "The Army in Palestine in the Eighteenth Century – Sources of Its Weakness and Strength," *BSOAS* 34 (1971), 42–4.

[15] Colin Imber, "Ibrahim Peçevi on War: A Note on the 'European Military Revolution,'" in *Frontiers of Ottoman Studies: State, Province and the West, vol. 2*, ed. Colin Imber, Keiko Kiyotaki, and Rhoads Murphey (London: I. B. Tauris, 2005), 7–22.

provincial levies that would become clear by Selim's reign reflected not the fighting spirit and skill of such troops but rather the advances in battlefield order, supply, command, weaponry (especially the use of field artillery), and the sheer scale of military forces that Christian Europe experienced in that century. Without further training, neither provincial levies nor janissaries could match – or stand against – the massed musketry and artillery fire of the Russian, Habsburg, or French armies that had developed such firepower to survive on Europe's battlefields; officers were similarly weak in strategy and tactics, in command and control in the field. Ottoman forces also could not be called into service at short notice, because terms of service for provincial levies had to be negotiated before recruits could be found.

Provincial notables played an increasingly important role in raising, supplying, and even leading the eighteenth century Ottoman military, just as they assumed growing importance in the malikane system. Again, this did not develop against the wishes of the imperial center, which set recruitment targets for its provincial officeholders. Locally influential families could provide valuable services to the state in wartime by using their knowledge of place and people to raise with greatest efficiency recruits and materiel to meet quotas assigned by the center. In both war and peacetime their knowledge and influence also made them well suited to act as tax collection agents for absentee malikane holders and arpalık governors, and as they built their own wealth through landholding or business with the state, they could bid for local tax farms, especially in auctions for relatively modest assets held outside Istanbul. Notables came to hold a variety of titles and official positions, and as they rose in rank, they often recruited military retinues that could grow to significant size.[16] This also performed a service for the state, in that provincial officials' households provided some of the military training and acclimation to regimented life that the state's temporary recruits otherwise lacked, and high officials called to campaign were expected to supply their household troops as the base of their district's quota of men for front-line service. The notables thus were not necessarily signs, let alone agents, of imperial dissipation but rather were actively tied to the state and Istanbul's interests.

---

[16] One such title was *a'yan*, now used as a generic term for "provincial notable" but actually referring to an urban notable who played an intermediary role between the state and the population of a town. *Derebey* was not an Anatolian equivalent of *a'yan* but referred to a rural, often tribal, leader.

Although commonly portrayed as rebellious, provincial notables considered themselves loyal to the sultan and accepted the guiding principle of *din ü devlet*. There were few who either declared rebellion against the sultan's rule (rather than being labeled as rebels by Istanbul) or openly turned to other states for help.[17] What many notables lacked was service in the imperial center (the sultan's palace, the elite households, or the bureaucracy), a shortcoming that may have lessened their ability to see issues clearly from an "imperial" perspective rather than in provincial terms, but the issue of perspective should not be exaggerated. Where it mattered was in notables' engagement in rivalries with neighboring peers that threatened the state's duty to protect the domestic peace – a problem that the imperial center sometimes encouraged, however, in part because the center itself was no stranger to factional rivalries as political households multiplied, but also because of policy choices made in the heat of wartime.

While malikane privatization of revenue collection ultimately proved more damaging to the state's fundamental interests than the rise of local notables, for the first two-thirds of the eighteenth century the Ottoman state continued to be quite capable of performing adequately its core tasks. As in the rise of provincial notables, malikane in itself did not mark decentralization because no centralization had ever really existed. At no time prior to 1695 had the state ever done other than delegate authority to collect taxes, and the system always worked to a reasonable extent as intended as long as the state had the power or will to revoke that authority from designees who abused their position, that is, those who were targeted by the *adaletnames* issued periodically by each sultan. Provincial notables similarly constituted little threat to imperial authority as long as the center exercised oversight.[18] It was not decentralization but the loss, or disavowal, of the center's regulatory power over both revenue collectors and political hierarchies that shaped the domestic aspect of the crisis besetting the empire in the wake of the crushing military losses of 1768–74 and 1787–92. It was these defeats that made evident the effects

---

[17] Egypt, which experienced an unusual degree of internotable rivalry in the eighteenth century, was most likely to produce such "traitorous" figures. See, for example, Jane Hathaway, "Ottoman Responses to Çerkes Mehmed Bey's Rebellion in Egypt, 1730," in *Mutiny and Rebellion in the Ottoman Empire*, ed. Jane Hathaway (Madison: University of Wisconsin Press, 2002), 105–13.

[18] For an example of how the central authorities reacted with alacrity to turmoil created by notables' disputes, see Antonis Anastasopoulos, "Lighting the Flame of Disorder: Ayan Infighting and State Intervention in Ottoman Karaferye, 1758–59," in Hathaway (ed.), *Mutiny and Rebellion*, 73–88.

of the system's slighting of military preparedness. The Ottoman center's disastrous foray into war making in 1768–74 did, in fact, destroy the stability of the system by crippling the center financially, militarily, and therefore administratively. It lost its ability to defend abroad, keep the peace at home, and provide justice for society.

THE MILITARY CRISIS OF THE LATE EIGHTEENTH CENTURY

Following acceptance of defeat in the war of 1683–99 against the Holy League, the Ottoman empire's fortunes in warfare against Christian Europe improved until 1768. It beat Russia in 1711, capturing Czar Peter the Great and his army (and then releasing them in return for modest territorial gains); it defeated Venice in 1715–18, retaking the Morea (southern Greece), but lost to the Habsburgs, who entered the war as allies of Venice and captured Belgrade; and it regained Belgrade in another war against the Habsburgs in 1736–9. This record of relative success may explain why Istanbul's governing elite decided on war with Russia almost blithely in 1768, with dissenters in the divan sidelined. Russia was unprepared for the conflict, but events showed that the Ottomans were even less ready to campaign. It was a war aptly described as "conflict between the one-armed and the blind."[19]

Istanbul's self-confidence failed to prepare it for the terrible shocks of the war, which affected the entire empire and particularly the European provinces. Such trauma went far beyond realization of defeat to include not only staggering casualties (500,000 dead on both sides) but also the tremendous strain of providing supplies under a rusty military logistics system.[20] With armies smashed at Hotin (1769), Kartal (1770), and Suvorovo and Shumen (1774), and a fleet sunk at Çeşme (1770), the conflict devastated the already frayed professional military, which was the main pool of manpower at least nominally dependent directly upon the sultan; the center had to rely ever more heavily upon levies from the provinces in order to keep forces in the field. It also suffered a critical shortfall of the money needed to raise and supply both seasonal and standing forces. This had crippling effects on the Ottoman system: Istanbul needed so desperately the help of provincial notables, the group crucial to meeting manpower and money needs, that it turned a blind eye to all but the

---

[19] Itzkowitz, *Ottoman Empire*, 108.
[20] Virginia Aksan, *Ottoman Wars 1700–1870: An Empire Besieged* (Harlow: Pearson Education, 2007), 142–60.

most serious misdeeds of those who proved able to supply troops and materiel. Without either money or strong forces directly under its own control, despite nominal repopulation of the janissary corps after 1774, Istanbul struggled to apply delayed justice to those in the provinces who had appeared to act against kanun and shari'a.[21] Several examples from the Balkans and Anatolia illustrate the degree to which the state felt its hands tied. In 1772 Istanbul ignored illegal acts of the notable who controlled Florina (Greece) because he was due to send five hundred men to the warfront. More striking was the case of Buşatlı Kara Mahmud Pasha, who held the essentially hereditary governorship of Shkodra (northern Albania) but faced a military campaign in 1787 to strip him of office due to turmoil he caused in neighboring regions. With the outbreak of war and a Habsburg drive into Bosnia, Kara Mahmud was not only reconfirmed in his position but given a promotion in rank and lucrative tax assets on condition that he assume the defense of southern Bosnia. Something similar happened in Anatolia, where in 1787 Divrikli Köse Mustafa Pasha, who had been accused of embezzling state funds and oppressing the population under his control, received promotion and higher offices, on condition that he repay his debt to the state and lead a motley army of tribesmen, Turks, and Caucasians against the Russians in Crimea.[22]

Lack of imperial attention to upholding the norms of administration compounded any problems caused by official malfeasance in the provinces, because the state turned a blind eye to feuding among notables, on the grounds that the winners in "survival of the fittest" contests would be best able to supply the army. One commander sent in 1790 to raise an army in Albania reported in disgust that most of the pool of potential recruits (and of the provincial revenues) was absorbed in squabbles between notables. Each district governor felt threatened by his neighbor, poured money into strengthening his own defenses, and then wanted to annex another district in order to afford the arms race. The officer's solution was to have the state make clear to each notable that it wanted the

[21] The treaty of Küçük Kaynarca that ended the war also included a secret clause committing Istanbul to paying a large war indemnity, worsening its financial problems.

[22] Frederick Anscombe, "Albanians and 'Mountain Bandits,'" in *The Ottoman Balkans, 1750–1830*, ed. Frederick Anscombe (Princeton: Markus Wiener, 2006), 98; Necdet Sakaoğlu, *Anadolu Derebeyi Ocaklarından Köse Paşa Hanedanı* (Istanbul: Tarih Vakfı Yurt Yayınları, 1998), 78–9. See also Antonis Anastasopoulos, "Crisis and State Intervention in Late Eighteenth-Century Karaferye (mod. Veroia)," in Anscombe (ed.), *Ottoman Balkans*, 24–5.

levy of soldiers that his district was assigned to raise, preferably with his help, but, if a neighbor showed greater willingness, then Istanbul would be happy to give that rival control over the region.[23]

With its toleration and even encouragement of turmoil at the upper levels of provincial government, Istanbul also found it difficult to uphold the justice system at other levels. Consider, for example, the case of Ömer Bey of Ioannina noted in the preceding chapter. One of the misdeeds that he committed in 1768 was coercion of the inhabitants of a tax-exempt *derbend* (mountain pass) settlement to accept that their village was his property (*çiftlik*). Istanbul effected his arrest and removal to prison simply by sending a courier with an order to be executed by the local governor. In 1786 Istanbul could do nothing about the forcible seizure of another village as çiftlik by a minor notable in the same province, other than refusing to recognize officially the land's change of status.[24] After 1768, the circle of equity came under increasing pressure as a result of war and faced imminent risk of breakdown by 1792. That the empire continued as a functioning political and economic unit was due, in a real sense, to the active loyalty and assistance of most of the later-reviled provincial notables. There certainly were some who took power in the provinces by force, but thereafter they flourished by providing Istanbul with its basic needs: men and money. The most capable of them also took care to support an effective system of justice for the population in lands under their control, even if they themselves did not submit willingly to all restrictions of edict from Istanbul.

Tepedelenli Ali Pasha, governor of Ioannina from 1787 to 1820 and one of the most famous provincial notables, illustrates this well. Already a significant, and often disturbing, influence in the province, he was first appointed governor on condition that he raise and lead troops against Kara Mahmud Pasha of Shkodra. Over the next three decades, he expanded by both fair and violent means his zone of direct or indirect control over much of mainland Greece and southern Albania. Istanbul was content to see him thrive in spite of the annoyance his local actions frequently caused because he served as a vital support for the empire's continued existence. He provided recruits for the military in a stream that grew to forty thousand men at the height of his territorial dominance in 1810–13 and remitted tax revenues (and even extraordinary additional

---

[23] Anscombe, "'Mountain Bandits,'" 97. Compare this to the attitude of central authorities in 1758–9 cited in Anastasopoulos, "Lighting the Flame."

[24] BOA, Cev.Dah 10372.

contributions) more effectively than the same lands previously under more fractured control had.[25] The population under his control, which included many Orthodox Christians, may not have loved him because of his strict rule, but they accepted his authority because he was more effective in keeping the peace, protecting both people and property, than the previous governors whom he displaced. The lands under his supervision formed an island of relative stability in the Balkans during the turmoil of Selim III's reign and the series of draining wars the empire faced after 1792. Istanbul recognized this, promoting him to the rank of vizier and even appointing him to the post of chief military officer of Rumeli (covering much of the Balkan peninsula), an office he performed very effectively for a year before Istanbul rotated the post to a rival to hinder his further rise.[26] Had Ali been a rebel or truly desired independence, he might well have succeeded in breaking free, and certainly the Ottoman center would have found its task of maintaining the empire's unity and autonomy much more difficult to accomplish.

SELIM III AND THE NEW ORDER

Selim III never experienced much relief from acute foreign and domestic pressures during his moderately long reign. He ascended the throne in the midst of a conflict that had been started by a foolhardy "war" faction in the imperial divan, and Ottoman military and governmental failures soon forced him to acknowledge defeat. Having signed peace agreements with the Habsburgs at Sistova (1791) and with Russia at Jassy (1792), Selim accepted that he commanded a military no longer capable of defeating major European Christian powers and did not have much money to build a force comparable to theirs, or even to pay the military that he still had. As a step toward recouping power, Selim asserted closer control over the factions that perennially complicated decision making. He could not dissolve the household system but rather manipulated it by rotating advisers and officers (he had nine grand viziers in his eighteen-year reign, with similarly rapid turnover in other high offices). The sultan adopted

---

[25] Frederick Anscombe, "Continuities in Ottoman Centre-Periphery Relations, 1787–1915," in *Frontiers of the Ottoman State*, ed. Andrew Peacock (Oxford: Oxford University Press, 2009), 245; Yavuz Cezar, *Osmanlı Maliyesinde Bunalım ve Değişim Dönemi* (Istanbul: Alan Yayıncılık, 1986), 241.

[26] Dennis Skiotis, "From Bandit to Pasha: First Steps in the Rise to Power of Ali of Tepelen, 1750–1784," *IJMES* 2 (1971), 219–44; Anscombe, "Centre-Periphery," and "'Mountain Bandits.'"

his reform program, the New Order, on the basis of proposals from an array of such advisers who were charged with suggesting plans to fix the empire's problems and restore the circle of equity. The New Order failed to achieve its goals for a variety of reasons: the scope of reform was too narrow, the relative importance and likely consequences of military and financial elements were not well gauged, and chaotic circumstances, both internal and foreign, gave little scope for trial and error. Selim's attempt to model the Ottoman future on the practices of the Christian enemy also struck many Muslims as a betrayal of all that the empire had recently fought to save.

Selim did not attempt to remake the Ottoman state; his main focus in trying to strengthen the state's ability to defend itself was the military, both army and navy. The main products of the New Order were a standing army corps that was clothed, trained, and equipped on the model of Christian European armies, and new ships for the navy. The state also established training programs, barracks, and munitions factories to support the new units. The new forces never made much impact, however: the naval reform had to wait until the army innovations gained momentum, and the army measures were slow to show much effect. In hindsight it appears that much of the reason for the slow pace of change lay in the relative superficiality of measures that failed to address some of the basic weaknesses in the military and imperial administration.[27] The New Order was essentially a reaction to Istanbul's perception of an existential threat to the empire's existence, and much of the modernization program reflected literal observation: scrutiny of enemy formations on the battlefield, where they performed much more effectively than Ottoman forces, and review of drill routines performed by captured soldiers in front of high Ottoman officials. One aspect of reform, the intensification of attempts to improve artillery, addressed a key need, but most of the elements resulting from observation – alterations in regimental order, drill, and appearance – were more effect than cause of Europe's military revolution. Areas of Ottoman backwardness that were less easily observable than poor artillery and weak rank-and-file discipline but were critical to Christian armies' superiority – officer training, battlefield command, staff work, and supply systems – changed little. Critical to the devastating advantage enjoyed by Russia in the "one-armed against

---

[27] For studies of how Christian countries addressed the structural challenges of military modernization, see Christopher Storrs (ed.), *The Fiscal-Military State in Eighteenth-Century Europe: Essays in Honour of P. G. M. Dickson* (Farnham, UK: Ashgate 2009).

the blind" war, for example, were experienced field commanders and a functional general staff; the Ottomans had no general staff, and by tradition field command fell to the grand vizier, who had no military experience.[28] Thus by 1806, state investment in the New Order had produced a new-style army corps numbering some twenty-four thousand men, but their performance in limited engagements against the French and domestic opponents was mixed. When on the march or in barracks, the soldiers of the new corps showed many of the signs of indiscipline characteristic of the janissaries, and they could only be as good as the still-poor quality of the commanding officers would let them.[29] In short, the new corps failed to repair the center's weaknesses, and the lack of visible progress, let alone military victories, left Selim and his coterie of reformers vulnerable to spreading popular discontent.

Financial turmoil caused by wars, defeats, and the expenses of military rebuilding contributed to dissatisfaction in capital and provinces alike, but the perception that the New Order and everything done on its behalf represented something akin to a betrayal by the sultan's regime added much of the heat to complaints. The first step of the New Order was the founding of a separate treasury (*İrad-i Cedid*) to be devoted solely to the new military projects, but the means of raising money for it were traditional. The new treasury received its income from a handful of sources: tax farms, notably those of at least moderate size that were already established but had lapsed; vacant timars that were turned into tax farms; and new taxes, particularly on commodities such as alcohol, cotton, wool and other textiles, and currants. The excise duties were intended to raise new funds, but the reallocated tax farms represented a gradual cannibalization of revenues due to the hard-pressed established treasury, since more tax farms would lapse over time and be transferred to the new treasury. Such tax farms were not reissued as malikane, however, marking a needed tightening of control over both valuation and administration of revenue collection. Confiscation of the estates of officials in both center and provinces who died or were disgraced raised further funds.[30] State finances remained overstretched, however, and Selim's regime tried to cover shortfalls by falling further in arrears in the payment of salaries and by debasing coinage, thereby inaugurating an extended period of

---

[28] Aksan, *Ottoman Wars*, 167–8.

[29] See, for example, Tolga Esmer, "A Culture of Rebellion: Networks of Violence and Competing Discourses of Justice in the Ottoman Empire, 1790–1808" (PhD diss., University of Chicago, 2009), 275, 277.

[30] Cezar, *Osmanlı Maliyesinde*, 161–92; Sakaoğlu, *Köse Paşa*, 129.

accelerating inflation that was inevitably to complicate tax farming and arouse anger among the wider population, particularly those on fixed salaries. The established military system again suffered most from Istanbul's changes to the financial system.

Selim's New Order aroused opposition almost from the moment of inception, and the most violent strands of such antagonism originated precisely in the military system that had fought the wars of 1768–74 and 1787–92. The hostility influencing Istanbul's (and foreigners') perspective makes the shape of protest difficult to decipher, but the three main centers of unrest all had distinctly military characters: Vidin (a frontier stronghold on the Danube in northwestern Bulgaria), whose commander, Pasvanoğlu Osman Pasha, defied Istanbul's authority; Belgrade, where janissaries terrorized the local population; and the highlands of Bulgaria and Macedonia, which became the domains of "mountain bandit" gangs, who included in their ranks numerous discharged provincial militiamen. This military identification suggests a link between the unrest and Selim III's experiment in military reform, which became much clearer in 1806–7, when Selim had to renounce the idea of introducing conscription into the new corps, then indeed disband the New Order, and finally give up the throne under pressure from rebellious troops in Istanbul. The military veterans who rose against their sultan and his programs had surprisingly widespread support and sympathy among the general population, however, which raises questions about standard explanations of rebels' motivations that center on janissaries' self-interest in wishing to preserve their pay and privileges.

Both the janissaries and the militia recruited for the campaign season had real reasons for discontent tied to their service in the wars against Christian foes and the inadequacy of state support for the military. Janissaries were nominally due both daily pay and bread rations, as well as an annual uniform subvention, but pay was chronically far in arrears throughout wartime, in peace the situation improved little, and the bread ration was essentially fictive in this era. If a provincial janissary was lucky enough to get his pay, by 1800 his daily wage barely covered the cost of a cup of coffee. Provincial militia were recruited on slightly better terms and received a signing bonus, but they too were regularly discharged from service without receiving the promised salary.[31] Both janissaries and the militia tended to have impoverished backgrounds, and

---

[31] Deena Sadat, "Ayan and Ağa: The Transformation of the Bektashi Corps in the 18th Century," *Muslim World* 63 (1973), 212; Anscombe, " 'Mountain Bandits,'" 91–2.

Istanbul's failure to pay its soldiers promptly or adequately had already exacerbated the problem of discipline among troops during the wars; it was such men who, when discharged from service without pay, formed much of the mountain bandit movement.[32] The news that the New Order involved taxes that disproportionately affected the poor to equip and pay a new military corps properly, which the state had failed to do for those who had fought in the war, must have been infuriating. It is no surprise, therefore, that at least some "mountain bandits" targeted particularly property of the central government, including storehouses, arsenals, and lands devoted to supplying the new army, and of officials serving it in the provinces.[33]

Perhaps less easy to comprehend from a modern perspective was the symbolic provocation presented by the New Order. This was an era of raised religious sensibilities, as both elite and less privileged Ottoman Muslims were conscious that the very existence of the empire as the Abode of Islam, territory under a Muslim ruler who could uphold shari'a, was threatened by superior Christian enemies. The state emphasized to the Muslim population the duty to rally to defense of the faith and the dynasty, *din ü devlet*; within the state elite itself, discussion of possible ways forward dropped the traditional concern for ensuring the circle of equity in favor of the more basic need to save *din ü devlet*, without which the circle of equity was a moot issue.[34] Wars against Russia, the Habsburgs, and France were jihad, declared by the commander of the faithful to protect the Islamic community, and all good Muslims were to rally to the cause.[35] This moral compulsion helps to explain why soldiers answered the call to arms in such significant numbers despite the state's bare treasury and poor military supply systems. The sense of the religious community in crisis became constant between 1787 and 1812: while the empire was repeatedly under threat of war with European powers, it also faced growing strife within its own borders. It saw the first outbreak of significant Christian revolt in 1804, when Orthodox Christians took up arms against the janissary garrison of Belgrade, and many provinces were

---

[32] Yücel Özkaya, *Osmanlı İmperatorluğunda Dağlı İsyanları* (Ankara, 1983); Anscombe, "'Mountain Bandits'"; Esmer, "Culture of Rebellion."
[33] Esmer, "Culture of Rebellion," 95, 284.
[34] Virginia Aksan, "Ottoman Political Writing, 1768–1808," *IJMES* 25 (1993), 53–69.
[35] Sultan Selim III's communications with officials convey the sense of duty to defend the borders of Islam against the infidels, a duty not just of the sultan but of all Muslims. Enver Ziya Karal, *Selim III.ün Hatt-ı Humayunları* (Ankara: Türk Tarih Kurumu Basımevi, 1942), 24–7.

wracked by banditry and political violence.[36] Perhaps most shockingly, even the Holy Cities were not safe: the Wahhabis, a radical movement in central Arabia that sought to enjoin pious practice on fellow Muslims, sacked Mecca and Medina between 1803 and 1806 and closed the pilgrimage route to Ottoman caravans. In this atmosphere of looming catastrophe, elements of the New Order seemed exceptionally provocative.

Irreligious facets to the project touted as the savior force for the Abode of Islam must have raised serious concern. That one of the most significant sources of funds for the project was the new tax upon alcohol, for example, raised ethical problems for Muslims hoping that God would grant the defense success.[37] The fact that mimicry of Christian Europe extended even to soldiers' clothing provoked perhaps the strongest reaction. At a time when Sultan Selim issued strict sumptuary decrees mandating that religious and social distinctions be maintained visibly through dress, the injunction to adopt Christian uniform incensed those who had fought for religion and dynasty.[38] Janissaries and militia had fought and died by the thousand in two unpopular wars rashly declared by the empire's commanders, and they had done so without receiving regular pay or supplies.[39] With the second war lost but only modest concessions to the Habsburgs and Russians accepted at Sistova and Jassy, Selim appeared to be using the peace to further enemies' interests by hollowing out that which had kept armies in the field, the willingness to fight for the faith. The New Order's supporters failed to address such complaints adequately.[40]

---

[36] Anscombe, "'Mountain Bandits.'"

[37] During the war against the Holy League (1683–99), a tax on alcohol was introduced to raise critical funds but then abolished as illegitimate. The collector of the tax, Ahmed Efendi "The Unbeliever," was publicly executed. Abdülkadir Özcan (ed.), *Defterdar Sarı Mehmed Paşa: Zübde-i Vekayiat* (Ankara: Türk Tarih Kurumu Basımevi, 1995), 298–9; Özcan (ed.), *Anonim Osmanlı Tarihi* (Ankara: Türk Tarih Kurumu Basımevi, 2000), 4, 10–11. In recognition of this danger of "spiritual" pollution, the alcohol tax under Selim was only to be collected by non-Muslims. In the first years of the New Order, the only source of revenue slightly larger than alcohol was profit from various tax farms. Cezar, *Osmanlı Maliyesinde*, table XII (p. 161).

[38] Donald Quataert, "Clothing Laws, State and Society in the Ottoman Empire, 1720–1829," *IJMES* 29 (1997), 410–12.

[39] That of 1787–92 was particularly unwelcome: the prospect of war had triggered unprecedented protests in the form of anonymous placards or posters placed on public buildings and mosques in Istanbul. Caroline Finkel, *Osman's Dream: The Story of the Ottoman Empire 1300–1923* (London: John Murray, 2005), 382–3.

[40] For an example of proreform propaganda, the work of Selim's court historian masquerading as a veteran soldier, see Aksan, "Political Writing," 61–2, and *Ottoman Wars*, 181–3.

Selim's diplomatic dalliances with Christian powers only reinforced the impression that he was betraying the struggle to save the Abode of Islam. Diplomacy offered yet another tactic in efforts to keep European threats at bay, but, as with the military innovations, it proved of little help. Selim diverted money from the war effort of 1787–92 to purchase alliance with Prussia, only to see Prussia join Russia and the Habsburg empire in partitioning Poland. Selim looked to France for help with training the New Order troops, only to have France later seize Egypt, an event that in turn produced an alliance with Britain and the Ottomans' emerging archenemy, Russia. Unpopular in both the Ottoman empire and Russia, the alliance fell apart quickly, and the former allies became again Istanbul's foes after the mending of Ottoman-French relations – a warming of relations that did not prevent Napoleon, after urging the empire to attack Russia in 1806, from concluding peace with the czar soon after Istanbul declared war.[41] Other than British aid in recovering Egypt, the Ottomans gained little from engagement with countries that seemed to revert to hostility at short notice, and such meager help was gained only at the cost of financial subsidies, trade concessions, and allowance of unprecedented freedom to move Christian forces around the empire and through its very center. A hostile British flotilla that appeared before Istanbul in 1807, preparing the scene for the military revolt that would overthrow Selim, was disturbing, but as shocking to Muslims had been the license given to Russia during the earlier alliance against France to maintain a Mediterranean fleet that passed, and was subsequently supplied, through the Bosphorus. Christian powers' movement at will in the waters of the Islamic empire only made manifest the weakness of the state despite Istanbul's various initiatives.

Ottoman Muslims might have accepted Selim's innovations, had his military experiment solved any of the threats to the Abode of Islam's safety, but with chaos in the Hijaz, Christians in revolt, and renewed war with Russia, rebellion against the New Order erupted as the state showed only rising vigor in pushing men and materiel into the "modern" but ineffective army. In 1805 Selim established another new treasury to fund modernization of the navy and in the following year tried to institute conscription for the New Order in the Balkans, rather than continuing to rely on recruits as in Anatolia and Istanbul – all at a time when

---

[41] Norman Saul, *Russia and the Mediterranean, 1797–1804* (Chicago: University of Chicago Press, 1970), and Anderson, *Eastern Question*.

war with Russia was evidently coming and the old army was ever less well served by the state. Janissaries and other Muslims of the Balkans blocked the force sent to institute conscription, and, in a significant turning point, the New Order fought Muslims and shelled the town of Çorlu, inflicting heavy loss of life before withdrawing. When war broke out, the Russians advanced with ease through Moldavia and Wallachia until blocked by a force under the provincial notable–governor of Ruse (northern Bulgaria), Bayrakdar Mustafa Pasha. The naval flotilla dispatched by Russia's British ally sailed past the unprepared Dardanelles defenses to anchor in the Sea of Marmara off Istanbul before retreating because of bad weather. Hordes of residents volunteered to man the walls in defense; when a rumor spread that the military reformers were going to impose the new, European-style uniforms on men of the shore batteries after their "victory," rebellion erupted. Traditional forces, primed to fight for *din ü devlet*, turned on the men who, they thought, had caused the state repeatedly to fail to support them materially and financially in their effort, having chosen instead to devote its resources to an ineffective venture in adopting the modes of the enemy – even to the point of turning these forces on the empire's own Muslim subjects.[42]

Absent from this account of the unrest that overthrew Selim and his New Order are the supposed agents of decentralization, the provincial notables. The rare figure to defy the central regime openly was Pasvanoğlu Osman Pasha, commander of the important stronghold of Vidin on the Danube frontier. Osman is usually depicted as interested only in plunder and power but is also acknowledged to have been genuinely popular among both Muslims and Christians, an apparent contradiction requiring explanation.[43] Despite the violence that he encouraged in lands outside his control, Osman seems to have become the champion of dissatisfied Balkan subjects by making himself a figure of a certain kind of Islamic morality. He appealed to the civilian urban and rural poor, both Muslim and non-Muslim, who suffered directly from the inflation and excise duties linked to the new treasury. Osman refused to levy any of Selim's new taxes (a practice followed by provincial notables elsewhere in less provocative fashion), restricting himself to the canonically legitimate

---

[42] Finkel, *Osman's Dream*, 413–17; Aksan, *Ottoman Wars*, 246–7; M. Şükrü Hanioğlu, *A Brief History of the Late Ottoman Empire* (Princeton: Princeton University Press, 2008), 53–4.

[43] Sadat, "Ayan and Ağa"; Rossitsa Gradeva, "Osman Pazvantoğlu of Vidin: Between Old and New," in Anscombe (ed.), *Ottoman Balkans*, 125–32.

agricultural tithe, the head tax on non-Muslims, and the livestock tax.[44] Being a janissary, as his father had been, he also defended the interests of those who had recently fought, albeit unsuccessfully, in defense of the Abode of Islam. Osman became a serious threat to the Ottoman order not because of his power as a frontier commander, but because of the widespread feeling that the state was failing to fulfill its responsibilities in the face of an existential threat from Christian Europe. Indicative of his sense of representing the true path of Islam against the wrongful innovations of Selim's ministers was his reaction to the outbreak of the Ottoman-Russian war of 1806–12. Osman apparently was insulted by not being given command of the Danube front against the Russians, a reaction that makes no sense given his long record of conflict with Istanbul other than as a sign of what he thought was due to the defender of true Islamic-Ottoman values.[45]

In contrast to Osman, most provincial notables refrained from open action against the center's projects, but they have nevertheless been blamed for organizing both subversion and those who did openly oppose the New Order.[46] The notables are assumed to have been disloyal and to have been motivated by greed. There is a tradition of linking the idea of troublesome notables to the empire's incorporation into the world economy, with local magnates seeking (illegal) control of land to maximize wealth from providing cash crops to Christian Europe. With their interests tied to foreign trade rather than to the Ottoman milieu, they were the drivers of "decentralization" and, because Selim's efforts to recentralize threatened their control over land and tax farms, they opposed the New Order.[47] There is little clear evidence for this scenario. The eighteenth century did see a significant rise in trade with Europe, but the peak was in midcentury; the supposed age of "recalcitrant notables" fell in a period of great disruption in both international and domestic trade at the end of the century. With limited exceptions, such as Zahir al-'Umar (d. 1775), a notable of northern Palestine who became a veritable magnate through

[44] Dina Khoury, *State and Provincial Society in the Ottoman Empire, Mosul 1540–1834* (Cambridge: Cambridge University Press, 1997), 164; Ariel Salzmann, *Tocqueville in the Ottoman Empire: Rival Paths to the Modern State* (Leiden: Brill, 2004), 170–2.

[45] Gradeva, "Osman Pazvantoğlu," 123.

[46] Fikret Adanır, "Semi-Autonomous Forces in the Balkans and Anatolia," in *CHT3*, 178–85.

[47] Sadat, "Rumeli Ayanlari: The Eighteenth Century," *JMH* 44 (1972), 346–63; Karen Barkey, *Empire of Difference: The Ottomans in Comparative Perspective* (Cambridge: Cambridge University Press, 2008); İlber Ortaylı, *İmparatorluğun En Uzun Yüzyılı* (Istanbul: Hil Yayın, 1987), 28.

exporting cotton, notables did not demonstrate a clear link between cash-crop foreign trade and a rise to local authority; even in the case of Zahir, his wealth gave him slight political importance in comparison to the 'Azm family, state-appointed notables of Damascus. It was not Zahir who made Acre a town of significance but rather a later governor, the Bosnian Ahmad Pasha al-Jazzar (The Butcher).[48]

Even were it true that "decentralization" derived from economic change and foreign trade, it would be hard to see a critical threat to provincial notables arising from Selim III's New Order. The most likely holders of wealth in this time were those with control over malikane, who benefited from accelerating inflation that lowered the real value of the tax payments that they owed to the treasury. With some exceptions, holders of such wealth were concentrated in the imperial center, not in the provinces. Indeed, given the uncertainties raised by Istanbul's manipulations of provincial rivalries and its weak powers of administration and upholding justice, few notables appear to have been sufficiently secure to avoid having to spend most of their incomes on maintaining their often precarious positions.[49] Although the state regularly seized the estates of disgraced or deceased officials in this period, it conducted no wave of tax farm confiscations that would have aroused antagonism by undercutting provincial officials' ability to maintain their positions; given the involvement in malikane by influential men at the center, any significant change in tax practice was unlikely. Since the new treasury was almost as incapable as the old of managing assets directly, moreover, opportunities continued for a handful of secure provincial contractors: Tepedelenli Ali Pasha, usually cited as the leading representative of provincial "decentralizers" and opponents of the New Order, was in a select group of seven men who contracted roughly half of the former timars leased from the new treasury.[50] If Ali had a financial interest in Selim's reforms, it would have made him a staunch supporter of the New Order. In truth, Selim was not undone by the notables but by the incensed military – indeed, a

---

[48] On trade, see Edhem Eldem, "Capitulations and Western Trade," in *CHT*3; Anscombe, "'Mountain Bandits.'" On Zahir, Dick Douwes, *The Ottomans in Syria: A History of Justice and Oppression* (London: I. B. Tauris, 2000), 53–4. For a notable growing primarily staples rather than cash crops, see Yuzo Nagata, *Tarihte Ayanlar: Karaosmanoğulları Üzerinde bir İnceleme* (Ankara: Türk Tarih Kurumu, 1997), 130–6.

[49] Sakaoğlu, *Köse Paşa*, 129; Fatma Göçek, "Ottoman Provincial Transformation in the Distribution of Power: The Tribulations of the Governor of Sivas in 1804," *SH* 35 (1994), 31–41; Anscombe, "Centre-Periphery," 240.

[50] Cezar, *Osmanlı Maliyesinde*, 179.

force that tried to rescue Selim in 1808 was led by a provincial notable, Bayrakdar Mustafa Pasha of Ruse.

One final factor frequently cited to explain Selim's failure to complete his reforms was his indecisiveness, but this does him an injustice.[51] His problem was not indecision but the narrow focus of the areas of his rule that he chose to change. The New Order did not touch the scope of the state's core concerns, and the fundamental machinery of state, the justice system, and even the methods of raising revenue remained essentially unaltered. His "indecision" in breaking dissenters derived from his own conformity to the established expectations of a sultan, which required adherence to standards of justice set by Ottoman-Islamic tradition.

This probably was not just force of circumstance but also his personal preference. The sultan was pious, personally devoted particularly to Mevlevi sufism, and very conscious of his responsibility not only to protect the Abode of Islam against infidel enemies abroad but also to perform his expected role as provider of justice at home.[52] He demonstrated the limits placed upon a ruler by the reigning sense of what constituted justice, which rested upon observance of shari'a and kanun. Although Selim exercised the ruler's recognized right of siyasa to punish summarily members of the 'askari class, he was unwilling to act arbitrarily against Muslims, let alone against the law. Selim was conscious of the unsettling effect of his new military, and he was careful in using it against Muslims until the fateful confrontation at Çorlu, despite the opportunities offered by Wahhabis, "bandits," and feuding officials such as Osman Pasvanoğlu. Osman illustrates some of the scruples observed by Selim, in that he was in the grasp of the center's officers on several occasions but was repeatedly spared, pardoned upon promising that he would mend his ways or upon the petition of the leading members of Vidin's population. As in the case of Ömer Bey of Ioannina, imprisoned repeatedly to encourage the mending of habits and character, Osman's expressions of remorse and promises for the future won release, and given the shari'a's commitment to promoting peace within the community, the expression of a unified opinion for or against a person by a community such as Vidin's Muslims was usually accepted by the state. Selim backed the New Order

[51] For a recent example, Finkel, *Osman's Dream*, 415. Şerif Mardin, *The Genesis of Young Ottoman Thought: A Study in the Modernization of Turkish Political Ideas* (Syracuse, NY: Syracuse University Press 2000), 147 correctly disputes the notion of Selim as mild or weak.

[52] Finkel, *Osman's Dream*, 394, cites a poem whose first line reads, "His Highness Han Selim who fashions perfect justice in his age."

and its expansion during his last war with Russia but still recoiled from the prospect of using his military against Muslims gathered to oppose it, going so far as to disband the new corps when he had no choice other than to engage in civil war if he wished to continue his project.

This sad saga illustrates Selim III's delicate position subject to powerful military, political, and emotive forces, and he could not save his throne with the premodern machinery of state available to him. The reforms stirred disquiet among the Muslim and non-Muslim population for a variety of reasons – ideological, financial, and simple exasperation over ineffectiveness – that Selim faced serious problems in countering. Beaten by waves of disillusionment with his leadership, Selim lost the throne to his cousin, Mustafa IV, a fate that he accepted with dignity. It was Mustafa who had him murdered as his own hold on the throne faced imminent challenge, also ordering at the same time the murder of the only other surviving male of the dynasty, Mahmud. Mahmud survived, however, as his executioners failed to find him before Bayrakdar Mustafa overthrew Mustafa IV.

THE DEED OF AGREEMENT

Mahmud II ascended the throne under dangerous circumstances, with violent mobs and provincial troops in the capital and hostile Russian forces on the Danube. The situation led to promulgation of an unusual document, the Deed of Agreement (*Sened-i İttifak*), which formed a pact to protect and bolster the royal center, in order that the state could concentrate on improving its forces in the field as quickly and effectively as possible. The nature of the deed as a program for settling domestic affairs and preparing the empire for the continuing conflict with Russia shaped the text.[53]

There were seven articles in the deed, according to which all signatories agreed to act as guarantors for proper observance of the prescribed practice. In summary of the important points, first was full support and protection for the sultan. Second, there was to be orderly recruitment of state soldiers. This point probably envisioned a force like the New Order, which the grand vizier planned to revive, but also was intended to

---

[53] Ali Akyıldız and M. Şükrü Hanioğlu, "Negotiating the Power of the Sultan: The Ottoman Sened-i İttifak (Deed of Agreement), 1808," in *The Modern Middle East: A Sourcebook for History*, ed. Camron Amin, Benjamin Fortna, and Elizabeth Frierson (Oxford: Oxford University Press, 2006), 24–30.

prevent notables from withholding troops to protect themselves against rivals. Third, revenue due to the center was to be protected and sped en route. This suggested that governors would gain more oversight of tax farmers, would actually levy taxes imposed by the center (as Osman Pasvanoğlu and others had not), and would protect the transit of money against the bandit threat that had plagued Selim's reign. Fourth, there was to be a clear chain of command at both imperial and provincial levels, with no official allowed to meddle in affairs outside his recognized purview; all signers were to be on guard against abuse of authority by the grand vizier, the recognized source of imperial orders. This addressed a significant problem of the imperial center, where factionalism had been rife and rivals were suspected of working secretly to subvert others' plans; provincial governors had to prevent similar factional manipulations. Fifth, Istanbul was not to set provincial rivals against each other, and no notable was to meddle outside his assigned region; anyone accused of meddling or stirring rivalries was not to be punished without proof and only upon the order of the grand vizier. By this notables gained security of tenure, made necessary by Istanbul's acceptance of violent seizures of position as long as the usurper promised resources for the war effort. Regime manipulation of notables' rivalries had hardly improved the situation. Sixth, any instance of janissary opposition was to be broken immediately. Seventh, provincial authorities were not to oppress the common people or "adjust" taxes in contravention of the shari'a and kanun. This addressed problems of tax farmers, and others who seized land illegally, gouging taxpayers under their control.

In addition to giving a perspective on the major problems threatening the empire's ability to defend itself, the form of the deed provides further insight on the mentality of the empire's governing classes. It represented above all a wish for an agreed set of rules by which all men involved in state affairs could serve the faith and the dynasty. The turmoil in the provinces and Istanbul that culminated in the overthrow and eventual murder of Selim indicated widespread discontent in the nonelite and provincial population, but the deed showed also a sense among the empire's upper echelons that too great a willingness to ignore imperial law and custom among their ilk had crippled the state. Unity of purpose and action could only come from freeing officials in both center and provinces from fear of the unpredictable, and only the rule of law and proper procedure could ensure this. It is also clear that the deed – its purpose of serving the faith and dynasty, its model of unity found in Muhammad and the early community of believers, and its sense of law and just practice – was a consciously Islamic agreement, the upholding of which was termed a duty (of faith).[54]

Events quickly overtook the deed, as yet another uprising led by disgruntled janissaries led to the death of the grand vizier, Bayrakdar Mustafa Pasha, the architect of the consultation that produced the agreement. The janissaries had seen no improvement in their condition since the dissolution of the New Order, as they had lost even the notional uniform allowance and had seen their salary sink to little more than four pounds sterling per annum by 1807.[55] Mustafa Pasha's moves to revive the New Order thus reignited violent protest. Mahmud II survived, perhaps only because he murdered his brother, the ex-sultan Mustafa IV, leaving the rioters without an alternate candidate to place on the throne. Without its architect, the Deed of Agreement never had an opportunity to have any effect, and Mahmud certainly displayed no interest in heeding its message about the "state of the state" and possible means to correct it.

With the overthrow of first Sultan Selim III and then Bayrakdar Mustafa Pasha, the experimentation with military modernization carried out within the generally accepted bounds of the premodern Ottoman state ended. Selim and Bayrakdar Mustafa tried to add to the extant military structure some elements of Christian Europe's field army practices that Ottoman observers had seen during a series of fruitless campaigns. For all the changes that they introduced, they left untouched the essential scope of the state and methods of its administration. They fell from power and died because of riots in the capital that probably were not premeditated but did feed on anger that the mood of existential crisis promoted. Rioters could overthrow a sultan because Selim's legitimacy had weakened for a string of interconnected reasons: he was unsuccessful in his duty to protect the Abode of Islam; he nevertheless spurned those who had fought for *din ü devlet*; he was unable to keep the peace at home, protect the poor and helpless (nonmilitary) population, and ensure that law and justice were upheld; and he wished to fund his experiment in a European-styled military by levying yet more (canonically illegitimate) taxes upon an already hard-pressed population. Even though it had been developing since 1768, the crisis of the Ottoman center claimed Selim as its most significant victim. There was an ideological element to the opposition to Bayrakdar Mustafa, since his legitimacy as "rescuer of the empire" – an image that could not hide the fact that he was at root a provincial

---

[54] Akyıldız and Hanioğlu, "Negotiating the Power," 23.
[55] Aksan, *Ottoman Wars*, 267.

notable with an army – was weak in the eyes of many contemporaries, and he suffered the usual fate of kingmakers, supported by neither his former equals nor his new, beholden sovereign.[56] He clouded the image of the *devlet* that Ottoman Muslims strove to serve, but there was also a personal aspect that made the *devlet* redeemable simply through his removal. There was also a personal element in the opposition to Selim, concentrated in the ranks of the janissaries, but his actions affected both parts of the tightly twinned couplet, religion and dynasty. His effective successor, Mahmud II, could have foreseen the recurrence of problems that might be forestalled by judicious action; he misread the source of his weakness, however, and took harsh measures against symptoms rather than causes of threats to the sultanate, thereby taking the state, built on service to religion and dynasty, to the point of collapse.

[56] For a view from the provinces, see Khoury, *State and Provincial Society*, 166.

3

The Breaking of the Premodern Islamic State

Historians commonly treat the reigns of Selim III and Mahmud II as a practically seamless whole, but despite some continuities, Mahmud ruled essentially in opposition to what he had seen of Selim's practice. Where Selim's attempts at state strengthening stirred resistance from the established Ottoman military, Mahmud's disdain for the limits on sultanic action that Selim had accepted spread disaffection and rebellion to a much wider population. Unlike Selim's, Mahmud's method of rule was to break extant systems, or at least to cripple them to ensure their subservience; his efforts to topple any power not obviously dependent upon his court created turmoil in both center and provinces, where his actions otherwise had small effect beyond his clients' seizing a greater part of the wealth of provincial notables while leaving to them, or their families, much of their local influence. In the manner and methods of provincial administration, he changed little on a systematic basis, and his rule brought the empire to the point of collapse.[1] Mahmud felt bound to observe few rules in his campaign to remake the empire into an entity better able to defend itself against its external enemies; in so doing, he alienated subjects who still held to the ideology legitimating Ottoman rule and did not share his conviction that he need not dispense, but rather could dispense with, justice. His decisions also accentuated Muslim ethnic identity by closing to Albanians, Bosnians, Kurds, and Arabs the ranks of the army he founded

---

[1] More effective change could occur on the local level, with notables continuing to play a role. Michael Ursinus, "Die osmanische Balkanprovinzen 1830–1840: Steuerreform als Modernisierungsinstrument," *Südost-Forschungen* 55 (1996), 129–60. Mahmud's tendency to want to see revenue collection in reliable hands, however, led to the undoing of some progress made by Selim in reducing the scope of malikane.

to replace the janissaries, a move that gave a lasting "Turkish" flavor to the empire. In another move that would prove more clearly damaging in future, he also surrendered much of Istanbul's long-treasured authority over commerce by concluding an ill-considered trade convention with Britain in 1838. Selim III's overthrow may have marked one of the low points in Ottoman imperial politics, but Mahmud's survival on the throne for thirty-one years did not mark an upturn in the empire's fortunes: at his death, he faced dethronement not by rioters but by a better-organized and cleverer underling, Mehmed (Muhammad) Ali, governor of Egypt. His successor, Abdülmecid I, had to issue a proclamation of intent not to rule as Mahmud had done in order to reconsolidate support for the throne among Muslim and non-Muslim subjects alike. Unlike the Deed of Agreement, this proclamation turned out to be lastingly significant.

MAHMUD II AND THE MILITARY

As noted in the last chapter, Mahmud's reign did show one distressing parallel with Selim's, in that it began in the midst of another war with Russia that the Ottomans were to lose, and the point of all that Mahmud attempted was the same as Selim's New Order: to improve the empire's ability to defend itself against Christian Europe. He failed to achieve much in military modernization, in spite of his most eye-catching move, abolition of the janissary corps and the remnants of the old timar-holding sipahi cavalry. He created a European-styled army that became the backbone of the state's land forces until the end of the empire, but as it suffered from many of the same flaws as the military system it had replaced, the new army did not become markedly effective until the era after Mahmud's death. Throughout his reign, therefore, Mahmud had to rely upon the same system of provincial militia levies that had distinguished the Ottoman military since the early eighteenth century. He openly tried to break that system, too, thereby inevitably damaging his hopes of preserving the empire and his own rule.

From the beginning, Mahmud's experience of military affairs was unfortunate, and he consistently showed more anger than insight in drawing conclusions from failure. In the war engaged before his accession, actual fighting had ground to a halt soon after its outbreak (allowing Bayrakdar Mustafa to march on Istanbul in 1807), but in 1809 the Russian czar's declared intention of annexing Wallachia and Moldavia stirred the renewal of hostilities. Istanbul had to rely on provincial notables to raise troops, as few janissaries arrived at the front lines, a confirmation of their final irrelevance to Ottoman battlefield calculations. Provincial troops and commanders fought effectively in some engagements, none of which was decisive, however. They succeeded in compelling Russian forces, weakened by redeployments to aid defenses against the expected French attack on Russia, to retreat from Bulgaria back into Wallachia by 1811. Urged by Mahmud to attack the Russian position in Wallachia, the grand vizier committed the classic error of splitting his army by moving roughly half his troops across the Danube and then waiting to see what would happen. The Russians simply crossed back to Bulgaria, surrounded the thirty thousand Ottoman soldiers there, and left the grand vizier's half-army stranded in Wallachia – and the war was over. It was another year before the Peace of Bucharest was agreed, however, as Mahmud refused to accept almost any significant Russian demand; in the meantime, the Ottoman troops stranded on the Danube suffered appallingly before the Russians took pity and offered them protection, rather than requiring surrender. Mahmud's maximalism perversely succeeded, in that the Russians dropped most of their demands, because they needed peace to confront Napoleon's invasion.[2]

Following the conclusion of peace, Mahmud launched a program of action that characterized the remainder of his reign: breaking every significant institution, group, or notable person that showed a willingness to act independently of the sultan. Throughout his reign Mahmud relied heavily upon a coterie of men whom he considered trustworthy, primarily from the eastern Black Sea region (Georgian, Abkhaz, Circassian), many of whom were literally his slaves. By relying so heavily on a palace-based network, he may have limited the scope for household rivalries at the top level of government. The most sustained target of Mahmud's plans for tying the rest of the empire to his authority, however, was the provincial notability, the backbone of the military and the leading representatives of the state outside Istanbul. Selim III would have recognized the core tactic of playing rivals against each other involved in this effort, although he would also have been impressed by the severity encouraged by the state in some cases. This severity was evident immediately after the war, when Yılıkoğlu Süleyman, one of the notables of Bulgaria, who was accused of involvement in provincial

---

[2] Aksan, *Ottoman Wars*, 269–81; F. Ismail, "The Making of the Treaty of Bucharest, 1811–1812," *MES* 15 (1979), 163–92.

rivalries and showing indifferent service against Russia, was hunted down and killed.[3]

Not all provincial notables targeted by Mahmud's regime suffered such an extreme penalty, but many paid a significant price to be allowed to maintain positions of any influence. The Karaosmanoğlu family dominated Manisa and Saruhan (western Turkey) and had a long record of largely dependable service to the center; the venerable Hüseyn Ağa was stripped of his official positions between 1812 and 1815, and upon his death in 1816, Mahmud ordered the seizure of much of his estate and the appointment of a man from another province to control of Saruhan. Only in 1822 did his descendants begin again to win appointment to office, but not within their home region. From 1829, as the empire suffered defeat again at the hands of Russia and faced the prospect of further turmoil in key provinces, however, a Karaosmanoğlu was once again appointed to Saruhan.[4] Thus were numerous notables tested for dependency upon Istanbul. Reduction of others continued in more brutal fashion, and the campaigns to reassert Istanbul's authority created in some instances turmoil as bad as any produced by provincial feuds. In Diyarbakır (eastern Turkey), for instance, Istanbul appointed as governor in 1819 a Kurdish tribal leader known as an enemy of the clan that traditionally ruled the area, and upon his arrival he reportedly announced to the assembled leaders of the town, "I was sent to destroy you, to scatter your belongings and to burn your houses." In the inevitable, months-long conflict that erupted, the town was devastated and up to a third of its population fell casualty, a trauma that marked it for decades.[5] Such brutal tactics, normally unacknowledged in imperial chronicles compiled under later sultans, were probably more widely used than most historians realize.

Violent suppression of established notables certainly triggered a major event in Mahmud's reign, the Greek revolt of 1821. Istanbul decided in 1820 to uproot Tepedelenli Ali Pasha, the governor of Ioannina, following Ali's success in winning from British control the last of four formerly Venetian enclaves on the coast of Epirus. Having served his purpose in securing the frontier and with the empire not engaged in a war for which it required his Albanian levies, Ali was declared a rebel and an army was dispatched to capture him. In spite of his patchy record in obeying

---

[3] İsmail Uzunçarşılı, *Meşhur Rumeli Ayanından Tirsinikli İsmail, Yılık Oğlu Suleyman Ağalar ve Alemdar Mustafa Paşa* (Istanbul: Maarif Matbaası, 1942), 33–9; Aksan, *Ottoman Wars*, 272.

[4] Nagata, *Tarihte Ayanlar*, 51–8.

[5] Salzmann, *Tocqueville*, 192–3.

orders from the center and in fighting with neighboring notables, however, Ali had never rebelled or failed to give the center the support needed from provincial governors, especially in the provision of men, money, and materiel during wartime. In 1812, Ali and his sons controlled much of mainland Greece and southern Albania, yet they accepted dismissal from many of their governorships in the years following the peace with Russia. In 1820 Ali's sons similarly submitted promptly to the forces dispatched from the center, and Ali did not turn his military might against the approaching army. His strategy was to retire to his fortress in Ioannina and wait for the central authorities to remember how valuable an asset he was formerly and could be again. To this end he encouraged Christian notables of Greece to launch a rebellion, hoping that Mahmud would restore him to his position of authority, since he was the one man with a demonstrated ability to keep the region in order.[6]

Ali's ploy might have succeeded, had Selim rather than Mahmud still ruled. The Christians of Greece had reasons for revolt, and the sheer brutality of the slaughter that the rebels visited upon the Muslims of Morea outraged many throughout the empire. Ali tried to tap into that anger, as can be seen in a proclamation he tried to distribute throughout the Balkans late in 1821, in which he stressed the violence committed against Muslims.[7] Ali's message touched a sensitive nerve in the Muslim community, subject as it was to ongoing fears for its future existence, and the central regime recognized the damage done to its own reputation in continuing the siege of Ioannina rather than concentrating on putting down the rebellion. Ali surrendered early in 1822 on terms that his life be spared, but Istanbul ordered that he be executed anyway (another incident damaging to the center's reputation), but the proclamation displayed beside his severed head in Istanbul specifically countered his proclamation by accusing him of being "a traitor to our religion ... who has sent huge sums to the infidels of the Morea ... to encourage them to revolt against the Muslims."[8] Ali's gamble did not save his life, but it helped to make the breaking of his power a debacle for Istanbul. In recognition of that, Mahmud held his heretofore most trusted adviser, Halid Efendi, responsible, having him executed and his estate seized. The Ali episode, however, did not die so quickly, as its consequences reverberated through the remainder of Mahmud's reign.

[6] Anscombe, "Centre-Periphery."
[7] BOA, Cev.Dah 14436 (1821). For an extract from the proclamation, see Anscombe, "Centre-Periphery."
[8] Finkel, Osman's Dream, 430.

FAITH AND NATION: THE GREEK REVOLT
AND OTTOMAN REFORM

Of the three matters that dominate most depictions of Mahmud II's reign in broader histories (the Greek revolt, the abolition of the janissaries, and the competition with Mehmed Ali), the Greek revolt seems the most important, apparently leading as it did to the latter two issues. The Greek revolt and ensuing developments show that religious identity continued to play a strong motivating role, despite the usual depiction of the rebellion as a nationalist liberation movement. The revolt, and Muslims' reaction to it, also showed the lingering effects of the earlier, essentially loyalist, Christian uprising in Belgrade province in 1804.

Belgrade's Orthodox population had taken up arms in self-defense against the depredations of janissaries who pillaged and committed murder among both Christians and Muslims serving Selim III's New Order.[9] It was Selim's appointed commander in Belgrade who had ordered that Christians arm themselves for protection, and from 1804 until 1807 the Christian leaders had pledged loyalty to the sultan and declared that until his authority could be reestablished, they fought only against those who defied Istanbul's orders. Combat against loyal Ottoman troops had occurred only when Istanbul ordered its forces to disarm the Christians following dispersal of the janissaries. The Christians had refused to disarm until Istanbul provided real surety that justice would be upheld in the province, and the surety they had sought was the guarantee of another power, either the Habsburg empire or Russia. This Istanbul could not accept. The two sides had reached a compromise solution in late 1806, however, and the confrontation had appeared resolved until Russia, again at war with the Ottomans, provided subsidies and persuaded the Christians to resume fighting. An armed movement that had had a loyalist character over its first three years then became a more conventional revolt, but from beginning to end it had been a Christian, not Serbian nationalist, affair.[10]

Christians in arms had alarmed Muslims in the capital as well as the provinces, and from an early point in the uprising Selim and his ministers

[9] On the Belgrade and subsequent uprisings, see Anscombe, "Revolutionary Age."
[10] Roger Paxton, "Nationalism and Revolution: A Re-Examination of the Origins of the First Serbian Insurrection 1804–1807," *EEQ* 6 (1972), 337–62; Gale Stokes, "The Absence of Nationalism in Serbian Politics before 1840," *Canadian Review of Studies in Nationalism* 4 (1976), 77–90.

had intended to punish militia leaders for their uprising.[11] Mahmud ruled when Belgrade was finally taken back under Ottoman control in 1813 and rebel leaders had fled. Contrary to the terms under which the province accepted the return of Ottoman rule, and to the expectation of Russia, whose latest victorious war against the Ottomans had concluded only in 1812, Istanbul's returning administrative and military forces did exact some revenge on Christians. This was all too reminiscent of the janissary oppression following the Habsburgs' return of Belgrade to Ottoman control under the Treaty of Sistova (1791) that had prompted the 1804 uprising, and rebellion erupted again. Russia applied pressure on Istanbul to withdraw its forces from Belgrade, and from 1815 the province became effectively self-administering under the leading figure of the second revolt, Miloš Obrenović. Muslims in the provinces resented this outcome and the manner of its determination. Just as the rebels who took up arms in the Morea in 1821 showed an awareness of the tortuous and treacherous course of events in Belgrade, adopting a much more aggressive, proactive stance against Mahmud's plans to assert Istanbul's authority over the provinces, so Ottoman Muslims showed equal ferocity in trying to crush the new Christian uprising.

There was much that the Christians of Greece, and especially the Morea, had to rise up against. Mainland Greece had suffered severely from the lawlessness seen in much of the Balkans around the turn of the eighteenth century, which Istanbul had proven incapable of controlling. No area suffered more than the Morea, which was pillaged regularly by Albanian gangs over the decades after 1770, despite Istanbul's repeated strictures against Albanians setting foot on the peninsula.[12] In the early nineteenth century security had improved, as Ali Pasha and his sons took control over much of the mainland. Ali never exercised a light touch in ruling Greece, but he offered predictability and a reputation for preserving order. Mahmud's decision to overthrow him threatened to remove this stability and return his territories to their earlier state of chaos, with the resumption of careless administration following the displacement of established local leaders. The devastation wrought on Epirus by marauding soldiers of the Ottoman army besieging Ali in Ioannina provided graphic evidence of the return of chaos. Christian notables were thus

[11] Mehmet Börekçi, *Osmanlı İmparatorluğu'nda Sırp Meselesi* (Istanbul: Kutup Yıldızı, 2001).

[12] Anscombe, "'Mountain Bandits'"; Süleymaniye Library (Istanbul), Esad Efendi 2419/2 (1779). On the chaos and the ineptitude of Istanbul's appointees in Greece in this period, see Skiotis, "Bandit to Pasha," 231–8.

threatened as much as their Muslim counterparts, and the retribution being visited upon Ali made those who had cooperated with him fearful of Istanbul's reassertion of authority. Mahmud's appointment of a trusted subordinate, Hurşid Pasha, to the governorship of Morea in 1820 was another sign of returning instability, because Hurşid could not assume the post in person, as he also was assigned command of the army sent to capture Ali. Hurşid had been governor of Belgrade when Ottoman rule resumed there in 1813 and thus bore responsibility for retaliation against former rebels.[13] When rumors spread that his army would turn to eliminating Christian local leaders in Greece after finishing with Ali, the dangers in rising up no longer clearly dwarfed those involved in trusting in future Ottoman administration.[14]

In its origins in self-defense against oppression, the Greek revolt resembled that of the Christians of Belgrade province in 1804; in the heated atmosphere of lingering Muslim-Christian tensions, and because the imperial center was now the apparent instigator of injustice, the uprising in the Morea quickly took a new direction. Revolt consisted of slaughtering non-Christians wherever found, culminating in the extermination of the Muslim population of Tripolitsa upon its surrender in autumn 1821. The Christians killed an estimated forty thousand Muslims (and an estimated five thousand Jews) in the Morea alone, and Muslims retaliated elsewhere, making negotiated settlement impossible.[15] Neutrality was no option, and the dividing line was between Orthodox Christian and Muslim, not "Greek" and "Turk."[16]

Ottoman Muslims clearly saw the conflict as one pitting their community against the Orthodox. Orthodox clergy were arrested, notables

[13] Gerolymatos, *Balkan Wars*, 155.

[14] For the role of Ali and Epirote events in the outbreak of revolt and the role of Christian notables, see Dennis (Dionysios) Skiotis, "The Lion and the Phoenix: Ali Pasha and the Greek Revolution" (PhD diss., Harvard University, 1971); "Mountain Warriors and the Greek Revolution," in *War, Technology and Society in the Middle East*, ed. V. J. Parry and M. E. Yapp (London: Oxford University Press, 1975), 308–29; and "The Greek Revolution: Ali Pasha's Last Gamble" in *Hellenism and the First Greek War of Liberation (1821–1830): Continuity and Change*, ed. Nikiforos Diamandouros et al. (Thessaloniki: Institute for Balkan Studies, 1976), 97–109.

[15] Avigdor Levy, *The Jews of the Ottoman Empire* (Princeton: Darwin Press, 1994), 95; Georges Castellan, *Histoire des Balkans (XIVe–XXe siècle)* (Paris: Fayard, 1991), 264–5.

[16] The one constant criterion by which "Greeks" defined themselves in the various constitutional documents adopted during the revolt was Christianity. Anna Couderc, "Religion et identité nationale en Grèce pendant la révolution d'indépendance (1821–1832): Le creuset ottoman et l'influence occidentale," in *La Perception de l'Héritage Ottoman dans les Balkans*, ed. Sylvie Gangloff (Paris: l'Harmattan, 2005), 24.

publicly humiliated, property plundered, and individuals killed or executed in many places around the empire.[17] In one incident well publicized in Christian Europe, Ottoman troops killed or enslaved much
of the Orthodox population of the Aegean island of Chios in 1821. In
another, Grigorios V, patriarch of Constantinople, was executed soon
after the outbreak of revolt, although he abhorred the uprising and pro-
nounced anathema upon the rebels. Most accounts portray his execution
as a simple lynching or as punishment because he had failed to keep the
Orthodox milla in submission, but he was killed because in the atmosphere of crisis he was suspected of taking part in the still-unfolding
"plot." The Orthodox of Istanbul, especially the Phanariote elite, were
indeed subjected to a calculated campaign of brutal harassment.[18]

Sudden and all-devouring violence such as that unleashed by the
Christians of the Morea and nearby areas touched the deepest insecurities felt by Mahmud, a sultan who had narrowly avoided being killed
by insurrectionists in 1808. He and his high officers were reportedly
appalled by some of the reprisals exacted by Ottoman forces such as
those who sacked Chios, but they actively promoted much of the oppression visited upon a population that they now regarded as wholly suspect.
The Phanariotes lost their privileged place in state and economic circles,
and the Orthodox dominance in the handling of foreign relations similarly ended, with Mahmud establishing a translation department to train
new (primarily Muslim) translators and diplomats. There is no doubt
that Mahmud and his officers also saw the empire once again involved
in an extremely dangerous religious conflict that threatened its future as
the Abode of Islam. The sultan himself displayed full signs of religious
devotion, including enjoining Muslims to pray; he took special pains to
rally his armies to follow the example set by the Prophet Muhammad,
commissioning and publishing an Ottoman translation of an early Arabic
treatise on the law of war. He must have been disappointed by the results,
however, as the war dragged on without clear success until the arrival of
troops from Egypt commanded by Mehmed Ali's son, Ibrahim.

---

[17] Bruce Masters, *Christians and Jews in the Ottoman Arab World: The Roots of
Sectarianism* (Cambridge: Cambridge University Press, 2004), 106–7; Ussama Makdisi,
*Artillery of Heaven: American Missionaries and the Failed Conversion of the Middle
East* (Ithaca, NY: Cornell University Press, 2008), 118; Richard Clogg, "Aspects of the
Movement for Greek Independence," in *The Struggle for Greek Independence: Essays
to Mark the 150th Anniversary of the Greek War of Independence*, ed. Richard Clogg
(Hamden, CT: Archon, 1973), 23.

[18] Christine Philliou, *Biography of an Empire: Practicing Ottoman Governance in the Age
of Revolutions* (Berkeley: University of California Press, 2011), 67–74.

Ibrahim's success in quelling the uprising in Crete and then the Morea must have been galling to Mahmud and his own appointed commanders. To have success gained by a provincial leader of the kind targeted in Mahmud's endless campaign to break the notables was embarrassing, especially under the clash-of-faiths conditions of the Greek revolt. As had Selim III, Mahmud had failed to recover Mecca and Medina from the detested Wahhabis, but Mehmed Ali had not only accomplished this, but had had his sons harry them across Arabia, freeing not only the Hijaz but the center and east of the peninsula from their control. Much of this had been accomplished prior to his launching in 1820–1 a conscription-based force modeled on the Ottoman New Order and trained by former French officers. Now Ibrahim used the new force in Greece and almost succeeded in crushing the traitorous Christians against whom the sultan had launched an ineffective jihad. The officers commanding Istanbul's land and sea forces were themselves embarrassed by this rubbing of salt in a long-open wound: the naval commander, Husrev Pasha, an illiterate but tough Abkhaz who served Mahmud in a number of high positions, had lost the governorship of Egypt to Mehmed Ali in 1805, a humiliation that drove a lifelong enmity for his victorious rival. The commander of Istanbul's land forces, Reşid Mehmed Pasha, was a Georgian slave of Husrev; the long-running rivalry in imperial affairs between men from the Balkans and from the Caucasus probably added to Istanbul's embarrassment in the Greek affair. It does seem that both Husrev and Reşid tried to hinder Ibrahim's efforts against the Christians, but the Egyptian troops nevertheless proved their efficacy.[19]

Mahmud's dissolution of the janissary corps was his decisive step toward correcting the state's military discipline problem, although it was both less and more than meets the eye. It was less not only in that the janissaries had lost their relevancy to campaign planning, but also in that janissary obstructiveness was concentrated primarily in Istanbul. Mahmud took care to secure the capital, where rebellion had overthrown Selim III and threatened Mahmud himself, in order to create space for a new army; he did not show as much concern for the problem of replacing fortress or frontier garrisons manned by the suddenly dissolved corps. Where Mahmud's military reform went further than simple destruction of the janissaries was in showing his intention to remake the entire military backbone of the state, shedding not only janissaries but the hired and

---

[19] Khaled Fahmy, *All the Pasha's Men: Mehmed Ali, His Army and the Making of Modern Egypt* (Cambridge: Cambridge University Press, 1997), 56–7, 285–9.

seasonal militias as well. He set strict limitations on who could join the new military, and under what conditions. Rather than seasonally hired, the new soldiers were recruited (and soon conscripted) to serve a minimum of twelve years; they also were to receive no pension unless they served until too old or infirm to continue.[20] The force was to consist of "Turks," by which usually derogatory term was meant the "ignorant and uncouth Turkish-speaking peasants" of Anatolia and the eastern Balkans.[21] Turkish peasants did not suffer from close identification with the old military institution; they also had less of the clannishness that contributed to the difficulties in command and control over the main military ethnic groups. Over several decades some military commanders had requested Turkish soldiers to leaven the formations under them that consisted of the more usual recruits, and Mahmud applied much more sweepingly this principle of ethnic reconfiguration to create a new army that would obey orders.[22] From 1826 until Mahmud's death, the Ottoman regular army was self-consciously Turkish, and this period of ethnicity-consciousness must have left its lingering imprint upon the military in subsequent decades, when succeeding regimes revised many of Mahmud's policies.

While Mahmud's decision to bar some ethnic groups from the new army may be understandable under the circumstances, one other restriction says more about his view of the challenges facing the state: the exclusion of converts to Islam.[23] Mahmud felt that internal and external Christian enemies threatened the existence of the empire and of the Muslim community itself. Given their unreliability, the janissaries must have lacked the true believers' sense of duty, and Mahmud apparently believed that they were indeed ineffective because they had been infiltrated by Christians. The bodies of some of the thousands slaughtered at the dissolution of the corps bore tattooed crosses, which Mahmud took as

---

[20] Erik Zürcher, *The Young Turk Legacy and Nation Building: From the Ottoman Empire to Atatürk's Turkey* (London: I. B. Tauris, 2010), 155.

[21] Lewis defined the term (*Modern Turkey*, 1–2) in relation to Anatolia but it applied to the Balkans as well.

[22] Aksan, *Ottoman Wars*, 357–8. Shortly before the abolition of the janissary corps, for example, the regime expelled unruly Kurdish guards of the naval yards and replaced them with Turks. *Vak'a-nüvis Es'ad Efendi Tarihi (Bâhir Efendi'nin Zeyl ve İlaveleriyle) 1237–1241/1821–1826*, ed. Ziya Yılmazer (Istanbul: Osmanlı Araştırmaları Vakfı, 2000), 533–4.

[23] Hakan Erdem, "Recruitment for the 'Victorious Soldiers of Muhammad' in the Arab Provinces, 1826–1828," in *Histories of the Modern Middle East: New Directions*, ed. Israel Gershoni et al. (London: Lynne Rienner, 2002), 193–4.

an explanation for their misbehavior. It was another plot: like the treacherous Greeks, the janissaries had worked for the Russians.[24] Since converts could not be trusted to have renounced their old ties, they were not to dilute the new army, the "Trained Victorious Muhammadan Soldiers." For the same reason, Mahmud also wanted born Muslims rather than (ex-)Christian Europeans to train the new troops; he requested appropriate instructors from Mehmed Ali, but the Egyptian governor claimed to have none to spare. Mahmud thus did employ a few Europeans but ordered strict limitations to their responsibilities, in order to minimize their opportunities to corrupt the army's zeal. He also ordered that each new regiment have a *mekteb*, or Islamic school, to instruct the recruits in religion.[25] He dispatched a handful of Muslims to study military subjects in France but enjoined them neither to learn French nor to reside in Paris, in order to avoid cultural pollution.[26]

In his effort to strengthen Muslim zeal and solidarity, Mahmud attacked the Bektashi sufi brotherhood three weeks after dissolution of the janissaries. The move is usually attributed to the identification of the janissaries with the Bektashis, but while this connection may have been close in an earlier era, it should not be exaggerated for the nineteenth century. Bektashism was stronger in Anatolia than in European or Arab provinces, an imbalance that did not reflect the geographic origins and distribution of the janissaries. Bosnia, the Balkan stronghold of the janissaries, had few Bektashis. The Bektashis were driven underground because of their perceived heterodoxy that purportedly carried elements of Christianity and Shi'ism (the empire fought its last war with Iran in 1820–3); much as in the times of crisis of the seventeenth century, when the antiheterodox *kadızadeli* movement agitated against sufism, the pressure to preserve the Abode of Islam led to steps for spiritual cleansing of the Muslim community. Such a motivation also led Mahmud once more to order Muslims to pray five times a day, saying that some people were failing to perform this duty because of "carelessness, ignorance, or falling for the seditions and perversions of assorted schismatics and heretics."[27]

---

[24] Aksan, *Ottoman Wars*, 321–2; Finkel, *Osman's Dream*, 437.
[25] Avigdor Levy, "The Officer Corps in Sultan Mahmud II's New Ottoman Army, 1826–39," *IJMES* 2 (1971), 23; Aksan, *Ottoman Wars*, 328.
[26] Hanioğlu, *Late Ottoman Empire*, 63.
[27] For the ferman of July 1827 sent throughout the Balkans and Anatolia, see *Maglajski Sidžili 1816–1840*, ed. Dušanka Bojanić-Lukač and Tatjana Katić (Sarajevo: Bošnjački Institut Fondacija Adila Zulfikarpašića, 2005), 529.

As virtuous as Mahmud's intentions to channel Muslim resources into the most determined defense of the community possible may have been, one action led to another and his decisions began to seem simply avaricious, arrogant, autocratic. The state seized the considerable assets of the Bektashis and confiscated the estates of the three richest Jewish bankers of Istanbul, who were executed on grounds of association with the janissaries (an act that devastated and impoverished the Ottoman Jewish community)[28]; when it subsequently took control over all religious foundations (*waqf*), the impression grew that greed was at work. The state was to continue to use the funds for the charitable purposes to which they were endowed, but in practice much of the income stuck to other hands. This feeling fed on the alacrity with which the sultan's officers seized the estates of executed or dismissed notables and men of the center, raising suspicion that some were executed only to enable seizure of their possessions.[29]

As in the time of Selim, reform required money, and Mahmud took advantage of every opportunity to raise cash. Having seen the rebelliousness of janissaries who felt unsupported by the state, the sultan's officers raised the salaries of soldiers in the new army more than fourfold over a janissary's pay, thereby creating an urgent need for new revenue. The regime raised the head tax paid by non-Muslims and levied a "market" tax akin to the sales tax now common in the United States, and in order to make it less easily avoidable established a number of commodity monopolies. The measures did not raise enough to cover the huge military budget, however, and the sultan faced the necessity to make good the shortfall from his own income. Mahmud therefore imposed levies on his own officials and sanctioned not only the seizure of waqf revenue and the estates of officials but also all land still classed as timar, turning the remaining now-landless sipahis into salaried cavalrymen of the new army.[30]

These actions swelled anger among the population, but this seems only to have pushed Mahmud to accelerate his innovations. The slaughter of

---

[28] Aron Rodrigue, *French Jews, Turkish Jews: The Alliance Israélite Universelle and the Politics of Jewish Schooling in Turkey, 1860–1925* (Bloomington: Indiana University Press, 1990), 27–8. The lasting damage to the community opened it later to the influence of wealthier Western Jewish communities.

[29] See, for example, Ahmed Lutfi, *Tarih-i Lutfi* (Istanbul, 1873), i, 243. Confiscation of the executed Jews' estates was a blatant example (Finkel, *Osman's Dream*, 438).

[30] Cezar, *Osmanlı Maliyesinde*, 246–50.

janissaries, including the summary execution of three hundred prisoners after the brief battle in Istanbul's barracks, brought to the capital's residents scenes of the shocking violence already seen by people in provinces targeted in antinotable campaigns. With seizure of waqf revenue and persecution of Bektashis added to this violent campaign, Mahmud's regime seemed embarked upon a violent struggle against both Muslims of the empire and key practices of the religion that legitimated the state. For a population still struggling under harsh economic conditions, the added financial burdens were oppressive, sparking hostility that led to revolt in several places, notably in Syria, and contributed to rioting in Istanbul in 1828. The extent of the perception that Mahmud had needlessly embroiled the empire in another futile war with Russia is hard to gauge, but it must have influenced opinion as well. Having broken the established army, the sultanate stood unprepared for the disaster of Navarino in 1827, when Anglo-French-Russian forces destroyed the fleet supporting Ibrahim Pasha's troops in Greece, causing Mehmed Ali to halt the campaign against the Christian rebels. Against his councillors' advice, Mahmud chose in 1828 as his response another foolhardy war with Russia.[31] As everyone could have expected, the Ottoman defense crumbled by 1829, and, with the Russians in Edirne and threatening the capital, the empire had to accept peace terms that led to independence for Greece, autonomy for Belgrade province, Russian rights in the Danubian principalities, and payment of a huge war indemnity. This disaster made Mahmud increasingly vindictive toward those whom he regarded as having failed to support the war that he had proclaimed to be a jihad to save the Islamic community.[32] Having lost control of Christians in fledgling Greece and Serbia, he turned on Muslims whom he considered "ignorant," too secure of their status, or associated with any institution that he found difficult to control directly.

Loyalty and dependence became the hallmarks of Mahmud's imperial order. The senior officers of the new military were from the sultan's household; untrained in modern military affairs and in some cases illiterate, they had all the critical faults of command that had plagued the old army. Junior officers were little better prepared.[33] In administration

---

[31] Mardin, *Young Ottoman Thought*, 149.

[32] For the jihad proclamation, see Hakan Erdem, "'Do Not Think of the Greeks as Agricultural Labourers': Ottoman Responses to the Greek War of Independence," in *Citizenship and the Nation-State in Greece and Turkey*, ed. Faruk Birtek and Thalia Dragonas (Abingdon: Routledge, 2005), 76–7.

[33] Aksan, *Ottoman Wars*, 328–9.

Mahmud made changes after 1829 that would eventually prove useful, such as organizing thematic ministries (war, interior, foreign affairs, and finances) and specialized consultative committees. These nominally "streamlined" administration of the empire, but their main purpose seems to have been to assign responsibility more effectively than did the old system, in which the divan discussed all and sundry matters.[34] The real purpose of the reform, in fact, seems to have been the breaking of the divan as an authoritative institution, with the council of august figures led by the grand vizier replaced by individual ministers answering to the sultan, who tried to buy their loyalty by awarding them staggering salaries (which the state could not afford to pay). From top to bottom of the revamped administration, bureaucrats received little training beyond what their predecessors had undergone.[35] Officials found wanting could still lose not only position but life and estate, and the extent to which the new "structure" still depended upon royal favor is indicated by the aftermath of Mahmud's death, when Husrev Pasha simply stepped into an institutional vacuum and claimed the grand vizierate for himself. One other noted reform of 1829, the introduction of the fez and the homogenization of clothing prescribed for officeholders and religious scholars, similarly subordinated officials to the sultan by attacking the sartorial means by which subjects could advertise any status independent of his state. This marked a startling change in custom, since sultans in times of public tension normally affirmed their roles as guardians of *din ü devlet* by ordering that shari'a-based regulations on differentiated clothing be strictly observed; Selim III had done this, as had Mahmud himself as recently as 1814.

Mahmud thus seemed to court opposition, and the resumption and intensification of his policy of breaking the provincial order finally ignited a response. The destruction and bloodshed visited upon loyal Muslims by Mahmud's army caused disaffection among the empire's main population that erupted into armed resistance against the center, a sure sign of the dire condition to which the state brought itself in the 1830s. Far from being unprincipled, resistance to Istanbul's actions grew directly out of the ideology that legitimated the regime: when the ruler acted against the ethics of the religion, then service to *din ü devlet* required protection of the religion from the lawless acts of the state.

[34] Mardin, *Young Ottoman Thought*, 153.
[35] Carter Findley, *Bureaucratic Reform in the Ottoman Empire: The Sublime Porte 1789–1922* (Princeton: Princeton University Press, 1980), 125–48.

REFORM, RELIGION, AND REBELLION: OTTOMAN EUROPE

Examination of unrest in European and Asian provinces reveals complex reasons for disquiet. It shows that "rebellion" was rare, being rather a label assigned initially by the imperial regime, and that provincial unrest often broke out as a reaction to repression by the center. From the conclusion of the war with Russia in 1829 until his death ten years later, Mahmud redeployed his remaining military to conquer anew the western sector of Ottoman Europe, eastern Anatolia, the provinces of Iraq, and the coasts of Libya. Mehmed Ali forestalled Mahmud in Syria and southwestern Anatolia, providing the most noted resistance to the policy of breaking the old order in Muslim lands. Mehmed Ali's defiance of the sultan may be well known, but of equal importance to the sustainability of Mahmud's rule was the turmoil elsewhere, especially in the Balkans, still the empire's most important region in terms of population and economic resources. Throughout the 1830s the Muslim population of the Balkans was restive, and particularly in Albania and Bosnia discontent led to much bloodshed as provincial forces battled Istanbul's armies.

Bosnia – the northwestern bulwark of European defense – had a population that was predominantly Muslim and highly militarized. With the loss of Hungary (1699), Belgrade (1718–39, 1790–1, and effectively from 1804), and in practice Montenegro, its vulnerability as a Muslim salient bordered by hostile and increasingly emboldened Christian powers and populations had grown over time. Bosnia's Muslims shouldered the load of defense against endemic raiding by neighboring Christians and had accepted primary responsibility for suppression of the Christian revolt in Belgrade province after 1804. Yet while these defense burdens increased, the Bosnian militia and janissary garrisons faced growing impediments to assuming them placed by policy changes originating in Istanbul. From the middle of the eighteenth century, the spread of malikane tax farming gradually alienated established funding sources from the Bosnian military, causing problems for defense of the frontiers.[36] In the early nineteenth century, because of great power protests, the imperial government tried increasingly to hinder Bosnian forces engaged in running conflicts with Christians across the province's borders. Within Bosnia, Istanbul's appointed governor manipulated

[36] Hickok, *Ottoman Military Administration*, 98–112, 152–75.

rivalries between local notables in order to keep Bosnian forces divided and thus malleable.[37]

Such interference seemingly designed to hamper self-defense in a vulnerable province prepared the ground for Bosnians' initial refusal to accept abolition of the janissary corps in 1826. The change had been announced in an insulting manner, moreover, by identifying the janissaries as little more than thieving crypto-Christians in league with the Russians; such aspersions were hard to accept in Bosnia, whose defenders had earned a better reputation in fighting the Habsburgs than any Ottoman force facing Russia.[38] Bosnians felt threatened at a fundamental level: the attack on the janissaries was taken as a sign that Istanbul intended to break Muslim society, stripping it of its rights, possessions, and even ability to defend itself. To replace the janissaries, Mahmud reintroduced the New Order army, which was to be developed in Istanbul; for the foreseeable future, it would not aid defense of an isolated province whose extant forces had been suddenly dissolved. Bosnian fears that the eradication of the janissaries meant their own demise were serious. Mahmud complained that Bosnians had great difficulty distinguishing between being Muslims and being janissaries – an ominous complaint, because in the aftermath of the corps's dissolution the failure to answer correctly the provocative question "Are you a Janissary or Muslim?" resulted in execution – but he did not understand why.[39] Given the security concerns and the military nature of the Ottoman system in Bosnia, the leap from the attack on the janissaries to one on wider Muslim society was all too credible.

Istanbul's methods of reconciling Bosnia's Muslims to the New Order deepened the impression that it no longer felt an interest in their well-being. In 1827 it dispatched a tough new governor supported by a large force to break Bosnian rejectionism. He executed a number of recalcitrants after his arrival in Sarajevo and demanded that notables of the region compile lists of all who played a role in resisting abolition of the corps – lists entitled "kill," "exile," and "fine." On the basis of such denunciations, incomplete though they were, more than one hundred people were

---

[37] Ahmet Eren, *Mahmud II. Zamanında Bosna-Hersek* (Istanbul: Nurgök Matbaası, 1965), 48–56.

[38] For the decree sent to Bosnia, see Bojanić-Lukač and Katić (eds.), *Maglajski Sidžili 1816–1840*, 534.

[39] Eren, *Mahmud II*, 76–7, 85; Virginia Aksan, "Military Recruitment Strategies in the Late Eighteenth Century," in *Arming the State: Military Conscription in the Middle East and Central Asia, 1775–1925*, ed. Erik Zürcher (London: I. B. Tauris, 1999), 33.

executed without trial. Hüseyn, commander of Gradačac (a stronghold in northeastern Bosnia), leader of the most significant Bosnian revolt a few years later, had been accepting of the governor and the new military order until this point but was among those notables refusing to draw up the lists, on grounds that they would be arbitrary and unjust.[40]

Like that of many other Bosnian Muslims, however, Hüseyn's transition to open resistance occurred only in 1829, following Istanbul's agreement in the Peace of Edirne to cede more Bosnian districts to the Christian province of Belgrade. Istanbul's attempts to carry out such transfers generated open opposition from Bosnia's Muslims. In the eyes of the "rebels," Bosnia was harassed by hostile Christians who raided across four frontiers, and Istanbul only pursued policies that weakened local self-defense. Rebel demands thus centered upon giving control over Bosnia's fate to Bosnian leaders and ending the diversion of its human and material resources to distant imperial interests. The support given these demands by a broad swath of the Muslim population was striking.[41] Hüseyn was thus able to raise a significant army that took the offensive against Istanbul's "modernized" forces in the Balkans.

Hüseyn and his supporters allied with Muslims elsewhere in the Balkans in 1830–1 to resist what had come to be seen as Istanbul's oppression. They found many potential allies, since tensions between the center and the European provinces had recurred frequently since the 1790s. In the case of Albanians, Mahmud and his officers distrusted their unruliness and blamed them for military failures in Greece in the 1820s.[42] Albanians had their own grievances against Mahmud's regime since it had sent the army against Ali Pasha that wreaked havoc on Epirus in 1820–2. As noted, Ali himself was no rebel, and the execution of the elderly pasha and his sons while in captivity smacked of treachery. The course of the whole affair and the precedence given the effort to break Ali over quelling the Greek revolt created lasting bitterness among Muslims of the region.[43]

---

[40] Eren, *Mahmud II*, 89–90.

[41] Eren, *Mahmud II*, 102, 115, 158–60.

[42] Hakan Erdem, "'Perfidious Albanians' and 'Zealous Governors': Ottomans, Albanians, and Turks in the Greek War of Independence," in *Ottoman Rule in the Balkans, 1760–1850: Conflict, Transformation, Adaptation*, ed. Antonis Anastasopoulos and Elias Kolovos (Rethymno: University of Crete, 2007), 213–40, and Anscombe, "'Mountain Bandits.'"

[43] Anscombe, "Centre-Periphery"; Yılmazer (ed.), *Vakanüvis Esad*, 711; BOA, Cev.Dah 8876 (1821), and HH 21638 (1829–30).

Officers involved in the attack on Ali commanded the Greek campaign, and under them served Muslim militia of the Balkans who bore the brunt of campaigning in a vicious war. As in other conflicts, command was flawed, the militia undisciplined, and the army ill supplied; troops fighting the rebels, and from 1828 the Russians as well, were also unpaid. The regime called upon their religious fervor in defense of the Abode of Islam to keep them in the field. Religious duty generated volunteers, but, given the poverty afflicting regions such as Albania that supplied much of the manpower for the army, lack of pay only exacerbated discipline problems. In these circumstances, Muslims who did not struggle to the full in defense of *din ü devlet* shirked a religious duty and could not be considered true believers, an attitude seen in the vituperative language regarding Albanians used within Mahmud's close circle of advisers and high officers. Albanian troops' demands for pay, even though recognized as both legitimate and necessary because of the poverty of their homeland, made them an "execrable nation" and, as Mahmud himself wrote, "without religion" (*dinsiz*).[44] The humiliation of the defeat by Russia and the loss of Greece only exacerbated Mahmud and his advisers' resentments, causing them to turn on the western Balkans as soon as the war ended.

Mahmud's commander for the reconquest of Albania was his new grand vizier Reşid Mehmed Pasha, one of the slaves of Husrev Pasha to fill important posts in Mahmud's government. Reşid had been a senior figure in the expedition against Ali Pasha, commander of Istanbul's land forces sent against the Greek rebels, and a harsh critic of Albanian troops.[45] He chose to attack the south first, and to judge by the actions of his selected targets, the population had no expectation of the punishment to which they would be subjected. Reşid invited the notables of the south whom he most despised to a meeting at his army headquarters in Bitola (Macedonia), offering them safe conduct. He staged for his guests a ceremonial demonstration of the gunnery skills of his troops, during which the soldiers turned their fire upon the notables. Some who survived were sent to Istanbul, while some of the wounded were executed in the town's bazaar as a warning to all (*'ibratan li'l-sa'irin*, a phrase used to justify

---

[44] BOA, HH 21513-G, 27 December 1828; HH 21433, 16 December 1829; HH 21554, 1830; Lutfi, *Tarih*, i, 261–2.

[45] BOA, HH 21513-G (1828). Erdem, "Perfidious Albanians," describes the growth of Reşid's venomous attitude toward Albanians during the Greek revolt.

executions according to siyasa).[46] Reşid carried out a similar massacre of Christian notables in Thessaly a few months later.[47] The massacres sent a powerful message across southern Albania and farther afield.

Reşid assumed command of the southern districts; control over administration and tax collection passed into new hands, but otherwise he altered little in the established system. Appointing his son to control of the south, he turned to the north, which was dominated by Buşatlı Mustafa Pasha, scion of the family that traditionally held the governorship of Shkodra. Unlike his predecessor and kinsman Kara Mahmud Pasha, Mustafa had always been demonstrably loyal to the sultan. He assisted operations to crush the Greek revolt, fend off the Russian attack on the Danube, and even mop up resistance to Reşid's takeover in the south; not an outspoken opponent of reform, he volunteered twenty thousand men to defend Mahmud's new military order against the Bosnians in 1826.[48] Given Mustafa's loyalty, Reşid needed to goad him into revolt, which he accomplished by having the districts around Shkodra transferred from men loyal to Mustafa to Reşid, endangering the governor's standing in the region. Mustafa tried negotiation and simple pleading for revocation of the order, but in vain.[49]

Mustafa raised the banner of revolt in the name of religion, in which he appealed to Islam's moral principles of peace, justice, and reconciliation within the community of believers. Mustafa asserted that the empire had been brought low by evil associates who were now instigating all sorts of injustices; he urged Muslims to unite "to render good service to our religion and state by annulling the innovations which have occurred in contravention of the blessed shari'a and kanun."[50] His call to arms, made in the name of "The Allied Muslims," met a ready response. Most of northern Albania supported him, as did much of the south. He established ties with the Bosnians and had strong support in Bulgaria, where the region of Sofia suffered greatly from a rebel assault.[51] If all of those

[46] BOA, HH 21518 (24 August 1830). The notables should have remembered an incident in 1828 when Reşid had his soldiers kill an Albanian notable invited to his residence. Erdem, "Perfidious Albanians," 234–5.

[47] NA, FO 78/203, 5–8 (5 January 1831).

[48] BOA, HH 22064 (25 December 1826) and HH 21911 (12 September 1830). The notion that Mustafa was responsible for the defeat by the Russians in 1829 seems a later scapegoating.

[49] BOA, HH 21472 (1831), HH 21412 (1831), and HH 21948-A (1831).

[50] BOA, HH 21173-D (15 April 1831) and HH 21173-E (12 May 1831).

[51] BOA, HH 21412-B (1831); Esmer, "Culture of Rebellion."

ready to rise up had been able to join forces, they could have destroyed Reşid's army.

Success barely eluded the revolt. Before the rebels could unite, Mustafa confronted Reşid in Macedonia. An attempt to assassinate Reşid on the eve of battle killed the wrong man, leaving the rebels mistakenly celebrating his death; they were then defeated by an attack launched to take advantage of the confusion. A rumor that four thousand rebels were summarily executed sapped the will to continue the revolt among Muslims of Bulgaria.[52] Past experience of the regime's readiness to execute Muslims made the rumor credible. The Bosnian rebels, however, reached Kosovo, where they defeated Reşid's forces. Not entirely enamored of their recent antagonist Mustafa, however, they were bought off by promises about Bosnian affairs that Istanbul had no intention of keeping. Reşid thus succeeded in capturing Mustafa, who benefited from Istanbul's apparent realization that continued ruthlessness would only widen fissures in society that European powers could exploit.[53] Mustafa was sent to Istanbul, where he was settled in a residence that he transformed into a salon for a wide circle of religious- and literary-minded friends.[54] Reşid removed Mustafa's men from all positions of influence, taking over their assets as he had done in the south.

When viewed from a perspective not centered on Istanbul and the upper reaches of the imperial government, such campaigning seemed unmerited and unjust. An imperial courier who traveled through Albania and Macedonia, for example, reported that Muslims there saw in Buşatlı Mustafa a loyal servant of the state who had performed his duties well and yet was stripped of posts and possessions – why should anyone else expect better treatment?[55] The Bitola massacre conformed to a wider pattern, with Muslims killed in summary fashion, and the assets of those out of favor seized by Mahmud's favorites. Reşid did not abolish tax farming or landed estates; as with political offices, he merely reallocated them to himself, his son, or his own political retainers. It appeared, in short, that the system had not changed, only the identities of those able to milk

---

[52] BOA, HH 21256-A (7 May 1831).

[53] BOA, HH 21644 (datable to 1830), HH 21519 (15 October 1831).

[54] After Mahmud's death, Mustafa was appointed governor of a series of provinces. He died in the holy city of Medina in 1860, and in 1865 the state returned to his sons (all high Ottoman officials of the Tanzimat) the property confiscated from their father in 1831. Mustafa Bilge, "Mustafa Pasha, Buşatlı," *İslam Ansiklopedisi* (Istanbul: Türkiye Diyanet Vakfı, 2006), xxxi, 345.

[55] BOA, HH 21412-B (1831).

it, with one set of amateurs replaced by another that was distinguished only by its loyalty to Mahmud, be that loyalty feigned, forced, genuine, or bought.[56] And while Mahmud's clique crushed those suspected of disloyalty and looted what remained of Muslim lands, all in the name of improving the state, they proved incapable of defeating Christians, be they Greek rebels or the Russian army. The janissaries had been slaughtered, but the new army was led by palace favorites and other officers as untrained and incompetent as the janissaries had been. Mahmud's methods raised a serious question: without justice and due process of law, what separated the Abode of Islam from its opposite, the Abode of War? The very definition of the Abode of Islam is land controlled by a Muslim ruler, since under a non-Muslim government shari'a – and thus justice – cannot reign. When Mahmud no longer enforced justice, Ottoman Muslims began to call him "Infidel Sultan" – and it was surely not coincidence that the sufi path to grow most vigorously in the early nineteenth century was the Naqshbandi, noted for its emphasis upon shari'a and strictly orthodox practice.

Mahmud recognized the threat to his legitimacy as head of state and commander of the faithful posed by such rebellions. He charged the shaikh al-islam with devising an Islamic theory of total obedience to the sultan. The shaikh duly derived an argument that, in times of "evil and corruption," shari'a regulations could be set aside so that the ruler could reestablish "civilization."[57] In Şerif Mardin's sardonic summation, this (despotic) theory "constitutes Mahmud's contribution to political philosophy."[58] In the case of the "Allied Muslims" revolt, Istanbul sent proclamations throughout the Balkans to counter Mustafa's claims and rally support to the sultan, stressing that it was a Muslim's duty to obey the commander of the faithful, and that those who sought to divide the community should die the death of the unbeliever, cut down by

---

[56] See also Keiko Kiyotaki, "The Practice of Tax Farming in the Province of Baghdad in the 1830s," in Imber and Kiyotaki (eds.), *Frontiers of Ottoman Studies*, i, 94. Mustafa Reşid Pasha, a leading figure of the Tanzimat era, commented dismissively on Mahmud's favoritism and idea of reform. "He had no knowledge whatsoever of the skills needed in administering the affairs [of state].... His mind lacked understanding. To flatter his pride and his vanity was to assure oneself of his approbation." Mardin, *Young Ottoman Thought*, 111.

[57] Kemal Karpat, "Ifta and Kaza: The Ilmiye State and Modernism in Turkey, 1820–1960," in Imber and Kiyotaki (eds.), *Frontiers of Ottoman Studies*, i, 29. 'Ulama were divided over Mahmud's reforms, with the support given by some holders of high office counterbalanced by hostility among humbler figures. Uriel Heyd, "The Ottoman 'Ulema and Westernization in the Time of Selim III and Mahmud II," *SH* 9 (1961), 69–77.

[58] Mardin, *Young Ottoman Thought*, 149.

the sword. They also noted a legal opinion issued by the shaikh al-islam condemning Mustafa's rebellion as unjust according to the shari'a.[59] Mahmud's government started the first Ottoman-language newspaper, the official gazette *Takvim-i Vekayı*, as a tool to strengthen its ability to guard public opinion against the spread of coffeehouse rumors about resistance to the regime's harsh "reforms." The array of military and propaganda measures deployed in the Balkans prevented a complete collapse of Mahmud's authority there, but it remained on insecure footing for the rest of the decade. This would be shown paradoxically by events in Ottoman Asia, where collapse loomed imminent at the time of Mahmud's death in 1839.

REFORM, RELIGION, AND REBELLION: OTTOMAN ASIA

Istanbul's actions in Asia created a situation there as volatile as that in Ottoman Europe, as Mahmud had restarted in the East the process of bringing provinces to heel, again arousing outrage over harsh methods. In Baghdad, for example, the "mamluk" (slave-soldier) regime that had governed the province and maintained defenses against Iran since the mid-eighteenth century was overturned, with all but fifteen mamluks and the governor executed in 1831.[60] Eastern Anatolia still seethed. The full nature of the danger posed by Mahmud's tenuous hold upon the loyalty of the empire's Muslims became clearer with the rise of a strong challenger to his manner of rule: Mehmed Ali.

Mehmed Ali's military power alone did not pose a critical threat to the empire, but when it was coupled with his ideological appeal to Muslims, he became a menace to Istanbul. He was the only significant ancien régime notable to escape Mahmud's humbling of provincial leaders, although as a military modernizer Mehmed Ali faced religiously inspired resistance in Egypt on grounds similar to those seen elsewhere in the empire.[61] His demonstration of military effectiveness showing that the old system could function under competent command, however, not only limited the domestic problems he faced in comparison to Mahmud's loss of authority but, combined with his position as last representative of

---

[59] BOA, Cev.Dah 7942 (mid-April 1831) and HH 21257-A (1831).
[60] Yusuf Halaçoğlu, "Bağdat – Osmanlı Dönemi," *İslam Ansiklopedisi* (Istanbul: Türkiye Diyanet Vakfı, 2006), iv, 435.
[61] Khaled Fahmy, "Mutiny in Mehmed Ali's New Nizami Army, April–May 1824," in Hathaway (ed.), *Mutiny and Rebellion*, 129–38.

the once-legitimate order and his wider image as a good Muslim and just ruler, enabled him to tap into the disquiet aroused by Mahmud.

As with Buşatlı Mustafa, part of Mehmed Ali's appeal lay in the fact that, by standards prevailing until Mahmud's reign, he remained a loyal and competent Ottoman official until the 1830s. Before Mahmud renewed his attacks on the provinces after his defeat by Russia, Mehmed Ali used his power to further Istanbul's interests as well as his own. He undertook the difficult and expensive task of restoring the sultan's control over Mecca and Medina. It was his liberation of the Holy Cities that allowed Mahmud to style himself not only as "Protector of the Holy Places" again but also as "Gazi."[62] The governor of Egypt brought Sudan into the empire. He almost rescued the Ottoman cause in fighting the Greek rebellion. The Greek experience proved a turning point, however, because Istanbul's unceasing demands suggested that the sultan would happily exhaust Egypt's resources to further his campaigns in the provinces. The methodical humbling of eminent men such as Buşatlı Mustafa left little doubt that Mahmud would crush him, in turn, once his military might was spent.

In 1831 Mehmed Ali launched into Syria an army under his son Ibrahim, securing thereby the only practicable invasion route for forces dispatched from Anatolia. He took advantage of the unrest to be seen in Ottoman provinces: he proclaimed that he was establishing "the just state" in Syria and charged Ibrahim to protect the Muslims, as Istanbul no longer could, leading the population to welcome his rule initially.[63] Ibrahim defeated in succession three armies mustered against him, and his victory at Konya left Istanbul at his mercy by the end of 1832. Yet Mehmed Ali refused to unleash Ibrahim upon the capital or to demand recognition of independence from the sultan. His hesitation stemmed from his sense of loyalty to the sultan as, echoing Buşatlı Mustafa, he blamed Mahmud's officers, especially Husrev, for causing tension between Cairo and Istanbul.[64] Mahmud's vulnerability, however, led the sultan to formal alliance with Russia in 1833, making the most reviled Ottoman foe the

---

[62] To gain the title "Gazi" (warrior for Islam) through victory over Muslims was emblematic of Mahmud's reign (Anscombe, "Age of Ottoman Reform," 170n28). The fatwa declaring that those who divided the community deserved to die the death of the infidel, however, applied to the militant Wahhabis more clearly than to Buşatlı Mustafa.

[63] Asad Rustum, "Idara al-Sham: Ruhuha wa Haykaluha wa Atharuha," in *Dhikra al-Batal al-Fatih Ibrahim Basha, 1848–1948* (Cairo: Matba'a Dar al-Kutub al-Misriyya, 1948), 107–10, 126; Judith Rood, "Mehmed Ali as Mutinous Khedive: The Roots of Rebellion," in Hathaway (ed.), *Mutiny and Rebellion*, 125; Douwes, *Ottomans*, 190, 195–7.

[64] Fahmy, *Pasha's Men*, 67–73, 285–9.

protector of the throne and the source of equipment for his "Victorious Muhammadan" army.

Mahmud's Russian alliance was unpopular among Ottoman Muslims, but he had little choice. He had exacted a heavy toll upon the empire's human and material resources in his effort to create an effective military, but the results were disappointing. His new army of Balkan and Anatolian Turks remained limited in size; when Ibrahim crushed that force, the state had to replenish its defenses with men of the wider Muslim population. But would they fight with commitment? Istanbul discovered at Konya that they would not.

Reşid Mehmed Pasha raised and led the army meant to drive Ibrahim from Anatolia and Syria. Despite his history in the Balkans, he ordered recruitment of seventy thousand troops from Albania and Bosnia. In order to make sure that they would fight, the regime interned numerous hostages. His rebuilt army outnumbered that of Ibrahim, but when they met on the battlefield of Konya, Ibrahim won decisively, with Reşid himself being captured.[65] The commander of the remnants of Reşid's army blamed the Albanians and Bosnians for the defeat, claiming that some of them fled the battle, while the rest fought indifferently.[66] There may have been scapegoating in the charge, since poor officer leadership was an important problem, but British reports support the charge of halfheartedness. The consul in Epirus stated that only an exceptionally severe frost and the Ramadan fast postponed renewed rebellion in Albania, while the consul in Salonica reported that Albanian troops being hurried to Istanbul's defense after Konya attempted to redirect their transport ships to join Mehmed Ali.[67]

Mahmud remained on the throne, courtesy of Mehmed Ali's restraint and the hasty deployment of Russian forces to protect the capital. Mahmud's position remained weak, however, since he could not rely on the support of his subjects. The protection of the Russians earned the sultan nothing but contempt.[68] Mehmed Ali, by contrast, rode high in the opinion of many Muslims, both within the empire and outside. In eastern Anatolia the advance of Ibrahim toward Konya had encouraged some dissatisfied with Mahmud's regime to rise against the sultan's

---

[65] BOA, HH 20330-A (1833), and HH 20076-C (13 January 1833); Fahmy, *Pasha's Men*, 160–7.

[66] BOA, HH 20036-F (23 January 1833).

[67] Levy, "Officer," 37–8; NA, FO 78/230, pp. 5–7, 25 January 1833; FO 195/100, 83, 28 January 1833.

[68] NA, FO 78/230, 26–9, 27 February 1833; Hanioğlu, *Brief History*, 66.

men; only Ibrahim's abstention from involvement restored a semblance of peace. In western Anatolia, where Ibrahim did have a strategic interest in extending his influence, he found both notables and ordinary Muslims happy to cooperate with him. Even in the Caucasus the governor of Egypt enjoyed striking support from Muslims waging a campaign against Russian domination.[69] Mahmud and his officers did not accept the status quo and periodically tried to weaken Mehmed Ali's position. They launched campaigns beginning in 1835 to assert direct control over lands and populations neighboring Mehmed Ali's expanded domain, including Tripolitania (Libya) and the large Kurdish-dominated southeastern quarter of Anatolia, where Reşid Mehmed again executed a violent campaign to destroy the old order. The governor of Egypt, in turn, played upon the disaffection among Muslims under Istanbul's tenuous control. Rebellion broke out anew in the western Balkans, for example, at least partially in response to messages of support from "His Excellency the Sultan of Egypt, Mehmed Ali Pasha."[70]

Mahmud thus could not afford to press too directly upon Egypt and Syria, but one of the sultan's acts hurt Mehmed Ali sufficiently to cause him to voice at last a desire for independence: the conclusion of a trade convention with Britain in 1838 that dissolved all Ottoman monopolies. Mahmud's regime had established monopolies over various commodities, but in its weak condition and facing popular opposition, its ability to enforce them was limited.[71] Uncomfortable with having to rely upon Russia to keep the sultan on the throne, Istanbul looked for additional assistance from Britain. Britain's price for closer involvement was the liberalization of trade in the empire, and Istanbul's poor profit from monopolization made it willing to agree. The Anglo-Ottoman Trade Convention accordingly established low maximum tariffs on imports and exports, abolished all monopolies and other restrictions on tradable goods, and opened all of the empire to British (and thereafter all European) merchants.[72] The convention's terms applied to Egypt and Syria, where

---

[69] Michael Meeker, *A Nation of Empire: The Ottoman Legacy of Turkish Modernity* (Berkeley: University of California Press, 2002), 241–2; NA, FO 195/101, 5 April 1833; NA, FO 195/88, 203–4, 20 February 1833; Andrew Gould, "Lords or Bandits? The Derebeys of Cilicia," *IJMES* 7 (1976), 488; Moshe Gammer, "The Imam and the Pasha: A Note on Shamil and Muhammad Ali," *MES* 32 (1996), 339.

[70] BOA, HH 21246-H and HH 21246-G (1 July 1835).

[71] See, for example, Ibrahim Poroy, "Expansion of Opium Production in Turkey and the State Monopoly of 1828–1839," *IJMES* 13 (1981), 191–211.

[72] J. C. Hurewitz (ed.), *Diplomacy in the Near and Middle East: A Documentary Record, 1535–1914* (Princeton: Princeton University Press, 1956), 110–11.

Mehmed Ali had established more effective monopolies that were crucial to maintenance of his military forces. Mahmud's agreement to Britain's terms damaged future Ottoman governments' ability to maintain economic independence from Christian Europe, but the convention aided him in the short term by winning closer British interest in imperial stability and in undercutting Mehmed Ali's means of raising revenue. The governor of Egypt had to push for independence or the overthrow of Mahmud. This brought the struggle to a climax when, shortly before dying, Mahmud ordered another assault on Ibrahim. Again the sultan's army suffered devastating defeat, leaving Istanbul vulnerable once more.

Muslims' reluctance to rally to Mahmud made his vulnerability painfully clear. Soldiers from Anatolia deserted from the Ottoman army during the short, lopsided battle.[73] The Ottoman navy subsequently defected to Mehmed Ali. There were few willing to fight on sea or land against the only effective Muslim leader left in the empire. Shortly before Mahmud's death, the British consul in Salonica had asked notables whether the sultan could raise thirty thousand Albanian troops to confront Mehmed Ali. The reply was striking: "'If the sultan was at war with any Foreign power not 30, but 100 (thousand) men, were ready for him, if he required them, but against Mehemet Alli, he would not be able to raise a single regiment.'"[74] Muslims would fight for the Abode of Islam but not to help the Infidel Sultan crush the idealized representative of all that Mahmud had failed to be. Mahmud thus bequeathed his successor a tough challenge: restore support to a teetering throne.

THE GÜLHANE REFORM DECREE

After Mahmud II died, his successor, Abdülmecid, addressed the grievances that had stirred decades of turmoil across much of the empire. Mahmud had embodied the stereotype of the distant "oriental despot," making momentous decisions based largely upon personality and regardless of both law and tradition; with his death, the imperial regime was freed to revise his debilitating administrative practices. Abdülmecid issued a decree, the Hatt-i Şerif of Gülhane, which made three promises to the empire's Muslim and non-Muslim populations that were to shape the Tanzimat period, the era of fundamental change in Ottoman government.

[73] NA, FO 195/112, 244–5, 13 July 1839.
[74] NA, FO 195/100, 403, 20 June 1839.

Gülhane's reassessment of government practice began with the startling admission with which the decree opened: that the power and well-being of the empire had declined because it had failed to uphold law.[75] The first of the three basic promises of the decree was that the government would henceforth rule only in accordance with law (the shari'a and regulations consonant with Islamic legal principles), and particularly in matters concerning the life, honor, and property of the sultan's subjects. These could not be touched without due process of law, and no one was too lofty or too humble to be either unconstrained or unprotected by law. Such a promise of justice openly and predictably applied addressed the most significant complaint of rebels, from Belgrade's Christians defending themselves against anarchy to the many groups that had resisted Istanbul's brutal reassertion of supremacy over the provinces. As the references to shari'a suggest, the decree targeted primarily the Muslims of the empire who had failed to rally to Mahmud's defense, but Christians also gained from the promise of legal procedure applicable to all.[76]

Gülhane's other two promises returned to the issues that had motivated the unsettling practices of Selim III and Mahmud II: the strengthening of the empire's defenses. The decree promised reorganization of tax collection to make it predictable, orderly, and sustainable. People were henceforth to pay taxes determined by their wealth and ability to pay and were to be protected against further exactions. The decree singled out tax farming for eradication. It cited the need to defend the empire's borders to legitimate the levying of taxes but also declared that the regime would formulate laws to limit expenditures on land and sea forces. Gülhane finally committed the government to take at least an initial step toward proper budgeting, which would be critical to any chance of meaningful military reform. The third promise of the decree was reorganization of military recruitment to make it, too, predictable, orderly, and sustainable. Conscription would be spread equitably (i.e., would no longer weigh only on the Turkish population but would extend to recently suspect groups such as Albanians, Bosnians, Kurds, and Arabs) and the length of service reduced from the minimum of twelve to four or five years, so that inductees would no longer be subject to despair.

---

[75] Lutfi, *Tarih*, vi, 61–4; Hurewitz (ed.), *Diplomacy*, 113–16.

[76] The Gülhane decree made no mention of Christian-Muslim equality before the law, which had not been the grievance of Christians in revolt: upholding the extant law had been the key issue.

Abdülmecid's short list of promises to his population provided the guiding principles of the most noted reform program in Ottoman history, the "beneficent measures to bring order" (Tanzimat-i Hayriye). These measures were effective in restoring domestic peace after an extended period of fratricidal conflict. Sultan Mahmud had begun his reign with essentially undisputed inherited legitimacy among his subjects, and the power of that legitimacy could be seen in the almost uniform loyalty of provincial notables, including Mehmed Ali prior to the 1830s. He then became the only late Ottoman sultan to come close to losing the empire to widespread internal, Muslim unrest rather than dismemberment at the hands of Christian powers. If filmed, his reign would be "Mutiny on the Bounty" rather than "The Alamo." None of his successors was to face such peril, even in the harrowing years after 1908. What they all confronted, however, was the external threat that had motivated Mahmud and his predecessor Selim to attempt radical methods of imperial defense. In facing the threat emanating from Europe's great powers, the Tanzimat state recouped some of the power once enjoyed by sultans in earlier centuries, but ultimately the contest proved impossible to win.

4

The Reconstructed Muslim State

For almost seventy years, from the accession of Abdülmecid in 1839 to the "Young Turk" revolution of 1908, the political history of the Ottoman empire revolved around the need to manage, if not resolve, a tangled knot of problems inherited from Mahmud's era: closing the rifts within the Ottoman Muslim community and thereby restoring the state's legitimacy in the eyes of its core population; using that legitimacy to intensify exploitation of the physical and financial resources of the population in order to strengthen the empire's military and administrative capacities; deflecting the often-conflicting diplomatic and economic pressures exerted by Christian Europe; and keeping the non-Muslim population sufficiently content to foreclose opportunities for interference by foreign powers. In comparison to regimes in Istanbul over preceding decades, imperial authorities after 1839 managed the challenges well, rebuilding the state as a modern, relatively efficient entity but with its domestic legitimacy as a power identified with the defense of Islam and of justice restored to an adequate level. The struggle to balance strengthening with observance of moral limits to state power never ended, however, and the tension caused by growing authoritarianism in government and weakening ability of the state to protect Muslim interests led to a peculiarly haphazard military coup in 1908 that signaled a change in the direction of governance.

In accordance with the plan outlined in the Hatt-i Şerif of Gülhane, law played the critical role in whatever success the modernization measures adopted by the state enjoyed after 1839. The Ottoman state showed scrupulous interest in devising and administering law through proper procedure. Ottoman administration, after all, was under intense scrutiny from various directions: from wary Muslim and non-Muslim populations that had felt harassed or treated unjustly in a variety of ways under pre-Tanzimat regimes, and from the Christian powers of Europe, whose presence and influence in Ottoman domains grew ever more obvious as the nineteenth century progressed. Foreign powers pressed Ottoman leaders to distance the state and its legal system from their religious roots, but to the extent that such pressure could be resisted, regimes maintained the Islamic identities of both the state and its rapidly developing institutions, from the military to the modern educational system founded during the Tanzimat. The evident loyalty of the Muslim population until the dissolution of the empire after the First World War suggests that Ottoman Muslims recognized the maintenance of the ideological identity of the state and its system of law at a fundamental level, despite periodic dissatisfaction with regime measures. That the empire saw almost no significant uprisings led by indigenous non-Muslims until the First World War suggests moreover that the state's commitment to improved law and legality repaired its legitimacy among Christians and Jews as well. The empire had appeared on the point of implosion at Mahmud II's death, but some eight decades later it was pressure from Christian Europe that killed it.

WESTERNIZATION OR MODERNIZATION?

Such a verdict on culpability for Ottoman collapse counters a common perception that Europe helped the empire, "the Sick Man of Europe," to survive for a century longer than otherwise it would have. Part of that alleged assistance derived from Europe's own internal divisions, with Ottoman rulers always able to find enough support among the powers to block dissolution of the empire. On a more prosaic level, however, Europe supposedly helped reformers by providing a model, and sometimes active support, for Ottoman westernizers in their desperate scramble to rescue their collapsing authority over restless peoples. The persistent tendency to describe the Ottoman state as "ramshackle" and much in need of reform modeled on Europe's mastery of rationalism and efficiency reinforces belief in the Ottoman desire for westernization. To view change in the empire as westernization, however, misses the point of reform.

Certainly instances of imperial "ramshackledom," or inefficiency and the lack of professionalism, are not hard to find. For example, a few years after the establishment of the Foreign Ministry an ambassador posted to Vienna, a capital critical to European politics, sent some fifty dispatches to the home secretariat – and received not a line in reply. On returning from his embassy, it was only on his third visit to the "ministry" that he actually found anyone there. Such lax oversight suggests why provincial or territorial governors launched domestic or foreign initiatives without recourse to the imperial capital, and should imperial orders reach them, they still felt secure to act against instructions, even in attacking neighboring territories. Good governorship, after all, provided no guarantee against cabals of personal or political enemies, as several accomplished governors forced to defend themselves in the capital against politically motivated charges could attest. Corruption was rampant in the form of officeholders' squeezing money out of "fees," or payments from supplicants, rather than relying on official salaries, which the state too frequently showed little willingness or ability to pay. Like the people applying for services from the government, holders of office in civil administration and of command in the military also advanced their interests – their careers – through personal connections and payments to those with powers of appointment. For any state concerned about effective administration of domestic affairs and ability to show strength abroad, such careless management suggests real cause for concern and may help to explain instances of rebellion in various territories.

Attempts to tighten control, improve military and civil efficiency, and organize predictable systems of administration to ameliorate such problems constituted the core of reform, but it is necessary to distinguish such a program from "westernization." All of the cited examples or patterns are drawn from British, not Ottoman, experience of the late eighteenth and early nineteenth centuries.[1] They are worth mentioning

---

[1] On Vienna, see M. S. Anderson, *The Rise of Modern Diplomacy 1450–1919* (London: Longman, 1993), 77. As one of Sultan Abdülhamid II's grand viziers noted (Frederick Anscombe, "On the Road Back from Berlin," in *War and Diplomacy: The Russo-Turkish War of 1877–1878 and the Treaty of Berlin*, ed. M. Hakan Yavuz with Peter Sluglett [Salt Lake City: University of Utah Press, 2011], 549), possession of India made Britain a first- rather than third-rate power – and yet British control there was decidedly ramshackle until well into the nineteenth century: management remained in the hands of the private East India Company, allowing directors in India tremendous latitude of action until mid-nineteenth-century telegraph and steamship technology permitted tighter oversight. Directors were nevertheless answerable to parliament, an arrangement that opened opportunities for political chicanery, as the trials of Robert Clive and Warren Hastings suggested. Others, such as Earl Cornwallis and Richard Wellesley, who launched campaigns of conquest against orders, suffered, by contrast, no rebuke. When the dangers of ramshackle control became too apparent to ignore with the "mutiny" of 1857, London finally took direct responsibility for India. It could also be said that the thirteen American colonies broke away in 1775–83 because of the ramshackle nature of British imperial control.

in part as a rebuttal to supercilious judgments of Ottoman inferiority rendered by nineteenth-century Europeans who, like villagers lately moved to the city, seemed too ready to put on sophisticated airs to denigrate later arrivals. The British examples also offer a reminder of the normality of Ottoman state structure and power: by the standards of today, every state of the eighteenth and even nineteenth century was distinctly ramshackle. Military competition spurred the rise of absolutism in ramshackle Christian Europe in the eighteenth century (eventually causing revolution in Bourbon France and near-collapse in Habsburg Austria), and the startling French might that Napoleon's innovative practices marshaled only intensified rivals' need to tighten governmental oversight and strengthen means of administrative control in the nineteenth. This was precisely the goal of Ottoman reformers after 1839. It would be nonsensical to describe the process in the former case as "westernization," and it thus seems right to describe kindred changes in the Ottoman empire only as "modernization." Some of the practices of improved administration, and much more clearly the technological advances that supported European powers' strength, may have influenced some Ottoman reforms, but these were adapted to suit Ottoman needs (a more open version of what today might be termed "industrial espionage," designed to capture secrets of the administrative trade) rather than adopted in the interests of "acting European."

European powers remained throughout the nineteenth century the greatest threat to Ottoman survival, and the strategic goal of modernization was to keep Europe at arm's length; "westernization" would only work against that purpose. Indeed, Muslims who aped elements of Western culture became figures of ridicule and distrust, as can be seen in various Ottoman novels.[2] To "become European" suggested the abandonment of morality, or even its active rejection, because in cultural terms it meant rejection of Islam and adoption of an ethic steeped in Christianity, since no nineteenth-century European state or country was anything but Christian.[3] Their identification with Christianity was repeatedly demonstrated in their behavior in Ottoman affairs. Indeed, Europe's concept of "civilized countries," among which the principles of international law must be observed, became much more consciously Christian in the nineteenth century, giving European regimes justification

[2] Ayşe Kadıoğlu, "The Paradox of Turkish Nationalism and the Construction of Official Identity," *MES* 32 (1996), 180–2.
[3] Anscombe, "Road Back," 540–3.

for ignoring such principles in their policies toward (and in) the Ottoman empire.[4] European powers pressed Ottoman regimes to strip Islam from state and law, but they applied no similar pressure to Ottoman Christians to distance themselves from their religious identity. Quite the opposite: the milla system, in which adherents of non-Muslim religions were guaranteed rights of autonomy in communal affairs, was created through the same imperial edict, the "Reform Decree" of 1856, that established the principle of full legal equality for all Ottoman citizens. This decree resulted from the demands of the empire's allies, Britain and France, as the Crimean War drew to a close; in a sense, Anglo-French interest thus hindered more than helped any stripping away of religion that the Ottoman state might have wished to encourage.

Previous Ottoman regimes had never shown any clear intention of "secularizing," of course, and those governing after 1856 showed little interest in conducting affairs in a manner truly blind to religion or in a way that would throw the Muslim identity of the state and its core constituency into serious doubt.[5] Yet the government did accede to the Anglo-French demand to remove all legal discriminations against non-Muslims in 1856, seeming to open that very question of Islamic identity. In addition to the simple fact of pressure from wartime allies, the value of the package proposed by Britain and France won Ottoman agreement to legal equality. In return for the promises about non-Muslim rights contained in the Reform Decree at the end of the Crimean War, the Ottoman empire won in the subsequent Peace of Paris recognition as a member of the Concert of Europe, the promise of equality with Christian powers under (Europe's) international law, and a guarantee of territorial integrity, to be enforced by British, French, and Austro-Hungarian arms, if need be. Since the threat of European conquest had driven all reform efforts since the reign of Selim III, the prizes offered at Paris were irresistible – an uncanny echo of the Protestant Henri of Navarre's decision in 1593 that "Paris is well worth a mass" as the price for recognition as King Henri IV of France.

---

[4] Richard Horowitz, "International Law and State Transformation in China, Siam, and the Ottoman Empire during the Nineteenth Century," *Journal of World History* 15 (2004), 462, 465.

[5] A partial admission of this can be seen in a report submitted to Sultan Abdülhamid II in 1880, after the loss of much of the Ottoman position in the Balkans. Feroze Yasamee, "European Equilibrium or Asiatic Balance of Power? The Ottoman Search for Security in the Aftermath of the Treaty of Berlin," in Yavuz (ed.), *War and Diplomacy*, 65.

Promised gains at Paris, however, did nothing to remove the most pervasive and deeply resented Christian European interference in Ottoman affairs on behalf of non-Muslims: the capitulations system. As legal safeguards initially designed to protect Europeans resident or traveling in Ottoman domains and, over time, their native-born interpreters and other employees, the capitulations became a critical tool in the European competition for influence within Ottoman lands. In the nineteenth century consuls issued documents bestowing honorary "citizenship" upon Ottoman non-Muslims in rapidly expanding numbers, by which the recipients gained immunities from Ottoman legal and tax authority. Successive Ottoman governments petitioned the European powers to end the capitulations but without success; indeed, post-Ottoman regimes in Muslim lands also had to struggle for years to end European privileges of protection over non-Muslims. The obvious and seemingly irreversible influence of foreign powers in Ottoman affairs helps to explain why the bargain sealed by the Reform Decree and the Peace of Paris did not appear to most Muslims to be as advantageous as it did to those at the top of government: Europe might have promised to respect the empire's territorial integrity, but observers across the country saw no sign that the powers had any intention of curtailing their everyday infringements on Ottoman sovereignty.

It is difficult to argue that the anger and suspicion of much of the Muslim population was more misplaced or misguided than was the relief of the state elite over the guarantee of territorial integrity. The full cost of the Ottoman promise to erect autonomous communal institutions (the milla system) in the 1856 decree only became clearer with time, for example: the creation of such institutionalized internal divisions complicated tremendously the very process of popular mobilization that nation-building states such as Germany, France, and Britain used to strengthen themselves politically and militarily. In return, the empire received little of what the powers promised at Paris. After 1856 no European power showed steady support for Ottoman independence, territorial integrity, or sovereignty: the dispatch of a military force to Lebanon in 1860 by France, one of the key guarantors of territorial integrity, suggested just how flimsy the promises made at Paris would prove in practice.

By their actions in Ottoman lands, European states and peoples confirmed that Christianity was integral to their self-identity, making the idea of westernization unattractive to most Muslim Ottomans – and providing no model of secularization to be emulated. Imperial leaders undertook instead modernization for the purpose of strengthening the state's ability to defend land and people, and the parameters within which regimes worked were the lines proclaimed to the Ottoman population in 1839. Seventy years of change reconstructed a modern but still Islamic state.

MEASURES TO CREATE ORDER

Ottoman self-strengthening after 1839 followed closely the promises made in the Hatt-i Şerif. This era and the steps taken to put matters in order (Tanzimat) have been more thoroughly studied than any others in Ottoman history, and there is little need to recount in detail measures taken. It is important to note, however, that the tendency to highlight the 1856–76 decades as the golden age of the Tanzimat is misleading, at the least: the 1839–56 years saw vigorous efforts to address core state concerns of revenue collection, military preparedness, and restoration of peace and justice among the population. These efforts continued unabated until the collapse of the empire; the 1856–76 period was distinctive only in that state-strengthening operated under the novel conditions shaped by the Crimean War alliance with Britain and France. As noted, these conditions promised to further, but in practice hindered, preservation of the empire.

Intensification of revenue extraction was a prime concern in the 1839–56 period, when some of the most significant experimentation in taxation measures occurred. Gülhane targeted tax farming as an oppressive practice to be abolished. Istanbul tried to replace tax farmers with salaried tax collectors dispatched from the center, but tax farming revived when the government realized that in some cases the salaried agents cost more than the revenue they collected. Tax farming continued until the end of the empire, but under much closer monitoring than it had received prior to 1839. An important part of the tightened control, and thereby also improved accrual of profit to the state, was the excision of the center from tax farming – the opaque and unwieldy farming structure of the malikane period, dominated by the political households of Istanbul, collapsed. The effective privatization of resources ended with the abolition of malikane, and the resumption of awarding farms on a short-term, renewable basis governed by the developing legal and administrative structures of the late empire ensured tighter control. The actual composition of the taxes to be collected underwent as much experimentation as the methods of collection, also with mixed results. The various customary taxes previously levied by timar holders and then tax farmers were consolidated into the cash *vergü*, and a wealth or profits tax was also introduced. Previous Ottoman rulers had hesitated to tax Muslims individually, dodging the problem by levying "extraordinary" dues upon notional tax households (*hane*) that made a group of people responsible for payment; the perceptible shift toward direct taxation after 1839 triggered reactions from some Muslims, because it suggested the head tax levied on non-Muslims. Over time, therefore, Istanbul maintained its primary reliance upon the traditional, canonic agricultural tithe, raising customs and excise duties as much as the 1838 Trade Convention permitted, and the profits levy transmuted into a tax on commerce. The changes in both collection and composition of taxes did lead to a significant rise in central treasury income, in terms of value and per-capita extraction.[6] Also beneficial to both government and the population was the taming of inflation through stabilization of the currency following adoption of gold and silver standards in 1844, although several later experiments with paper currency failed. Improvements in state finance never closed the revenue or military gap with modernizing Christian powers, however, and the empire finally turned to borrowing (on extremely disadvantageous terms) on European financial markets in 1854. By 1875 it was effectively bankrupt as a result.

Much of the borrowed money was spent on the military, the most critical area of concern since Selim III's reign, and the Ottoman army grew progressively stronger from 1839 to 1908. From 1843 the army relied upon conscripts, drawn by lot from the Muslim peasant population of most of the empire and required to serve comparatively short terms (ultimately two or three years). This active force had a strength of circa 230,000 prior to the First Balkan War (1912) – a powerful body, but still stretched relatively thin by the extent of territory to be defended. Active units were organized into army corps stationed at strategic points around the empire. These front-line forces were backed by a larger system of reserves, and in the provinces there was another large garrison/local security organization. Much of the money invested in the army, however, was spent on weaponry and materiel that needed frequent updating in an era of rapid technological change. While the late Ottoman military was truly modern in many respects and incomparably more effective than the pre-1839 imperial army, it remained hobbled in comparison to its potential

---

[6] K. Kıvanç Karaman and Şevket Pamuk, "Ottoman State Finances in European Perspective, 1500–1914," *Journal of Economic History* 70 (2010), 621–3.

foes, suffering particularly from underdeveloped transport. A modern military was powerful only if it could be concentrated at the right place at the right time, and operations of any duration needed effective systems of supply and medical support.

It was such "ancillary" concerns about improving military effectiveness and the efficiency of the state in exploiting the empire's resources that drove many other aspects of modernization in the era. Significant changes in taxation required an immediate, significant growth in imperial bureaucracy, not only in unprecedented employment of salaried tax collectors but, more significantly, in creating systems to collect and collate information about what was taxable. Having practically privatized tax collection in the eighteenth century and then lost effective control over much of its territory prior to 1839, Istanbul had little reliable information on what revenue potential it actually had. Early surveys collected data on what had been taxed under the old regime as well as what assets could be identified for assessing the new wealth tax. Later, particularly after land law was clarified in 1858, cadastral surveys became the next monumental task. The regime dabbled in industrial policy as well as agricultural extension services but with limited effect, largely because it lacked the funds needed to stimulate growth, seeing instead these efforts as geared primarily toward increasing tax revenue. To carry out such tasks, as well as the other functions of government, education was reshaped to produce fewer lawyers (via the medrese) and more bureaucrats via a full range of new state schools. Even more effort went into establishing rigorous training systems for military officers, which led to creation of a corps of men skilled in staff work. Finally, great investment was made in improving communications, including roads, ports, telegraph, and railways. Much of this was financed in arrears, with initial funding from European firms that took repayment and profits from operation of the finished project. This meant that schemes tended to be oriented toward commercial exploitation rather than imperial military and administrative needs, but they nevertheless furthered progress toward melding the provinces into a controllable empire. It was in the system of law used to exercise that control that the Islamic character of the realm remained evident.

LAW AND ISLAM

Ottoman reform's fundamental concern with law and legal administration after 1839 has been recognized by observers and historians since the nineteenth century, with the focus resting on the adoption of new statutes and codes and the creation of a new system of courts.[7] This very recognition of the importance of legal innovation makes seemingly incredible the proposition that the Ottoman state maintained its religious identity after 1839, because no state that forsakes the path of correct conduct – the shariʿa – can rightly claim Islamic legitimacy. As every student of Islam knows, "innovation" in sharʿi matters is objectionable without jurisprudential justification. By this pattern of reasoning, Ottoman legal reform, and indeed the Tanzimat as a whole, must have constituted a program of secularization. Legal reform operated in the long-established, legitimate sphere of kanun, however, and avoided contravention of sharʿi norms, although in some instances only through justification of acting "for the public good."

Law functioned simultaneously as lubricant for, and legitimator of, modernization. Reform after 1839 aimed to improve the state's fiscal-military machinery, and an important component of this drive was the creation of uniformity in administration and law, to increase the efficiency that resulted from homogenization and to speed the operation of both systems, making them more responsive to state needs. The state not only increased its fiscal-military power through such improvements, but, with the development of fully articulated legal forms and institutions, it also hoped to show Christian powers that it was sufficiently "civilized" to be accorded the protections of international law, and to persuade Ottoman non-Muslims to give up the privileges they gained from the milla and capitulations systems. The imperial center also wanted from legal development and administrative efficiency increased ability to throttle internal disputes before they widened into opportunities for foreign intervention. The growth of a well-modern bureaucracy from perhaps two thousand in 1800 (and not significantly more in 1839) to thirty-five thousand to fifty thousand members by 1900 suggests the scale of change thus wrought in administration. Legal change in the post-1839 period involved the extension of homogenized, statutory law and the way in which law functioned rather than significant revision of the moral basis, or religious roots, of the system of justice. Of the three main areas of change – the extension of the defined legal net, the elaboration of legal process, and the training of those administering law – none required the expunging of Islam.

Because of the religious injunction against unwarranted innovation, the codification into statutory law of a flexible system based upon

---

[7] Carter Findley, "The Tanzimat," in *CHT4*, 16.

jurisprudential interpretation seems most difficult to reconcile with Islam.[8] What Ottoman legists did marked a variation on practices associated today with Arab scholars of the mid- to late-nineteenth century and labeled as Islamic modernism. Muslim society had grown vulnerable to non-Muslim foes, suggesting that there must be flaws in understanding of shari'a, the path of God that assured well-being for the society of believers. Since the Qur'an is unchanging and eternally true, the errors must have arisen through subsequent interpretations that were valid for the times of their formulation but, being "man-made," were not eternal. The core requirements of Islam contained in the Qur'an must be observed, but the principles thus revealed must be interpreted anew to fit the conditions of the modern period. And one of the pressing conditions of the age was precisely the need to standardize law, both to empower the state through fiscal-military efficiency and to preempt Christian powers that threatened to fill what they, with different religiously grounded concepts of law, saw as a legal vacuum.[9] The figure most associated with modernism, Muhammad 'Abduh, rector of al-Azhar in Egypt, favored choosing among interpretations of all schools of jurisprudence to find those most suited to current conditions; Ottoman codifiers sifted variant opinions within Hanafi thought to craft law both jurisprudentially sound and suited to state interests.[10]

As in the case of the Reform Decree of 1856, some of the legal codification that still suggests westernization resulted from European pressure or was introduced to forestall further assertions that Ottoman law was biased against Christians. Several law codes adopted during the Tanzimat drew upon European models, notably the commercial code of 1850 and maritime code of 1863, and the criminal code of 1858. Since long-distance (largely maritime) trade by midcentury was dominated by European firms and the burgeoning non-Muslim mercantile class with whom the Europeans conducted business, adoption of familiar laws for

---

[8] Aharon Layish, "The Transformation of the Shari'a from Jurists' Law to Statutory Law in the Contemporary Muslim World," *Die Welt des Islams* 44 (2004), 85–113.

[9] On the continuing Christian character of Britain's law and legal system, see Didi Herman, *An Unfortunate Coincidence: Jews, Jewishness, and English Law* (Oxford: Oxford University Press, 2011).

[10] On 'Abduh, see Albert Hourani, *Arabic Thought in the Liberal Age 1798–1939* (Cambridge: Cambridge University Press, 1983), 130–60. Modernist interpretation fed a nineteenth-century conservative counterargument that "the gate of ijtihad (interpretation)" had closed in the medieval period. Indira Gesink, "'Chaos on the Earth': Subjective Truths versus Communal Unity in Islamic Law and the Rise of Militant Islam," *American Historical Review* 108 (2003), 710–11.

those to be controlled by the first two codes mentioned was relatively uncontroversial, indeed sensible for a state incapable of resisting combined great power pressure. Adoption of the 1858 criminal code, apparently based on a French code of 1810 but with extensive alteration to meet Ottoman conditions, was a more sensitive step to take.

This example of "westernization" again resulted directly from British and especially French pressure on behalf of foreign and Ottoman non-Muslim interests. Such pressure had been only heightened by the 1856 Reform Decree's promise that all Ottoman subjects were equal before the law, which gave some justification for foreign powers' representations. Ottoman reformers had already attempted compilation of a clear codification of law based upon Hanafi interpretation in 1855 precisely for the purpose of making law less mysterious and thus daunting, particularly for non-Muslims, but the effort failed.[11] Adaptation of French law was the next step, because further delay fostered only greater European penetration of the empire. It was in this period, when Anglo-French rivalry with Russia was played out most visibly in the Crimean War, that Britain and France greatly expanded their recruitment of protégés among Ottoman non-Muslims, driven by the perception that they needed to compete for influence with Russia, which had already gained large numbers of clients among the Orthodox.[12] Adoption of a code resembling a European model would apply countering pressure against British, French, and Russian claims that their protégés needed special legal protection, and perhaps even end the system of European consular courts that had jurisdiction over real and nominal foreigners. Egypt, still Ottoman but autonomous, felt this same need to counter European interference on behalf of non-Muslims and took similar steps, adapting European laws from the 1860s until the onset of British occupation in 1882.[13] That the foreign powers were a – or indeed the – intended audience for such legal innovation was indicated in the Ottoman case by the inclusion in the 1858 code of the right of defendants to demand that cases be heard by their religious courts.[14] Since there was no tradition of non-Muslim religious courts enforcing law, this proviso must have been intended to reassure Muslims that they still had the option of the qadi and shariʻa.

---

[11] Cevdet, *Tezâkir* 1–12, 63.

[12] Maurits van den Boogert, *The Capitulations and the Ottoman Legal System: Qadis, Consuls and Beratlıs in the 18th Century* (Leiden: Brill, 2005), 104.

[13] Nathan Brown, *The Rule of Law in the Arab World: Courts in Egypt and the Gulf* (Cambridge: Cambridge University Press, 1997), 26–31.

[14] Ortaylı, *İmparatorluğun En Uzun Yüzyılı*, 142.

Unlike Egypt, the Ottoman empire retained its independence long enough to see that such adaptation of European statutes would not suffice to reverse foreign influence, and the crowning achievement in legal innovation was the Ottoman Civil Code, the *Mecelle*, based upon Hanafi jurisprudence and formulated by a special committee that met regularly for some years. The committee was chaired by a member of the *'ulama* and contained other religious scholars; its chairman considered it the greatest achievement in European legal codification, surpassing even Justinian's Code (also a product of Constantinople), because it was not devised by mere legal scholars but by *'ulama* who combined expertise in shar'i jurisprudence with insights gained through all the developments seen up through that time.[15] Testifying to the strength of ties between the Mecelle and shar'i interpretation was the decision by Kuwait, an Ottoman territory that was not required to adopt the codified law rather than its traditional Shafi'i practices, to apply the Mecelle – beginning in 1938.[16] The Ottoman state interests served by codification of shari'a included the hope that the growing transparency and predictability of law and legal procedure would persuade the European powers and their protégés that exemption from Ottoman state control was unnecessary (recruitment of protégés did slow from the 1880s, aided by an Ottoman law barring dual citizenship), but Istanbul's needs were also more immediate than that tantalizing prize.[17]

Ottoman reform aimed to give the state the means to squeeze money and manpower efficiently from the population without creating the fissures in society that Mahmud II's rougher methods had opened. Law had to empower the state but also protect the population to be squeezed and win its respect as legitimate. No longer could the state afford the loose process of shari'a dispute resolution such as was applied in the 1760s to Ömer Bey of Ioannina, sentenced to repeated spells in prison to encourage repentance and moral reform. The Tanzimat era state's new attitude was exemplified in Delvina, a district neighboring Ioannina, where in 1846 as part of the introduction of the Tanzimat program a committee was appointed to reconcile killers with the heirs of people killed over the previous eighteen years (roughly the time since Mahmud's destructive intervention crippled the Ottoman order in Albania): 170 men and 6 women killed and 12

---

[15] Cevdet, *Tezakir* 1–12, 64.
[16] Brown, *Rule of Law*, 149–50.
[17] Zürcher, *Young Turk Legacy*, 67.

wounded. Shari'a offered three basic solutions in cases of unlawful killing or wounding: the heirs could inflict retaliation (kill or maim the perpetrator), accept blood money, or forgive the guilty party, with each option governed by various circumstances such as intent and social status. The committee in Delvina ignored the circumstances and simply imposed payment of blood money, compelling killers and heirs then to reconcile publicly. The state's interest in restoring peace as quickly as possible governed its choice in making one of the possible shar'i options the uniform standard, but the roots in Islamic interpretation seen in this simple solution (aided by the fact that Hanafi jurisprudence made no distinction in the value placed upon Muslim and non-Muslim lives) increased the likelihood that the state-imposed solution would last.[18] A population riven by feuds or disagreements would not prosper and could not pay the taxes or provide the soldiers needed by Istanbul; local disturbances also provided opportunities for interference by foreign powers. The Tanzimat state's interpretation of shari'a aimed to fix both problems as quickly as possible.

Fear of foreign intervention influenced the state's stance on a range of legal matters. Apostasy or conversion from Islam was a particularly delicate problem that illustrates the calculations that had to be made in crafting law and legal procedure to promote defense of the realm. In the early Tanzimat period, there was an apparent wave of forced conversions, especially targeting Orthodox Christians, carried out ad hoc at local level in the provinces. This probably resulted from the popular fears for the religion that had grown during the futile wars against foreign powers and Christian rebels, as well as the perceived injustices wrought by the state itself, and this generated antagonism toward European real or perceived protégés among local non-Muslims. Forced conversions and other signs of inequality for Christians upset the European powers, and they pressed Istanbul to protect Christians and to stop punishment of Muslims who converted to Christianity. The Ottoman regime had to bow to the foreign demands, repeatedly reminding Muslims that "there is no compulsion in religion" and decreeing that cases of apostasy be decided in Istanbul. The masterful stroke in handling competing external and internal pressures occurred in the transfer of accused apostates to the capital: their guards allowed the prisoners ample opportunity to escape custody before reaching Istanbul, where a trial would arouse both domestic and foreign

[18] BOA, Cev.Dah. 8872, 21 March 1846.

passions.[19] This neat solution to a delicate problem, preserving the correct position of the Islamic state in the eyes of the majority of the population and yet deflecting the anger of stronger Christian powers abroad, showed the benefits of Istanbul's assertion of tighter control over legal procedure and punishment, the focus of Tanzimat law reform.

In the several instances mentioned previously, the state's mastery over law and its agility in applying it ameliorated potentially explosive situations, and one of the characteristics of post-1839 codified law was its preference for resolution of problems over harshness of retribution – a characteristic that indicates on another level a continuity with shari'a. The Mecelle fit this pattern in choosing among Hanafi interpretations, but in the majority of instances preceding the issuance of the Civil Code as well, punishments meted out were less harsh than those imposed in the decades prior to 1839. In 1859, for example, a widespread conspiracy to overthrow Abdülmecid and his ministers in order to combat European influence and "restore the shari'a" came to light. Mahmud II's regime probably would have executed all suspected of complicity, but the Tanzimat government of Grand Vizier Ali Pasha treated the military and religious figures implicated in the "Küleli" plot relatively leniently, executing none.[20] Arguably the most controversial case of retributive justice in late Ottoman domestic affairs was Sultan Abdülhamid II's order to kill former Grand Vizier Midhat Pasha in 1882, precisely because the direction of legal development since 1839 hindered such action. Midhat had organized the ouster of two sultans in 1876 and the placement of a third, Abdülhamid, on a throne threatened by domestic tensions and the imminent likelihood of war with Russia, and Abdülhamid delivered the fate often dealt to king makers. Midhat's death might have made him feel more secure from overthrow, but Abdülhamid could never dispel the dirty deed from public memory or completely overcome the resentment it stirred among Ottoman citizens.

Other instances of hasty execution occurred in the Tanzimat period and angered many, but the most egregious instances resulted yet again from foreign pressure, to which the government acquiesced more meekly than many Muslims liked. The years following 1856 were particularly

---

[19] Selim Deringil, "'There Is No Compulsion in Religion': On Conversion and Apostasy in the Late Ottoman Empire, 1839–1856," *Comparative Studies in Society and History* 42 (2000), 547–75.

[20] Roderic Davison, *Reform in the Ottoman Empire* (Princeton: Princeton University Press, 1963), 100–2.

suited to fast-developing confrontations, as perceptions that Istanbul was succumbing to European pressure to de-Islamicize, or even Christianize, the empire aroused muttered or loud protest. No act did more to damage the reputation of the sultan and his ministers among Muslims than the Reform Decree of that year. To Muslims this marked a craven submission to Christian powers' demands and, as in the case of reaction against Selim III's European-styled New Order, was taken as a betrayal of all that Muslims had struggled for over the decades.[21] Each of the famous grand viziers of the Tanzimat era, Mustafa Reşid, Fuad, and Ali Pashas, was eventually burdened with the nickname "Infidel Pasha," and in 1861 Muslims in Syria reportedly cried, "Islam is saved!" upon hearing of the death of Sultan Abdülmecid, who was undoubtedly pious and the issuer of the Islamically sound Hatt-i Şerif of Gülhane.[22] Dissatisfaction over the Reform Decree was immediately apparent in Istanbul, leading to the plot to overthrow the regime in 1859, but it was the flaring of anger in the provinces that sparked the harshest reaction from Istanbul, precisely because European governments took steps to intervene.

Two incidents illustrate the galvanizing effect when the possibility of foreign interest became reality. In 1858 rioters in Jidda, the port for Mecca and Medina, killed the British and French consuls following tensions capped by a British warship's seizure of a vessel in the harbor. The mob also killed a score of other Christians, and the British government demanded immediate execution of the killers or else would seize Jidda – and its warship returned to shell the town until some executions were hastily arranged as soon as an Ottoman plenipotentiary arrived to confer Istanbul's blessing (Tanzimat era law required Istanbul's confirmation of all death sentences). Salt in the wound was an Anglo-French-Ottoman commission's majority decision to award TL315,360 (by comparison, total Ottoman expenditures in the Hijaz in 1862–3 were TL236,485) in damages to Christian claimants while rejecting the Ottoman commissioner's attempt to discuss compensation for victims of the British warship's bombardment.[23] In Syria in 1860, resentment of Maronite Catholics' perceived flaunting of new privileges led to pogroms launched by Druze and Sunni Muslims in Mount Lebanon

---

[21] Finkel, *Osman's Dream*, 459; Cevdet, *Tezakir 1–12*, 68.

[22] Efraim Karsh, *Islamic Imperialism: A History* (New Haven, CT: Yale University Press, 2007), 97.

[23] William Ochsenwald, *Religion, Society, and the State in Arabia: The Hijaz under Ottoman Control, 1840–1908* (Columbus: Ohio State University Press, 1984), 137–51, 173.

and Damascus. Fuad Pasha, the foreign minister, went to Damascus to oversee the rapid prosecution of rioters against Christians and, after perfunctory legal proceedings, the execution of several hundred Muslims deemed guilty of violence and murder. Such action, barely acceptable under the Hatt-i Şerif of Gülhane guidelines, was necessitated by France's dispatch of a military force to Beirut to protect the Catholics of Syria; it was not coincidental that it was the Ottoman foreign minister who conducted the retributive campaign. The French eventually withdrew because Fuad had settled affairs so quickly, but foreign pressure led to creation of an autonomous, Maronite-dominated and French-protected Mount Lebanon in 1861. This series of events helps to explain why Abdülmecid's death around this time caused such satisfaction in Syria. The impotence of the Ottoman regime in both situations – with the Jidda garrison remaining quiet while a British warship lobbed shells into the town, and Fuad Pasha acting as proxy for France and failing to block the creation of an autonomous, Christian-dominated Mount Lebanon – could not but raise questions about Istanbul's determination to act in Muslim interests.

It also helps to explain the origins of the most noted Muslim protest group, the Young Ottomans, a small but vocal clique of journalists and bureaucrats. The focus of their criticisms of the state in the 1860s, mainly penned and published abroad, was Ottoman leaders' persistent failure to defend more vigorously the empire and its Muslims against foreign and Christian pressures. Such apparent heedfulness of foreigners was hard to accept, because the regime seemed all too capable of ignoring the views of Ottoman Muslims, who objected to the concessions made to Christian interests in Ottoman lands ranging from Serbia to Crete to Lebanon and decried the harshness with which the government treated Muslims in places such as Syria. The Young Ottomans tend to be remembered because of their advocacy of liberal ideas, including constitutional parliamentarism, under which Ottoman leaders would find it much more difficult to silence or ignore Muslim opinion. The regime neutralized the Young Ottomans through co-optation, but the idea of constitutionalism as a means of closing the gap between state and population influenced the small elite group who persuaded the newly enthroned Sultan Abdülhamid II to issue a constitution in 1876. Isolated abroad, unsure of the depth of popular commitment at home, and facing again the threat of war with Russia, Ottoman leaders needed the constitution to rally Muslims to activism in a time of crisis, as well as to entice Britain to support Istanbul against the Russian threat. It was this latter point that led Midhat Pasha, the leading architect of the constitution, to end a lengthy debate on non-Muslim representation in parliament by opting for inclusion.[24]

Constitutionalism, the crowning achievement of the Tanzimat period, thus marked a point on a continuum of actions taken to shore up the relationship between state and population in the face of severe external pressure upon the empire. Those who directed the state took care to maintain its religious identity, especially through retaining commitment to the principle of Islamic morality as the guiding force for growing state power. Muslims reacted strongly against state action when that power appeared to break the constraints of law and turn despotic, notably in instances of hasty and harsh retribution against Muslims seemingly at the behest of Christian powers. All that changed in this regard in the post-Tanzimat reign of Abdülhamid II was that the regime made little attempt to downplay its Islamic identity in either internal or foreign affairs. The actions of the powers that had sworn to protect Ottoman territory in return for legal equality of non-Muslims with Muslims, after all, had shown by the beginning of his reign that the empire had little to lose from open espousal of a religion reviled by Europe's Christians.

OTTOMAN AND FOREIGN CHRISTIANS

If state and core society identified with Islam throughout the post-1839 decades, it seems safe to assume that the non-Muslim population must have grown increasingly restive under the discomfort of second-class status. While non-Muslims as well as Muslims certainly had reasons for periodic dissatisfaction, the evident relative equanimity of Ottoman Christians and Muslims requires explanation. It is worth emphasizing that the empire never confronted a successful, or even significant, nationalist rebellion throughout its existence prior to the First World War, and that it lost territory and finally its life only at the hands of the Christian powers of Europe. That nationalism in the empire was "the dog that did not bark" begs the question of why the creature that everyone thinks "must have been there" failed to emit more than an occasional whimper.

Traditional views of the late empire as the "Sick Man of Europe" rest upon two assumptions or perceptions characteristic of nineteenth-century Christian Europe that, as the discussion so far suggests, should be

---

[24] Engin Akarlı, "The Problems of External Pressures, Power Struggles, and Budgetary Deficits in Ottoman Politics under Abdülhamid II (1876–1909)" (PhD dissertation, Princeton University, 1976), 99–100.

treated with skepticism. The first of these, that the Ottoman empire was too ramshackle to survive, has already been considered; it was only fitting that Russia, the state ruled by the most famous propounder of the "Sick Man" dismissal, collapsed before the Ottoman state did.[25] The second assumption is that Ottoman non-Muslims yearned for independence in their own nation-states, which meant that separatist nationalism doomed to failure any attempt at "Ottomanism," or the creation of a nonsectarian common identity and unificatory loyalty to the imperial regime. Yet there is no good reason to think that nationalism was an unmanageable problem for the empire, because the nation-state offered very little that could resolve any problem of serious concern to any section of the population. No Ottoman regime from 1839 to 1908 (and arguably to 1923) devised or applied policy based upon ethnicity rather than upon religion. Anyone who sensed discrimination or persecution at government hands would have felt it first as Christians or Jews, not as members of an ethnic group; humiliation from nonofficial pressure would have conformed to this pattern as well, given the strength of Muslim supralocal identity demonstrated in incidents ranging from forced conversion to assaults on Maronite Christians in Damascus. Such nongovernmental oppression was usually too localized and short-term to create revolutionary eruptions among non-Muslims, and the generally favorable, indeed privileged, treatment accorded them in the application of government policy limited the appeal of insurrectionary schemes. Most non-Muslims had too much to lose through revolution for an aspiration that lacked a compelling, practical rationale.

Despite the indisputably horrible experiences of Christians caught up in rampages in places such as Damascus and Jidda, Ottoman non-Muslims as a whole had the unusual experience of modernization as a process of noticeable gain with little added pain. A significant number grew wealthy through their dominant roles in the empire's booming trade with Europe and their associated readier access to credit, which allowed them to purchase land and build fixed assets at rates far higher than Muslims'. The developing wealthy class was that which assumed the status of protégés of Christian powers, which afforded them protection against much of the Ottoman state's effort to collect more tax revenue.[26] Poorer non-

---

[25] Czar Nicholas I of Russia used the term in trying to persuade London not to impede Russian plans against the Ottoman empire before the Crimean War.

[26] For an example of how European powers became aware of the problems caused by the system that they promoted, see Steven Rosenthal, "Foreigners and Municipal Reform in Ottoman Istanbul: 1855–1865," *IJMES* 11 (1980), 227–45.

Muslims gained from the principle introduced with the Tanzimat that tax burdens should vary with ability to pay. All non-Muslim males benefited also from exemption from the other burden borne by populations across modernizing Europe, compulsory service in the military. Non-Muslims, in short, felt little of the growing weight of servicing the modernizing state and its expanding military power that promoted the growth of nationalism elsewhere in Europe. For non-Muslims the modernizing Ottoman state remained much as it had been: an authority responsible for upholding law and preserving the peace at home and defending against threats abroad. As long as the otherwise-remote state performed these functions adequately, the fact that it was commanded by Muslims was of marginal significance. This certainly was true for the great majority of the population that was illiterate, but among the literate as well, including even those educated abroad or in schools established in the empire by foreign governments or missionaries that preached the message of national identity, many saw in the ideal of "national liberation" little practical advance over their current condition.

One serious exception to this pattern did occur, where the state failed to uphold its basic responsibilities in keeping the peace and upholding law. In 1894–6 turmoil beset parts of Anatolia with significant Armenian Christian populations, especially six provinces in the East. There the Ottoman state failed to control two large, antagonistic groups that had lived in some degree of harmony for centuries: Kurdish tribes and Armenian peasants. There had been a long-standing hierarchy of tribes, with a few leaders able to control much of eastern Anatolia, but the centralizing programs pursued by Istanbul, beginning with brutal campaigns led by Reşid Mehmed in the 1830s, had chipped away the authority of these great notables. The Ottoman center was not powerful enough to replace the authority of the local commanders, however, inviting continuous struggle among other tribes seeking to fill or exploit that vacuum. Armenian peasants became a favored target of plunder. Sultan Abdülhamid made this unrest worse by organizing tribal cavalry units, the Hamidiye regiments, attempting thereby to limit the turmoil, attach the tribes to Istanbul, and turn their fighting abilities to defense of the state's interest along rough frontier terrain. When appeals to Istanbul to control the tribes produced no lasting improvement in their situation, some Armenians began to organize in self-defense. All of Istanbul's deep insecurities about Christian designs upon territory were aroused, matching the fears about Christian intentions so widespread among the Muslim population. This bloody history of flawed central control, heightened local enmities, widespread suspicion, and Armenian vulnerability triggered pogroms in the 1890s that would recur in the following decade and, most gruesomely, during the First World War. As in the cases of Christian unrest before 1839, however, this pattern of turmoil was not driven by a concerted Armenian bid for independence but rather simple self-preservation in the face of repeated persecution that Istanbul failed to halt.[27]

Other instances of unrest made famous by the attention given by Christian Europe, by contrast, would not have occurred without incendiary – and usually bloody – agitation by small numbers of nationalists who had little standing in the communities that they wished to "liberate." In eastern Hercegovina, tensions rose among the mainly Orthodox peasant population due to tax demands in 1875 that were impossible to meet because of harvest failures in preceding years; sympathetic responses from the Ottoman administration defused the situation, until several bands of agitators dispatched by Serbia and raiders from neighboring Montenegro launched attacks to radicalize the situation, forcing villagers to choose sides in a conflict that they had not started or wanted.[28] In the pattern grown familiar during the Tanzimat, the Ottoman response was subdued, because the unrest quickly drew the attention of Christian Europe. Austria-Hungary and Russia proposed a reform program sympathetic to those in revolt, which Istanbul accepted to bring the rebellion to a close; the rebels refused, however, and in 1876 the Ottoman military moved decisively to crush the unrest.

Even better known among such agitation-led incidents was the "April uprising" of 1876, which led to extensive Muslim attacks upon Christians in what is now central Bulgaria, known as the "Bulgarian horrors" after the British Liberal leader William Gladstone's adoption of the event as a campaign weapon against the Conservative government of Benjamin Disraeli. What Gladstone's rhetoric described was essentially myth. Bulgarian nationalists resident abroad, especially in Romania, attempted to start a rebellion as the Ottomans finally moved against the unrest in Bosnia-Hercegovina. They failed almost completely. A few villages did

[27] Selim Deringil, "'The Armenian Question Is Finally Solved': Mass Conversions of Armenians in Anatolia during the Hamidian Massacres of 1895–1897," *Comparative Studies in Society and History* 51 (2009), 344–71.

[28] Hannes Grandits, "Violent Social Disintegration: A Nation-Building Strategy in Late Ottoman Hercegovina," in *Conflicting Loyalties in the Balkans: The Great Powers, the Ottoman Empire and Nation-Building*, ed. Hannes Grandits et al. (London: I. B. Tauris, 2011), 110–34.

take up arms, goaded by rumors spread by the nationalists that Russia had invaded the empire and the Muslims were coming to slaughter Christians before the Russians could arrive; in such villages the promoters of rebellion killed some waverers and resident Muslims to persuade the rest to commit themselves to the uprising.[29] The uprising itself consisted mainly of murdering Muslim civilians in or near those villages.

One village, Batak, came to symbolize the April uprising. Some of Batak's residents armed themselves and went into the surrounding forests to kill Muslim travelers. When a couple of unarmed gendarmes from a neighboring, mainly Muslim village arrived to ask what was going on, they too were killed. The Pomaks (Bulgarian-speaking Muslims) of several neighboring villages then also took up arms, and the two sides negotiated; as part of the rebels' demands, the Christians of neighboring villages were to be helped to move to Batak. Those Christians refused to leave their homes. For almost a week nothing more happened, but then the Pomaks under the local notable Ahmed Ağa, commander of the two gendarmes who had been killed, attacked, and Batak's defense soon crumbled. That the nationalists' main organizer of the rebellion absconded early in the fighting must have sped the collapse of an already ill-planned effort. Batak's remaining Christians negotiated a surrender, but Ahmed Ağa's men then massacred them.[30] Hundreds died, slaughtered in a hopeless struggle devised by incompetent romantics for a cause poorly, if at all, understood by its victims. The ferocity of the Pomaks' counterattack offers further evidence, however, of the tensions within the Muslim population concerning Christian threats to their ideals of the religion and the state. Yet as brutal as the episode may have been, in imperial terms such a revolt as that staged in Batak and a handful of other villages that suffered less thorough retribution was a "tempest in a teapot," quickly quelled by local Muslims. That Ottoman rule over part of Bulgaria ended in 1878 was the result of the Russian invasion the year after Batak.

Underneath the patina of national liberation struggle superimposed on nineteenth-century history by post-Ottoman states, incidents such as the "April uprising" do show the only real threat posed to the empire by nationalism: that almost any provincial disturbance by Christians could draw a disproportionate response from local Muslims, providing

[29] Richard Millman, "The Bulgarian Massacres Reconsidered," *Slavonic and East European Review* 58 (1980), 218–31.
[30] Tetsuya Sahara, "Two Different Images: Bulgarian and English Sources on the Batak Massacre," in *War and Diplomacy*, ed. Yavuz and Sluglett 479–510.

a pretext for intervention by European powers. Ottoman leaders came to be almost obsessed by the threat of nationalism precisely because incidents could arise seemingly without warning, and, unless the state reacted quickly enough to stop not only the instigators of unrest but the Muslim retaliation, territory and population would be stripped away by Russia, Britain, France, and/or Austria.[31]

Ottoman paranoia had justification, because foreign intervention was the sole instrument responsible for stripping territory from the empire. As noted previously, the cores of Serbia and Greece gained their autonomous or independent existence through Russian, British, and French intervention on behalf of Christian rebellions over injustice. Montenegro existed in defiance of Ottoman authority through Russian financial subsidies and the political protection of several European powers until being granted independence following the Russian victory in 1878. The defeat of the Ottomans in that year also created an autonomous Bulgaria and added territory to Serbia and Greece, even though the former had been utterly defeated after declaring war on the empire (an act hardly defensible under European international law, since Serbia was still legally Ottoman territory) and the latter had not even joined the conflict. Whenever those creations of foreign powers sparked disputes with the Ottoman empire, the European powers defended them. Montenegro tried to seize Ottoman territory in 1853 but itself lost land to an imperial counterattack, until Russia and Austria pressed Istanbul to withdraw its troops. Ottoman forces repelled Serbia's invasion of Bosnia in 1876, broke the forces defending Belgrade, and were advancing on that city when Russia again issued an ultimatum to Istanbul to withdraw. Greece, involved for years in instigating unrest in Ottoman Crete, declared war on the empire during renewed turmoil on the island in 1897; having trounced the Greeks, the Ottomans again had to withdraw from their reconquests upon the demand of European powers. Not only did Greece regain its lost territory but Crete was made autonomous under a Christian governor. Other territories simply passed directly into foreign hands. Russia annexed the northern Black Sea littoral and Crimea in the late eighteenth century and from there extended its control over the Caucasus in the nineteenth. Austria-Hungary occupied Bosnia-Hercegovina and the subprovince of Novipazar while Russia was still engaged in fighting the Ottomans in 1878. Britain occupied Cyprus as "compensation" for promising support

---

[31] A readily recognized parallel to the obsession with nationalism was the "red under the bed" fear in the United States that generated McCarthyism during the 1950s.

to Istanbul against the extension of Russian control over northeastern Anatolia in 1878 – an occupation pure and simple, because Britain had already agreed with Russia a slightly altered disposition of the recently conquered Anatolian territories.[32] France started its conquest of Algeria in 1830 and occupied Tunisia in 1881. Britain occupied Egypt in 1882 and Sudan in 1899, the same year in which it established an effective protectorate over Kuwait. Every one of these actions was "justified" by citing the duty to protect Christians from oppression (valued so clearly above the loss of life or homeland by the Muslims killed in or expelled from "liberated" territories) or balance of power politics or simply because the European powers felt that they could.[33] Might, it seems, did make right.

ABDÜLHAMID II AND ISLAMISM

If Christians generally tolerated the modernizing state and showed little readiness to abandon their position as Ottoman citizens enjoying a range of privileges and protections, relations between Muslims and the state, while more intimate, showed more complexity. Abdülhamid II stressed the importance of Islam as the bonding force between the state and its core population, and with that he built strong loyalty among most of his Muslim subjects; his autocratic methods of rule, however, generated tensions in some circles that carried echoes of earlier periods of protest against authoritarianism.

That Abdülhamid should have faced Muslim opposition seems surprising, because he became the most recognized champion of Islam in public life of any nineteenth-century Ottoman leader. His open attachment to Islam was a reflection of his own belief but also met a simple necessity: after the disastrous 1877–8 war with Russia, which stripped the empire of significant Christian populations and forced resettlement within the empire of hundreds of thousands of Muslim refugees from lost territories, failure to appeal to Islamic solidarity would have been foolish. The empire's population was more clearly Muslim-majority, any illusion that Christian Europe would accept the empire's right to exist had dissolved, and the confidence of the tax- and service-rendering Muslim population

---

[32] B. H. Sumner, *Russia and the Balkans, 1870–1880* (Oxford: Clarendon Press, 1937), 485, 491, and Richard Millman, *Britain and the Eastern Question, 1875–1878* (Oxford: Clarendon Press, 1979), 600n.14.

[33] On the partiality of European humanitarianism, see Davide Rodogno, *Against Massacre: Humanitarian Interventions in the Ottoman Empire 1815–1914* (Princeton: Princeton University Press, 2012), 8–16.

had been severely damaged. Abdülhamid succeeded in reviving spirits and rallying the Muslim population to the state, but the intellectual and emotional ferment among those grappling with the question of how the Islamic community was to be saved was so strong that no sultan could have conjured unity of thought.

When faced with a serious problem, it is the rare group that knows exactly what must be done to remedy the threat; for Muslims of the nineteenth century, the challenge posed by a militarily dominant Christian Europe provoked a variety of proposed responses for self-strengthening, each of which could be given a seemingly familiar but misleading label. As noted in discussion of the Mecelle, one school of thought could be termed "modernist," using God-given reason in jurisprudential interpretation to protect the well-being of the community under the novel conditions of the age. There was a related "fundamentalist" approach, as well, which agreed with the modernists that the accumulated lore of jurisprudence contained too many errors to be emulated uncritically, but rather than simply reinterpreting to meet the needs of the day, it stressed a return to the origins – the Qur'an and the example of Muhammad and the early community of believers – as the only reliable guide to how the floundering Islamic community could right itself. This developed into the "salafi" stream of Islamic thought. There was also a "puritanist" view, which did not focus so clearly on debating jurisprudence and the "true essence" of Islam as it did on purifying practice to restore the moral strength of the community and make it worth being saved. This was Abdülhamid's approach. He emphasized strictly orthodox views on proper behavior, shunning the experimentation that the "modernist" and "fundamentalist" proponents advocated. It is tempting to see in Abdülhamid yet another sultan who saw himself in the role of "renewer of the faith" for the new century (the Muslim lunar calendar year 1300 occurred in 1882–3), and his determination to style himself as caliph emphasized this persona. His attempts to convert Shi'is and other Muslim schismatics to Sunnism showed his sense of purpose, as did lesser steps such as barring the import of Qur'ans printed outside the Abode of Islam (Russia, and even Egypt under British domination) or by schismatics who favored different readings of the text (Iran).[34]

---

[34] Selim Deringil, *The Well-Protected Domains: Ideology and the Legitimation of Power in the Ottoman Empire, 1876–1909* (London: I. B. Tauris, 1998), surveys Abdülhamid's efforts to ensure moral probity, albeit treating his concern for religion as a quasi-nationalist program for rallying popular support.

Abdülhamid's convictions complicated his relations with scholars of Islam. Some members of the 'ulama favored a more experimental approach to strengthening the community, earning his mistrust, especially since both modernists and salafists seemed ready to question his right to lead the community as caliph. His problem was compounded by his tendency to paranoia, which also made him suspicious of the 'ulama, given the visible role played by medrese students and some scholars in the constitutional movement of 1876. He therefore courted the conservative mainstream who supported his claim to the caliphate, but he favored even more strongly leaders of sufi brotherhoods, who generally accepted unquestioningly his claim to the caliphate and had a greater influence in the everyday life of the Muslim population than did the 'ulama.

Reliance upon sufi networks strengthened attachment to the sultan among the population but made such devotion even harder to ensure among both salafi and literalist scholars who deplored sufi practices and those "modernists" who favored more vigorous, less tradition-bound interpretation of law. The antagonism between the scholarly mainstream led by Abdülhamid and proponents of the other currents of thought about Islamic regeneration, many of whom escaped the sultan's control by residing in Egypt, devolved into a petty spat, with the sultan and his adherents accusing their opponents of being supporters of the British occupation of Egypt, and the modernists and salafists reviving early interpretations of caliphal succession, which barred the obviously non-Qurashi Abdülhamid from legitimate claim to religious authority. Yet for salafi and modernist scholars who regarded the sultan with suspicion, it was Abdülhamid's methods of rule and his insistence upon unquestioning obedience, rather than his person, that lay at the root of antagonism.[35]

Such protest carried at least echoes of the resistance aroused by Mahmud II, and indeed strong parallels link Abdülhamid to Mahmud; the differences between them, however, suggest the extent of transformation in the practices of the Ottoman state since 1839. Both came to the throne in the midst of crises in foreign and domestic affairs, not ascending to the seat of authority but rather placed there by king makers. The sudden deaths of recently unseated predecessors, combined with narrow escapes from further coup plots shortly after their enthronements, entrenched the new monarchs' sense of insecurity. Both remained as deeply suspicious of domestic subversion as they were of foreign powers, but despite their

[35] İsmail Kara, "Turban and Fez: Ulema as Opposition," in *Late Ottoman Society: The Intellectual Legacy*, ed. Elisabeth Özdalga (London: RoutledgeCurzon, 2005), 162–200.

fears, they remained on the throne for more than three decades. Mahmud presumably attributed his longevity to ruthless action upon suspicions, but Abdülhamid enjoyed no such authority to act so decisively: legal reform had neutralized siyasa. Less an oriental despot, Abdülhamid was rather a curiously timid authoritarian. The murder of Midhat Pasha still stands out because it was so extraordinary. Abdülhamid's norm in quelling perceived domestic opponents consisted primarily of censorship, bribery (buying loyalty through appointment to official positions providing little scope for troublemaking), and exile. Exile was internal, in order to keep suspects under close observation, and one of his primary institutions of personal protection was a system of spies who reported on suspected subversives. Given the stress placed upon law and legality since 1839, which Abdülhamid could not rescind and remain true to his open commitment to Islam, he could not flout the law or tamper too egregiously with legal procedure; aside from legal restrictions of censorship, much of his security system teetered in a murky area between zones of public life covered by the empire's evolving legal framework.

Much the same could be said of Abdülhamid's methods of imperial administration. Mahmud II relied heavily upon a coterie of officials with close connections, and unquestioned loyalty, to him, assigning members of the small, palace-centered bureaucracy responsibility but limited power. Abdülhamid, by contrast, developed significantly the bureaucratic system that had grown during the Tanzimat and gave it both responsibility and to a significant extent the power to fulfill its duties – modernization's goal of strengthening the state's ability to defend the empire required no less. He nevertheless bypassed it in recruiting unofficial networks of supporters in the provinces, particularly among Muslim notables in potential trouble spots.[36] Such a system may have helped to secure the throne against any threat of widespread disaffection or disloyalty, but it also (re-)created opportunities for administrative inefficiency. Not only had provincial governors to beware the possibility that the palace might pursue through its own channels activities that undercut local administrative plans, but favoritism from royal circles could decide intrabureaucracy disputes on inconsistent grounds.[37]

---

[36] Butrus Abu Manneh, "Sultan Abdulhamid II and Shaikh Abulhuda al-Sayyadi," *MES* 15 (1979), 131–53.

[37] For examples, David Kushner, "Ali Ekrem Bey, Governor of Jerusalem, 1906–1908," *IJMES* 28 (1996), 349–62, and Frederick Anscombe, *The Ottoman Gulf: The Creation of Kuwait, Saudi Arabia, and Qatar* (New York: Columbia University Press, 1997).

Abdülhamid's various measures were sufficiently effective to give him endurance and a relatively successful record in keeping the empire intact. His reputation for having done well under the many disadvantages besetting him – the loss of so much economically and strategically valuable territory between 1878 and 1882, and state bankruptcy in effect from 1875 and openly acknowledged in 1881 – is arguably well deserved. Yet it is equally clear that those very tools used by the security-obsessed palace aroused dissatisfaction in parts of the population, including not only scholars who resented Abdülhamid's zeal in smothering opinions about the need for real change in the way that Muslim society regulated itself, but also members of the bureaucracy and the military, who saw the contradiction between the murkiness of Abdülhamid's measures and the precepts of law and justice promoted since 1839. And in tune with the complaints voiced by the Young Ottomans in the 1860s, some critics of Abdülhamid felt that he failed to use his authoritarian powers against the targets most deserving of resolute treatment, the Christian powers and their local protégés.

These sometimes-overlapping themes constituted the main lines of opposition to Hamidian rule, represented in two factions of the Committee of Union and Progress (CUP), the expatriate group that eventually recruited the army officers who would curtail his power. The faction usually labeled as "decentralist" or "liberal" sought to ease the open and covert repression associated with autocracy, while the centralists wanted to push more energetically Abdülhamid's methodical efforts at state strengthening and to be more proactive in using that power. For both factions, the goal became the restoration of the constitution that Abdülhamid had suspended in 1878: for decentralists, constitutional rule suggested the consent of the governed and the accountability of those governing, and centralists' ambitions carried echoes of previous constitutionalists who wanted to mobilize the population for greater efforts on the state's behalf. As in the case of Young Ottoman protest against the statesmen of the Tanzimat, pressure from Christian Europe stoked the full range of discontent with Abdülhamid's rule. Such pressure reached its peak in Macedonia, the conflict zone that undermined his authority.

MACEDONIA AND THE YOUNG TURKS

Following the great carve-up of Ottoman Europe sealed by the Berlin peace treaty of 1878, Macedonia, Thrace, and Albania were the only territories remaining under Ottoman control and thus drew the attention of acquisitive neighbors; of these areas, Macedonia became the most hotly contested, because of its location and variegated population. Macedonia also illustrates the limited appeal of nationalism and the continuing threat to the empire posed by the Christian powers of Europe. Each of the post-Ottoman states created by those powers adopted a program of irredentism as an important part of creating the nation. All Macedonian territory was claimed by one or more of its neighbors: Greece, Bulgaria, Serbia, Montenegro, and even Romania.

One feature making Macedonia an unusual arena for anti-Ottoman irredentism, however, was the role acknowledged to the views of those targeted for redemption. Under the terms of the creation of the Bulgarian Exarchate (1870), Orthodox parishes could decide which church authority they wished to follow, the Slavic Exarchate or the "Greek" Patriarchate of Constantinople. This caused the neighboring states, especially Greece and Bulgaria, to devote major efforts to educating Orthodox Macedonians that they were really Greek or Bulgarian. Serbia also staked a claim on a cultural-religious basis, arguing that Macedonian Slavic Christians shared with Serbs the cult of St. Sava, a "Serbian" saint, and Romania claimed an interest in the Vlach population.[38] Suitable instruction was provided through educational and cultural missions, and through paramilitary (and also regular military) violence targeting villagers who did not answer satisfactorily the question "Who are you?" Such guidance was necessary, as the experience of one activist from Greece illustrates. When he asked villagers whether they were Greek or Bulgarian, he received unhelpful responses from the puzzled peasants: "Asking each other what my words meant, crossing themselves, they would answer me naïvely: 'Well, we're Christians – what do you mean, Romaioi or Voulgaroi?'"[39] The pressure applied to the population, often descending into thuggery, meant that even after the terms "Greek" and "Bulgarian" were absorbed, some villagers hardly altered their answer to the question: "'We are neither Rum nor Bulgar, we are Christians.'"[40]

---

[38] Vlachs spoke a Romance language and were mainly livestock herders (Wallachia, now part of Romania, derived its name from its Vlach population).

[39] Mark Mazower, *The Balkans: A Short History* (New York: Modern Library, 2000), 39.

[40] Ipek Yosmaoğlu, "Counting Bodies, Shaping Souls: The 1903 Census and National Identity in Ottoman Macedonia," *IJMES* 38 (2006), 69. See also Paraskevas Konortas, "Nationalisms vs Millets: Building Collective Identities in Ottoman Thrace," in *Spatial Conceptions of the Nation: Modernizing Geographies in Greece and Turkey*, ed. Nikiforos Diamandouros et al. (London: I. B. Tauris, 2010), 161–80.

Such disgust helped to spur creation of the Internal Macedonian Revolutionary Organization (IMRO), whose slogan "Macedonia for the Macedonians" reflected resentment felt toward alien irredentist powers as much as toward Istanbul. Given the strength of religious identity as a factor complicating the struggle to convert Macedonians into various nationalities, there was also inevitably a suggestion that an explicitly Ottoman autocephalous Macedonian Orthodox church should be established that would undercut Bulgarian national claims deriving from the Exarchate.[41] IMRO and other streams of political thought among Christian Macedonians thus fit a decentralist model better than the separatist-nationalist, and indeed IMRO showed some openness to the liberal stream within the CUP, holding discussions with Young Turk representatives about the restoration of constitutional rule to the empire. This goal was achieved in July 1908, much to the surprise of almost everyone inside and outside the empire, as Sultan Abdülhamid chose to restore the constitution when an open conflict with Muslims in Macedonia suddenly arose.

Abdülhamid's quick accession to constitutionalists' demands is the most curious feature of the 1908 revolution. As a "revolution," the event had almost none of the turmoil and bloodshed normally associated with such movements. Other than the shooting of several commanding officers charged by the Istanbul regime to investigate and quell CUP activities in Macedonia, and of some security officers sent by the Porte, there was little violence. Several CUP-led bands formed in the hills and issued demands regarding imperial reform and the rejection of foreign interference in Macedonia, but these bands were recruited from Muslim villagers who believed that they were mustered to fight against Bulgarian agitators and to combat the threat that Macedonia might fall under Christian control. This was not entirely subterfuge, because the CUP network had been prompted to act by news of Anglo-Russian discussions concerning further reform in Macedonia. Given that Abdülhamid had acceded to intrusive Austro-Russian reform proposals of 1903 that legitimated the obvious influence of Christian powers in Macedonia's security, administrative, and taxation affairs, the CUP had reason to fear that the sultan would not resist further encroachment on Ottoman sovereignty.[42] Their contempt for Abdülhamid's lack of will to resist nevertheless could not

---

[41] Alexander Maxwell, "Krsté Misirkov's 1903 Call for Macedonian Autocephaly: Religious Nationalism as Instrumental Political Tactic," *Studia Theologica* 5 (2007), 165–7.
[42] Zürcher, *Young Turk Legacy*, 31–40.

have prepared them for his quick capitulation to the demand for the constitution's return to force.

It seems that the sultan stayed true to the habit that he had followed throughout his reign: when confronted by discontent among Muslims that could not be broken or suborned quickly, give way. The alternative would reopen the internal divisions that had so damaged Mahmud II, as domestic turmoil would only create opportunities to be exploited by Christian powers. Warned by his ministers that combating the unrest would take time and scarce resources, and heeding his grand vizier's suggestion that if the root of dissatisfaction was the suspended constitution, then it might as well be restored, the sultan promptly took that step. Abdülhamid was to prove similarly phlegmatic in accepting the demand that he abdicate in 1909.[43]

With Abdülhamid's acceptance of revived constitutionalism in 1908 and, more definitively, his deposition the following year, imperial politics entered an unprecedented phase that lasted until the empire's effective demise in 1918. The seventy years after 1839 had wrought tremendous changes in the state, which had grown into a truly powerful, modern institution, and equally impressive was the fact that such alterations had been accomplished without inflicting lasting trauma on the state-society relationship. Successive regimes accomplished this feat by adhering to the promises laid out in the Hatt-i Şerif of Gülhane as fully as their international vulnerabilities permitted, taking care that the intensifying exploitation of the empire's human and material resources was modulated by the perceived need to act legally and justly. The Ottoman state of the modernizing period reestablished the imperial allegiance to Islam as the moral pole of dynastic rule. After 1908, however, that Islamic code of morality and justice came under increasing pressure. CUP leaders, propelled to political activism by their sense of foreign threats, continued to value Islam as a balm for soothing the state-society relationship but increasingly ignored the moral brake that religious scruples exerted upon state action. Themselves creatures of the modernization programs implemented by the Tanzimat and Hamidian regimes, they wanted above all to use the strength that the state had gained. Much as Mahmud II had discovered, they would see disaster result from their radicalism.

[43] Anscombe, "Age of Ottoman Reform," 189; Küçük Said Pasha, *Said Paşa'nın Hatıratı*, 2 vols (Istanbul: Sabah Matbaası, 1328), ii/2, 445; Finkel, *Osman's Dream*, 517.

5

End of Empire

Eagerness to apply the strength that the Ottoman state had gained since 1839 led to the empire's collapse a decade after the Committee of Union and Progress (CUP) came to power. This sorrowful end was caused in large part by growing pressure from foreign powers, of course, but the dominant clique in the CUP weakened the state's and population's ability to withstand such forces. The regime damaged state-society relations by undercutting the legal safeguards against autocratic rule that had been instituted since 1839, and the harsher, more violent administration that resulted troubled parts of the population even before the disasters of the First World War. The CUP thus hastened precisely what it had intended to prevent: the loss of land, people, and ultimately independence.

Mutinous military officers' opposition to Abdülhamid's rule originated in frustration over his pusillanimous submission to what many Muslims regarded as Europe's bullying, but others in state service who welcomed restoration of the constitution had grown weary primarily of his autocratic tendencies. Still others, particularly in the general Muslim population, had had no desire for fundamental change in the extant system, which had appeared to function reasonably well outside Macedonia. Abdülhamid actually gained in popularity following his decision to restore the constitution, indicating the weakness of popular alienation from him personally as dynastic leader. It thus did not take long for serious divisions to emerge between groups wishing for progressively more liberal rule, a return to sultanic-caliphal primacy, or more assertively centralizing authoritarianism. The clique of the CUP that was to establish dominance over imperial affairs by 1913 and was therefore placed to decide any lingering dispute over future direction was rooted in the military, a background that encouraged them to favor centralization and authoritarianism. The important figures in the clique who were not graduates of the military staff college had studied medicine or been trained as bureaucrats, and their education may have inclined them to favor the pseudoscience of positivism as much as the army officers did. Another source of common perspective was familial background in the Balkans and northwestern Anatolia, the regions recognized as the most vulnerable to Christian threats. Positivism and belief in the power of the state led the ruling clique to bridle against the moral authority of Islam as a check upon regime action, and compounding the risk associated with subverting such authority was the CUP's lack of serious interest in building popular support for its methods. The 1908 revolution thus produced a noticeable alteration to the background, mind-set, and tactics of those who decided imperial policy, and the ruling nouveau-élite had to learn again nineteenth-century lessons about the dangers of authoritarian state strengthening. A decade after the CUP triggered the return of the constitution, its rule collapsed, effectively taking the empire down with it.

POSITIVISM AND MILITARY RULE

To be blunt, the disastrous situation of 1918 could have been foreseen: when men who have never ridden anything but a 50-cc motor scooter try to drive eighteen-wheel trucks, bad things happen. Aged in their twenties and thirties at the time of the revolution, the key figures then and subsequently in the CUP's Central Committee were junior officers, who had commanded companies or battalions of soldiers, and low-level bureaucrats, who had supervised a handful of clerks. Such experience hardly prepared them for the task of running a complex empire. Of the men who were to form the "triumvirate" of the First World War, Enver and Cemal were army majors and Talat was the head of the Salonica telegraph office in 1908. They achieved the pinnacle of power by executing a coup in January 1913. By 1914 the first two were generals and ministers (of war in Enver's case and of the navy in Cemal's) and Talat was minister of the interior. Enver devised the greatest Ottoman military disaster of the war, the invasion of the Caucasus in the winter of 1914–15; Talat was the most deeply involved in the destruction of the Armenian population of eastern Anatolia; and Cemal commanded a poorly planned offensive against Egypt in 1915 and then did more to alienate the Arab population than any other figure by his brutality and questionable decision making as military governor of Syria. None was stupid, but their record showed that each lacked some element of the training, experience, and sense of perspective that had been expected of previous appointees to such positions of power.

It is tempting to see in both positivism and military training important ingredients of their belief that they could perform tasks so far beyond what their education and experience had qualified them to do, and in performing those tasks ignore what precedent had established as good practice. In essence, military training is about how to reach a goal that is ultimately political but through means that are simply brutal, destroying animate and inanimate objects obstructing the most direct path to the target while minimizing the pain suffered in the process. At critical points in execution of military plans there is no time for considered debate and no freedom given to participants to do as they choose, putting a premium upon discipline and unquestioned hierarchy of superior-subordinate. The military sphere, shaped by command and obedience, produces people practically guaranteed to fail at politics, which grinds to a halt without the lubricant of persuasion and negotiation. Talat the telegraph-clerk-turned-pasha retained his great influence in the CUP because he was the only member of the Central Committee with the political skill to maneuver rival cliques to some form of common ground. For a soldier like Enver, who was the most dynamic force in the CUP throughout the 1908–18 period, the conviction that Abdülhamid and his followers were cooperating with those obstructing achievement of the objective (maintenance of Ottoman Muslim control over Macedonia) moved him and fellow junior officers to shove the sultan out of the way. Firm action was needed, not the equivocation of a timorous autocrat. Familial ties to territories most threatened by Christian powers or already lost to them sharpened the sense of urgency to act and thus helped to overcome the subordinate officers' cultivated instinct to obey, not override, their commanders. The rapidity with which Abdülhamid caved in to their demands seemed only to confirm that decisive action was key to achieving goals. Enver continued to favor boldness thereafter, sometimes to success (the 1913 coup and, arguably, the negotiation of alliance with Germany in 1914) and sometimes to disaster (the Caucasus offensive in 1914–15 and, again arguably, the alliance with Germany).

Officers' faith in decisive action to implement rational and efficient change was reinforced by the strains of positivist thought that influenced some members of the CUP. Positivism and its derivatives stressed rationalism and science as keys to the solution of problems and the achievement of progress, and by extension favored a strong, controlling state to prevent interruptions of the scientific process. It is possible to see its influence in most of the military planning carried out in Europe prior to the First World War. Germany's Schlieffen Plan for victory in a two-front war through rapid mobilization and campaigning to destroy France before Russia could mobilize was a noted example of military positivism, but similarly Russia's inability to stop mobilization once it had commenced in 1914 showed the value placed on scientific planning and the construction of a clockwork military system. German influence in training the Ottoman army grew in Abdülhamid's reign, especially after Kaiser Wilhelm II began to court Istanbul's favor in the 1890s, increasing exposure to the views on science and rationalism dominant in the German military. Civilian CUP figures also gained exposure to the exaltation of science but primarily through schooling or residence in France, where positivist streams of philosophy were strongest. Several of the most influential of these civilian figures were medical doctors and by training favored the glorification of science associated with positivism. For them, sultanic despotism was an affliction weakening the empire; as medical science showed, amputation of a diseased limb was sometimes necessary to save life, and squeamishness over such tasks only hurt the patient in the long run. This attitude perhaps explains why one such medic, Dr Bahaeddin Şakir, was intimately involved in the annihilation of Armenian communities in eastern Anatolia in 1915–16.

One putative effect of positivism on CUP members was encouragement of nationalism as a force to keep together the myriad elements that made up the empire's "body." The extent to which members of the CUP were Turkish nationalists is much debated, but with a few possible exceptions, the ideas about "the Turks" that seem to have been most commonly held in the empire fell far short of nationalism. Traces of the "reliable Turk" views of the early nineteenth century echoed in military and bureaucratic circles after Mahmud II's reign, but wherever belief that the Turks were the "backbone of the empire" surfaced, there was no sign of such ethnic sense leading to any desire for a nation-state. Rather than Turkish nationalism, this was "Turkist Ottomanism." Among the important figures of the CUP who showed signs of ethnic sentiments, their views are best termed "cultural Turkism," which focused primarily upon language.[1] For the positivists in the military and the bureaucracy, a program that stressed language as a unifying element held obvious appeal because of the efficiency that universal knowledge of Turkish would add to state

[1] M. Şükrü Hanioğlu, "The Second Constitutional Period, 1908–1918," in *CHT4*, 101.

action.[2] While the army shared an Ottoman-Turkish vocabulary for ranks, maneuvers, or other routine terms, the unpredictability of military operations made the lack of a common language a problem. When Sultan Abdülaziz was deposed in 1876 (a necessary step toward introduction of the constitution), for example, the plot almost went awry when Arab guards kept his intended successor, Murad, at bayonet point outside the palace because they could not understand what was afoot.[3] It is thus easy to see why the early "Turkist" journal *Genç Kalemler* (funded through subsidy by members of the CUP) stressed the importance of language and the need for linguistic reform/simplification.[4]

Those few people who advocated rather confused and derivative notions of nationalism that went beyond language were fringe figures from border areas threatened by foreign powers or indeed not native to the empire. Nationalism promised support for their local communal interests through solidarity with larger groups beyond the fractured populations in which they lived. The most well known of these, Mehmed Ziya (Gökalp), was born in eastern Anatolia, an area of turmoil throughout the nineteenth century and particularly after 1878, when the well-being of its Armenian population was specified in the Treaty of Berlin as a formal issue of international interest. Ziya was of mixed Turkish and Kurdish parentage and initially preached for Kurdish solidarity against the Russo-Armenian threat. The Kurds, divided by tribal, linguistic, Muslim sectarian, and international barriers, ignored him. With that failure, he took up Turkism. He wrote for several journals, including *Genç Kalemler*, but he remained an activist with limited influence outside some CUP circles until the Kemalist decision to adopt Turkish nationalism. Other figures had similarly fluid agendas for rallying communal solidarity but were even less well positioned to influence Ottoman public opinion. Ahmed Ağaoğlu, Yusuf Akçura, and Hüseyinzade Ali were Russian emigrés, and Moiz Tekinalp was Jewish. Even among those circles of the CUP who were sympathetic to the Turks-are-the-backbone-of-the-empire

[2] The Habsburgs also faced this problem. The efficiency-seeking "enlightened despot" Josef II (1780–90) tried to make German the administrative language across the empire, a program abandoned because of intense opposition and never fully revived. CUP interest in linguistic standardization similarly stirred resentment and had to be relaxed after the Balkan Wars.

[3] Robert Devereux, "Süleyman Pasha's 'The Feeling of the Revolution,'" *MES* 15 (1979), 27–8.

[4] Murat Belge, "*Genç Kalemler* and Turkish Nationalism," in *Turkey's Engagement with Modernity: Conflict and Change in the Twentieth Century*, ed. Celia Kerslake, Kerem Öktem, and Phillip Robins (Basingstoke: Palgrave Macmillan, 2010), 27–37.

view, expatriates' dreams of pan-Turkish solidarity had no practical effect.[5] The CUP leaders, a group originating in, and most directly concerned about, the western wing of the empire, simply did not rank highly concern for distant regions such as the Caucasus, and even Anatolia only gained much interest from them after almost all the European provinces were lost in 1913.[6] With that change, however, the Arab provinces also gained in relative importance, and the CUP regime stressed the Islamic, not ethnic, elements of their version of Ottomanism in their calls for communal solidarity.[7]

Calls for Islamic solidarity were not simply propaganda, as most of the CUP leadership accepted without question the Muslim identity of the empire and its main constituency, Turkish or not. The CUP figure with by far the highest public profile was Enver, who gained much of his popularity from his reputation for notable piety, and from being a truly "loyal Ottoman," to which his marriage to a princess of the dynasty attested. The few "atheists" or determined materialist secularists in the CUP, such as Dr. Abdullah Cevdet (one of the four [non-Turkish] founders of the movement), were marginalized after 1908.[8] Yet, despite the firmness of the Islamic Ottoman identity that CUP leaders held, their relatively brief period of control over the empire did mark a shift away from the Islamic identity of the state and of its methods of rule. Part of this weakening of religious identification resulted from the high practical priority that the CUP placed upon abolishing the array of privileges that various groups, including notably non-Muslims, had enjoyed under previous regimes. It thus broke the effective Muslim monopoly on the army, an anomaly for a supposedly "Turkish" party that is to be explained as a conscious shifting of some of the burden of military service onto those parts of Ottoman

---

[5] A. Holly Shissler, *Between Two Empires: Ahmet Ağaoğlu and the New Turkey* (London: I. B. Tauris, 2003); Michael Reynolds, "Buffers, Not Brethren: Young Turk Military Policy in the First World War and the Myth of Panturanism," *P&P* 203 (2009), 137–79.

[6] Zürcher, *Young Turk Legacy*, 118–21.

[7] Hasan Kayalı, *Arabs and Young Turks: Ottomanism, Arabism, and Islamism in the Ottoman Empire, 1908–1918* (Berkeley: University of California Press, 1997), 141–3. On increasingly strident identification of Ottomans with Islam from 1913, see Eyal Ginio, "Paving the Way for Ethnic Cleansing: Eastern Thrace during the Balkan Wars (1912–1913) and Their Aftermath," in *Shatterzone of Empires: Coexistence and Violence in the German, Habsburg, Russian, and Ottoman Borderlands*, ed. Omer Bartov and Eric Weitz (Bloomington: Indiana University Press, 2013), 283–97.

[8] Abdullah's views on Islam were complicated, and eventually he undertook to reconcile the religion with science. M. Şükrü Hanioğlu, "Blueprints for a Future Society: Late Ottoman Materialists on Science, Religion and Art," in Özdalga (ed.), *Late Ottoman Society*, 48–61.

society that had thriven through privilege. Yet it was their attempts to reshape Ottoman law, in particular, that reduced the effective identification of the state with Islamic principles.

Positivism and its scientistic variations shaped the "corporatist" approach to law and imperial administration favored by the dominant clique of the CUP. In legal matters, this view prompted a marked shift from the Tanzimat and Hamidian era emphasis on preventing or repairing breaches of harmonious relations within society, not only because domestic disputes created opportunities for the "world's policemen," the Christian European powers, but also because that emphasis reflected a prime purpose of shari'a. The "scientific" and "biological" views of many in the CUP (founded by medical students in 1889) disposed them to sympathize with social Darwinism, which viewed the nation, or however the supralocal community identified itself, as a corporate whole. When in power, the CUP did not try to rescind shari'a-based law by, for example, eliminating the Mecelle, and they made public breaking of the Ramadan fast a criminal offense punishable by a fine or up to one month in prison.[9] But, as the treatment of those breaking the fast suggests, the CUP view of how law was to be applied was as a tool to preserve the health of the corporate whole. Criminals were not to be reconciled with their victims but were to be excised or quarantined from the morally healthy parts of society. CUP regimes grew ever more reliant on issuing new laws or rules regarding application of law by means of temporary decree, confirmed by royal assent, rather than through parliamentary action, in order to put this corporatist view into effect.[10] They also showed greater willingness simply to kill opponents, judicially where they could, through assassination where law offered no quick solution.

Although the very fact of the officer-led 1908 "constitutional revolution" indicated the CUP's readiness to ignore legal restrictions, it was the "counterrevolution" of the following year that decisively influenced their attitude toward the boundaries imposed by extant law. In April 1909, a protest movement in Istanbul that combined disgruntled soldiers with a civilian "Society of Muhammadan Union" demanded the removal of the CUP regime and "the return of shari'a." The slogan's suggestion that shari'a, including the Mecelle, had been suspended was false, but it represented the impression that the "revolution" had broken the rules holding

---

[9] Ruth Miller, *Legislating Authority: Sin and Crime in the Ottoman Empire and Turkey* (New York: Routledge, 2005), 88.
[10] Hanioğlu, *Brief History*, 163.

society together. Not only had the Muslims' military rebelled against the Commander of the Faithful, but events since the restoration of the constitution also motivated the society, including the perceived loosening of morals condoned by the new regime, the presumably CUP-authored assassination of a leading opposition journalist, and the reduction of the shaikh al-islam to the status of government minister answerable to parliament. The movement enjoyed a brief victory, and the lack of any popular countering force rallying to defend the CUP deeply disturbed its leaders. They were restored to power, however, by an army dispatched to Istanbul from Macedonia. In marked contrast to the restrained reaction of the Tanzimat era regime that survived the 1859 Küleli incident, the CUP on resumption of control summarily tried by court-martial those accused of participating in the uprising and executed many of them. The regime also used the occasion to arrest members of the main parliamentary opposition, the Liberal Party, and to engineer the deposition of Sultan Abdülhamid. Apparently not satisfied with imposing restrictions on the press, the CUP was suspected of responsibility for further assassinations of journalists. The aftermath of the affair thus saw the real onset of the CUP's restrictive measures on public life, the turn to legal authoritarianism, and the growing restraint upon the authority of shari'a courts.[11]

CUP actions clearly aimed to empower the state, and the authoritarian nature of their innovations demonstrated the committee's disinterest in public perceptions of damage to the state-society relationship. Positivist beliefs promoted CUP leaders' conviction that responsibility to rule lay with those sufficiently enlightened to understand the virtues of science, and that the delusions of the ignorant masses could not be allowed to stand in the way of progress. After April 1909, religious "reactionaries" became particularly feared as disturbers of the leaders-followers relationship. That the CUP survived as long as a decade while applying such an abrasive, and therefore dangerous, concept of administration owed much to force: its main support was the army, whose non-CUP commanders abhorred the complications for imperial defense caused by disorder in Istanbul. It also owed much to the foreign threats to Ottoman territorial integrity that gave urgency to CUP plans for strengthening the state because that peril – so widely recognized by both the traditional spokesmen for morality, the 'ulama, and the wider Ottoman population – provided

---

[11] Zürcher, *Young Turk Legacy*, 77–9, 289; David Farhi, "The Şeriat as a Political Slogan: Or 'the Incident of the 31st Mart,'" *MES* 7 (1971), 175–99; Hanioğlu, "Second Constitutional Period," 70–1; Findley, *Turkey*, 197.

some degree of protection against protest over authoritarianism. Failure to repel such pressure, however, would cause discontent, as it had repeatedly since the late eighteenth century.

THE CUP AND IMPERIAL DISINTEGRATION

Unprepared for the realities of responsibility that their quick ascent to power gave them, the leading figures of the CUP suffered a string of failures to preserve imperial territorial integrity. These setbacks pushed the CUP to ever-greater radicalism, culminating in the unconstitutional dictatorship of 1913–18 and the extreme violence of the First World War.

European interference in Macedonian affairs slackened slightly with the uncertainties besetting Istanbul from the time of the CUP uprising in July 1908; the neighboring states continued their ventures in Ottoman territories, however, and by October other sources of pressure appeared to rattle the new constitutionalist regime. In quick succession, autonomous Bulgaria proclaimed its independence in union with Eastern Rumelia; Austria-Hungary annexed Bosnia-Hercegovina, which it had occupied since 1878; and Crete's Greek leadership declared union with the Kingdom of Greece. The CUP government could do nothing to prevent quick international recognition of the first two of these faits accomplis, although they did gain some financial reparation from Austria-Hungary and, indirectly, Bulgaria. The CUP's failure, which in some eyes contrasted unfavorably with Abdülhamid's success in keeping these territories at least legally within the empire, contributed to the discontent that would manifest itself in April 1909.

Following the imposition of much tighter controls on public life in 1909, dissatisfaction grew especially in distant provinces and other circles where the ideas of the decentralist faction of the original CUP would have been more readily welcomed. Revolt erupted in Albania, where the aggressive efforts of the regime to disarm the population, tighten control over public life, and increase extraction of taxes and military recruits excited strong opposition. Northern Albania in particular had been spared much of the effect of measures enacted since 1839 to intensify exploitation of the empire's resources, but the CUP abolished such privileges. With expansionist pressure from Greece, Serbia, and Montenegro continuing, if not intensifying, moreover, Istanbul's refusal not only to countenance any Albanian self-defense effort that could be misconstrued as a step toward autonomy, but even to relax its efforts to disarm the population, angered many. The regime failed to pacify the area completely, despite trying first harsh repression and then a conciliatory visit of the sultan to Kosovo.[12]

Timed in part to coincide with the distractions offered by unrest in Albania and in southwestern Arabia, where northern Yemen and 'Asir were again in revolt, Italy invaded Tripolitania (Libya) in 1911. The regime could not provide significant support to the area's defense, but various officers and CUP members (including Enver and Mustafa Kemal, the future Atatürk) traveled incognito via Egypt to help organize resistance. The Italians struggled to assert their control and so used their naval superiority to widen the conflict, seizing Rhodes and shelling Ottoman ports such as Beirut. Evident popular dissatisfaction with CUP rule led it to employ widespread intimidation during the parliamentary election of 1912, but the spread of anti-CUP feeling to important parts of the military officer corps meant that the CUP cabinet formed after the rigged election had to resign almost immediately. CUP control gave way in July 1912 to a cabinet that bore a resemblance to the kind of safe bureaucrat-and-honored-ex-military-officer government that had typified Abdülhamid's era. This government essentially capitulated to Italian demands when it became clear that the Balkan states were on the point of invading Ottoman Macedonia, Thrace, and Albania. With Russian encouragement, Montenegro, Serbia, Bulgaria, and Greece had signed mutual defense pacts that, rather than aimed against Austro-Hungarian expansion in the region as Russia hoped, contained secret clauses committing each party to act against the Ottoman empire. The First Balkan War thus soon erupted in October 1912, with Bulgaria invading Thrace, Serbia and Greece invading Macedonia, and Montenegro and Greece attacking Albania.

In just a few weeks the Ottomans lost their European lands beyond the defensive lines around Istanbul; only the besieged cities of Shkodra and Ioannina in the west and Edirne in the east held out. Although the war was a disaster for the empire, it was beneficial for the CUP, even though it bore a great part of the blame for the fiasco. One of the agendas pushed by the CUP since achieving power in 1908 was the effective purging of those deemed loyal to Abdülhamid from both the bureaucracy and the military officer corps. The acrimonious politicization of the officer corps meant that, despite greatly increasing the money spent on arms and equipment (unlike the Hamidian period, in which budget deficits were small, the CUP era saw deep deficit spending despite increases in tax revenues collected),

[12] On Sultan Memed V Reşad's visit, see Zürcher, *Young Turk Legacy*, 86–92.

the pre-Tanzimat problem of poor leadership recurred to cripple military effectiveness. One of the main criteria by which political reliability was judged was the route to promotion followed by officers: those who had been promoted from the ranks were purged, to be replaced by graduates of the military staff academy. In addition to the problems of poor morale and politically driven distraction caused by such culling, the emerging post-1908 military came to have many officers well trained in staff work but relatively few with practical field command experience. When the Balkan states invaded in 1912, the Ottoman military response showed the effects of the upheavals of the preceding years, with the prepared plans for withdrawal to defensible positions in Thrace and Albania to await reinforcements from Anatolia not being followed. The chief of staff who had drawn up those plans had been posted to Yemen early in 1912 as punishment for opposing the harshness of repression in Albania, and the new minister of war in the "safe" non-CUP government was unfamiliar with them. As a result, and in line with the CUP propensity to resist any concession such as withdrawal would have suggested, the Ottoman forces in Europe stood and fought each invading army; badly outnumbered everywhere, they lost every battle.

Not being in power at the time, the CUP escaped the worst of the ignominy of defeat, and luck in the form of the Second Balkan War would boost their fortunes. Having already agreed an armistice with the victorious Balkan allies, the non-CUP regime entered multilateral negotiations in London; CUP leaders' fears that the government would accept the loss of Edirne to the Bulgarians triggered their staging of a coup in January 1913. Enver and a handful of others burst into a cabinet meeting, shot the unfortunate war minister, and compelled the grand vizier at gunpoint to resign "at the instance of the people and the armed forces."[13] The new regime, with the non-CUP general Mahmud Şevket as grand vizier, fought on until the capitulation of Edirne in March 1913, after which Istanbul had to sue for peace.[14] Then in June 1913 Bulgaria attacked its recent allies, acting rashly on its justified perception that it had done most of the fighting to defeat the Ottomans but that Serbia and Greece had seized far more than their share of the spoils in Macedonia. Bulgaria's redirection of military forces to the west and north, where Romania also attacked

[13] Hanioğlu, "Second Constitutional Period," 82.
[14] Mahmud Şevket, whose relations with the CUP were often prickly despite their history of cooperation at crisis points, clearly found the determination of some cabinet ministers to voice hard-line views on military matters hard to accept. *Sadrazam ve Harbiye Nazırı Mahmut Şevket Paşa'nın Günlüğü* (Istanbul: ARBA, 1988), 9–10.

them, and then its defeat allowed the Ottoman army to march back into Edirne. Any such victory after the comprehensive disaster of the First Balkan War seemed ample justification for the CUP's course of action since January.

Any such vindication, however, hardly negated the desperate condition in which the empire found itself and the profound anger and misery affecting large sections of the population at the end of the wars. The army had been badly mauled, and the loss of much of the cadre of experienced noncommissioned officers only worsened the problems already caused by the CUP's purging of the officer corps. The civilian population of the now-lost provinces had suffered similarly in a war that became infamous for the brutality inflicted upon civilian as well as military "enemies of the nation." One serious attempt to extrapolate the number killed from before-and-after census figures, checked against reports of massacres and figures of resettled refugees, concluded that more than 600,000 Muslim civilians died during the wars and in their aftermath – 27 percent of the Muslims living in the conquered lands in 1911.[15] More than 400,000 refugees poured into remaining Ottoman lands, recalling the massive dislocations caused by Russia's defeat of the empire in 1877–8, and much like the earlier refugees, many of the uprooted of 1912–13 were scarred by the violence, loss of homeland, and years of uncertainty and impoverishment in unfamiliar zones of resettlement. When the Republic of Turkey was founded in 1923, more than twenty percent of its population were resettled refugees and their children. The loss of 155,000 square kilometers of territory that had been Ottoman for more than half a millennium and had been home to two and a half million Muslims at the time of the concerted invasions of 1912 struck popular morale as surely as the disasters of 1878 had.[16] Anger simmered along with despair, and the cold realization of how precarious the empire's position was in facing an expanding array of fundamentally hostile states prepared both government and population for fast and drastic action.[17]

Perhaps inevitable results of the Balkan disaster were a simultaneous intensification of exploitation of the remaining imperial human and

---

[15] Justin McCarthy, *Death and Exile: The Ethnic Cleansing of Ottoman Muslims, 1821–1922* (Princeton: Darwin Press, 1995), 164.

[16] Findley, *Turkey*, 202, 204. Findley's figure of 435,000 refugees is slightly larger than McCarthy's (c. 414,000).

[17] Mustafa Aksakal, *The Ottoman Road to War in 1914: The Ottoman Empire and the First World War* (Cambridge: Cambridge University Press, 2008), 19–41, gives a good account of the atmosphere, at least in CUP-favored publications and in political debates.

material resources and adoption of a less abrasively centralizing style of administration. While taxes were raised and military conscription was intensified, the government under Mahmud Şevket issued new provincial regulations that allowed greater local control over some issues, including the administration of taxes, and again allowed Arabic as a language of administration.[18] Such changes reflected realization not only of the default growth in importance of the Arab provinces of the shrunken empire, but also of the damage done to Ottoman preparedness by the heavy-handedness of policy in places such as Albania. The regime nevertheless had to press the provinces for more resources, and much of the money raised through taxation went to the central government's intensive rebuilding of the military. Mahmud Şevket requested assistance from most of the great powers of Europe; Germany took the lead in army reorganization and training, Britain a similar role in naval affairs, and France in training the internal security forces of the gendarmerie. Enver, who became war minister after Mahmud Şevket was assassinated in June 1913 (although Russian support for the plot was suspected, his killing may have originated with the CUP's domestic opponents in retaliation for the January coup), supplemented such efforts by founding in November 1913 a formal paramilitary organization, the Teşkilat-i Mahsusa (Special Formations/Forces Speciales), which banded together the most ardent and self-sacrificing of the CUP's activists, a group dominated by refugees and sons of refugees. Enver estimated that the various reform and retraining programs would ready the military for another war by 1919, but again international pressures required a renewed mobilization little more than a year after the Second Balkan War ended. The First World War was to be the final disaster, from which the empire did not recover.

THE FIRST WORLD WAR AND IMPERIAL COLLAPSE

With some reason Enver usually receives much of the blame for the empire's entry into the war and therefore its demise, but enough uncertainty surrounds the questions of whether, when, and how Istanbul should have chosen to participate to make definitive judgment impossible. Had the empire followed the same path as its neighbor, Greece, a country also insecure about its military strength and torn by divided domestic inclinations toward the two alliances, then it might have gained as much as Athens did through its vacillation. Perhaps the most significant reason

[18] Kayalı, *Arabs and Young Turks*, 130–43.

for blaming Enver was not his leadership in concluding alliance with Germany but rather his practically unilateral decision to activate the alliance by attacking (to no direct military effect) Russia in November 1914. His predilection for bold action was to trigger tremendous pain to the empire, and not for the last time. One of the unanswerable questions of the period is whether the imperial regime would have followed a less precipitous course of action, had the more experienced military commander and grand vizier Mahmud Şevket not been assassinated.

Several factors suggest, however, that the CUP regime might not have been allowed to vacillate for as long as Greece did. While Greece was struggling to absorb the extensive territories gained in the Balkan Wars, it did not face any pressing external threat. Istanbul, by contrast, was painfully aware of the blindingly obvious: it was militarily weak, it had severely compromised autonomy within its remaining borders, and no external state felt any compunction about trying to seize further Ottoman territories or would lift a finger to prevent other states from doing so, except to "preserve the balance of power" (which might as easily entail distributing still more lands to rivals as reversing illegal seizures). Its very military weakness meant that neither bloc was inclined to bid for its allegiance – the CUP regime proposed alliance to each of the five great powers, and, with the exception of Germany (after initial rejection), each spurned the approach – but both would feel free to offer Ottoman land as enticement to still-uncommitted Christian states, as indeed happened in the case of Italy in 1915 and, ultimately, Greece. Neutrality offered no safeguard. A lesson drawn from the Balkan Wars, and indeed the 1877–8 war with Russia, was that Istanbul's only hope of protection other than self-strengthening lay in formal alliance with a great power, a fact recognized by all in the Ottoman cabinet. Once the empire joined the German-Austro-Hungarian alliance, Germany in particular made its expectation of rapid engagement with Russia clear, in hopes of salvaging some element of the already-failing Schlieffen Plan.

Once Enver committed the empire to war, it showed unexpected endurance and even energy in response. In common with populations in most, if not all, combatant countries, Ottoman citizens who embraced the war concentrated on the justice of their cause and the possible advantages to be won from defeating opponents. As an indication of what could be gained, the regime had annulled the capitulations from 1 September 1914, having secured a German commitment to support their abrogation as one of the conditions of alliance. This move was tremendously popular, at least among the Muslim population. Exuberance after the start of the war reached Enver as well, who directed the opening of fronts against the Russians in the Caucasus and the British in Egypt, with another front already having been opened by a British-Indian invasion of southern Iraq in November 1914. Each front was thus undermanned and undersupplied. The Egyptian campaign was entrusted to Cemal, who held simultaneously the positions of naval affairs minister, military governor of Syria, and commander of the Syria-based Fourth Army. British forces were surprised by the attack in February 1915 but after a couple of days were able to dislodge the poorly equipped Ottoman forces who had managed to gain the western bank of the canal. Enver himself went to eastern Anatolia to command operations against Russia and was thus directly responsible for the extremely risky offensive launched into the Caucasus in the winter of 1914–15. His dead-of-winter surprise attack upon the superior Russian forces centered on Sarıkamiş led to the loss of at least sixty thousand men, some two-thirds of the Third Army, most of which had not even been equipped with winter uniforms.[19] Given that the Ottomans reached the point of mobilizing one million men only in 1916, such losses hurt deeply. With the exception of some limited counterattacks (most notably in the entrapment and capture of British Indian forces at Kut al-'Amara in Iraq and a second attack upon Suez, both in 1916), the Ottoman army lacked thereafter much ability to launch offensives until the disorder brought to the Russian side of the eastern Anatolia front from November 1917.

Ottoman military weakness extended beyond sheer shortage of manpower due to the relatively small population available for conscription, as damaging as that proved to be. The empire mobilized some 2.6 million men over the course of the war, but this number conveys no sense of the armed forces' size, given ravages of disease and desertion. Disease killed one-seventh of these recruits and, as the war drew to a close, the deserters afoot in the provinces outnumbered the soldiers still under arms by three or five to one. Desertion resulted from chronic and severe shortages of food, medical care, clothing, and other basic necessities, all of which were affected by the underdeveloped transport system. The fact that a disproportionate percentage of Ottoman railway track had been built in now-lost European provinces, and that much of the remaining road and

---

[19] Michael Reynolds, *Shattering Empires: The Clash and Collapse of the Ottoman and Russian Empires, 1908–1918* (Cambridge: Cambridge University Press, 2011), 124–8. Zürcher estimates 72,000 of 90,000 in the army as lost (*Young Turk Legacy*, 166). He also estimates that the Ottoman armed forces never exceeded an effective strength of roughly 800,000 (*Young Turk Legacy*, 174)

rail network was oriented for trade purposes to port cities (made useless by enemy coastal blockade), made concentration of manpower and supplies at any point exceptionally difficult. A four-front war (as it was while Britain pushed the Gallipoli campaign in 1915–16) was simply not possible for the empire to wage effectively. Disease and desertion inevitably combined to sap Ottoman military strength much more seriously than combat with the enemy.[20]

Acute awareness of such weakness helps to explain in part the ruthless brutality with which the regime treated several sectors of the population. The disaster of Sarıkamiş led to a veritable collapse under Russian pressure on the eastern Anatolian front, and the seizure of the city of Van by armed Armenians raised the terrifying specter of a strong fifth column aiding the Russian advance by destabilizing the Ottoman rear and its precarious supply system. (It is still unclear whether the Van incident was truly a rebellion or simply a self-defense move by a frequently persecuted population whose sense of insecurity reached an intolerable level with the collapse of military organization and discipline following Sarıkamiş.)[21] The British-led landings at Gallipoli in April 1915 simultaneously threatened Istanbul itself, and the wartime regime made preparations to abandon the capital and retreat into Anatolia. True to the established CUP philosophy of rule, the regime adopted a program of resolving the internal security problems of threatened areas in the most direct manner possible, choosing to isolate or indeed amputate sources of infection in order to cure the rest of the body. The regime had already started to compel much of the Greek population of western Anatolia to resettle in the interior before the war began in 1914, and the arrival of the enemy at the Dardanelles seemed only to confirm the wisdom of such preparations. Following the failure of the attack on Suez in 1915, Cemal implemented in Syria a campaign of executions and the deportation to Anatolia of an estimated five thousand families suspected (on generally flimsy grounds) of French sympathies, with a second and expanded round of executions staged in 1916. Cemal's actions targeted mainly Muslims but were comparable, albeit on a much smaller scale, to the violent measures unleashed upon the Christians (Armenians and Assyrians) of eastern Anatolia at about the same time.[22] This latter program was executed in the most direct manner possible: killing enough of them to stampede the others

[20] Zürcher, *Young Turk Legacy*, 174–87; Hanioğlu, "Second Constitutional Period," 93–4.
[21] Reynolds, *Shattering Empires*, 146.
[22] Kayalı, *Arabs and Young Turks*, 192–6.

toward their designated "zones of resettlement." Most who managed to escape immediate killing but could not flee to Russian-controlled territory ended their flight in arid zones of Iraq and Syria, where many died of hunger and disease. This terrorization and "ethnic cleansing" effort rapidly extended to other parts of Anatolia.[23] It is impossible to know how many people died or to discover the exact details of the campaign against Armenians and Assyrians because of the inadequacies of surviving documentation, but the best estimate is around 650,000, or 45 percent of the prewar Anatolian Armenian population.[24] The questions not only of formal responsibility for the effective destruction of the communities of Christians in eastern Anatolia (the fact of those communities' disappearance seems inarguable) but also of intent have become key points of dispute between those who insist on use of the term "genocide" and those who refuse to do so.

Discussion here will not resolve the interminable dispute: proponents of both sides are sure that they are right, and nothing newly discovered offers startling fresh evidence. Both sides have plausible grounds for their positions, as well. For the proponents of the term "genocide," there is the simple fact of destruction of large-scale communities by death and forced movement, which fulfills basic criteria of the crime as first defined in the Geneva Convention of 1948; regardless of whether it is termed genocide or "merely" murder, manslaughter, and ethnic cleansing on a massive scale, it was certainly a "crime against humanity," as it was labeled at the time by the empire's foes in the war.[25] A standard countering claim that much of the loss suffered by the Armenian population resulted from the famine, epidemic disease, and endemic violence of the war zone that also killed a staggering percentage of the Muslim population is hard to accept unquestioned: famine and therefore disease were undoubtedly worsened by the uprooting of the significant Christian percentage of eastern Anatolia's peasant population. Most of the Christians were gone by the end of 1916, moreover, therefore making comparison with the scale of deaths of Muslims over the course of the entire war problematic. Assignment to Kurdish tribes of the blame for the endemic violence that killed so many is again only partially plausible: Kurdish oppression of Armenians had been a very real problem for decades prior

---

[23] Ryan Gingeras, *Sorrowful Shores: Violence, Ethnicity, and the End of the Ottoman Empire, 1912–1923* (Oxford: Oxford University Press, 2009), 41–45.

[24] Reynolds, *Shattering Empires*, 155. Zürcher, *Turkey*, 171, estimates between 600,000 and 800,000 Armenian deaths.

[25] Reynolds, *Shattering Empires*, 148.

to 1915 (and helps to explain why the Armenians of Van might have chosen to organize in self-defense), but given the Turkish Republic's repeated vilification of the Kurds since the 1920s as the group most resistant to accepting "Turkish" identity, the assertion that "the Kurds did it" seems a suspiciously neat conclusion. Indeed, one side's minimizing claims that 300,000 Armenians died tries to make plausible the theory of death by unorganized violence, disease, and famine, while the other side's exaggerating claim of two million dead makes conscious planning by those in power impossible to deny: the deaths of even half that number in a targeted population would have been a physically difficult and time-consuming task that would have required planned, concerted action.

Yet that very fact of determined action being necessary for the scale of death seen gives ground to those refusing to label the Armenians' fate a genocide, because the rate of morbidity among Muslims in the region indicates conscious campaigns of killing and ethnic cleansing by Christian forces as well. In the immediate aftermath of Sarıkamiş, Russian forces and paramilitaries (especially Cossacks and Armenians) appeared intent on ethnic cleansing of all Muslims from reconquered land. They killed an estimated forty-five thousand of the fifty-two thousand Muslims resident in the Chorokhi valley, for example, and deported to inhospitable and isolated areas many Muslims living along the Ottoman frontier.[26] Extermination of Muslims appeared to be the goal of Russia, and especially its paramilitaries, and the fear of "it's us or them" must have influenced the CUP leaders' decision to crush the Armenian and Assyrian communities of the east, the reservoirs of potential paramilitaries made threatening by the approaching Russian forces. Recent experience from the Balkan Wars, the Macedonian Question, the 1877–8 and still earlier conflicts, in which paramilitaries were the worst perpetrators of ethnic cleansing and killing of Muslim civilians, only deepened the fear and the determination to act. It was hardly coincidental that the CUP's own paramilitary force, the Teşkilat-i Mahsusa, organized the persecution of the Armenians and included disproportionate numbers of Muslim refugees from the Caucasus and the Balkans within its ranks. Once the breaking of the eastern communities was under way, the CUP extended the campaign to other parts of Anatolia except the largest cities, reflecting both the cold-blooded thoroughness of the regime and the depth of animosity toward Christians, the religious group that seemed close to achieving their suspected historical aim of destroying the Muslims.

---

[26] Reynolds, *Shattering Empires*, 144.

It is this piecemeal quality of the expanding effort to break the Christians, and indeed the nature of the persecution as a conflict between two religious rather than ethnic-national groups, that also works somewhat against the case for describing the campaign as genocide. The timing of the definition of genocide, a term coined by Raphael Lemkin in 1944, was hardly fortuitous, and the effort to define the crime clearly reflected the experience of the Holocaust. Compared to the Nazi campaign to annihilate Europe's Jews, the effort to destroy Anatolia's Armenians and Assyrians lacked such a single-minded, absolute intent to exterminate. Christians who were not killed were to be resettled either in isolation or in small groups that presented no threat to the surrounding Muslim majority or could even be absorbed into it. This echoed CUP policies on dispersing and resettling non-Turkish Muslim refugees.[27] Regardless of the difficulties inhibiting the process, assimilation was a marginally foreseeable option that was never open to Jews in Nazi Europe. Some Armenians who converted to Islam were spared, particularly women and children but also Armenians serving in the Ottoman military fighting against the British in the Arab provinces.[28] Despite Adolf Hitler's purported rhetorical question "Who remembers the Armenians?" when formulating his "final solution," it is the unique quality of the Holocaust that has presumably legitimated the stance against official designation of 24 April as "Armenian Holocaust Remembrance Day" taken by important political figures and organizations identified with Jewish causes in the United States.

Leaving aside the sheer war criminality of what the dominant clique of the CUP regime perpetrated against multiple sectors of its own population, it may well be argued that such extreme internal security measures hurt the war effort more than they helped to prevent treachery. Famine and ensuing epidemic disease crippled Anatolia and Syria in part as a result of the havoc wreaked upon the civilian populations in these regions, and such conditions made disintegration of the eastern and southern fronts more likely. The east was saved only by the October Revolution in St. Petersburg and Russia's subsequent withdrawal from the war. The Syrian front collapsed in the late summer of 1918, and the lands from north of Jerusalem to Anatolia were lost in a few weeks. In Iraq, a British army, reinforced after the loss at Kut al-'Amara, took Baghdad in March 1917 and finally broke through Ottoman defenses to

[27] Gingeras, *Sorrowful Shores*, 47–52.
[28] Zürcher, *Young Turk Legacy*, 173.

the north in early summer 1918. Final defeat for the empire, however, occurred with the collapse of its ally Bulgaria in September 1918, which opened a hole in imperial defenses that there was no military manpower left to repair. Talat first made overtures for peace in early October but no negotiations commenced until late that month. The empire's negotiators accepted surrender on terms by 30 October, and the news of the end of the war brought relief to most of the population – except the leading figures of the CUP regime, who left Istanbul on board a German ship bound for the Black Sea. Talat, Cemal, and Bahaeddin Şakir were later assassinated in an Armenian revenge campaign, and Enver was to die fighting the Bolsheviks in the Caucasus.

While the empire was traumatized and exhausted, it had been defeated without being comprehensively destroyed. Of all of the defeated powers, it was the only one to resume fighting soon after signing the armistice, and in this ultimate phase of the struggle, it was the allied powers of the First World War who had to withdraw from the conflict and make concessions to the victors. Yet that ultimate phase of the decade of war for the empire (1911–22) culminated in the emergence of yet another post-Ottoman state, this time out of the totality of the domains still remaining to the Ottoman sultan. The empire's death resulted from the allied powers' (and notably Britain's) resistance to heeding several of the main concerns that the Ottoman negotiators had raised during armistice talks in October 1918, which the British negotiator Admiral Calthorpe had addressed in a letter of reassurance to the grand vizier and sultan at that time: that the allies not occupy the capital, Istanbul, and especially that Greek troops not be allowed among any occupying force.[29] London was to encourage the Greek occupation of western Anatolia in 1919, and with the upsurge of resistance to the partition of Anatolia into Christian-controlled spheres, Britain and France were to occupy Istanbul in 1920, stripping the sultan's regime of any façade of authority to govern. The hypothesis that Britain and France set the stage for the Second World War through their demands on Germany encapsulated in the Treaty of Versailles is well known, and the reignition of conflict in Anatolia after a much shorter interlude can be similarly attributed to the victors' determination to destroy any possibility of future revival of their defeated opponent. After more than a century of heavy pressure upon the empire, Christian Europe finally inflicted the wounds that proved mortal after 1918.

[29] Zürcher, *Young Turk Legacy*, 191.

PART II

FROM OTTOMAN TO POST-OTTOMAN STATES

Truly the Ottoman empire must have been the Sick Man of Europe, because no healthy entity could have spawned such a sickly brood as the post-Ottoman states proved to be – and in most cases still are. Almost all young post-Ottoman states were weak, in that they struggled to win the active allegiance of more than narrow sections of their populations, facing from the majority of their citizenries either indifference or, worse yet, alienation. This flaw was apparent from the birth of practically every post-Ottoman country, because almost none was created by its people's struggle to achieve independence, rather than by the decisions of European rulers. The population of each country created by external powers lacked a clear sense of what the new regime's purpose was to be, trust in its capacity to improve public life and private well-being, and coherent leadership that could mold a vision and inspire such trust. The country that may be said to have broken the pattern was Turkey, which did have a leader with prestige, Mustafa Kemal (Atatürk), who lived long enough to shape a nation-state out of the remains of the Ottoman empire. Yet even in the case of Turkey, where Atatürk remains the most important political figure some three-quarters of a century after his death, elements of his vision of what it means to be a Turk were sufficiently alienating for parts of the population to create political instability over that three-quarter-century period.

Atatürk, credited with having led an exhausting liberation struggle, also had the advantage of support from a large, experienced administrative and political organization inherited from the late Ottoman regime of the CUP; this ensured that Turkey was better prepared than other new states to address the problems resulting from separation from the empire.

The dissolution of the empire had been a long, drawn-out drama, and the transformation of provinces into post-Ottoman countries also proceeded fitfully, and messily. Nowhere had this blood-soaked transition been accomplished without tremendous disruption that continued well past the achievement of formal independence. The length and difficulty of transition had multiple facets, including the breaking of economic, social, and communications ties that had developed in a great empire and suddenly had to adapt to the shrunken arenas created by new frontiers. The groups that had wrested authority in the new states, including Turkey, had to find a means to justify their own acquisition of power and either persuade the population to accept the reality of the new borders or offer the hope that they would be redrawn. New rulers needed, in short, purpose and ideological legitimacy. Nationalism was the natural method, because it grew rapidly as the ideological justification of choice in strong states of western Europe from the middle of the nineteenth century, and it was the principle cited by those states to legitimate their creation of post-Ottoman countries. Given the awkward size of the new entities – too large to be able to benefit from the local identities that their populations held but too small to match religion's supralocal community of believers – nationalism also could be tailored more easily than old allegiances to instill in populations across young countries loyalty to new rulers in new capitals.

Authorities in new states knew that among populations to be shaped into conscious nations, Muslim or non-Muslim, religion and locale provided much stronger identities than ethnicity. The early measures taken by post-Ottoman regimes, therefore, aimed at reworking these established foci of identity into forms more useful to the state. This pattern first manifested itself in the Balkans and then in Anatolia; by contrast, Arab lands suffered abnormally long transitions due to post–First World War occupation by victorious European powers, and the task of building national identities there thus became even more difficult, lagging decades behind the Balkans and Turkey.

Success in Balkan and Turkish regimes' immediate steps to reorient extant identities and allegiances toward the state depended upon sustained, longer-term campaigns. Crucial first steps included the creation of explicitly national "churches," institutions dependent upon the new nation-state, aiding the transformation of Orthodox Christians into Greeks, Serbs, Romanians, Bulgarians, or Slav Macedonians and of Muslims into Bosnians, Albanians, or Turks. They co-opted local notables by providing them with political offices and associated material rewards or commissions in the oversized armies established by most of the new states, assuming that the central figures in networks of local allegiances could deliver the loyalty of their clients. The great majority of the population, the illiterate peasantry, was largely ignored, except as a source of conscripts into the armed forces that were to teach young men the need to defend a sacred homeland much larger than their home districts; members of the ethnoreligious minority communities remaining in all ex-Ottoman territories were excluded from state attentions, except as subjects of surveillance and harassment. And to strengthen their ability to control populations with suspect identities, both "minorities" and the new "national" majorities, states undertook thorough regime-strengthening revisions to law.

Within the ranks of those targeted for development into the ethnically "sound," the ultimate success of efforts to create a new, state-centered national identity depended upon converting the young and impressionable, who were not yet firmly settled into alternative loyalties beyond their families. All new states stressed education, schooling children in the largely artificial language and history, and thereby the embryonic civic culture, of the nation. In the field of history, regimes commissioned the reworking of interpretations to cast events, recent and long-past, as episodes in the life of the nation, which then were presented as truth to youth who had no personal knowledge or experience of the times discussed.[1] In Bulgaria, generations of students have known about life in the Ottoman period through reading *Under the Yoke* – a novel that features the requisite stereotypes of bad Turks and good Bulgarians (as well as traitorous Bulgarians, whose treasonous attitude might explain why Bulgarians had failed to liberate themselves) published fifteen years after the country was established. In Serbia, the project of training the nation's youth began in earnest under the first minister of education and religious affairs, Stojan Novaković, in 1882. Novaković was nineteenth century Serbia's foremost historian and wrote the first secondary school reader himself; born in 1842, well after Serbia gained autonomy from the empire, and given the name of Costa, he had no more hesitancy in rewriting history to build the nation than he did in reinventing himself by adopting the more

---

[1] For an unusually direct case study of propagandistic reconfiguration of the past, see Uğur Üngör, *The Making of Modern Turkey: Nation and State in Eastern Anatolia, 1913–1950* (Oxford: Oxford University Press, 2011).

"authentically Serbian" name Stojan.[2] Arab nationalism was similarly first promoted in a meaningful way through education, notably through the efforts of Sati' al-Husri, a former Ottoman bureaucrat whose mother tongue was Turkish but who promoted Arabism after 1918 as director-general and then minister of education under King Faysal, first in Syria and then in Iraq, the two states that came to be most lastingly associated with Arab nationalism. In Turkey, Atatürk supported the creation of the Turkish Historical Society, which developed the Turkish History thesis that all civilization worth mentioning in the history of the world origi-nated with the Turks – a view propagated in schools in Atatürk's remain-ing years and still traceable in textbooks to the end of the century.[3]

While not every rewriting of history to build ethnic national conscious-ness was as obviously improbable as the Turkish History thesis (whose lack of concern for the limits of credibility suggests the inchoate nature of any sense of Turkish nationalism inherited from the Ottoman era), almost all of them hurried to achieve their goal by applying the most effective means of arousing common emotion: fostering the sense of having been unjustly hurt or oppressed by evil and powerful (yet somehow decadent) enemies. Writing the nation through history involved dwelling upon a long-past period of cultural glory and worldly power that could be appro-priated for the nation (Athens, Alexander the Great, and the Byzantine empire for Greeks; the realms of the Nemanjić dynasty and Stefan Dušan for Serbs; the kingdom of Simeon and Samuil for the Bulgarians; the Islamic world from the time of the Prophet Muhammad to the fall of the Umayyad caliphate for Arabs; and seemingly all great civilizations of the world for Turks), which was brought to a catastrophic halt by a demon-ized enemy, usually "the Turks" (Turkey, by contrast, portrays the Turks as a strong, positive force in history that was then subverted by overclose

---

[2] Charles Jelavich, *South Slav Nationalisms: Textbooks and Yugoslav Union before 1914* (Columbus: Ohio State University Press, 1990), 33; Victor Roudometof, "Invented Traditions, Symbolic Boundaries, and National Identity in Southeastern Europe: Greece and Serbia in Comparative Historical Perspective (1830–1880)," *EEQ* 32 (1998), 455. Roudometof also discusses nineteenth-century Greek nation-building historiography.

[3] For examples from Turkish schoolbooks (and from comparable nation-building Greek texts), see Hercules Millas, "History Textbooks in Greece and Turkey," *History Workshop* 31 (1991), 21–33. See also Umut Özkırımlı and Spyros Sofos, *Tormented by History: Nationalism in Greece and Turkey* (London: Hurst, 2008), 91–7; Büşra Ersanlı, "The Ottoman Empire in the Historiography of the Kemalist Era: A Theory of Fatal Decline," in *The Ottomans and the Balkans: A Discussion of Historiography*, ed. Fikret Adanır and Suraiya Faroqhi (Leiden: Brill, 2002), 115–54; and Hercules Millas, "Non-Muslim Minorities in the Historiography of Republican Turkey: The Greek Case", in *idem.*, 155–92.

association with Balkan and Arab peoples). Standard narratives in the Balkans suggest that the nation submitted outwardly to "the Turks" only after desperate and honorable struggle, and that the nation's sacrifices saved the rest of Christian Europe from the infidel horde. The Ottoman period is then dismissed as centuries of darkness for the nation that toiled under the yoke, except for fulsome discussion of every peasant jacquerie that could be rechristened a national uprising. The pace slows drastically again for discussion of "the national revival" period that presaged the ultimately victorious struggle for independence. The Arab version of national history follows a similar path, albeit with different emphases: decay set in with Persian infiltration of the Abbasid movement that overthrew the Umayyads in 750 and accelerated with the rise to power of Turkish slave soldiers in the ninth century. The Ottomans thus merely maintained the established pattern. In Arab national history, the dead weight of "the Turks" was also responsible for the nation's backwardness, but for the Arabs there was less active, vindictive oppression than asserted in the Balkans.[4]

With time, these efforts took effect, creating populations aware of national identity and indeed, in some sectors, strongly nationalistic, but the sense of the nation's past, present, and future has always been insecure, thus helping to explain why the states that depend upon such a shared sense of nationhood have proven weak. In the Balkans, one of the accomplishments of the nation-building effort was transformation of the idea that Christians had suffered oppression under the Ottomans – a perception grounded in reality for some periods – to the conceit that the people were persecuted because of their ethnicity. Such blurring of the line between national and religious identities was eased by the messianic undertones of the nationalism inculcated by Balkan states: the (Christian) nation had dwelt in the Garden of Eden (classical Athens, Nemanjić Serbia, etc.), suffered a fall and endured the vale of tears, and then been redeemed and admitted to paradise (independence in the nation-state); another interpretation could be more personal, in that the nation lived

---

[4] This distillation is necessarily simplified, but readers familiar with any of these nations' historiographic traditions or school texts will recognize the elements cited. A trenchant dissection of one national historiography is in Machiel Kiel, *Art and Society in Bulgaria in the Turkish Period* (Assen: van Gorcum, 1985), ch. 1. On these traditions and the place of the Ottomans within them, see Maria Todorova, *Imagining the Balkans* (Oxford: Oxford University Press, 1997), 182–3; Rifaat Abou-el-Haj, "The Social Uses of the Past: Recent Arab Historiography of Ottoman Rule," *IJMES* 14 (1982), 185–201; Frederick Anscombe, "The Ottoman Empire in Recent International Politics – I: The Case of Kuwait," *IHR* 28 (2006), 537–45.

IMAGE 1 King Ferdinand I of Bulgaria, preceded by scripture and Orthodox clergy, enters Mustafa Pasha (now Svilengrad, Bulgaria) following seizure of the town in the First Balkan War (1912)

the virtuous life, suffered death and then centuries of purgatory, only to be reborn in paradise.[5] Even more obvious as reworking of religious into ethnic identity is the common Balkan myth that the church had served as preserver of the nation through the dark centuries under the yoke. In illustration of the tight link between state and church, nation and faith, see Image 1. Such a messianic vision of the nation, with a history that stresses past glory as evidence of greatness but also a litany of injustices and oppression inflicted by powerful enemies – and their local collaborators – creates reservoirs of resentment against outsiders and distrust of fellow nationals. The ultimate lesson was that the new state stood between those menacing forces and the threatened population, which therefore was bound by duty and self-interest to support the nation's leaders and bear their demands on the people. Yet such retellings of oppression and treachery in history tended also to make the sense of common identity on which the state had to rest too brittle to withstand much stress.

[5] Gunnar Hering, "Die Osmanenzeit im Selbstverständnis der Völker Südosteuropas," in *Die Staaten Südosteuropas und die Osmanen*, ed. Hans Georg Majer (Munich: Südosteuropa-Gesellschaft, 1989), 360–1.

Part of the weakness in post-Ottoman national identity that also has made the nation-state insecure is the difficulty of reconciling the record of the vale of tears with the lack of a successful liberation struggle waged by the oppressed nation, heightening national insecurity by suggesting inadequacy – or betrayal by fellow nationals and supposed friends. In the case of Greece, for example, eight senior military officers and politicians who had been involved in Greece's failed campaign to occupy Anatolia against Mustafa Kemal's Ottoman-Turkish liberation movement in 1922 were tried for high treason and six were executed, a process so blatantly unjustified that it destroyed Greece's political unity in the interwar period. By contrast, Mustafa Kemal led a successful liberation struggle, not only giving him the prestige to shape the new nation, but also allowing the nation to draw self-confidence from its achievement to ameliorate, compared to the grievance-laden Greek nation, the expected sense of outrage against the peoples who supposedly had sapped the vitality of the Turks in the Ottoman period. The sense of grievance is directed instead against those enemies whom neither Ottomans nor Turks clearly defeated, the great powers of Christian Europe, an attitude distilled into the "Sèvres complex" of deep suspicion directed against the states who helped to destroy the empire in the nineteenth century and then tried to dismantle what remained of it (i.e., Turkey) through the harshest of the peace treaties concluding the First World War. The message of the Sèvres complex is that such enemies stand ready to try again in future.

With national identities being shaped as work-in-progress, and bedeviled by insecurities and grievances, most post-Ottoman regimes failed to add to their daunting challenges by attempting to define what membership in the nation meant, or what the purpose of the nation might be. The crude form of post-Ottoman nationalism, created and applied from above, had little ethical content to guide people on how to act as members of the national community; the messianic quality of nationalism also encouraged communal passivity, in that redemption is conferred by the grace of the savior, be it God or the state. It proved tempting to nation-building regimes to cater to the taught grievances by, for example, pursuing irredentism abroad rather than to build consensus on domestic affairs, such as strategies for economic and social development. The lack of attention to bettering the lot of all members of the nation may follow naturally from the various myths of long-past golden ages in which the nation demonstrated its perfections before being forced to its knees by barbarous enemies – for all romantic nationalism's glorification of the peasantry as the repository of authentic national lore, the peasants' superstitions, impure language, and uncultured demeanor made them an embarrassment to the nation, the slow-witted brothers to be kept hidden rather than given the attention needed to improve their circumstances. Political leaders or parties that made an effort to address the concerns of the embarrassing majority of the nation (the Agrarian National Union and after 1945 the communists in Bulgaria, the Obrenović dynasty and then the Radicals in Serbia, Jamal 'Abd al-Nasir in Egypt) did well, falling not to popular protest but to the pressures of nationalist activists.

In the main, however, politicians failed to make significant efforts to raise consciousness of the nation's moral responsibilities toward all of its members, and as a result politics too often had relatively little content, with stable parties being slow to develop to displace cliques. Democracy requires an established sense of nationhood, but the brittle, superficial quality of post-Ottoman national identity tempted few regime leaders to test through competitive elections the strength of the bond they hoped to have established with the wider population. Rather than rousing the passive nation in hopes of building stronger support, political figures who won control of the state tried to buy clients through state employment. The problem of patron-client relationships – it is who, rather than what, you know that procures advancement – had characterized the Ottoman empire, but it worsened in insecure, weakly legitimate post-Ottoman systems.

As seriously flawed as most post-Ottoman nation-states were, their problems were hardly unique. Given the sense of superiority so often evident in western or central European pronouncements on the Balkans, Turkey, and the Middle East, it is salutary to remember that the post-Habsburg states created by Anglo-French directive after the First World War, for example, were just as unnatural, insecure, and undemocratic nation builders as post-Ottoman regimes. Just as they played a decisive role in breaking Ottoman territory into post-Ottoman "national" countries, Britain and France saw fit to create a cordon of large countries to the east of Germany that could help to contain the power of that state (and quarantine Bolshevism to the east); they used in this project the principle of "national self-determination" where it was helpful and ignored it where it would be inconvenient. Poland, Czechoslovakia, Romania, and Yugoslavia were all awkward Anglo-French creations, and they exhibited the stridency and the intolerance of minorities that characterized post-Ottoman nation builders. Post-Ottoman states may have proven themselves to be weak and barely competent in forming lasting, strong bonds with the populations that nominally they represent, but they are only typical products of eras that marked the apotheoses of the nation and of the state.

6

The Post-Ottoman Balkans

With Yugoslavia's bloody disintegration in the 1990s, the Balkans have come to be associated in the Western public mind with the worst excesses of nationalism in past and present. This perception, which is hardly fair in light of much of the rest of Europe's appalling record in this regard from the late nineteenth to mid-twentieth centuries, results in part from widespread ignorance of the region and its history but also in part from the preponderance of national identity in shaping the published accounts of the area's development that do exist. Those that speak of Greeks, Serbs, Bulgarians, or Romanians as distinct collectives in the Ottoman or earlier eras gloss over the vagueness of such ethnic identities prior to the creation of post-Ottoman states that undertook zealous nation building.

Under Ottoman rule, Orthodox Christians lived in an anational ecumene that reached across the peninsula.[1] Christianity in the Balkans was organized according to the combined interests of the Ottoman state and the state-sanctioned church hierarchy, neither of which had any reason to "preserve" or promote ethnic identity. The languages that helped to create the ecumene, liturgical Greek and Slavonic, could be spoken by the educated but were not mother tongues for anyone, a situation with some parallel elsewhere in Europe in the Catholic Church's use of Latin.

---

[1] Georges Castellan, *Histoire des Balkans (XIVe–XXe siècle)* (Paris: Fayard, 1991), 145–6; Maria Todorova, *Imagining the Balkans* (Oxford: Oxford University Press, 1997), 179; Paschalis Kitromilides, "Orthodox Culture and Collective Identity in the Ottoman Balkans during the Eighteenth Century," *Oriente Moderno* 18 (1999), 131–45; Richard Clogg, "The Greek *Millet* in the Ottoman Empire," in *Christians and Jews in the Ottoman Empire: The Functioning of a Plural Society*, ed. Bernard Lewis and Benjamin Braude (New York: Holmes and Meier, 1982), i, 185–207.

As in the tenacity of Catholicism's linkage to Latin (relinquished as the sole language of the liturgy only in the 1960s but still used in church services, documents such as Papal encyclicals, and even a Vatican Web site), the religious rather than ethnic character of the languages written by the literate was clear – and indeed dangerous to question, as shown by the collapse of the Greek government in 1901 following "Gospel riots" over plans to translate scripture into the vernacular.[2] Since liturgical Greek and Slavonic were learned languages, there was no insuperable ethnic bar to entry into the church hierarchy.

There were no standardized "national" languages, thus permitting a multitude of linguistic divisions across the peninsula, but relatively few of these divides were very sharp or unbridgeable. Intuition suggests that the clearest division lay between the Greek, Slavonic, Romanian, and Albanian families of dialects, but large commonalities of everyday vocabulary helped to overcome those barriers, as did the convergence of grammatical structures in what linguists have termed "the Balkan Sprachbund." Prior to standardization, vernacular "Bulgarian" had a vocabulary estimated to be 50 percent Turkish, with many other words adopted from Greek; indeed, well into the nineteenth century Karamanlı (Turkish in Greek script) texts "served urban Bulgarians' spiritual needs better than purely Greek or Church Slavonic ones."[3] Other Balkan dialects similarly shared terminology. The standardized literary languages of today – adopted, adapted, and promoted by the post-Ottoman states – may have lost some of the commonalities of vocabulary, but many terms are still shared across the peninsula, especially those referring to everyday items such as food and household goods. Some of the overlapping vocabulary in other fields not quite so closely tied to home life has been erased by borrowing from less ideologically suspect foreign sources (i.e., Russian words adopted into modern standard Bulgarian to replace most of the Turkish, or Latin/French/Italian terms adapted into Romanian to replace Slavic and Turkish). Another common means of linguistic "purification" was the creation of neologisms, purportedly reviving "authentic" words that had died out during the centuries of Turkish oppression. Standardization also involved choosing between adopting a specific dialect to serve as the backbone for a modern literary language or adapting a

[2] William Miller, "The Changing Role of the Orthodox Church," *Foreign Affairs* 8 (1930), 280.

[3] Vivian Pinto, "Bulgarian," in *The Slavic Literary Languages: Formation and Development*, ed. Alexander Schenker and Edward Stankiewicz (Columbus, OH: Slavica, 1980), 46.

"classic" form of the written language (Church Slavonic and Attic or New Testament/Byzantine Greek) to suit modern needs. Modern Bulgarian was based on the dialect of east-central Bulgaria, which throve economically and culturally in the mid-nineteenth century, for example, while Serbian's dialectal basis was Hercegovinan, with some later adaptation toward Belgrade speech (cf. German and Dutch, which became distinct languages through standardization of separate Germanic dialects). This geographic separation and concomitant dialectal variance, along with the Bulgarian adoption of many Russian words, explain much of the difference between modern Serbian and Bulgarian (Serbian nouns retain case endings, for example, which Bulgarian lost when, after much discussion among early linguists, the dialectal practice of attaching the definite article to the end of the noun was adopted as the literary standard). The independent state of Greece vacillated between demotic and the modernized-archaic Katharevousa until finally opting for the former as the official language in 1976, and demotic itself had no common form until the independence period. Modern Albanian and Romanian similarly resulted from ultimately state-supported standardization.

Yet the Balkans did form an ecumene, regardless of linguistic variety, and Orthodox Christianity bound the commonality together. Modern nationalism avers that the church kept alive national consciousness during the dark centuries of Turkish oppression, but such claims are unproven and almost certainly unprovable. There was no ethnic monopoly on appointment to supposedly national church positions (the "Serbian" patriarchate of Peć [Kosovo] and the "Bulgarian" archbishopric of Ohrid [Macedonia] had no ethnic nature either formally or in practice), and the church as an Ottoman-dependent institution had no interest in stoking disruptive ethnic divisions.[4] With few exceptions, the figures of early

---

[4] Frederick Anscombe, "The Ottoman Empire in Recent Politics, II – the Case of Kosovo," *IHR* 28 (2006), 758–93; Paschalis Kitromilides, "'Imagined Communities' and the Origins of the National Question in the Balkans," in *Modern Greece: Nationalism and Nationality*, ed. Martin Blinkhorn and Thanos Veremis (Athens: ELIAMEP, 1990). The notion that the Peć patriarchate was Serbian derives from the "Serbian" origin of its Bosnian-born founder, the vizier Sokollu Mehmed Pasha. Mehmed was not serving Serbian interests but his own, by consolidating control over a key part of the empire at a time of imperial uncertainty and turmoil in the Balkans. Serbian historiography notes that Mehmed appointed a brother or cousin to the new patriarchate but never mentions that he also placed another (Muslim) relative, Mustafa Pasha, in the governorship of Buda from 1566 to 1578, thus securing one of the most important offices in the Balkans, that of commander of the frontier with the Habsburg empire. Claudia Römer, "On Some Hass-Estates Illegally Claimed by Arslan Paša, Beglerbegi of Buda 1565–1566," in Heywood and Imber (eds.), *Studies in Ottoman History*, 299.

Balkan national "awakening" either were not Ottoman subjects or were expatriates who discovered their ideas of national identity while living and studying in cities such as Paris and Vienna; the main exception was the founding figure of Bulgarian nationalism, Paisii (1722–73), a monk in Hilandar (part of the complex of monasteries at Mt. Athos in northern Greece – a monastery now viewed by Serbs as having been "Serbian"), who wrote a *Slaveno-Bulgarian History* in 1762. Even this work reflected a foreign source, as it drew heavily upon a Russian version of *The Realm of the Slavs* by the Dalmatian Catholic monk Mauro Orbini (1601), and it appears to have been a reaction to Graecophony in the late eighteenth century Orthodox Church, rather than a clarion call to national self-determination. Although numerous copies of his manuscript survive, it was not published until 1844, and Paisii's history aroused little reaction until well into the nineteenth century.

Activists who developed their nationalist ideals abroad and crossed into Ottoman territory to awaken the nation made little discernable impact upon the stability of the empire. Rhigas Velestinlis, for example, was a pamphleteer, poet, and early apostle of "Greek" (meaning in effect Orthodox Christian) nationalism who lived in Vienna. From his Habsburg base he tried to spark a revolution among the Ottoman Orthodox, but, having no success, he attempted to cross into Ottoman territory to start an uprising in 1797. Appalled by Rhigas's reckless scheme, a "Greek" merchant in Trieste told the Habsburg authorities about his plans before the revolutionary could cross the border; Velestinlis was arrested and transferred to Ottoman authorities in Belgrade, who ensured his ignominious end. In the later nineteenth century the Bulgarian revolutionary Georgi Rakovski (1821–67) had no more effect than Rhigas had – and, given his lack of stability, this should cause no wonder. Christened Subi Rakoval, Rakovski subsequently adopted almost a dozen different names, took up a succession of national citizenships, and adapted his still-fluid literary "Bulgarian" to reflect his identity or residence of the moment. He altered his surname to *Rakovski* in order to sound Polish, but, in the absence of an independent Poland, he had to be content at various times with Greek, Serbian, Romanian, or Russian citizenship and a name to match. The need to escape creditors prompted many of these changes of name and nationality. Rakovski was the archetypal impractical romantic, incapable of either planning or organization, and was a failure in business, politics, and revolution.[5] Vasil Levski (1837–73),

---

[5] Mari Firkatian, *The Forest Traveler: Georgi Stoikov Rakovski and Bulgarian Nationalism* (London: Peter Lang, 1996).

another Bulgarian revolutionary, was more noteworthy than Rakovski and Rhigas in that he actually traveled in Ottoman territory to prepare an uprising, but, his location possibly having been given to Ottoman authorities by a priest, he was arrested and executed as a common criminal.[6] Both Rakovski and Levski achieved fame posthumously through promotion by post-Ottoman regimes that anointed them heroes of the nation. The Macedonian Jane Sandanski (1872–1915) of IMRO was killed by rival revolutionaries, thus meeting the same fate that he had inflicted on several onetime colleagues. He, too, was championed posthumously by a regime building its own legitimacy, in this case the post-1945 communist government of Bulgaria, which renamed the (overly Orthodox-sounding) town of Sveti Vrač after him. Of this short but sordid roster of activists, only Sandanski could plausibly be said to have had any impact while alive, given the importance of the Macedonian Question in late Ottoman history.

Creating a clear national identity was a significant challenge to the newly independent states of the Balkans following their creation by the great powers of Europe. The nineteenth-century post-Ottoman Christian states were weak, insofar as they all struggled to find a natural ideological basis of legitimacy that could support a stable relationship between rulers and ruled. With a short-lived exception in Serbia, no head of state or government had won independence through heading a successful liberation struggle, none was a native leader who had inherited a traditional leadership status through royal or even "aristocratic" birth, and none was elected by popular mandate. All were placed in authority by action of European Christian powers or simply were in the right place at the right time; many of those who sought political influence were fringe figures, nonnatives either from non-Ottoman Europe or from elsewhere in the empire. All regimes therefore adopted legitimacy-building programs that depended on teaching the people that they formed a great nation fated by the cruelty of others to need a strong state that could protect them and finish the liberation of unredeemed members of the nation and its ancestral homelands. Until the people absorbed that lesson and accepted the legitimacy of the national regime, each of the new-found states adopted a program of irredentism, giving a purpose to the massive expansion of

---

[6] Maria Todorova has written a study of the mantle of Levski as an object of competition for the Bulgarian church since the end of the communist period (*Bones of Contention: The Living Archive of Vasil Levski and the Making of Bulgaria's National Hero* [Budapest: Central European University Press, 2009]) but, reflecting the scantiness of evidence about Levski, gives little account of his life rather than his image.

bureaucratic and military institutions that were designed to consolidate the state's hold over newly won territory and population.[7] As the first step of such consolidation, and in order to give the nation-building program any chance of success, the new states co-opted the church, the focus of the main sense of identity beyond the local level that most of the population had ever felt.

GREECE

As Greece was the first independent country, its response served as a model for later states including Serbia, Bulgaria, Romania, Albania, and, in the twentieth century, Macedonia. Greece won independence after the Russian defeat of the Ottoman empire recognized in the Peace of Edirne in 1829. Those who had borne the main burden of fighting against reassertion of Ottoman control had no clear idea of struggling for creation of a new but equally distant national regime, and the first president of the Greek republic, Ioannis Kapodistrias, originally from Corfu but by profession a diplomat for Russia who had spent most of the period of the Greek revolt in Switzerland, quickly alienated notables who had fought, leading to his assassination in 1831. His brother tried to succeed him but failed to establish order; the solution to the infighting was the importation of a Bavarian prince, patently non-Greek, to become king of Greece. No Greek was party to the Anglo-French-Russian-Bavarian negotiations and agreement to install Prince Otto von Wittelsbach. The simple choice of Otto's capital illustrated the absence of indigenous Greek influence on arrangements: in 1834 Athens was a village of between two thousand and four thousand inhabitants.[8] Otto (who became King Othon in 1833) and his entourage of German ministers, supported by a large force of German and Swiss mercenaries, created a state modeled on what they had known from post-Napoleonic western European practice, setting up the principal tools to be used to forge the disparate regional and ethnolinguistic grouplets into a national unit: an educational system to provide compulsory schooling, a national army, a national church, a national university to take the message of Greekness to Ottoman Orthodox populations

[7] Victor Roudometof, "The Social Origins of Balkan Politics: Nationalism, Underdevelopment, and the Nation-State in Greece, Serbia, and Bulgaria, 1880–1920," *Mediterranean Quarterly* 11 (2000), 144–63.

[8] Konrad Clewing and Oliver Jens Schmitt (eds.), *Geschichte Südosteuropas vom Mittelalter bis zur Gegenwart* (Regensburg: Verlag Friedrich Pustet, 2011), 531.

outside the new state's borders, and a national law code to empower the new institutions.[9]

It would have made little sense for either the brief-lived republic or the monarchy to have justified itself ideologically by championing Orthodox Christianity, because only a small minority of the Ottoman Orthodox population lived within the new country's borders and the Patriarchate of Constantinople, which still exerted strong influence over the Orthodox within the new country, had an unremittingly hostile attitude toward first the revolt and then the independent state. In working to build national identity, therefore, Othon began by prompting the creation of an explicitly national autocephalous church in 1833 and then protecting it in the face of opposition from the Patriarchate, which refused to acknowledge it even implicitly until 1850, when Russia mediated an agreement. The beleaguered condition of the new church made it wholly dependent on the state, and it was run by a synod whose members from 1833 until 1852 were appointed by the monarchy; thereafter, no decision of the reformed synod was valid until signed by the state's representative. The church paid for such dependency by adopting fully the state's vision of the nation, and from the late nineteenth century until today, the church has taken a lead role in all nationalist initiatives.[10]

Until 1923, nationalist initiatives related in some way to the Megali Idea (The Great Idea), which was adopted by the state as its mission from 1844: the liberation of unredeemed Greeks still under Ottoman (and patriarchal) control (for the scope of the Megali Idea as conceived in the early twentieth century, see Map 2). The term "Great Idea" was coined in 1844 by a politician, Ioannis Kolettis, during parliamentary debate on a new constitution introduced by Othon following a military coup. The coup showed the frustration of autochthonous (native-born) notables who, freed of Kapodistrias, found themselves subordinated to an equally alien monarchy that, insofar as it drew "Greeks" into power, relied upon Phanariotes and other nonnatives, including many like Kapodistrias from the diaspora in Europe. One of the significant changes introduced after the coup was the reservation of most state offices to autochthons. With

---

[9] The following discussion draws on Paschalis Kitromilides, "'Imagined Communities'"; Clogg, "Greek Millet"; Barbara Jelavich, *History of the Balkans, vol. I, Eighteenth and Nineteenth Centuries* (Cambridge: Cambridge University Press, 1983); Victor Roudometof, "Invented Traditions"; William McGrew, *Land and Revolution in Modern Greece, 1800–1881: The Transition in the Tenure and Exploitation of Land from Ottoman Rule to Independence* (Kent, OH: Kent State University Press, 1985).

[10] Kitromilides, "'Imagined Communities,'" 166.

the Megali Idea Kolettis, born in Epirus and thus a heterochthon (not native to the area that became the Kingdom of Greece in 1833), justified the continued presence of nonnatives in Greek public affairs. Othon naturally supported his fellow nonnatives and made Kolettis prime minister in 1844.[11] His embrace of the heterochthon Megali Idea ensured its influence, despite its audacity; in the state's new liberation mission "Greek" had no ethnolinguistic meaning but signified Orthodox, presenting a direct challenge to the Istanbul patriarchate as well as the Ottoman state.

Having an audacious reason for being helped the monarchy to achieve what the republic had failed to do: give a plausible rationale for drawing the array of military bands left over from the revolt under some element of central control. The new army performed several vital functions in nation building. First, while it was still dominated by the German and Swiss mercenaries, it gave the state the military supremacy, if not a monopoly over the use of force, that it needed to gain internal and foreign recognition. Second, it legitimated the redirection of remaining military bands and bandits away from the kingdom's present territory toward neighboring lands – a pressing need, because the pastoral economy of populations that had provided much of the fighting forces of the Greek revolt had been badly damaged by the imposition of new, constricting borders.[12] Third, through mandatory military service for all Greek males, it trained its variegated recruits not only militarily but educationally, in language and national thinking, drumming into soldiers the belief that they were all part of a new community, regardless of their fellows' strange speech or ways, and posting recruits away from their home region to make them familiar with the idea of a bigger homeland than they previously could have conceived. This kind of conscripted army, whose primary purpose was political rather than military, did not create a very effective fighting force but did help in forging the nation; it also became an increasingly popular model for ordering the military in other countries from the late nineteenth century, not only in the post-Ottoman Balkans, Turkey, and Arab states but around the world.

---

[11] On heterochthon-autochthon rivalry, see Socrates Petmezas, "From Privileged Outcasts to Power Players: the 'Romantic' Redefinition of the Hellenic Nation in the Mid-Nineteenth Century," in *The Making of Modern Greece: Nationalism, Romanticism, and the Uses of the Past (1797–1896)*, ed. Roderick Beaton and David Ricks (Farnham: Ashgate, 2009), 123–35.

[12] John Koliopoulos, "Brigandage and Irredentism in Nineteenth-Century Greece," in Blinkhorn and Veremis (eds.), *Modern Greece*, 79, 84.

With time, the educational mission of the Greek military could build upon the basic schooling that also became compulsory from 1834. Othon's government set up a system of primary schools that expanded over subsequent decades, and the net of secondary schools also grew, although the latter were less effective in their mission of teaching students useful skills than the primary schools were in spreading knowledge of spoken and rudimentary written Katharevousa Greek. Katharevousa was the natural choice over local demotic for a state shaped by Bavarians and other nonlocals who came to champion the Megali Idea, a program directed as much toward other Ottoman lands as toward the kingdom's population, and a program whose expansionism was legitimated by classical, Byzantine, and church history. Drawing upon the forms of Greek associated with those three histories, however, Katharevousa proved an awkward literary language, as writers developed a range of styles according to which form(s) they chose to emulate.[13] In line with teaching Katharevousa, schools naturally also preached the idea of the nation and the citizen's duties to it.

Capping the education of Greek citizens in the ethos of the nation and simultaneously providing active outreach to the unredeemed Orthodox of Ottoman lands was Athens University, founded in 1837. The university had two main functions: providing trained graduates fit for government service and educating unredeemed Greeks, both by recruiting candidates from Ottoman lands to study in Athens and by training teachers to staff schools abroad. Such schoolteachers, imbued with the ethos of the nation, became active proselytizers of the Megali Idea among the Ottoman Orthodox, although their efficacy in building Greek national identity in the unredeemed population remained limited.

None of these new institutions resonated with the bulk of the population outside Athens, which appeared content to continue living according to local custom. The Bavarian monarchy therefore introduced by 1835 a revised version of the Code Napoléon, Bonaparte's "greatest achievement," devised as a tool to unify the French "nation" and tie it to the state. The alien code was often disappointing in practice, but nevertheless it did ultimately prove an important tool for building the nation and subduing the recalcitrant population to the center's control, in this sense empowering the state. The courts established to enforce the imported law

[13] W. B. Lockwood, "Language and the Rise of Nations," *Science and Society* 18 (1954), 250. Roudometof, "Invented Traditions," 441, notes the curriculum of secondary education, which stressed instruction in classical Greek.

were notoriously ineffective and arbitrary in most matters throughout the century, but in order to ensure that the two main compulsory nation-building tools would be effective, the state judicial system prosecuted more zealously anyone who tried to evade either school or military service than it did many other criminals.[14]

By grafting a new identity upon the entrenched Christian and local sensibilities of the still largely rudely lettered and peasant population, the independent monarchy of Greece achieved its reason for being and its mission, but these crudely artificial props, and the essentially sterile and self-serving nature of the mission, gave the state neither stability nor prosperity. Othon, a devout Catholic, did not convert to Orthodoxy and was never fully accepted because of his foreign faith and advisers. He had to dismiss his expensive German mercenaries by the end of the 1830s and his Bavarian aides by 1843, when effective bankruptcy and the coup by the Athens garrison forced him to accept a constitution that would make the state more "Greek." In addition to agreeing to a basic constitution at that time, it was also then settled that any offspring who might succeed him would be raised in the Orthodox faith. Remaining childless, however, and still well placed to play a very active role in state affairs, he was dethroned by another military coup in 1862, to be replaced by a Danish prince who resolved the religious issue by marrying a Russian princess and ensuring that successors in his line would be Orthodox. Since Othon resisted giving any real authority to ministers, who served at his pleasure, his opponents had little to gain from political creativity or stability, and political cliques remained so clearly tied to the foreign powers that had created the state and still had leverage with the king that they were known as the French, Russian, and British parties. Only one prime minister, Charilaos Trikoupis (who favored "autochthon" policies while in office, repeatedly but often briefly, from 1875 to 1895), showed much interest in improving the administration of the state and the well-being of its citizens – an effort that, as in the Ottoman empire, quickly led to officially acknowledged bankruptcy. Much of his reform program, moreover, was undone by his main rival of the 1880s and 1890s, Theodoros Deligiannis, who reasserted the prime importance of the Megali Idea.[15] The Great Idea soon led Deligiannis and the military into the ill-judged

---

[14] McGrew, *Land and Revolution*, chap. 6; Kitromilides, "'Imagined Communities,'" 164–5.

[15] Thanos Veremis, *The Military in Greek Politics: From Independence to Democracy* (London: C. Hurst, 1997), 39–40.

attack on the Ottoman empire in 1897 that did much to destroy whatever credibility remained to a state whose legitimacy had been tied to its role as leader and defender of the nation.

In the absence of mature civilian politics, the military was the most influential secular institution created by the state over the nineteenth century. Supported by all political contenders, from the monarch to ministers such as Deligiannis and even Trikoupis, the military absorbed much of the state budget and suffered no retribution for its periodic interventions in politics. This condition led to a seemingly peculiar but ultimately typical result, in that the military was necessary and successful in the project of building the nation, but in the longer term its prominence damaged the country and the members of that nation. Maintenance of the large army that nation building and the Megali Idea required consumed more than half of the Greek state budget, straining resources and helping to crimp economic development. The wealth spent on the military nevertheless did not buy war-making efficiency, as the experience of 1897 demonstrated.

In that year Istanbul was preoccupied by a Christian insurrection in Crete sparked in part by agitators sent to the island from Greece, providing Deligiannis and the military an opportunity to probe the viability of seizing new territory in pursuit of the Great Idea. This was not the first time that Greek governments and military leadership had been tempted to take revanchist action, but in the past Greece had been spared most of the negative results that could be expected from such adventurism. Signs of Greek mobilization at the beginning of the Crimean War and in 1885, when Serbia attacked Bulgaria, had drawn British naval blockades to warn the government and military not to attempt provocative action. This did not happen in 1897, however, and the army invaded neighboring Ottoman territory on the mainland. The military's amateurish performance in the ensuing brief war gave Greece a humiliating defeat. Great power intervention prevented the loss of any significant territory (and indeed pushed Crete closer to absorption into Greece), but Greece had to pay a war indemnity, which only worsened the country's financial woes. Much as they did to the Ottoman empire after the Treaty of Berlin in 1878, the powers imposed a financial control board on Greece to ensure the repayment of state debt to foreign bondholders, sealing the collapse of legitimacy of the state as the leader and defender of the nation.[16]

---

[16] Thanos Veremis, "From the National State to the Stateless Nation 1821–1910," in Blinkhorn and Veremis (eds.), *Modern Greece*, 15.

Unlike the civilian-run state, the military did not suffer a similar collapse in stature or political power, leaving it as the most influential political force outside the monarchy until it imported Eleftherios Venizelos from Crete to Athens as the new face of government in 1910 following a coup. Like Kolettis a heterochthon, Venizelos became an accomplished politician by proving more astute at rallying public emotion across the kingdom than any previous figure, becoming thereby the dynamic force of Greek politics until 1920 – but at base the ideological element of his success was little more than revitalization of the Megali Idea, which the disaster of 1897 had tainted. Venizelos was a populist, in that he addressed himself to the entirety of the kingdom's population as well as the ethnic nation outside the borders – indeed, he traveled through the country as no other politician had – but he, too, achieved surprisingly little to better the lot of the population. His main achievements at this time were in military and revanchist affairs: the seizure of Salonica and southern Macedonia in the Balkan Wars, Greece's entry into the First World War on the side of the Entente in 1917, and the campaign to seize western Anatolia launched in 1919. The first two involved relatively little fighting or other costs, and Venizelos left office before the Anatolian campaign ended in disaster. Within the country, he introduced modest change at best.[17]

One of his shortcomings was his failure to develop a mature party that could represent a clear idea or ideology beyond irredentism. His adherents were not liberals, conservatives, or agrarians; they were Venizelists. His most significant nonroyal rival in the 1910s, Dimitrios Gounaris, did represent an idea of pursuing progress within the kingdom, much in line with what Trikoupis had attempted, but he had little opportunity to implement his plans for improving the lot of workers and the underclass. He formed a government after Venizelos's fall in 1920 and was in power when the Anatolian campaign collapsed, for which "act of treason" against the nation he was executed in 1922. Venizelos's era thus maintained in large measure the personal nature of politics seen since the decades of the French, Russian, and British parties.

Another reason why Venizelos's favorable reputation has survived fairly well was that he entered Greek politics at a time when, under a constitution revised in 1911, some of the worst effects of the political system began to be controlled. The constitution included clauses designed to

[17] Mark Mazower, "The Messiah and the Bourgeoisie: Venizelos and Politics in Greece, 1909–1912," *Historical Journal* 35 (1992), 885–904.

stop the wholesale discharge of bureaucrats when government leadership changed. Whenever government had changed party hands, there had been a mass changeover of state employees, an exchanging of the clients of the ousted party with those of the new. This practice had promoted both bureaucratic inefficiency and government expenditure, helping to keep Greece mired in underdevelopment throughout the nineteenth and into the twentieth century. Given the slow growth of agriculture and the low level of manufacturing, however, for many Greeks this personal characteristic of politics offered the best chance for an improvement of circumstances through gaining employment by the state itself, and the key to finding state employment for people of nonnotable background was attachment to a patron.

Patronage was the product of the system of government established after 1833, and its ill effects extended beyond the distribution of state jobs to those whose qualifications might not go far beyond correct clientage. Othon and his Bavarian advisers devised from nothing a state that they hoped would survive; nationalism was cultivated to legitimate it and was an ideology into which the various factions of the revolutionary and post-1833 eras could be co-opted (or, if necessary, bought into), but the imported monarch needed to keep the levers of power in reliable hands. Until 1843, this meant mainly Bavarian hands, but even after the constitution took effect, Othon appointed ministers according to their potential for causing turmoil if ignored and then dismissed them before they could become entrenched in power – a system that encouraged political hopefuls to build portfolios of both clients and patrons, including the ambassadors of foreign powers. Only in the later nineteenth century did elections clearly influence the shape of government. Office inevitably became a spoils system used to consolidate and expand client networks. Patronage also guided the legal system: the courts may have pursued those who avoided military service and schooling, but in other matters the legal system prosecuted or let drop cases according to the influence of the parties involved.[18] Lacking a professional bureaucracy, the state relied for collection of revenues upon loosely policed tax farmers who, much like those in the pre-1839 Ottoman empire, absorbed a significant part of the money due the state and frequently gouged the payers. In addition to the fact that the state treasury never received the full sums nominally due

[18] Rodanthi Tzanelli, "Haunted by the 'Enemy' Within: Brigandage, Vlachian/Albanian 'Greekness,' Turkish 'Contamination,' and Narratives of Greek Nationhood in the Dilessi/Marathon Affair (1870)," *JMGS* 20 (2002), 50.

it, peasants suffered in that they found themselves paying more in Greece than they had in the Ottoman empire, and the bleak prospects for any improvement in their lot prompted a steady exodus back into Ottoman lands.[19]

One further bone of contention in the countryside was control or ownership of land, and support for those trying to make the land productive. The notables who led the fight against the Ottomans took some of the land previously held by the Muslims who were killed or driven out, and the state took the rest. Lacking any understanding of Ottoman law, the Bavarian monarchy in its new law code classed practically all peasants as sharecroppers, stripping them of heritable tenancy rights and increasing dues to their "landlord," the state (which fortunately was frequently too weak or disorganized to collect). The state lacked the will to take land from the notables and could not risk using the army for such a purpose, and more damningly it did not attempt to distribute its own holdings, as had been promised by leaders during the revolt to encourage recruitment. It delayed a cadastral survey of the kingdom (Greece still has no effective land registry), and without it peasant property rights were practically unenforceable, even were the court system in better health. The state offered to sell land to cultivators, but, since most lacked the necessary sums, it rented fields on a sharecropping basis instead. If a farmer occupied land for thirty years without paying the usufruct fee to the state, he could claim ownership, and by the late nineteenth century a significant but almost accidental transfer of land to peasant smallholders occurred, boosted by the land squatting encouraged by poor oversight by the bureaucracy.[20] Agriculture consistently constituted more than 70 percent of Greek gross national product in the nineteenth century, but the state practically ignored the sector. It established no agricultural bank, agricultural school, or other significant support structures or extension services prior to the twentieth century, except for projects initiated by Trikoupis to improve transport infrastructure. In effect, the nation-building state looked to its own survival and its interests in the "unredeemed" part of the nation still in Ottoman lands, leaving the bulk of the population in the kingdom essentially unattended.

Greece's experience was replicated in other emerging post-Ottoman countries, with minor variations. The model of the state was imported from elsewhere in Europe, constructed quickly and with the goal of

---

[19] Clogg, "Greek Millet," 195.
[20] McGrew, *Land and Revolution*, 215–24; Roudometof, "Social Origins," 147

survivability in an unsettled environment, and legitimated through the molding of the population to match a simple ideology of the nation. Serbia and Bulgaria followed the same route, although neither suffered as severely from pressures of time and circumstance as Othon's Greece had.

SERBIA

Serbia's path to independence was more attenuated than Greece's, offering both benefits and drawbacks to political development. It gained autonomy from 1829 but won independence only in 1878, when the Treaty of Berlin ended Ottoman suzerainty. Its half-century of limited sovereignty might be seen as hampering national and state development, but the form of national identity fostered during this transition period was more clearly drawn than in the case of Greece, where the only crucial ingredient required for potential membership in the nation was Orthodox Christianity. Serbian nationalism certainly shared this defining religious characteristic, but to it was added an ethnolinguistic element. Serbian nation-building regimes adopted a revanchist program, much as Greece had done, but it was more clearly targeted at specific adjoining lands than the Megali Idea, which was to propel Greece to the Anatolian debacle of 1919–22.

Some of this slower, more practical development can be attributed to the extended period of rule by Serbia's first "royal," Miloš Obrenović. Unlike any other post-Ottoman leader in the Balkans, Miloš had some claim to having achieved position by demonstrating accomplished leadership in service of "his" people. Like Karadjordje Petrović, the leader of the 1804 Serbian uprising, Miloš was an illiterate former minor provincial notable; he replaced Karadjordje as "leader of Serbia" from 1814, after Karadjordje had fled to Bessarabia via Habsburg lands and Belgrade had once again been reclaimed to Ottoman authority. When Ottoman reprisals triggered renewed rebellion, Miloš provided the leadership (and killed Karadjordje, who returned to Belgrade to try to reclaim his old position in 1817). It was Russian pressure on Istanbul that assured Miloš's survival and the loosening of Ottoman pressure, but nevertheless he was firmly entrenched in his leadership position by the time autonomy was won in the Peace of Edirne. He ruled his princedom according to the stereotype of a "Turkish pasha," treating "state" property as his own and bolstering his authority by upholding Orthodox Christian faith and practice. After autonomy was assured, he asserted control over the local church hierarchy, naming his own secretary as metropolitan of Belgrade, but unlike Othon in Greece he did not court opposition by severing ties to the ecumenical patriarchate in Istanbul. He blocked potential secular rivals from establishing control over rural areas by outlawing seizure of farm homesteads for debt; he also established a system of village grana-ries to prevent serious famine and distributed land to immigrants. With these measures he consolidated among the peasantry a lasting inclination toward the Obrenović dynasty that other royal houses in the Balkans could not really match.

In other respects, however, Miloš showed little interest in active devel-opment of the country, promotion of the well-being of it population, or expansion of the state. He was, in short, a premodern ruler with the very limited "state" interests characteristic of that age. Little investment went into education, the bureaucracy, or even the military; these developments were to come later. As in Greece, where Othon's "Bavarian regency" fos-tered frustration among aspirers to influence, Miloš's domination irritated notables, who petitioned Istanbul for new regulations of government. Istanbul obliged by issuing a "Turkish Constitution" for the autonomous province in 1838, causing Miloš to abdicate in 1839 rather than accept diminution of his authority. On his resignation, his household "state" had 672 employees, of whom 201 were police; by 1842, the number of state employees grew to 1,151. Since the population of Serbia remained over-whelmingly illiterate through much of the nineteenth century (in 1866 the literacy rate was still below 5 percent), the growing cadre of civil servants came from the Serbs of Habsburg Vojvodina.[21]

It was these "heterochthons" who pushed first and most strongly the idea of Serbian nationalism, at least at government level and in urban areas, as a means of strengthening their own position and legitimacy as authorities in a land to which they were not native.[22] In this they had a de facto ally in the prince enthroned in 1843, after Miloš's young son was ousted: Aleksandar Karadjordjević, a son of Karadjordje, who also had weak roots in the autonomous land, having grown up and been schooled in exile, returning only on Miloš's abdication. Perhaps because of the Obrenović stature in the rural areas, neither the prince nor the expanding bureaucracy exhibited much interest in the peasant mass of

[21] Roudometof, "Invented Traditions," 444; Jelavich, *History of the Balkans I*, 242; Palairet, *The Balkan Economies, c. 1800–1914* (Cambridge: Cambridge University Press, 1997), 88.
[22] Stokes, "Absence of Nationalism."

the population, concentrating instead on the small urban and mercantile sectors. They wrested from the Orthodox Church control over education, and hence gained the ability to shape a nation-building curriculum, but much of the population, particularly those resident in villages, remained unserved by the school system. In the period of bureaucratic dominance, the state took the first clear steps toward building national identity in the towns, but the main focus was on the expansion of the civil service and improvements in its conditions of employment, the strengthening of the state's domestic power through the police and the legal system (the Vojvodinan bureaucratic leaders introduced in 1844 a national law code derived from the Austrian adaptation of the Code Napoléon), and the breaking apart of trade monopolies previously held by Miloš.

Under the influence of the Vojvodinan bureaucrats, the state did adopt a program similar to the Megali Idea in 1844, although any concrete effort to realize it was long delayed, in part as a result of Serbia's liminal status of autonomy but not independence. The program was laid out in the *Načertanije* (the Draft), which called for the liberation of all Orthodox Slavs still under Ottoman rule, as well as those in Habsburg lands (for the territory that Serbia would claim by the early twentieth century, see Map 3). It was composed on the order of the interior minister Ilija Garašanin, who was a native of Habsburg Vojvodina, but Franjo Zach, the author of the document, was even more clearly nonnative. Zach was Czech and was in Serbia at the time only as an emissary from Prince Adam Czartoryski, the Polish aristocrat and notable figure in liberal-national politics of Europe in the 1830s–40s.[23] Czartoryski had sent Zach with the aim of stirring national liberationist sentiment, hoping to use an activist Serbia as a tool to distract Russia and Austria, the powers that controlled much of Poland.

It was under Miloš's son Mihailo (1860–8), who assumed the throne after his father had returned briefly to authority following the fall of Aleksandar Karadjordjević in 1858, that Serbia first took steps that could lead to activation of the *Načertanije* program. Mihailo introduced a form of military conscription and adopted a newly assertive stance toward liberation of the autonomous homeland from vestiges of Ottoman control. True to the Obrenović practice of relying on the rural population for support, the early efforts to boost Serbia's military strength involved little more than distributing guns to the peasants, who then formed a

---

[23] Gale Stokes, *Politics as Development: The Emergence of Political Parties in Nineteenth-Century Serbia* (Durham, NC: Duke University Press, 1990), 109.

militia-cum-nation-in-arms. In political terms, Serbia under Mihailo (who was assassinated by Karadjordjević supporters in 1868) and his successor Milan devoted much of the 1860s to pressing for the removal of the remaining Ottoman garrisons in his autonomous domain, efforts that ultimately proved successful, and consequently the 1870s became the period in which the Serbian state first adopted seriously a program of revanchism abroad.

Under Milan Obrenović, a very young ruler who had been schooled in France and had become an enthusiastic proponent of the nation-building project, the state encouraged the placement of educators or agents in Ottoman lands targeted in the *Načertanije*. Teachers dispatched into Bosnia, for example, toured villages around Sarajevo to persuade peasants to stop calling themselves Orthodox Christians and declare themselves Serbs. These nation-building efforts were only marginally successful in overcoming established identities by the time of the uprising in Hercegovina and Bosnia that sparked the eastern crisis of 1875–8, but nevertheless the revolt has come to be portrayed as a rebellion of Serbs (and Croats) against the Turks.[24] As noted in Chapter 4, moreover, armed revolutionaries dispatched from Serbia had played a crucial role in sparking and then fanning the uprising. The money spent by Mihailo and Milan on boosting the army's strength (much of it wasted) led Milan into declaring war on Serbia's suzerain in support of the rebels in Bosnia, a disastrous decision that required great power intervention to save Belgrade from Ottoman reconquest. Military collapse incurred no penalty, however, as Serbia gained both independence and further territory from Russia's victory over the Ottomans in 1878.

Gain after defeat meant that far from discouraging revanchism, the military debacle led to much greater investment and attention given to the army, a step that also required at last that serious attention be given to the mass of the population (84 percent in 1900) who worked the land and had been left little affected by the course of Serbian politics and national development since 1829. The urban sector, dependent so heavily upon state employment, was too small (Belgrade's population in 1874 was a mere twenty-eight thousand) to fund or man significant military expansion, and thus the rural population had to be drawn into the political arena. Formal independence eased the expansion of efforts to boost the nation, including through increased outreach to the rural population,

---

[24] Roudometof, "Invented Traditions," 451, 455–7.

which was a useful tool for boosting extraction of resources from the countryside. Added purpose and resources were directed into education to teach the youth of the nation its language, history (with the epic of the 1389 Battle of Kosovo stressed), and geography, which included lands still in Ottoman hands. History became the second-most-studied subject at Belgrade University, after law (another lively field in young post-Ottoman states). Nation strengthening also generated more open avowal of intentions to expand in accord with Garašanin's *Načertanije*. One sign of this new push was the regime's decision to change (again) the standard literary language to adopt the "South Serbian" dialectic pronunciation found in the region around Skopje, an area that became a more desirable avenue for expansion after Austria-Hungary occupied Bosnia in 1878. Belgrade's confidence in its ability to realize any such territorial expansion rose with signs of success in efforts to reach the rural population: in addition to providing the manpower for the expanding army, per capita taxation of the rural population rose by 76 percent from 1879/81 to 1887/91.[25]

Intensification of nationalization also necessitated maintenance of the bonds between state and church. The national curriculum taught through the expanding school system, for example, continued to include substantial study of Orthodox Christianity and Church Slavonic.[26] The state's achievement of independence in 1878, however, led to its tighter control over the church, helping to tie the hierarchy more firmly to the nation-building project, as had happened in Greece. The church became a fully "Serbian" institution, being granted autocephaly by the patriarchate in Istanbul in 1879; cutting the last links to the patriarchate left the hierarchy isolated in any effort to resist state dominance over the church. In 1881 King Milan succeeded in dismissing the metropolitan of Belgrade and his four bishops for thoroughly worldly reasons of state and nation building, namely, their refusal to levy a new state tax on church appointments. The dismissals caused a rancorous, drawn-out dispute, but Milan and his government prevailed. Thereafter the church maintained its active profile in public affairs but as an institution fundamentally loyal to the Serbian state. This loyalty led the Belgrade regime of the new Kingdom of Serbs, Croats, and Slovenes (Yugoslavia) to subsume into the Serbian

[25] Palairet, *Balkan Economies*, 305.
[26] Jelavich, *South Slav Nationalisms*, 32–40, 144, 269–70; Stokes, *Politics as Development*, 217–19.

church the various Orthodox hierarchies in the territories awarded it after 1918.[27]

Orthodoxy's centrality in the self-image of the developing Serbian nation, however, meant that Milan's dispute with the church damaged his reputation, especially among the rural population that had favored the Obrenović line. The harm done by the dispute was subsequently worsened by a long-running series of open conflicts between Milan and his wife that deflated the monarchy's image across the country, and Milan's legitimacy as leader of the nation that was being so assiduously promoted suffered from another embarrassing military defeat in 1885–6. In 1885 autonomous Bulgaria united with the Ottoman province of Eastern Rumelia (now southern and eastern Bulgaria, including Bulgaria's second city, Plovdiv), thereby greatly increasing its size and regional consequence and thus sparking a diplomatic crisis; Milan opted to attack Bulgaria in hopes of using the crisis to seize territory as compensation for Sofia's gains. Against all expectations, the Bulgarians defeated the Serbs convincingly.

Milan's multiple failings opened possibilities for parties to exploit, particularly in the onetime pillar of Obrenović rule, the countryside. Early political groupings had formed in part according to pro-Obrenović versus pro-Karadjordjević inclinations, but formal parties only became legal in 1881. The delayed opening to party politics did help to ensure that enough variation in interests and perspectives among seasoned politicians existed to give parties somewhat clearer ideological purpose than in Greece; such ideological competition was focused upon the nationally and politically "aware" urban population, however, leaving the peasant majority unaddressed. Two of the three main post-1881 parties, the Liberals and the Progressives, retained the urban sector's condescending attitude toward the peasantry, but the third, the Radicals, courted the countryside more actively and established itself as the main party by establishing links to the rural bulk of the population.

Like the other parties, the Radicals embraced the *Načertanije* program and thereby also built close ties to the strongly nationalist officer corps of the expanding military, which proved an even more valuable relationship in the long term. The officers grew increasingly alienated from the Obrenović monarchy because the king insisted upon warm relations with

---

[27] Paschalis Kitromilides, "The Orthodox Church in Modern State Formation in South-East Europe," in *Ottomans into Europeans: State and Institution-Building in South-East Europe*, ed. Alina Mungiu-Pippidi and Wim van Meurs (London: Hurst, 2010), 46.

Austria-Hungary. Austro-Hungarian intervention had saved Serbia from more serious losses following the bungled attack upon Bulgaria in 1885. The Obrenović relationship with the far more powerful Austria-Hungary and continued scandals in royal family lives led a cabal of army officers to execute a grisly coup in 1903, during which the last Obrenović, Aleksandar, and his wife were brutally killed.[28] The army once again brought back a Karadjordjević from exile to take the throne, but the military and the Radical Party dominated Serbia from 1903 through the First World War; the Radicals were thus well positioned to extend their preeminence through the first decade of Yugoslavia's existence.

With their party program shaped by pro-Russian, anti-Austrian nationalism and the drive to expand Serbia's borders toward the Adriatic and Aegean, the Radicals ultimately failed to speed the social and economic development of the country, and particularly its dominant rural sector, in part because of the destructive conflicts that the party's nationalism triggered: the economic "Pig War" with Austria-Hungary of 1905–11, the First and Second Balkan Wars (1912–13), and the First World War, in which roughly half of Serbia's adult male population died. The experience of cold and hot conflicts with neighbors carried out since 1876 in the name of the Serbian nation helped to embed the national ideal in the population, however, as did continuing improvement in literacy, which by 1914 had reached 40 percent of the population.[29] This identification of people with nation and thus with the government that protected the nation met the need for legitimacy of the monarchy, the political parties, and the bureaucracy, which helps to explain the stronger support for the interwar Yugoslav monarchy seen in Serbia, as well as the dominant role in Yugoslav affairs played by Serbia under the monarchy.

In practice, the Radical Party, the Karadjordjević dynasty, and indeed all Serbian political institutions were to view the creation of the Kingdom of Serbs, Croats, and Slovenes (Yugoslavia) as the natural culmination of the *Načertanije*. Serbia, which already had taken Kosovo and much of geographic Macedonia in the Balkan Wars of 1912–13, was on the

---

[28] Castellan, *Histoire des Balkans*, 329–30.

[29] The literacy rate was highest among young adults (11–30 years), who constituted 53% of the literate in 1900. Jelavich, *South Slav Nationalisms*, 40. This cohort was the most important in establishing lasting national identity, as they and their children shaped post-1918 Yugoslavia. On the enduring influence of the initial wave of ideological education on political loyalties, see Keith Darden and Anna Grzymala-Busse, "The Great Divide: Literacy, Nationalism, and the Communist Collapse," *World Politics* 59 (2006), 83–115.

eve of the First World War the only independent country other than tiny Montenegro in the lands to be shaped into post-1918 Yugoslavia; at the end of the war, emerging leaders in Slav territories of the Austro-Hungarian empire (Croatia, Bosnia-Hercegovina, and Slovenia) had to look to Serbia's extant army and state institutions as their only effective means of keeping rival claimants to their lands (notably Italy and Hungary) at bay. In a process foreshadowing the absorption of the provinces of the dissolved East Germany into the extant state of West Germany in 1991, these lands and Vojvodina became attached to Serbia. Although most non-Orthodox parties and populations apparently preferred a federalist structure for the postwar state, mainly Orthodox parties (with critical support from the main Bosnian Muslim party, which associated the Croats with Habsburg rule and was promised concessions by Orthodox parties) voted to accept a constitution creating a strongly centralist state headed by the Serbian monarchy (to the chagrin of Montenegro's king). Parliamentary government proved dysfunctional, however, largely because of the dissatisfaction of mainly Catholic parties over Serbian domination of the kingdom. To resolve this ongoing issue decisively in favor of Belgrade, the king, Aleksandar Karadjordjević, abolished parliament in 1929 to establish a monarchical dictatorship that continued until the Nazi occupation of Yugoslavia in 1941. The experience of the Kingdom of Yugoslavia (as it was known between 1929 and 1941) as essentially the "Great Serbia" of the *Načertanije* was to influence Josip Broz Tito, founder of the postwar Republic of Yugoslavia, and the questions of national identity that were to tear post-Tito Yugoslavia apart in the 1990s.

BULGARIA

Independent Bulgaria was created in 1878 by the Christian powers of Europe, more than half a century after they had enforced recognition of Greece and Serbia. Like Serbia, Bulgaria gained some advantage from this later start to national life, but in general it echoed patterns and problems seen in the other Balkan states. The rate of literacy among Bulgarians in some parts of the new country was slightly higher than in Greece and particularly Serbia at independence, especially in eastern parts of the country that had benefited from the textiles-led economic expansion of the Tanzimat period. In Turnovo province, for example, one in fifteen adults was literate in 1881; elsewhere, however, the figures were much more grim, with one in two hundred twelve adults in Vratsa province considered literate.[30] The Bulgarian economy was relatively diversified, with a more substantial industrial base complementing the strong agrarian sector that also characterized the economies of Serbia and Greece. Bulgaria nevertheless faced challenges familiar to the other new states: the strengthening of a weak state, the inculcation of national identity as a means of shoring up the government's base of legitimacy, and the weakening of rival centers of allegiance and identity, including local notables and the Orthodox Church.

Although Bulgarian historiography stresses the importance of the "April uprising" of 1876 in the creation of the independent country, at least in indicating that Bulgarians could no longer tolerate a future within the Ottoman domains, the revolt was essentially irrelevant to the founding of independent Bulgaria, which resulted from Russia's defeat of the Ottoman empire in the war of 1877–8. In the San Stefano peace treaty (1878), Russia forced Ottoman acceptance of an independent Bulgaria covering almost all of the eastern Balkan Peninsula south of the Danube, including Macedonia, but this new country was scaled back by the other European powers in the Berlin peace conference. Macedonia returned to Ottoman control, the southeastern third of San Stefano Bulgaria became the Ottoman province of Eastern Rumelia to be administered by an Istanbul-approved Christian governor, and only the northern third centered on Sofia gained autonomy. The Russians still occupied the scaled-down country and were given leave to remain until they had established a stable state; this proved a challenge, because under the terms of the Berlin accord they could not continue to administer it themselves, but no Bulgarian organization capable of assuming authority existed. Bulgarian nationalist groups were made up of expatriates in Romania, among whom Georgi Rakovski had been a leading and all-too-typical figure, but they lacked size, standing, and organization in Bulgaria itself and were also viewed skeptically by the Russian authorities. The Russian interim administration drafted a constitution based on those of Serbia and Romania and submitted it for consideration by an assembly of Bulgarian religious and secular notables, many from abroad but also significant numbers from within the country.

Much like Serbia, Bulgaria faced the need to import administrators, but rather than recruiting them from neighboring populations, it looked

[30] Roy Heath, *The Establishment of the Bulgarian Ministry of Public Instruction and Its Role in the Development of Modern Bulgaria, 1878–1885* (New York: Garland, 1987), 278.

largely to Bulgarians who had left their home provinces to study and then stayed away thereafter. The number of expatriate educated Bulgarians was itself not large: perhaps five hundred received an education in Russia over the period 1840–78, for example.[31] Of such graduates, many had chosen not to return to Bulgaria but had found employment closer to their places of education, such as Marin Drinov, an academic schooled in Russia who taught history in Kharkiv and became the only Bulgarian member of the Central Chancery organized by Russia to oversee the transfer of authority to a new Bulgarian state. Drinov himself thought that Bulgarians were not yet prepared for a parliamentary government and preferred that authority be vested in a monarch for the first seven years. The new state that was certified by the constitutional assembly, however, was more liberal than Drinov thought fit, but this was not the result of focused pressure from Western-educated intelligentsia. The American-run Robert College in Istanbul was long thought to have exerted a liberalizing influence on the assembly through its alumni, but by 1878 a total of just forty-five Bulgarians had earned degrees there, only four of whom were appointed or elected to the constitutional assembly.[32] The relative liberalism resulted rather from resistance to the idea of a very powerful monarchy among the disparate notables attending the assembly, much like those of Greece whose dislike of Othon's autocratic rule had forced the king to accept constitutionalism in 1843–4 and those of Serbia who had protested to Istanbul over Miloš's despotism in 1838.

As in Greece, there was no dominant party in the assembly, and the political parties that formed to contest parliamentary elections were similarly incoherent and unstable, essentially becoming groupings aligned with personalities rather than distinctive ideologies other than views on proper relations with foreign powers, notably Russia. All necessarily subscribed to the new national ideal that legitimated the creation of an independent country, were "urban" (Sofia had just twenty thousand inhabitants in 1878), and sought to win votes in the countryside by gaining the support of local landowning or mercantile notables who could deliver blocs of peasant votes. The prime means for buying such support was patronage, which led to the rapid expansion of the bureaucracy and the military; the collapse of much of the economic progress made over the preceding decades as most school leavers entered government service rather than

---

[31] C. E. Black, *The Establishment of Constitutional Government in Bulgaria* (Princeton: Princeton University Press, 1943), 28–9.
[32] Ibid., 60, 70–1.

applying their newly acquired skills to manufacturing, trade, or farming; and the adoption of aggressive revanchism abroad as a goal of state.[33]

After Eastern Rumelia merged with Bulgaria in 1885, Macedonia was the main target of this revanchism, and the Macedonian problem influenced the Bulgarian state's relations with the church in a manner unseen in Greece and Serbia (for Bulgarian territorial claims, see Map 4). In response to pressure from both Bulgarian Orthodox circles and Russia, the Ottoman state had sanctioned creation in Istanbul of a Bulgarian Exarchate in 1870, before Bulgaria itself was established. After 1878, the new state in Sofia faced the problem of gaining control over a church structure already recognized as the domain of the Bulgarian Orthodox nation but headquartered in Istanbul and headed by an exarch appointed by the sultan. The solution eventually agreed between Sofia and the exarchate was that the affairs of the church within the new country's borders would be governed by a synod of local bishops in Sofia. Meeting in the capital, the bishops would be vulnerable to pressure from the government – indeed, in 1889 the authoritarian prime minister Stefan Stambolov (1887–94, assassinated by Macedonian activists in 1895) had a meeting of the synod broken up and the bishops involved escorted back to their sees by the police – but they were nevertheless still part of a hierarchy headed by the exarch. There thus recurred tensions between Bulgarian political authorities and the exarchate over issues such as the authority and identity of the ruling prince, and relations between church and state became increasingly prickly as the century drew to a close. Unlike in the cases of Greece and Serbia, however, Sofia could not afford to establish a new, captive national church, because the authority of the exarch in Macedonia gave weight to Bulgarian irredentists' claim to that Ottoman territory. The regime in Sofia and the exarch also did not agree on much concerning Macedonian affairs, and the exarchate even made a point of naming Serbs to bishoprics in Macedonia on several occasions in order to show its irritation with the aggressive campaigns of agitators based in, and supported by, Bulgaria. Although relations between the exarchate and the Bulgarian government varied in degrees of warmth or coolness, they thus remained intact as long as nationalist revanchism in Sofia kept alive the dream of gaining Macedonia, with autocephaly declared only in 1945.

---

[33] John Bell, *Peasants in Power: Alexander Stamboliski and the Bulgarian Agrarian National Union, 1899–1923* (Princeton: Princeton University Press, 1977), chap. 1; Roudometof, "Social Origins"; Palairet, *Balkan Economies*.

It is hard to gauge how committed the preponderance of the population was to the revanchist program in Macedonia. Certainly the religious nature of identity remained quite high in rural areas: peasants in Ruse, for instance, knew that the minister of education, Konstantin Jireček, was Czech but also that he had written a famous history of Bulgaria, an act that in their eyes meant that he must have been Orthodox.[34] Over time, however, as in Macedonia, Orthodoxy was not enough: the regime pressed Christians within the young country to declare their Bulgarian identity on the basis of adherence to the exarchate, with those who remained loyal to the ecumenical patriarchate being identified as "Greek," a process that could make even brothers members of different "ethnic" groups.[35]

As in the cases of Greece and Serbia, Bulgaria certainly had success in the state's enduring drive to inculcate the national ideal in the largely anational population, but there were signs that the well-publicized, mainly urban, zeal for the national project, and therefore also for the governments that led it, simply overshadowed currents of discontent. In Greece, where high taxes after Trikoupis's fall simply fed an expanding bureaucracy and voracious military, large numbers of the nation's citizens emigrated to Ottoman Anatolia or to the west. Some 350,000, almost all of whom were adult males and constituted nearly one-sixth of the total population, left between 1890 and 1914.[36] In landlocked Serbia, where emigration was not a ready option, a large peasant revolt erupted in 1883 over the government's attempt to take back the muskets distributed by Prince Mihailo in the 1860s, but underlying this was resentment of the state's domination by urban commercial interests that treated the rural population as little more than a flock to be fleeced. The revolt helped to propel the Radical Party, which succeeded in tapping rural discontent, to power.[37] In Bulgaria, there was no major revolt and large-scale emigration was no easier than in Serbia, but the author Aleko Konstantinov reflected social and political tensions of the early post-1878 decades in his stories about a character named Bai Ganio, who became an enduring

---

[34] Heath, *Bulgarian Ministry of Public Instruction*, 289.

[35] Theodora Dragostinova, *Between Two Motherlands: Nationality and Emigration among the Greeks of Bulgaria, 1900–1949* (Ithaca, NY: Cornell University Press, 2011), 2. Dragostinova cites elsewhere other examples of the malleability of national identity under pressure from government (in Bulgaria) or paramilitaries (Macedonia).

[36] Stevan Pavlowitch, *A History of the Balkans 1804–1945* (London: Longman, 1999), 154; Barbara Jelavich, *History of the Balkans, vol. II* (Cambridge: Cambridge University Press, 1983), 44.

[37] Jelavich, *History of the Balkans 2*, 31; on the blatant favoritism shown to urban traders over the peasantry, see Palairet, *Balkan Economies*.

national icon. The early, comic stories show Ganio as a quintessential Bulgarian as viewed by the educated, "European" Bulgarians who dominated the upper levels of government: half-Turkish in appearance and speech, uncultured and unaware that he needs improvement. In the later, darker stories he remains unimproved but has become an unscrupulous operator in public life: a sycophant to anyone in power but a drunken thug toward ordinary citizens.[38] Bai Ganio seems emblematic of not only the majority of the population's lack of connection to the westernizing, nation-building state but also the governing elite's attitude toward the "everyman" of the nation, who was an object of ridicule, contempt, and fear, rather than a person whose views and well-being were of significant interest. Konstantinov's stories hint at the radical changes resulting from the shift from Ottoman to post-Ottoman eras: their elevation of the westernized and denigration of the native contrast sharply with Ottoman novels that vilified those who forsook communal mores for westernized immorality.

Succeeding Bulgarian regimes' failure to provide significant improvement in much of the population's standard of living, or even political and economic stability, prompted grassroots organization among the disaffected, including notably the peasantry. Rural discontent led in 1899 to the formation of the Agrarian Party, which drew increasing electoral support in the predominantly rural population. The Bulgarian Agrarian National Union (BANU), as it came to be known, argued against militarism abroad, boosting its popularity, particularly after the debacle of Bulgaria's experience in the Balkan Wars and the First World War. It formed several governments from 1919 to 1923 before nationalists organized a military coup in which several Bulgarian army officers and members of IMRO tortured to death BANU's leader, Prime Minister Aleksandar Stamboliski; his brother; and various associates. By one estimate up to sixteen thousand BANU supporters and communists were killed between 1923 and 1925.[39] The state returned to the control of the urban sectors that had dominated it from 1878 to 1919, but the bloody BANU episode showed how badly the regime's nationalist credentials had failed to sink deep roots of legitimacy in the largest part of the population.

---

[38] Roumen Daskalov, "Modern Bulgarian Society and Culture through the Mirror of Bai Ganio," *Slavic Review* 60 (2001), 530–2. Soon after the Bai Ganio stories were published, Konstantinov was assassinated during an attempt on the life of a politician – killed by his own creation, as contemporaries noted.

[39] Bell, *Peasants in Power*, 244–5.

The dismal and sometimes bloody record of government in Greece, Serbia-Yugoslavia, and Bulgaria both before and after the First World War suggests that revanchist nationalism won the state committed support from some, particularly urban, parts of the nation, but that the ideological base of such support was narrow. Failure to achieve the revanchist goals by any and all means stripped leaders of legitimacy, leaving them open to not just rejection but retaliation. All of these revanchist plans for liberating lands and people abroad had been constructed according to the idealized visions of aspiring politicians and inevitably suffered disappointment. Even Serbia, which appeared to have achieved most of the aims of the *Načertanije* in the creation of Yugoslavia, soon found that non-Orthodox populations in the new kingdom would resist absorption, keeping the revanchist goal still open to dispute. Regimes that had justified autocratic rule by highlighting irredentism thus would find continued reason to rule harshly in the decades after 1918, when the programs of revanchism effectively ended.

ALBANIA

It is perhaps an oversimplification to divide post-Ottoman lands into Christian and Muslim countries, because not all new states cleansed their territories of significant religious minorities. The time and manner of transfer from Ottoman to post-Ottoman authority affected the potential for ethnic cleansing. Countries such as Greece and Serbia killed or expelled practically all Muslims from territories acquired by 1830, and lands taken in 1878 and 1880 were also soon emptied of most native Muslims. Bulgaria, however, despite the massive wave of refugees who fled as Russian forces advanced in 1877–8, retained a significant Muslim population in Dobrudja (northeastern Bulgaria/southeastern Romania) thereafter and gained more in 1885 with the union with Eastern Rumelia, which had a large Muslim population concentrated in the Rhodopi Mountains. Greece, Serbia, and Montenegro all gained territory with Muslim populations in the Balkan Wars, a significant proportion of whom survived and were not expelled, although most Muslims remaining in Greece were sent to Turkey in the population exchange agreed in 1923. Turkey sent most of its surviving Orthodox Christians to Greece in the same exchange, by which time the last Ottoman government had already driven out or killed most of Anatolia's Armenians. Bulgaria and Greece exchanged their Orthodox "minority" populations after the First World War. Those future countries whose formerly Ottoman lands passed into the control of another imperial power, by contrast, including Arab territories, Serbian/Yugoslav Macedonia, and Bosnia, could not attempt such purges and thus remained multireligious. Only one people, however, the Albanian, consciously attempted to build directly a post-Ottoman nation without trying to set the religion of the majority, Islam, at the core of the new identity. The legitimacy problems seen in Christian post-Ottoman nation-states were thus magnified in Albania.

Although there had been repeated clashes of authority and occasionally arms between Istanbul and Albanian provinces, there was no anti-Ottoman liberation struggle that could create a recognized leader able to wield authority when Albania came into being in 1913, an orphan of the Christian European politics of the Eastern Question. If anything, a continued tie to their Ottoman past was arguably the most appealing option for most Albanians, but no power would support such an idea. Britain at least insisted that the core of Albanian territories should not be absorbed by Greece, Serbia, and Montenegro after the Balkan Wars, but London had no interest in organizing a new state in the manner Russia did in Bulgaria in 1878. A member of a surplus German minor royal family, Wilhelm zu Wied, a captain in the German army, was found to act as king; he lasted but months in the country. He left under pressure from a strong Muslim movement under Haxhi Qamili, a now rather obscure figure from the region of Tirana who may have been a sufi shaikh, and Musa Qazimi, the mufti of Tirana. Their movement established a regime enforcing Islamic law in the center of the country in 1914, fought against and ousted the new Christian king, and sought appointment of a member of the Ottoman ruling family as monarch. This movement has been slighted in histories of Albania, because its religious nature and Ottoman sympathies contradicted the subsequently developed official image of the Albanian nation, but clearly it was a significant force in 1914–15, after which Albania was under foreign occupation. Insofar as the Muslim-Ottoman movement has been studied, it has been described as a class revolt, as a peasant uprising against the great landholding families of Albania.[40] It was eventually defeated by forces of Esad Pasha Toptani, a notable who sought to establish his own claim to rule and was aided by the Serbian army, which moved into much of northern Albania in 1915. Haxhi Qamili, Musa Qazimi, and other leaders of the Muslim movement

---

[40] Gazmend Shpuza, *Kryengritja fshatarësisë së Shqipërisë së Mesme dhe udhëhequr nga Haxhi Qamili* (Tirana: Shtëpia Botuese 8 Nëntori, 1979).

were captured and executed. Thus ended one of the few potentially meaningful popular movements in the history of Albania.

With the political stage emptied of a viable broad-based movement
during the Balkan Wars–First World War period, various local notables
and expatriates from the diaspora competed for authority after the collapse of the Austro-Hungarian occupation. The lack of potential political
leaders with more than local appeal and the chaotic aftermath of the
wars made formation of more than the simulacrum of a state and government extremely difficult. The process began with formation of a committee of regents (because Wilhelm had not abdicated formally), through
which members of notable families such as the Toptani and expatriates
such as Fan Noli rose and fell from positions of autocratic, albeit limited,
power.[41] Ahmet Zogoğlu/Zogolli (later Ahmet Zogu and, as ruler, King
Zog), a notable from Mati in northern Albania, finally overshadowed
all rivals, becoming president in 1925 and then king in 1928. He faced
an enduring struggle to win and keep legitimacy as ruler, however, living almost as a recluse in Albania and escaping numerous assassination
attempts.

In such a turbulent, makeshift political arena, great attention was paid
to building national identity, an effort that has never ceased. Occupation
by various foreign powers (first Serbia and Greece, then Austria-Hungary,
and always there lurked a very interested Italy) from the Balkan Wars
through the First World War gave momentum to the search for nationhood among Albanians of all faiths, but major practical problems made
progress a challenge. There was no geographic, social, or political focus
for the country. The Balkan Wars had taken two of the four largest cities
of nineteenth-century Albania (Ioannina, now in Greece, and Prizren in
the north, which with the rest of Kosovo passed to Serbian control until
the end of the twentieth century) and saw a third, Shkodra, crippled in
a drawn-out siege and occupation by Montenegrins. Only Vlora in the
south survived in good shape but, as a port, was particularly vulnerable
to foreign powers, being occupied by the Italians until 1920. The regency
therefore moved to Tirana, at that time a minor town that was far from
a natural center for a national government, despite its importance in having produced Haxhi Qamili and Musa Qazimi. One advantage Tirana
had was its location near the linguistic frontier between the Gheg north
and Tosk south. It was only in the hard-line communist state after the

---

[41] Born in Ottoman Thrace but a resident of the United States most of his life, Fan Noli
started the Albanian Orthodox Church there in 1908.

Second World War that standard literary Albanian took its final form (influenced heavily by Tosk, as could be expected, given Enver Hoxha's regime's roots in the south) and was taught to enough of the population to make it an effectively national language. Arguably more damaging were the religious divisions among a population that is conventionally estimated to have been (and to be still) 70 percent Muslim, 20 percent Orthodox, and 10 percent Catholic.

Expatriates and some native nationalists provided the most promising approach to resolving the tensions between religious and national identities, the glorification of Bektashism as a specifically Albanian religion that was rooted in both Islam and Christianity. In some ways it made a good vehicle for transmitting the message of solidarity against outside forces, because it had taken root in southern Albania with the persecution of Bektashis ordered by Mahmud II in 1826, which prompted many to flee to the area. Adopting Bektashism therefore carried an undertone of defiance against Istanbul that could be turned against other outside powers, such as Greece and Italy. Although Bektashis embraced the linkage of their sect with the nation, the idea never worked very effectively, in part because the Bektashis had never had much influence in the northern half of the country, and because as a "national faith" it still offered enough significant differences from both Christianity and mainstream Sunni Islam to dissuade many people from "converting." This led, in turn, to still greater propaganda extolling the myth that "Albanians never cared much for religion," represented by two much-noted dicta, one by Vasa Pasha that "the faith of the Albanians is Albanianism!" – a phrase either profound in its simplicity or just profoundly vapid – and the other a heavily-promoted aphorism, "Where the sword is, is the faith" – meaning that Albanians think nothing of changing religion to suit circumstances.[42]

King Zog tried to place religion under the control of his state in a manner familiar to other post-Ottoman rulers. He asserted the right to dismiss Orthodox metropolitans appointed by the ecumenical patriarchate in Istanbul, although his efforts to win recognition of autocephaly for the Albanian Orthodox Church succeeded only in 1937. By that time he had

---

[42] On attempts to reconfigure religious issues into elements of nation building, see Stephanie Schwandner-Sievers and Bernd Fischer (eds.), *Albanian Identities: Myth and History* (Bloomington: Indiana University Press, 2002), especially chapters by Ger Duijzings, "Religion and the Politics of 'Albanianism': Naim Frashëri's Bektashi Writings" (60–9), and Noel Malcolm, "Myths of Albanian National Identity: Some Key Elements, as Expressed in the Works of Albanian Writers in America in the Early Twentieth Century" (84–7).

already taken control over all education in the country, an act that had been opposed by Greece and the Orthodox Church, whose network of schools in southern Albania provided the best education in the country. In the field of law, Zog arrogated to himself the exclusive right to initiate legislation, ensuring that the indirectly elected parliament remained a weak force in national politics. Under his direction and in accord with his wish to westernize the country, Albania adopted new legal codes based upon Western European models, and the wearing of the veil was banned. Although Kemal Atatürk derided Zog's elevation to monarch, the Albanian king adopted a program of westernization that bore strong resemblance to that pushed in other Muslim countries such as Turkey and Iran in the interwar period.

"Westernization" as a conscious goal became the norm for post-Ottoman states in the Balkans, as it would also in Turkey. The politics and culture of the powers that collectively brought about the collapse of the empire became, through their resoundingly demonstrated superiority, the models to be emulated by new states seeking the most direct route to strengthen themselves. They adopted both institutions and ideologies from non-Ottoman Europe. This phenomenon was perhaps only to be expected in the Christian countries of the Balkans, which had less pre-existing prejudice against European powers and even imported much of their nation- and state-shaping leadership from non-Ottoman countries. That the latecomer of the Balkans, Muslim-majority Albania, followed an essentially Westernizing path was perhaps also understandable in light of the conditions under which it achieved independence. More unexpected would be Turkey's commitment to the same path under Mustafa Kemal Atatürk after abolition of the Ottoman dynastic sultanate-caliphate.

7

Post-Ottoman Turkey

Viewed from today, Turkey's construction from the rubble of the Ottoman empire appears to have been a natural step, given Istanbul's loss of its remaining "non-Turkish" provinces in Europe (Albania, Macedonia, and western Thrace), Asia (the Dodecanese islands, Iraq, eastern and western Arabia, Transjordan, Palestine, and Lebanon), and Africa (Libya, Egypt, and Sudan) between 1911 and 1918. The twelfth of Woodrow Wilson's famous fourteen points that provided an ostensible blueprint for reshaping the world after the Entente's victory in 1918 called for secure sovereignty for Turkish Muslim parts of the Ottoman empire. Turkey seems the natural embodiment of this point, but its construction featured arguably the most traumatic direct transition of any part of the empire to nation-state. Unlike in most of the Balkans except Albania, there was serious conflict between native aspirants to political power and between adherents of competing visions of the future. Unlike in Albania, where King Zog gained critical financial and material assistance from Italy, none of the Entente states supported the efforts of any party to restore stability to Anatolia, and indeed some, notably Greece and Britain, showed fierce hostility. The one state to render assistance was another outcast of Europe, Bolshevik Russia, leading to the seemingly odd fact that the eventually strongly anticommunist republic signed its first treaty of friendship with the Soviet Union. Turkey also had advantages compared with Albania and other Balkan post-Ottoman countries, however, that helped it to achieve stable statehood after independence, because Turkey's founders inherited established political and administrative traditions that were not only recognized but welcomed by a population traumatized by a decade of war, and because the victorious struggle against various hostile powers gave key figures, notably Mustafa Kemal (Atatürk), a degree of legitimacy that no other leader of a country emerging from the Ottoman empire enjoyed. These assets served Atatürk well in his postindependence campaign to make Turkish politics and society into seamless wholes that would be under the full control of a powerful state.

Anatolia was shattered by the First World War, with an estimated loss of more than 20 percent of the population through combat, massacre, disease, and deprivation. The Ottoman government had to accept an armistice that permitted Entente powers to occupy strategic points as they saw fit (the most noted case being Britain's seizure of Mosul and much of its associated province after the armistice was signed); after the CUP wartime leadership fled the country, a series of new cabinets had to accept the occupation of the capital and much of the country, which was formalized in the Ottoman surrender signed at Sèvres in 1920.[1] According to the Sèvres agreement, the secure sovereign homeland for Turks was to be north-central Anatolia, with other parts of Anatolia and eastern Thrace taken or protected by Greece, Italy, France, and projected Armenian and Kurdish countries in the east. Istanbul itself was subject to occupation by Entente forces, and the straits were internationalized. Of all the states in the losing alliance of the First World War, the Ottoman empire faced the harshest peace terms.

Opposition inevitably arose in reaction to the drastic changes imposed on the empire, despite the disarray besetting Anatolia. Wartime preparations for mounting military operations in Anatolia, undertaken by the CUP regime in 1915 when it faced the possibility of losing Istanbul to Britain's invasion at Gallipoli, proved crucial in organizing the opposition and providing them with the wherewithal to act. CUP men – members of the Special Formations (Teşkilat-i Mahsusa), the paramilitary network reconstituted at the end of the war as the General Revolutionary Organization of the World of Islam, and provincial administrators – provided leadership, although usually drafting local notables and religious figures to act as the public face of each region's "committee for the defense of rights." Such committees appeared first in areas that were designated for assignment to an Entente power or to Armenia and Kurdistan, and each committee convened an assembly (dominated by CUP appointees) to pass a resolution that the area was Muslim and wanted to remain part of the empire.

---

[1] On poor Ottoman negotiation at Sèvres, see Syed Tanvir Wasti, "Feylosof Riza," *MES* 38 (2002), 83–100.

In both the organization of resistance and the mobilization of popular support, there was far more emphasis upon Muslim than Turkish ethnonational identity and solidarity. This is suggested by details such as the renaming of the Special Formations to identify the organization with the Islamic world and the choice of religious leaders, particularly muftis, to act as heads of the defense of rights committees. The committees themselves also stressed Muslim identity, with the terms later used to refer to "national" and "the nation" (*milli* and *milla*) so noted by later historians being practically impossible to separate from their established connotations of a religious community.[2] Criticism of the "milli" resistance in Anatolia leveled by the Ottoman government in occupied Istanbul charged the "nationalists" not with ethnicism but with atheism, because they had established contacts and received arms from the godless Bolsheviks of the Soviet Union, a charge that the nationalists rebutted by such means as deploying the "Green Army," a group of emigré Russian Muslims who demonstrated that support from, and for, the Bolsheviks did not require abandonment of the faith.[3] Over the years a small but steady stream of scholars have recognized the basic fact that the "Turkish war of liberation" fit the Ottoman mold of a Muslim movement against Christian attack, except that organization rested in the hands of the remaining CUP party provincial network rather than with the sultan or any other figure in Istanbul. The notion that Atatürk and other CUP-based figures invoked Islam only as a ploy to galvanize resistance to Christian invaders could conceivably be true but is irrelevant. Nationalism had little power to motivate "the Turks" prior to the establishment of the post-Ottoman nominal nation-state; Islam, by contrast, mattered to the mainstream population.[4]

What Atatürk, like most CUP figures, most firmly believed in was the same major goal desired by Ottoman rulers since the beginning of the nineteenth century: a strong state capable of protecting the country in an ever more hostile political environment. Post-1918 leaders had no doubt that the country was to be of and for Muslims but were less united on the question of whether Islam could still suffice as the source of political

---

[2] Hasan Kayalı, "The Struggle for Independence," in *CHT4*, 122.

[3] Paul Dumont, "La Revolution Impossible: Les Courants d'Opposition en Anatolie 1920–1921," *Cahiers du Monde Russe et Soviétique* 19 (1978), 145–6.

[4] Şerif Mardin, "Ideology and Religion in the Turkish Revolution," *IJMES* 2 (1971), 198–9; Kayalı, "Struggle for Independence," 129,143; Andrew Mango, "Atatürk," in *CHT4*, 160; Erik Zürcher, "The Ottoman Legacy of the Turkish Republic: An Attempt at a New Periodization," *Die Welt des Islams* 32 (1992), 244–6.

identity. The empire had endured for centuries because it rested not on Islam alone but on two pillars, *din ü devlet* (the religion and the dynasty), and the leadership of the war of liberation struggled to find equally secure supports for their movement. They asserted their role as representing both *din* and *devlet* while Istanbul was under Christian Entente occupation and the sultan-caliph was not free to lead the struggle himself, and under this cover they pushed aggressively to establish unchallengeable dominance over Anatolia.

While the 1919–23 period is traditionally termed the era of national liberation struggle, it also was a transition period in the development of a new, authoritarian state that deepened the CUP's intolerance of dissent. Christians were obviously subjected to repression – the early organization of resistance took place in the east, targeting the remaining or returning Armenian population that hoped to establish their nation-state foreseen by the treaty of Sèvres, and the Greek invasion galvanized the mass Muslim resort to arms – but the new state extended its severe repression just as readily to its fellow Muslims. This aided the decision to turn to nationalism. The strictures of the Ottoman Istanbul regime against the resistance movement forced the "milli" leaders to develop in new directions their strategy for ensuring their own legitimacy. Attachment to the sultan-caliph, the defender of the faith even while under Christian control, led to the emergence of loyalist groups in rivalry with the milli movement and thereby triggered murderous struggles in some provinces.[5] Violence between Muslims created severe problems for resistance to Christian occupation, and the milli movement inevitably shifted to direct attack upon Istanbul's authority in the provinces and the consolidation of power in the hands of a few leaders within the milli ranks. Significant military resources were diverted to crushing Muslim loyalist groups, and the new Grand National Assembly in Ankara commissioned summary "independence tribunals" to silence critics of Mustafa Kemal and the direction of the milli movement.

With the suppression of differing viewpoints among the Muslim population, the assembly itself became a theater of political competition. The assembly legitimized its own formation by asserting that "sovereignty belongs unconditionally to the milla," but this did not prevent its extraordinary transfer of much of its power to Mustafa Kemal as leader of the efforts to stop the Greek drive toward Ankara and to annul the treaty

[5] For a study of fighting between Muslims during the "national liberation struggle," see Gingeras, *Sorrowful Shores*.

of Sèvres. Mustafa Kemal's autocratic tendencies, however, spurred the growth of opposition within the assembly, leading it to refuse to renew those powers in 1922; the leader simply refused to accept the assembly's attempt to claw back authority, raising the specter of halting the campaign to expel the Greeks. The assembly thereupon reversed itself and renewed his powers. It was not yet permanently cowed, however. After the army expelled the Greeks and the treaty of Sèvres was opened to renegotiation at Lausanne in 1922, the assembly declared that it alone had the authority to enter the negotiations and that the political authority of the Ottoman dynasty was at an end, abolishing the sultanate. More problematically, the assembly then objected to some of the points agreed by Mustafa Kemal's appointed negotiator, İsmet (İnönü); Mustafa Kemal thereupon ordered its dissolution and had the ensuing elections so closely controlled that only his supporters were reelected. The state that reached agreement at Lausanne in 1923, therefore, was already dominated by a few key figures, of whom Mustafa Kemal was by far the most important.

Victory over the Greeks was crucial to elevating Mustafa Kemal and associates such as İsmet to dominance, because many even from the old CUP objected to their ascendancy and decisions that they made. Military victories rallied enough support in the assembly at key moments when opposition began to appear threatening. The years after Lausanne were therefore devoted to institutionalizing Mustafa Kemal's authority over the state, and the state's control over the population. The great Atatürkist reforms of the 1920s aimed to crush all potential rivals for influence and then to extend the state's authority further than it had gone before. When the sultanate was abolished, any advocacy of its return became high treason, but inevitably the Ottoman caliph, whose remaining nominal leadership role was religious, became the focus of hope for those dissatisfied with Mustafa Kemal's dominance; the new leader therefore abolished the caliphate as well, as soon as circumstances were favorable and a suitable pretext arose. Mustafa Kemal mooted the possibility of establishing formally a republic, thereby making practically inevitable the abolition of the caliphate, in January 1923, long before two Indian Muslims wrote a public letter in support of the caliph's leadership of the *umma* (the nominal cause of the caliphate's abolition). The timing of the declaration of a republic with a president (i.e., Mustafa Kemal) as unassailable as any Ottoman sultan-caliph had been was determined, however, by the absence from the assembly of most other significant figures of the "liberation" period (at least those remaining in the assembly after the managed election of 1923) who might not support the move.

Their opposition was indeed swiftly voiced thereafter. The defense of rights movement, which had begun and fought until 1923 to protect what remained of the Muslim Ottoman empire, suddenly found that it had liberated the land not only from Christian occupiers but also from the last living link to that empire. The postliberation state in the 1923–4 period engineered the death of the old "oriental despotate" resting upon *din* (Islam) and *devlet* (the Ottoman dynasty) as the ideal of public life and created, not a true or democratic republic, but merely a new, ever-more-muscular state resting upon an updated and more "European" version of the twin pillars: the nation and the parvenu authoritarian.[6]

Aside from his undoubted legitimacy as the man credited with expelling Christian occupiers and sloughing the burden of Sèvres, Mustafa Kemal (from 1934, Kemal Atatürk) was a far from unique post-Ottoman ruler, but circumstances gave him a legacy more lasting and fortunate than most. His time in power, the interwar period, saw the rise of the authoritarian "strongman" across southern, central, and eastern Europe (the Middle East, being largely under Anglo-French control, was less affected, except Iran, where a semiliterate cavalry officer became Reza Shah Pahlavi and subjected his country to a program of forced modernization patterned on Mustafa Kemal's Turkey). Almost all of the countries created in the vacuums left by old empires before and after 1918 fell under the control of militaristic nationalist leaders who took to heart the fascist model of enforced unity. Mustafa Kemal's contemporaries in the post-Ottoman Balkans were General Ioannis Metaxas in Greece, King Aleksandar Karadjordjević of Yugoslavia, a succession of military officers and Czar Boris III in Bulgaria, and General Ion Antonescu and King Carol II in Romania – dictators all. King Zog in Albania was too weak and poor to accomplish much but otherwise fit the autocratic pattern.[7] Like many of his contemporary strongmen, Mustafa Kemal was a military man; although as president he resigned from active service and barred serving personnel from politics, his rule over Turkey showed his roots in the positivist late Ottoman officer corps that spawned the CUP

[6] Kayalı ("Struggle for Independence," 144) notes the irony in Turkey's being named a republic only after genuine republican impulses of the independence struggle were stifled.

[7] On many of these contemporaries, see Bernd Fischer (ed.), *Balkan Strongmen: Dictators and Authoritarian Rulers of Southeastern Europe* (London: Hurst, 2007). Feroz Ahmad contributes a chapter on Atatürk that gives the standard admiring view.

circles that (mis)ruled the empire after 1908. Indeed, the political elite of the early republic was even more heavily dominated by men of military background than the CUP leadership of 1908–18 had been.[8] Even many of Atatürk's admirers admit that he was inclined toward autocracy, both personally and politically, being sublimely sure of his own correctness, to the point of alienating superiors, associates, and finally friends. He certainly did not meet any standard definition of either a democrat or a liberal.[9] As a man who eventually had only followers, Atatürk remains a surprisingly distant, even mythic figure who has inevitably attracted biographers but whose image remains carefully tended by successor governments. One important way in which Atatürk differed was in governing a country that was not drawn into the Second World War, another conflict as cataclysmic as the 1914–18 war and one that broke the state in almost all fascist-inclined countries. The period of his rule and his legacy to Turkey have therefore never been really seriously subjected to reconsideration within the country, where criticism of him became a criminal offense in the 1950s.

It is no exaggeration to say that Turkey itself is his legacy. This can be seen not only in the country itself, which resulted from the successful liberation struggle that gave Atatürk so much of his legitimacy, but also in the effect he had in creating a strong sense of Turkish nationhood. As noted previously, the liberation movement had been supported by people defending the Muslim empire, not fighting for the Turkish nation, and even in the CUP network that organized the struggle, the establishment of an ethnic national "Turkey" was far from the clearly established goal. The determined effort to convert the citizens of the new state into members of a unified nation would not – could not – have happened without the determined direction of Mustafa Kemal, from 1934 named appropriately *Kemal Atatürk*, "Perfection Father-Turk." Mustafa Kemal took an officer's typically functional approach to problems, including the challenges of the politically possible: whatever stood in the way of a target was to be removed quickly, and any tool that could help to achieve the goal was to be adopted. The goal that he ultimately sought was inherited from earlier generations of Ottoman reformers: a powerful state capable of defending itself; nationalism, like most of the noted reforms of the 1924–9 period, was simply a tool used to achieve it.

---

[8] Zürcher, "Ottoman Legacy," 242.
[9] Assertions to the contrary rarely argue the point in detail. See, for example, C. H. Dodd, "The Development of Turkish Democracy," *BriJMES* 19 (1992), 16–30.

At the founding of the national republic, a basic question surfaced that has never received a very clear answer: "Who, or what, is a Turk?" It certainly was not the old category of uncouth Turkish-speaking villager: the aphorism (command) of Atatürk that to be able to say "I am a Turk" is a source of joy, engraved on public buildings across the country and now the national subconscience, attacked both that negative connotation and any other prerepublican ethnolinguistic affinities present in the variegated population. The immutable part of the answer to "Who is a Turk?" has always been "a Muslim." It is possible to be a (noncitizen) Muslim and not a Turk, but in practice it has been impossible to be a Turk and a non-Muslim. Non-Muslim citizens of Turkey have always been treated as "minorities," and their numbers have dwindled through emigration to their "real" homelands. All Muslims within the borders of Turkey are deemed to be Turks, but members of Muslim minorities in formerly Ottoman lands also have been welcome to return "home," whether their mother tongue was Turkish, Greek, Bulgarian, Bosnian, or Albanian (Muslim Arabs, by contrast, have not been as welcome, because the end-of-war agreements partitioning former Ottoman lands in the Middle East required residents who considered themselves to be "Turks" to emigrate within two years to Anatolia). This basic reality shaped the population exchange agreed by Turkey and Greece in 1923, with deportees selected by the religious, not ethnic or linguistic, criterion. The fundamental content of Turkishness thus did not really change from the religious element that had shaped Ottoman identity, but the practical import of the relabeling of religious as national identity was great. The state would henceforth be the only permitted channel for expression of the identity and would police aggressively all alternative paths for formation and demonstration of social awareness. Atatürk's republic nationalized Islam.

As soon as the assembly abolished the caliphate, it started to dismantle large parts of the religious infrastructure inherited from the Ottoman empire. Along with the caliphate went the office of chief mufti and head of the imperial religious establishment, the shaikh al-islam, and the ministry of pious endowments (waqf). Religious schools or medreses were dissolved, and the state became the sole legal purveyor of schooling. The constitution of the republic adopted in 1924 still proclaimed Islam to be the religion of the state and acknowledged a place for shari'a law, but these references were removed in 1928. Abolition of the caliphate and partial dissolution of the official infrastructure of religion angered many in the country, prompting most notoriously a rebellion in eastern

Anatolia in 1925 that was primarily religious in nature (it was named the Shaikh Said rebellion after its leading figure, a noted sufi), although it also fed off Kurdish resentment over Turkification. Mustafa Kemal, never one to doubt visibly the wisdom of his own choices, responded with intensification of his ambitious program of change. Not only was the rebellion crushed, but all sufi brotherhoods were formally abolished and their assets seized by the state, and the regime reconstituted the summary "independence tribunals" that had been used to crush Ottoman loyalists in 1920. The Progressive Republican Party, a new grouping of deputies from Mustafa Kemal's People's Party who objected to abolition of the caliphate and other signs of growing authoritarianism, was dissolved.

With one-party rule established and protected by what was essentially martial law until 1929, all remaining facets of public life and society that had clearly religious origins or connotations were banned or, in the case of veiling by women, strongly discouraged, to be replaced by consciously Western European innovations. Swiss civil and Italian penal codes replaced Ottoman era shari'a-based law; indeed, among the signs of how far the authoritarian early republican state diverged from Ottoman practice were the many amendments to the Italian code subsequently introduced to make Turkish criminal law match the Italian fascist code introduced in 1930.[10] Comportment in public life was similarly westernized, with the fez outlawed and Western-style dress enjoined, women pressed to leave the home and mingle with men socially and at work, and the Christian European calendar and clock adopted. The small remaining Christian communities also did not escape attention, with the state attempting to create a Turkish Orthodox Church not under the control of the ecumenical patriarch, much like the churches established in post-Ottoman Balkan countries.[11] The highest-profile reform of the time, however, was the linguistic engineering that began in 1928 with introduction of a Latin-based alphabet to replace the Arabic script used in the Ottoman period.

Historical accounts that discuss Turkish linguistic reforms in more than the briefest of terms almost uniformly deem the program, and especially the new alphabet, to have produced major improvements over the established script and language. This might be true, but the case to be made for this judgment is not as obvious as often assumed, because assessments of what is "right" or "natural" tend to be closely tied to what modern

[10] Miller, *Legislating Authority*, 108–9.
[11] Miller, "Role of the Orthodox Church," 278.

Turkish has become. The usual criticisms of Ottoman heard today are that orthography and pronunciation were ill matched – vowels were not clearly marked and certain Turkish consonants could be represented by multiple Arabic letters – and that the language was just too complicated, too full of Arabic and Persian loanwords. Each criticism has some validity, but none is as significant as is now thought (note that this is stated in English, a Germanic language enriched by massive derivation of vocabulary from French, and whose promiscuity of relationships between spelling and pronunciation is positively immoral – but is nevertheless the "world language" today). The apparent redundancy in Ottoman consonants was useful, because many of the Arabic-script letters indicated possible neighboring vowels as well. In Ottoman, *olmak* [to become/be] and *ölmek* [to die] would not be confused because different letters represent the sound that modern Turkish can only give as "k," thus obviating some of the need to mark the vowels as explicitly as modern Turkish must. The gap between Ottoman orthography and modern pronunciation has also been exaggerated by the extensive restructuring and formalization that the language has undergone, especially since the founding of the republic, which has made modern Turkish at least as "artificial" as any of the Balkan literary languages that have been formulated in the course of nation building. In adjacent areas not subjected directly to republican-era reform, pronunciation of Azeri and of Turkish elements surviving in Balkan languages tends to retain closer ties to Ottoman written forms than the Turkish of modern Turkey, suggesting that Ottoman did reflect spoken Turkish of the time more closely than is often now recognized. This assertion holds even when it is remembered that there was no more a uniform colloquial Turkish than there were standard spoken forms of Bulgarian, Greek, or Albanian before the founding of the nation-states, but rather rich palates of dialectal pronunciation and vocabulary.

Atatürk and his supporters in the language reform that started in 1928 nevertheless argued that "Ottoman" Turkish as it then existed was too complicated and separated from the common man, and thus prevented the spread of literacy, but the experience of the reforms belies their stated rationale.[12] Their purpose was to sever the people from their Islamic and Ottoman past in order to aid their conversion into a Turkish nation. At a most obvious level, the abolition of the accepted system of writing and introduction of a radically new pattern, a change instituted over

---

[12] See, for example, Frank Tachau, "Language and Politics: Turkish Language Reform," *Review of Politics* 26 (1964), 191–204.

a mere two months (a law of 1 November 1928 ruled that all public communication must be in the new script by 1 January 1929), made much of the nation's literate minority at least temporarily as illiterate as their unschooled fellows. This problem was probably soon corrected, because the state pressed both children and adults to learn quickly the new "national" script (had it applied the same effort and resources to schooling the illiterate before the start of the reform, literacy rates would also have risen). Functional literacy remained stubbornly low thereafter, however, because the reform's supposed purpose of lessening the gap between the common man and the language only created more confusion, as the reformers turned to cleansing Turkish of its "undesirable" elements: words of Arabic or Persian origin. This was not part of purifying the language of foreign words, because words with European (especially French) origins were safe and even multiplied; it was rather a campaign focused upon severing ties with the Islamic past. If these alien words resulted from the affectations of the old Ottoman ruling class and were incomprehensible to the common Turk, as the reformers claimed, then they should have had little trouble in finding colloquial Turkish equivalents, but despite great efforts to scour Turkey for any "native" equivalents for "alien" Arabic and Persian words, relatively few were found. Reformers had to "revive" long-dead Turkish words spotted in old manuscripts or simply create neologisms to replace the Arabic and Persian elements that had become integral parts of Turkish. The result was a language at least as alien as Ottoman had supposedly been, as became evident in a series of incomprehensible speeches given in neo-Turkish by Atatürk in 1934.[13]

None of the Atatürkist religious, linguistic, and other reforms designed to create a Turkish nation won the immediate acceptance and admiration of the bulk of the population, and the authoritarianism of the state alienated many.[14] Dissent received little official recognition, although there clearly was unrest independent of the Shaikh Said rebellion in a number of towns south and east of Ankara late in 1925, which led to numerous death sentences passed by independence tribunals.[15] The regime hardly

---

[13] Özkırımlı and Sofos, *Tormented by History*, 66. At this time he dropped his (Arabic) given name of *Mustafa* but retained his equally Arabic adopted name of *Kemal* ("perfection") with a dubious assertion of its Turkishness; the surname he also adopted in 1934 was unique, and legally so: even members of his family could not have it.

[14] Meeker, *Nation of Empire*, chap. 9, gives a view of the provincial experience of the Atatürk period.

[15] Gavin Brockett, "Collective Action and the Turkish Revolution: Towards a Framework for the Social History of the Atatürk Era, 1923–38," *MES* 34 (1998), 44–66.

matched the expectations of the majority of a society still rooted in an Ottoman past, and Atatürk never explained properly why he had chosen the path for the country that he did. He tried to remedy this with his six-day-long *Nutuk* (speech – subsequently retitled with the neologism *Söylev* after the Arabic *nutuk* was purged from modern Turkish) in 1927, a paean to himself that recounted his version of history since 1919 and avowed that his nation building and reform program had been the purpose behind the liberation struggle. He came to realize that skepticism and discontent nevertheless continued and thus in 1930 allowed for the first time since the state of emergency declared in 1925 the creation of a token opposition party, to be led by an old associate, Fethi; when the new party was swamped by applications for membership, however, he told Fethi in effect to dissolve it, as Fethi duly felt compelled to do just a few months after the party was founded. Muzzled opposition to the current regime continued, but on at least one occasion it found violent expression. In the western Anatolian town of Menemen in December 1930, protesters led by a sufi shaikh called for the restoration of the caliphate and shari'a, and they killed an officer commanding a handful of troops who had shot a protester. Harsh repression quelled the dissent, although Atatürk's order that Menemen be burned to the ground and rebuilt was fortunately not executed (but conceivably could have been; in the 1930s Kurdish regions were subjected to campaigns of killing and mass relocation reminiscent of that targeting Armenians and Assyrians during the war).[16] The state under Atatürk reacted to signs of discontent (beyond stifling expression of it) not by amendment of reform measures and methods of administration but rather by intensification of the drive to empower the state and to form the nation that it nominally served. Single-party rule resumed, the last dissident newspaper was closed, and all remaining organizations outside state control were abolished, including even the nationalist Turkish Hearth association and the Turkish Women's Union.

To provide a clearer rationale for the regime's actions, the sole party, the Republican People's Party (RPP), adopted in 1931 and then inserted into the state constitution in 1937 the "six principles of Kemalism," all of which provided ideological support for the absolute ascendancy of

---

[16] Norman Itzkowitz and Vamik Volkan, *The Immortal Atatürk: A Psychobiography* (Chicago: University of Chicago Press, 1984), 290–1; Üngör, *Making of Modern Turkey*, chap. 3.

the state: republicanism, secularism, nationalism, populism, statism, and revolutionism. The first two made clear that loyalty and service to "devlet" meant to the state, not to a deposed dynasty, and that "din" had no role other than as a prop of the state. Even by loose definition, this was not secularism: there was neither separation of "church" and state nor even simply the making of religion a personal issue not to intrude in public affairs. The state barred religious figures, parties, and even dress from public areas and affairs but recognized no limit to its ability to intrude in religious matters. It dissolved sufi brotherhoods, took control over training and licensing of religious figures, tried with partial success to replace Arabic by Turkish within the mosque, and even directed the contents of Friday noon-prayer sermons. Yet in the state's view religion also could not be considered a private matter, a question of personal discretion. Its various restrictions and harassments targeting Muslim religious observance and thought show this, as does its treatment of the remaining non-Muslim communities, whose members have never been accepted as equal with Muslims, as fully Turkish. Examples of disparity in treatment are easy to find. Non-Muslims have always been viewed as alien minorities, while the largest Muslim ethnic minority, the Kurds, have been blithely labeled "Mountain Turks." During the first half of the Second World War, all non-Muslim males aged eighteen to forty-five were rounded up and deported to camps in the Anatolian interior, and a "wealth tax" was levied on the urban middle class that non-Muslims paid at a rate up to ten times that levied on Muslims – indeed, the main point of contention in the national assembly was the propriety of making Muslims pay anything at all.[17]

Islam thus provided the true base for national identity, but the state tried hard to decorate that identity with enough nonreligious elements to disguise its origins. This was the principle of nationalism, and the means of building it included not only language reform but the development of theories of the Turkish nation through history, including pseudoscientific notions such as the Sun Language theory (Turkish was the original language from which other languages are descended) and the related Turkish History thesis (Turks formed the world's first high civilization in Central Asia; when forced to migrate by climate conditions, they founded high civilizations in China, India, Mesopotamia,

---

[17] Hugh Poulton, *Top Hat, Grey Wolf and Crescent: Turkish Nationalism and the Turkish Republic* (London: Hurst, 1997), 117–19.

and Europe).[18] Atatürk embraced these notions, and although some of their more outrageous claims were allowed to fade after his death in 1938, they continued to influence the content of school curricula for decades thereafter.

Acceptance of new ideas and practices, no matter how odd or repugnant to old sensibilities, constituted the revolutionism principle of Kemalism; populism was another peculiar principle, because neither the RPP nor its predecessor, the CUP, was a party that tried to mobilize the masses of the nation.[19] Kemalist "populism" meant unity and thus justified the state's reluctance to allow any form of organized opposition, including parties other than the RPP, or indeed any other milieu in which dissidence might coalesce, from Masonic lodges to village tea houses.

Statism, at least, fit its most common meaning, that the state should play a leading or directing role; the only remarkable element in this principle of Kemalism was the emphasis placed on state direction of economic development, which became a serious issue in the worldwide depression that began in 1929. It is difficult to see that the state, which followed in most years the directives of military men (Kemal Atatürk and İsmet İnönü) ignorant of economic affairs, achieved as much as it could have but, given the scarcity of funds for investment during the depression (already a problem prior to 1929, following the effective destruction of the old non-Muslim commercial class in 1914–23), even misguided state projects provided practical training for managers and workers that might not have otherwise been available in the 1930s.

Kemalist ideology, as expressed in the six arrows, explained the rise of an unchallengeable state, but it did not dissolve all dissatisfaction with the authoritarian regime. Atatürk's personal legitimacy and authority, based upon his role as leader of the anti-Greek struggle and reviser of the Sèvres treaty, complemented by his undeniable charisma, had made the growth of the state tolerable, but after the Second World War ended, his successor, İnönü, had to loosen ties between the state and the RPP and to lessen some of the firmness of the state's grip on the life of the

---

[18] Özkırımlı and Sofos, *Tormented by History*, 91–9. On the nation-building pressures placed upon history and other fields of study after the founding of the republic, see Üngör, *Making of Modern Turkey*, chap. 5, and Arzu Öztürkmen, "Folklore on Trial: Pertev Naili Boratav and the Denationalization of Turkish Folklore," *Journal of Folklore Research* 42 (2005), 185–216.

[19] Zürcher, "Ottoman Legacy," 243.

nation. In the first National Assembly elections relatively free of state and RPP manipulation, in 1950, the young Democrat Party won a resounding victory, and the RPP was consigned to ineffective opposition until the DP was overthrown by Turkey's first military coup in 1960. By 1950, however, the Atatürkist state had had almost three decades of uninterrupted control in which to entrench the ideas of Kemalism in at least some sectors of society, and indeed the DP had explicitly accepted the six principles of Kemalism before its first election victory. Age played a role in the entrenchment: Atatürk appealed directly to the youth of the nation to act as agents and guardians of his program, and as in other post-Ottoman states in the Balkans, the education system and the military (two institutions most strictly controlled for ideological purity) trained the young to their role. Teaching the new alphabet to the population in 1928–9 indeed depended upon the armed forces' educating recruits to a basic level of literacy and then returning them to their villages with instructions to tutor both young and old. In towns where more than the most rudimentary schools were to be found students ingested an intensely Kemalist education, beginning with the *Nutuk* as a basic text and history lessons based upon the Turkish History thesis. Graduates who had absorbed sound views had various routes to professional advancement open to them, most of which depended upon the state directly or indirectly. Thus the sectors of society that became the advocates of Kemalism became the bureaucracy, school and university staff, the press, the legal and medical professions, the management levels of commercial and manufacturing establishments, and the military officer corps, which had been formed by the ideologically unblemished triumvirate of Atatürk himself, İnönü, and the third most powerful figure in the first decades of the republic, Marshal Fevzi Çakmak.

Unbroken control from 1923 to 1950 thus helps to explain why Turkey's transition from Ottoman territory to post-Ottoman nation proved successful, despite the considerable turmoil created by the rapid, forced changes imposed upon the country. Despite Atatürk's personal and political flaws, he does deserve recognition for his signal achievement in shaping the new country and ensuring its survival. Unlike the first post-Ottoman leaders of any country in the Balkans, he had a genuine claim to legitimate leadership based upon personal rootedness in the culture and experiences of the new country's society, and upon meaningful achievement in struggling for that population's future; his public persona made him well suited to filling the central political void created by the departure of centuries-old Ottoman rule. He was, in fact, a highly competent and accomplished leader (but perhaps not quite as brilliant as he thought himself). The majority of his new nation embraced him as leader but did not fully accept his vision of the future, and especially two elements: the hard authoritarianism of the state, and the harsh subjugation of religious institutions and faith to the dictates of that state. Both issues have surfaced repeatedly in political tensions ever since Atatürk's death and especially since the end of the Second World War.

8

The Post-Ottoman Arab Lands

Of all the post-Ottoman countries, those of the Arab region had the most peculiar – and disadvantageous – beginnings. While the independent states of the Balkans and Turkey felt the need to develop or adapt forms of government to fill the vacuum left by the collapse of Ottoman rule, they at least had the chance to create regimes to control the new, nominally national, countries. Arab lands had little such opportunity. Rather than transiting from Ottoman provinces to post-Ottoman countries, they left the empire only to enter political purgatory, set officially on paths to the eventual recognition of independent nation-states but left in fact to practically open-ended British and French control. This twilit existence continued for roughly three decades, a period not of completely suspended animation but rather of misdevelopment or ultimately directionless drift. One of the most important issues that suggested such aimlessness was the choosing of a model that the construction of post-Ottoman supralocal identities should adopt.

During their European imperial interlude, the populations in the Middle East started with most of the disadvantages seen in the Balkans and Turkey but few of the opportunities to execute any of the measures taken elsewhere to build new senses of identity. As in other formerly Ottoman lands, there was little legitimate native leadership above the local level, and in some cases the European powers again proved decisive in establishing the authority of nonnative leaders (as they had done for Otto Wittelsbach and Georg Glücksburg in Greece, Alexander Battenberg and Ferdinand Saxe-Coburg-Gotha in Bulgaria, and Karl Hohenzollern-Sigmaringen and Ferdinand Hohenzollern in Romania, and almost did for Wilhelm zu Wied in Albania); rarely did they accept the rise of local notables to supralocal influence (as Miloš Obrenović in Serbia, Ahmet Zogu in Albania, and Mustafa Kemal in Turkey were able to do). Given that European control over the Middle East was established for the purpose of founding sustainable nation-states, nationalism was as logical or "natural" a choice of political ideology after the Ottoman collapse as it was elsewhere. Yet in the absence of true, legitimate native leadership and without fully autonomous regimes, no state existed capable of undertaking any serious nation-building program that would or could mold the populations within the European-drawn borders into distinct peoples. This meant that versions of nationalism emerged around the region, and the one to achieve surprising influence after midcentury was Arabism, an ideology impractical as anything other than a motivational tool for expelling the European powers (with the focus transferred after 1948 to Israel, seen as the most egregious remaining vestige of imperialism) and for erasing European-imposed borders. Arab nationalism is the world's only "pan"-national movement to have won serious support as a political ideology, and its lack of tangible results suggests why such grandly inclusive ideologies failed elsewhere. It has offered little, if any, of the state legitimation that nationalism provided other post-Ottoman countries, and the impossibility of matching the borders of the nation with those of the state has only heightened long-term political instability.

THE EUROPEAN IMPERIAL PERIOD

Except in the case of Iran's borders with Iraq and Turkey, today's map of countries in the Middle East and North Africa was drawn by the leading European powers on the winning side of the First World War, Britain and France. The Franco-British border-drawing exercises were not entirely unreasoned, since some countries of today (such as Egypt and Iraq) reflect geographic identities established in earlier centuries, or indeed millennia. Yet the very nature of modern frontiers made the drawing of the map unreasonable. Nationalism often gains strength from identifying what the community is not, and borders gain importance not just from the lands and peoples drawn together within them but from those excluded. All Franco-British borders were arbitrary, because they created real barriers to the movement of people and goods where none had existed in the Ottoman period, rendering familiar faces and places suddenly "foreign," and were made that much more arbitrary by the justification for stripping lands and people away from Ottoman control that was advanced by Britain and France during the world war. Britain in particular trumpeted the cause of liberating the Arab nation from Turkish oppression, only then to engineer with France the division of that nation into discrete protocountries. Yet the idea of the "Arab nation" had roots in the Ottoman past that were almost as weak as those of Franco-British borders.

Much as in the Balkans and Anatolia, the Arab provinces of the Ottoman empire did not form an ethnonationally distinct part of the empire; the term "Arab provinces" seems suitable mainly because of its brevity compared to "Ottoman West Asia and North Africa." As elsewhere in the empire, the strongest senses of loyalty were local (kinship, locale, and the social networks upon which professional and religious communities depended) and religious. "Arabness" carried slight practical weight. In Ottoman usage, which followed a pattern of assigning negative connotations to ethnic terms, especially for Muslim populations deemed troublesome or uncivilized (such as the uncultured "Turk" villager), "Arab" normally referred to bedouin tribesmen rather than Arabic-speaking settled people, and this usage underwent only modest change in the last years of Ottoman rule. The "Arab" provinces also had significant populations that were not ethnolinguistically Arab, including Kurds, Turks, Circassians/Caucasians, and Armenians in western Asia and Berbers in North Africa. For the Arabic-speaking population, moreover, language was a relatively weak unifying factor. Like the church versions of Greek and Slavonic, literary Arabic was a liturgical language that the educated could speak but differed significantly from the colloquial dialects used in daily life. It seems indeed ironic that the word implying in Ottoman usage a section of the population that was splintered by clan and tribe allegiances, and often hostile relations with settled people, should become the nominal rallying point for the sedentary masses across a huge expanse of the Middle East and North Africa, almost none of whom really spoke the nation's language. Yet under the conditions created by the extension of European control over the southern tier of Ottoman provinces, Arabism became the default supralocal identity rather than regional or religious solidarity.

Much of the responsibility for Arabism's rise lay with Britain and the Hashimite sharif of Mecca. The Ottoman sultan-caliph's declaration of jihad against Britain and its allies had pushed the British to arouse a counterjihad, which led them to press Sharif Husayn to start an anti-Ottoman uprising in the Hijaz. This revolt was religious, not ethnonational. The Hijaz was a region "singularly lacking" the economic, intellectual, political, and military prerequisites for the emergence of nationalism even among the elite, and Husayn cast the revolt as a religious movement from the beginning.[1] Echoing Mehmed Ali's critique of Mahmud II as defender of faith and justice, Husayn charged the CUP regime with failing to uphold shari'a, oppressing and killing Muslims, and losing lands from the Abode of Islam.[2] Like Mehmed Ali, Husayn and his sons launched rebellion because of feeling trapped: to remain quiescent in the Hijaz was to invite overthrow by either Istanbul or the British. There was certainly an element of opportunism in Husayn's response to British overtures, but he and his sons had real concerns that the CUP regime might remove them because of their failure to commit themselves wholly to the war effort, whereas their vulnerability to rivals in Najd and 'Asir made doing so difficult; perhaps more importantly, Mecca had to import food and other basic supplies through Jidda, which was very vulnerable to British blockade. Indeed, once Husayn sided with Britain, his ability to distribute Egyptian grain to tribes equally vulnerable to British blockade generated much of the revolt's fighting force.[3] That Muslims' response was much cooler than that given Mehmed Ali suggests that Husayn lacked his legitimacy as a leader and the CUP's reputation was less dire than Mahmud II's; that Husayn made Mecca, the holiest city, implicitly subordinate to his new patron, infidel Britain, also sapped credibility from his claim of fighting for the religion.[4] The revolt therefore soon had to adopt Arab nationalism, however ill defined, as a legitimating principle. This shift occurred also because Britain maintained consistently throughout the war the ethnonational purpose of liberating "the Arabs" from "the Turks" and gave no support to any alternate view. Husayn himself seems to have had little trouble accepting the British terminology because he and his sons 'Ali and 'Abdallah understood their "Arab" project primarily in a geographic sense: they wanted to be amirs of Arabia (Hijaz and its neighboring lands).[5] For Husayn's third son, Faysal, who took the Arab revolt out of the Arabian Peninsula and had no real political future

[1] William Ochsenwald, "Ironic Origins: Arab Nationalism in the Hijaz, 1882–1914," in *The Origins of Arab Nationalism*, ed. Rashid Khalidi et al. (New York: Columbia University Press, 1991), 190. See also Mary Wilson, "The Hashemites, the Arab Revolt, and Arab Nationalism," in Khalidi et al. (eds.), *Origins of Arab Nationalism*, 213–14.
[2] G., "Textes historiques sur le reveil arabe au Hedjaz," *RMM* 46 (1921), 4–10.
[3] Tariq Tell, "Guns, Gold, and Grain: War and Food Supply in the Making of Transjordan," in *War, Institutions, and Social Change in the Middle East*, ed. Steven Heydemann (Berkeley: University of California Press, 2000), 33–48.
[4] For pro-Ottoman propaganda making this point, see G., "Textes," 14–17, 22.
[5] C. Ernest Dawn, *From Ottomanism to Arabism: Essays on the Origins of Arab Nationalism* (Urbana: University of Illinois Press, 1973), chap. 1, and Wilson, "The Hashemites," 215–16.

without British support, however, the British perspective was to become the only one tenable.

After Russia's withdrawal from the war in 1917, Britain was the only opponent of the Ottomans that mattered in deciding the struggle in the East, and Britain's vision of the Arab nation shaped the postwar political order; the Hashimites and even France had to accept Britain's lead. Britain's disposition of formerly Ottoman lands followed its own imperial interests but, beyond that constraint, reflected the Arab ideal far more than the local or religious identities dominant within the population. Obscuring Britain's role in fostering Arabism was its commitment to promises of postwar payoffs to real or prospective allies. These promises were infamously ad hoc and mutually irreconcilable: Britain would back a division of Ottoman Arab lands into French (in the North) and British (from Egypt to Baghdad and Basra in the South) zones of control or influence, with Palestine under international administration (Sykes-Picot Agreement, 1916); it would aid the creation of an Arab kingdom under Sharif Husayn that would incorporate much of this same territory (Husayn-MacMahon Correspondence, 1916); and it would support the creation of a Jewish homeland in Palestine (Balfour Declaration, 1917). Britain struggled to reconcile its package of promises without damaging its own imperial interests but ultimately satisfied none of its wartime interlocutors. It acquiesced to French control of what is now Syria and Lebanon but retained Palestine and northern Iraq. It backed the immigration of Zionists to Palestine but without setting any clear goal of creating an independent Israel, Arab Palestine, or "binational" state. It did least for Sharif Husayn, failing to create an "Arab kingdom" for him or even to offer protection against Sa'udi pressure on the only territory Husayn really valued, the Hijaz. He had to accept a Sa'udi ultimatum that he go into exile in 1924, and Britain refused to aid his son 'Ali's efforts to retain the Hijaz, abandoned under Sa'udi pressure in 1925. Britain did place two of Husayn's sons on thrones established in British-controlled territories elsewhere, however: Faysal in Iraq and 'Abdallah in Transjordan.

Having created these "Arab" monarchs, however, Britain balked at permitting Faysal and 'Abdallah the freedom to build independent states or cultivate any clearly viable political culture that would build legitimacy in the eyes of the populations placed under their nominal authority. Having invested in material and immaterial terms so much in the liberation of "Arab lands" from the "Turkish yoke," and thereby removing the threat to British imperial interests that the weak or hostile "Turks" had posed, Britain had no desire to jeopardize the war's results by permitting "the Arabs" the freedom to decide their course in the international arena or even how they wished to manage their "national" affairs. Fear of the resurgence of "Turkish" – and thereby Bolshevik – influence only confirmed the determination to retain control over post-Ottoman lands in the region. The postwar disposition indicated Britain's prime concerns: India and oil. Baghdad and Basra had been destined for British control since the outbreak of war in the Middle East (Britain's first military move against the Ottoman empire was the invasion of southern Iraq in November 1914), because one of the two direct routes from Britain to India led overland from the Syrian coast to the Euphrates and then followed the river to Baghdad, Basra, and the head of the gulf. Mosul's evident oil riches caused reconsideration of the Sykes-Picot Agreement's prevision of that province coming under French influence, leading to its occupation and then retention by Britain after the war (although Mosul was still in Ottoman hands at the armistice in 1918, British forces seized it soon thereafter).

Britain was most stubborn in defending its control over the key points controlling the Suez Canal and the Red Sea, the most heavily used direct route to India. The British had occupied Egypt since 1882 but did not challenge the land's legal status as Ottoman territory until the outbreak of war in 1914; at the end of the conflict they showed every sign of intending not to recognize Egypt's independence but rather to absorb it into their own empire. Widespread and continuing Egyptian protests and campaigns of noncooperation with the occupiers led London to a unilateral declaration that Egypt was independent, but Britain reserved to itself control over key matters, including the defense of the canal and control over the Sudan, which had been subject to an Anglo-Egyptian "condominium" since 1899. Sudan was of interest because it was the other significant riverain territory of the Red Sea north and west of its Bab al-Mandab entry point, which in turn Britain already policed from its base at Aden (occupied since 1839). It again changed the terms of the Sykes-Picot Agreement to retain control over southern geographic Syria (Palestine and Transjordan), the land route for any power wishing to threaten the canal or Egypt. As long as it held India, Britain refused to relinquish its dominant voice over the external and security affairs of these lands and retained also its willingness to intervene in internal matters where these posed any risk of creating turbulence. Without control over the core interests of any state, no "native" regime under British influence could claim either real independence or legitimacy.

Having occupied Egypt since 1882, Britain had taken actions there that foreshadowed its practice of "indirect" but firm control across the region. It had assumed direction of Egyptian security and international affairs from the outset of occupation and had inserted British advisers in departments of the reigning khedive's government that dealt with domestic affairs. At the outbreak of the war, Britain deposed the khedive of the day because he was too conspicuously Ottoman (he issued a call from Istanbul for Egyptians to rise against the British) and replaced him with an elderly uncle upon whom it bestowed the title of sultan; the declaration that Egypt was now to be a British protectorate, however, vitiated the prestige of the new title. Throughout the war, in which the British campaigns against the Ottomans west of Iraq were run from Cairo, Britain kept Egypt under tight military control, legitimated by a declared state of emergency. It requisitioned labor and agricultural produce, there were widespread shortages of goods induced by the strain of the war effort, and inflation rose rapidly. The British government had debated annexation of Egypt at the start and late in the war, and the postwar constitutional arrangements suggested that this idea would be enacted in all but name. The high commission in Egypt proposed a reworking of the institutions of government known in the khedival period, replacing them with new bodies under full British control.

When the end of the war produced no sign that the tightening of the British grip would be loosened, the wave of unrest began that led to Britain's decision to accept Egyptian independence provided that the country accepted a constitutional arrangement suitable to London's imperial interests. From 1922, when the main Egyptian "nationalist" party, the Wafd, accepted Britain's conditions, Britain retained control over imperial communications (i.e., the Suez Canal), Egypt's international security, protection of minorities (i.e., continuation of the capitulations, which Britain had wanted to annul while it ran Egypt for the same reason that the Ottoman empire had, because they made coherent administration impossible), and Sudanese affairs. Some 575 British civilian and at least 5,000 military personnel remained stationed in Egypt through the 1920s and 1930s to maintain supervision of London's declared interests.[6] It was no surprise that demands for renegotiation of these four points, and complete withdrawal of British personnel, formed one of the few constants in Egyptian politics until the early 1950s, because these issues

---

[6] Yoav Alon, *The Making of Jordan: Tribes, Colonialism and the Modern State* (London: I. B. Tauris, 2007), 62.

had enormous implications for the independence and territorial integrity of Egypt's nominal nation-state.

As in Egypt, so in Palestine and Transjordan. Being a territory that had little value other than as a transit route or buffer between regions with higher population densities, strategic value, and economic productivity, Transjordan had slightly more freedom from pervasive interference. It was originally part of the Palestine Mandate, and the mandatory authority there did not divest itself of all oversight of affairs on the Jordan's East Bank, including notably control over the main military force. Payment of a stipend to 'Abdallah, who controlled little other revenue potential, ensured that Transjordan was governed in accord with British interests, despite the lack of outright occupation. In Palestine, by contrast, there was no attempt to disguise the open-ended and thorough nature of British control, as it was the only territory governed under a League of Nations mandate that contained no stated goal of preparing the population for eventual independence – a vagueness necessitated by the Balfour Declaration's espousal of creation of a Jewish national home without prejudice to the civil and religious rights of non-Jews in Palestine. The declaration indeed was incorporated into the terms of the Palestine mandate. The close control exercised by the British, coupled with their commitment to aid Zionism, caused the outbreak of riots by Palestinians in 1920 and 1921, carrying echoes of the protests in Egypt.

It was Iraq that offered the closest parallel with Egypt, however, beginning with the eruption of a widespread rebellion in 1920 that killed several thousand British and Indian troops and required months (and much bloodshed caused by brutal tactics) to quell. As in Egypt, the unrest pushed Britain to relinquish plans to absorb Iraq fully into the empire. It installed as king Faysal, the main field commander of the Arab revolt, and pressed him to accept a nominal form of independence much like that imposed upon Egypt. British authorities retained a decisive role in security, financial, judicial, and international affairs. This dominance was loosened but not broken by the Anglo-Iraqi treaty of 1930 that Britain required before proposing to the League of Nations that Iraq be recognized as independent and admitted to the league. Britain retained a decisive military role in the country, although from 1932 the newly independent state was permitted to begin development of its own military forces.

Britain's close monitoring of key affairs that should have been the primary concerns of any truly independent state in the post-Ottoman Middle East seemed almost lax in comparison to the pervasive control exercised by France in what is now Syria and Lebanon. At a most basic level the degree of French control could be seen in the repeated redrawing of administrative borders: France created Lebanon by adding significant territory to the Ottoman era district of Mount Lebanon, diluting the district's Christian majority by adding mainly Muslim-populated areas but giving the new (still Christian-dominated) Lebanon greater heft. It had to fight to extend control from the coast to Damascus. Once the remaining parts of Syria were in hand, the French arranged and rearranged local districts into separate administrative "states" (see Map 5). Each administrative zone had a range of French commissioners and advisers who decided important issues according to French interests. Two of the most contentious areas of expatriate control were security and judicial affairs: French military forces numbered at least fifteen thousand men from the early 1920s, with French officers commanding an additional "native" corps, and French judges presided over all legal matters that involved any non-Syrian national, inspected the "native" civil courts, and ran military tribunals that tried political opponents of the French regime.[7] Such opponents certainly existed, as the eruption of a widespread revolt in 1925 indicated.

It might be argued that Anglo-French arrangements in the Middle East paralleled the great powers' actions in establishing the post-Ottoman countries of the Balkans, not only in deciding who should be placed in nominal control of new states but even in active administration of national affairs. Nowhere in the Balkans, however, did such direct control last as long as in the Middle East: Russia had to withdraw its military and administrators from Bulgaria one year after the 1878 Treaty of Berlin, and in Greece the Wittelsbach monarchy had to dismiss its Swiss-German Praetorian Guard and Bavarian administrative staff within ten years of its founding in 1833. Perhaps more importantly, even in Greece, the Balkan country subjected longest to foreign control, the Bavarian-"Greek" monarch pushed aggressively the creation of effective nation-building tools, which neither the French nor the British had any interest in promoting in the Middle East. Part of this coldness toward nation building presumably resulted from the lack of connection to the European powers' own senses of identity: the Greeks were the Orthodox, misguided but still Christian, and Greece was Athens, Sparta, Delphi, and Thebes. A Bavarian king whose "enlightened" views nominally originated in these classical-era cultural centers could persuade himself of the illusion of "coming home"

---

[7] Philip Khoury, *Syria and the French Mandate: The Politics of Arab Nationalism, 1920–1945* (Princeton: Princeton University Press, 1987), 79, 82–3.

to Greece. Arabs, by contrast, were Muslim and therefore had been until recently (when it became convenient to think of them otherwise) "Turks," and Arabia was Baghdad, Damascus, Cairo, and the deserts of the bedouin, which, unlike the classical sites, were neither conveniently united in one country nor part of the "European heritage" taught to colonial officialdom between spells on the playing fields of Eton. The uprisings against European occupation soon after the end of the First World War also raised the awkward possibility that the lack of rebellion among the overwhelming majority of Ottoman Arabs during the war was not just a sign of their meekness or docility. This led to the post-Ottoman paradox of the Middle East: Britain had built wartime policies upon the idea of the Arab nation, but after 1918 neither the British nor the French considered that nation mature enough to manage its own affairs, and any nation-building efforts would inevitably damage Anglo-French interests in the region. Post-Ottoman identities in the Middle East thus developed in a more haphazard fashion, and under more inhospitable conditions, than in either the Balkans or Turkey.

ARAB NATIONALISM AND ISLAM

Three significant avenues for the development of post-Ottoman identities existed in the lands under British and French control: continuation of the religious identities inherited from the Ottoman past, the boosting of geographically defined regionalism, or the nationalism in whose name Britain had fought the Ottoman empire. All showed vitality, but Arabism achieved the strongest growth, in part because it addressed forcefully the issues of the postwar settlement that most troubled significant parts of the population: European control and the newly imposed borders. Like nationalisms in the Balkans and Turkey, it also succeeded because it retained a close link to the dominant faith, Sunni Islam – and even included some of the same weaknesses that persuaded leaders of new states not to adopt religion as the basis of political identity, including the impossibility of controlling a nonhierarchical religion shared by populations outside country borders. Those fragile post-Ottoman states that adapted themselves to Arab nationalism as they struggled to rid themselves of lingering European control attempted the redirection of religious identities into national ones but failed to gain the levels of mastery over religion seen in the Balkans and Turkey. Islam, particularly the "populist" form reflected in sufism, remained a force more independent of the state than anywhere in other post-Ottoman countries, as the rise of the

Muslim Brotherhood in Egypt after 1928 and subsequent spread to other Arab lands under European influence showed. The option of regionalism might have made possible an experience that more closely paralleled that of the Balkans or Turkey, but the political circumstances of the time undermined its potential strength everywhere but in Egypt.

Ottoman Middle Eastern lands had historically well-established regions: geographic Syria, Iraq, and Egypt had been distinct territories throughout the Islamic period and indeed reaching back into the pre-Islamic era. Post-Ottoman Iraq and Egypt approximate the respective historical units, but geographic Syria has split into Syria, Lebanon, Jordan, and Israel-Palestine. The inhabitants of each region shared dialectal affinities, with numerous variations across its area but nevertheless forming a recognizable colloquial language that distinguished Syrian from Egyptian or Iraqi. In the Ottoman era natives of each region also showed forms of geographic "homeland" identity, both regional and subregional.[8] This was most developed in Egypt, which had a great asset in the Nile, the major thoroughfare binding the narrow band of densely settled, rich land from south to north. Egypt's exceptional early experience of practical autonomy after Mehmed Ali won the hereditary governorship of the province in 1841 boosted the sense that it was a distinct entity. After Mehmed Ali's grandson Ismail had to accept that Egypt was bankrupt in 1876 and submit to tighter external control, first by Istanbul and then much more intrusively by European powers and bankers, a "native" (not speaking Turkish as mother tongue) army officer, Ahmad 'Urabi, mounted an "Egypt for the Egyptians!" uprising in 1881 that was crushed the following year by British forces, thus beginning the British occupation of Egypt. This movement found subsequent echoes in the anti-British National Party, associated notably with Mustafa Kamil (1874–1908), whose experience as a student in France, where he had much exposure to radical European ideas of nationalism, sharpened his views. Yet his "nationalism" was not adamantly focused upon Egyptian independence but rather fit within the anti-European tradition, as he favored Egypt's reintegration into the Ottoman empire.[9] Ottoman Syria or Iraq also had "decentralists" who wished to see more control over local affairs granted to the inhabitants of these regions, but none of Mustafa Kamil's stature.

---

[8] Haim Gerber, "'Palestine' and Other Territorial Concepts in the 17th Century," *IJMES* 30 (1998), 563–72.

[9] Peter Sluglett, "The Mandate System: High Ideals, Illiberal Practices," in *Liberal Thought in the Eastern Mediterranean: Late 19th Century until the 1960s*, ed. Christoph Schumann (Leiden: Brill, 2008), 33.

While Egyptian regional nationalism grew in vitality in the post-1918 period, when Britain's incomplete withdrawal widened the viable scope for distinctly Egyptian politics, no post-Ottoman political leaders in a position to build upon such regional identities in Syria or Iraq really wished to do so in any determined fashion. In Syria, mutual suspicions emanating from subregional or local identities (notably between Aleppo and Damascus) made calls for Syrian solidarity less straightforward than might have been expected.[10] Being divided under the control of French and British wartime allies still suspicious of each other presented further complications, since the mandatory authorities allowed little latitude to push cross-border initiatives. Insofar as France encouraged any group identities in the populations under its control, they were religious: Lebanon was created for the benefit of the Uniate Catholic Maronites, and among the statelets established in what is now Syria were entities for the 'Alawis and the Druze. After the end of French control following the Second World War, however, one of the political parties that showed strength in electoral and subversive politics in both Lebanon and Syria was the Syrian Socialist National Party of Antun Sa'ada, which championed reunification of the region.[11] Syria's non-Maronite religious minorities generally found the idea attractive. The notables of Jabal Druze, for example, were readier to look to 'Abdallah of Jordan than to the "Arab nationalist" notables of Damascus as their rallying point.[12] 'Abdallah in turn dreamed of acquiring the Syrian throne held briefly by his brother Faysal, but in 1924 British authorities told him in ominously clear terms to desist from agitation toward French mandated territory.[13] It was only in 1948 that he was able to absorb another slice of Syria, seizing the West Bank of the Jordan River during the war over the creation of Israel. In Palestine, as in French Syria or indeed the post-Ottoman Balkans, there was no native candidate capable of establishing his leadership within the territory, let alone directing attention to reuniting with other parts of the region. The only figure remembered by most non-Palestinians as a "leader," Hajj Amin al-Husayni, owed his influence to the British, who installed him as mufti of Jerusalem and more importantly vested that

---

[10] Joshua Landis, "Nationalism and the Politics of Za'ama: The Collapse of Republican Syria, 1945–1949" (PhD dissertation, Princeton University, 1997).

[11] Daniel Pipes, *Greater Syria: The History of an Ambition* (Oxford: Oxford University Press, 1990).

[12] Landis, "Politics of Za'ama."

[13] Eugene Rogan, *The Arabs: A History* (London: Allen Lane, 2009), 183–7.

religious office with unprecedented political authority to "speak for the community."

Iraq under King Faysal was better positioned to achieve success in building regionalism, which might have been the best choice for an identity to legitimate the new state in the eyes of its citizens. Influential Shi'i scholars favored a religious identity for the new state, but the fact that the Shi'a constituted the largest religious group made religion a questionable rallying point for the Sunnis whom Britain placed in power during the mandate; Britain's support of the Hashimites as champions of Arab nationalism implied Sunni domination, which in turn made the idea of Arabism problematic for some Shi'a, as of course it was for the Kurdish and Turkish populations in the north of the country. (In Basra, distrust of the dominant Sunnis competed with dislike of colonial control, yielding no decisive edge in notables' backing between the ideas of inclusion in Iraq or autonomy under looser foreign control akin to Kuwait's status under British protection.) Yet no form of Iraqi identity could realistically be stressed, precisely because of Britain's choice of leadership: Britain legitimated placing on the new throne a Hijazi, Faysal b. Husayn (the charade of a referendum that Britain arranged had no bearing on the issue), purely on the basis of Faysal's and Iraq's common "Arab" identity. One of the few points upon which most groups in Iraq (except the Assyrians, among whom the British had recruited their local military auxiliary force soon after occupying the country) had actually demonstrated agreement was the desirability of breaking European control, moreover, and Faysal's intimate connection to Britain only heightened suspicions about his allegiance to local Iraqi interests.[14] Some of his advisers were Iraqis who had joined the Arab revolt mainly through recruitment from British prisoners of war, but neither they nor Faysal could stress an identity from which birth or recent history excluded them; like Kolettis in Greece, who first proposed the expansive Megali Idea to justify his participation in Greek politics, the heterochthon Faysal had to adopt a "big tent" ideology. Arab nationalism was thus essential to the new regime's survival, despite its weak suitability for the internal conditions of Iraq.

Faysal had limited means available for identity building. As long as the mandate lasted, Britain refused to support Iraqi plans for conscription

---

[14] Mahmoud Haddad, "Iraq before World War I: A Case of Anti-European Arab Ottomanism," in Khalidi et al. (eds.), *Origins of Arab Nationalism*, 120–50; Charles Tripp, *A History of Iraq* (Cambridge: Cambridge University Press, 2000), 48–9, 74–5. Many of the Assyrians were refugees who had been driven from eastern Anatolia at the same time as the CUP regime destroyed the Armenian population there.

to create a significant military force, knowing full well that a large army would both increase the powers of coercion of the central regime and be an institution likely to boost anti-British sentiment, given inevitable antagonism toward British control over defense matters. Dislike of the Sunni Arab nationalism promoted by the regime led Shi'a and Kurds also to object to the conscription plan, which was thus not realized until the aftermath of a Kurdish revolt in 1930 and an Assyrian bid for independence in 1933; the Kurdish revolt had shown the weakness of the army, and the widespread distrust of the Assyrians, viewed as armed servants of the British, made the parliament more sympathetic to the needs of the military forces that crushed their uprising. Conscription may have strengthened the military and thereby furthered the inculcation of Arab nationalism, but it also stirred repeated rebellions by tribes, non-Sunnis, and non-Arabs. These developments involved the military in politics, and the first of many coups in post-Ottoman Arab lands was executed in 1936. The military, as in the CUP period and in some other post-Ottoman countries, soon became the real force in politics, and as a Sunni-officered force shaped by Faysal and, after his death in 1933, by his Arab-revolt associates, what ideology it displayed was Arab nationalism.

Prior to the mid-1930s, Baghdad had had to rely heavily upon the educational system to build identity, and the intentions of successive governments under Faysal in this regard were made clear by appointment of the most noted figure in the development of Arab nationalism, Sati' al-Husri, to the Directorate-General of Education (1923–7) and thereafter to a series of posts that enabled him to dominate educational affairs until the Second World War.[15] That someone of Husri's background became the most influential proponent of Arab nationalism says much about the late development, alien roots, and artificial nature of the ideology, much as the origins of the proponents of Balkan and Turkish nationalisms indicate the foreign construction of those movements. Husri's father was an Ottoman jurist serving in Yemen when Sati' was born. While his father was a native of Aleppo, the family spoke Turkish at home – Arabic was Sati''s third language (French his second), and he always spoke it with a strong Turkish accent. He "discovered" nationalism as an important force while serving as an education bureaucrat in the Ottoman Balkans during the height of the Macedonian Question in the early twentieth

---

[15] On Husri, see William Cleveland, *The Making of an Arab Nationalist: Ottomanism and Arabism in the Life and Thought of Sati' al-Husri* (Princeton: Princeton University Press, 1971).

century; the emphasis that Bulgarian and Greek cultural missions placed upon the power and importance of "national" languages would be replicated in his own views of Arabness. Husri remained a loyal Ottoman and influential figure in education until the empire's defeat in 1918. At that point he decided that Arabism and its figurehead, Faysal, were the best means of rallying opposition to European occupation. He joined Faysal during his brief reign in Damascus and then followed him to Iraq in 1921. Faysal intended to have Husri revive and expand the Iraqi educational system, which Britain had severely curtailed until that point, but British opposition to his nationalist views helped to delay his assumption of any official role for two years.[16] His vision of Arab nationalism (he was one of the few to articulate any such vision prior to the 1930s) was hardly subtle and formed the basis of a history curriculum that was almost as blunt, if not so incredible, as the Turkish History thesis that Atatürk was soon to promote. Anyone who spoke Arabic was part of the Arab nation, the Arab nation had a glorious past but needed to unify in order to have a glorious future, and divisive forces (foreign imperialism, regionalism, and even religious identity) must be overcome or absorbed into Arabness. He attacked the established association of "Arab" with "bedouin" and argued vigorously against the suggestion that formal and colloquial Arabic bore a relationship similar to that between Latin and French (or Katharevousa and demotic Greek). He therefore stressed the need to teach, and for people to use in conversation, the formal language. He also mandated that schools teach history only as it related to Iraq and the Arab nation, requiring, for example, that sixth-year students learn about national unification movements in places such as Germany and Italy to build the idea that Iraq was to be the Prussia or Piedmont of the Arabs.[17]

Such ideas might naturally appeal to military officers and gained civilian adherents over time, but Arabism was slower to blossom even with government support in Iraq than in Syria, despite the lack of powerful promoters in that European-controlled region. One critical problem also seen in some Balkan countries was that Faysal, his associates, and his successors concentrated in domestic politics upon building – or buying – the allegiance of Iraq's local and tribal notables, practically ignoring the preponderance of the population. The growing disparity in landownership

---

[16] Malik Mufti, *Sovereign Creations: Pan-Arabism and Political Order in Syria and Iraq* (Ithaca, NY: Cornell University Press, 1996), 28–9.

[17] Cleveland, *Making of an Arab Nationalist*, 116–48.

between the Hashimite-notable elite and the rest of the population was but the most obvious indication of the regime's strategy for survival. Arab nationalism offered little to the nonelite. Ending British dominance was desired by much of the population other than the non-Muslim minorities, but the weakness of confidence in the central regime lessened the urgency of expelling a power with significant influence over Baghdad. Arabism's other main objective, erasing borders, could appeal to residents of Mosul province, which in the Ottoman period had commercial and social connections to Aleppo in Syria and Diyarbakır in Anatolia – but much of the population was Kurdish- or Turkish-speaking. Removing the border between Basra and Kuwait might appeal to some in the south (Faysal's successor, King Ghazi, first raised Iraq's claim to Kuwait in 1938 as a populist move), but the idea of opening the region also to Saudi Arabia, whose zealous Wahhabism posed historically a lethal threat to the Shi'a and was little better loved by Iraq's Sunnis, would struggle to win hearts or minds. It was thus perhaps only to be expected that Sati' al-Husri recruited teachers for his nation-building curriculum from kindred "heterochthons," primarily political refugees from geographic Syria.

Syria, the land that was to become "the beating heart of Arabism," faced the conditions that a "pan-"nationalism seemed suited to address. The extreme fracturing, and the longer duration and greater immediacy of first European intervention and then colonial control, made the widest possible unity movement that promised expulsion of imperial powers and erasure of borders most attractive, despite the lack of any real government backing. Iraq's very possession of (admittedly limited and heterochthon) self-government and then achievement of formal independence raised interest in identifying with the "Arab" kingdom in territories under more open-ended European control. French and British mandatory authorities frowned upon nationalist school texts but, given the lack of any clear political authority charged with policing education, schools found it relatively easy to adopt books influenced by the views of both Husri and the renowned American Egyptologist and Arabophile James Breasted.[18] Perhaps the most heavily stressed element of the nation-building school texts was the necessity of overcoming internal divisions that resulted not only from Western imperialist manipulation but from the Arabs' well-known "tribal élan" ('*asabiyya*). Such a message had a greater potential impact in fractured Syria than in Iraq or Egypt, and

---

[18] C. Ernest Dawn, "The Formation of Pan-Arab Ideology in the Interwar Years," *IJMES* 20 (1988), 68–72.

it was hardly coincidental that the first truly Arab-nationalist political party, the Ba'th, was founded in 1941 by two young (French-educated) Syrians, Michel 'Aflaq and Salah al-Din al-Bitar.

'Aflaq and Bitar had their views on the nation sharpened under the tutelage of Zaki al-Arsuzi, a (French-educated) nationalist agitator who campaigned against, and was radicalized by, the cession of the district of Alexandretta to Turkey in 1938–9.[19] Alexandretta's ethnically and religiously mixed population led to competing Syrian and Turkish claims, and in the tense international atmosphere prior to the Second World War France permitted a referendum open to Turkish official manipulation to decide whether its inhabitants wished to be "Arab" or "Turkish" – a move driven by France's wish to woo Turkey away from its inclination toward Germany. As in the Greco-Bulgarian competition over Macedonia, the short menu of identities devised by outsiders hardly fit the local reality, as suggested by the violence of a street-level argument in 1938 between acquaintances who had chosen opposing identities – conducted in Kurdish.[20] Arsuzi had no objection to the menu's limitations but rather to giving the opportunity to manipulate choices to the authoritarian nationalizers of Ankara, and his disgust grew with suspicion that the locally focused notables of Damascus had accepted the resulting "loss" of Alexandretta, in return for French promises of more autonomy or independence for the rest of their mandated territory. His homeland's vulnerability and then loss to Turkish nationalism fueled his commitment to Arabism. As with the Turkism of Ziya Gökalp and Yusuf Akçura, parochial interest intensified identification with an expansive nationalism, in Arsuzi's case also influenced by the intellectual ferment of interwar Paris.

This was, in short, a far cry from Ottoman era Arabism. The identification with Arabness and the Arabic language that manifested itself from the last years of the nineteenth century spread in limited, and still loyally Ottoman, elite circles. This Arabism was specifically Islamic: it originated in the perceived need to reexamine and reinterpret the foundational texts of the religion, making sophisticated understanding of Arabic and historical linguistics a critical skill, heightening in turn consciousness that God chose to disclose his final revelations to the tribal Arabs. Rediscovering

[19] Keith Watenpaugh, "'Creating Phantoms': Zaki al-Arsuzi, the Alexandretta Crisis, and the Formation of Modern Arab Nationalism in Syria," *IJMES* 28 (1996), 363–89.
[20] Sarah Shields, *Fezzes in the River: Identity Politics and European Diplomacy in the Middle East on the Eve of World War II* (Oxford: Oxford University Press, 2011), 3.

the secret power of that revelation would revive Muslims' fortunes, just as it had united the Arabs and empowered them to conquer the mighty empires of Rome and Iran.[21]

Following the collapse of the Islamic empire and especially after Mustafa Kemal's abolition of the caliphate-sultanate, the Islamic elements in Arabism were diluted by early proponents who were non-Sunnis (Arsuzi, 'Aflaq) or simply felt that Islam in the "Arab" lands, hemmed in as they were by emerging ethnonational countries in Turkey and Iran, was too divisive of the community (Husri, Bitar). Arsuzi, for example, not only was a member of the minority Muslim sect of the 'Alawis but also had to base his conviction that Alexandretta was clearly Arab on melting all non-Turkish elements (including 'Alawis, Armenians, other Christians, and Jews) into one unit.[22] For Muslims elsewhere, and Sunnis in particular, there were two factors that weakened the practical attraction of continuing to identify politically with religion. First was the destruction of what remained of the Ottoman empire by Mustafa Kemal, who dissolved the sultanate and the caliphate and then built the national Turkish Republic; recreation of the Ottoman order in the Arab provinces became a practical impossibility when the old imperial center foreswore the project, alienating Muslims outside the new republic and encouraging development of anti-Turkism (as Arab nationalism, with its myth of Turkish oppression, certainly promoted). There also was the crystal-clear realization that, unless non-Muslims and particularly Christians could be weaned from European patronage, the imperial powers would perpetuate the system of capitulations that had proven so debilitating to Ottoman sovereignty and self-strengthening efforts. France's carving of northern Syria into statelets dominated by religious minorities, of which the expanded Lebanon was only the most egregious example, suggested this, as did Britain's championing of Zionism in

---

[21] Hourani, *Arabic Thought*, stresses Egyptian examples. On this intellectual ferment in arguably its leading Ottoman center, Damascus, see David Commins, *Islamic Reform: Politics and Social Change in Late Ottoman Syria* (Oxford: Oxford University Press, 1990), and Itzchak Weismann, *Taste of Modernity: Sufism, Salafiyya, and Arabism in Late Ottoman Damascus* (Leiden: Brill, 2001). Dawn, the preeminent authority on the origins of Arab nationalism, also identifies unequivocally the Islamic modernist roots of pre-1914 Arabism ("The Origins of Arab Nationalism," in Khalidi et al. (eds.), *Origins of Arab Nationalism*, 8–11).

[22] Arab nationalist interpretation of French figures of the mid-1930s labeled 46% of the population as "Arab" (Sunnis, Alawis, and Orthodox Christians), 39% as "Turkish" (overwhelmingly Sunnis), and 15% other (mainly Armenians). Watenpaugh, "Creating Phantoms," 366.

Palestine. Britain's shift from resenting the capitulations as the greatest barrier to administration of Egypt prior to 1914 to including continued capitulatory rights in the points reserved for its control after declaring Egypt's independence in 1922 removed any doubt about the powers' intentions in this regard.[23]

As in the Ottoman period, however, any distancing of some elite circles from explicit identification with religious interests should not be mistaken for the loss of religious identities throughout society. Some of those elite who came to be labeled Arab nationalists were actually promoters of the continuing dream of Islamic solidarity.[24] Ottomanism, with all the religious significance implied by the term, seems to have exerted a stronger attraction on the popular imagination in Syria than did the "Arab" forces under Faysal, not only during the First World War but during the liberation efforts of the "milli" forces in Anatolia that would only later adopt a Turkish rather than Muslim identity.[25] Muslims in Aleppo province organized self-defense committees just like those in Anatolia, and these committees helped to drive the French out of territories now part of Turkey, such as Antep and Mersin – and would have liberated the district of Alexandretta as well, had Ankara not had to divert resources to fighting the Greeks, leading it to agree a division of territory with France. After Ankara turned its back on opponents of French control in Syria, the "nationalist" leaders there couched their statements to the French and the League of Nations in terms of secular nationalism, but they still called upon Islam to motivate the majority of the population.[26] The two most significant elements of the 1925 Syrian revolt against French control drew on religious identity: the Druze under Sultan al-Atrash in the south and Fawzi al-Qawuqji's Party of God (*Hizb Allah*), based initially in Hama.[27] Religious identity, and both Ottomanism and the ideal of Islamic solidarity against foreign control, were not the preserve of Sunnis but included "schismatics" such as the Druze and 'Alawis (and indeed some Orthodox Christians).

[23] Brown, *Rule of Law*, 34–5.
[24] See, for example, William Cleveland, *Islam against the West: Shakib Arslan and the Campaign for Islamic Nationalism* (Austin: University of Texas Press, 1985).
[25] Kayalı, *Arabs and Young Turks*, 202–5; Keith Watenpaugh, *Being Modern in the Middle East: Revolution, Nationalism, Colonialism and the Arab Middle East* (Princeton: Princeton University Press, 2006), chaps. 5–7.
[26] Khoury, *Syria and the French Mandate*, 205.
[27] For a summary of the revolt, see Rogan, *Arabs*, 227–32.

As in Syria, so in Iraq, where the Shi'i religious hierarchy initiated resistance to British rule between 1918 and 1920 and were driven into exile for years as a result.[28] Sunni opposition similarly centered on mosques, and Britain had either to exile or to co-opt leading religious notables of Baghdad and Basra to restore order under their appointee, Faysal. In both Iraq and Syria preemptive and punitive repression by mandatory authorities weakened the established religious orders, just as it was to prove to have done to the entire class of local notables, and the growing consolidation of political opposition around less explicitly religious ideas of nationalism also blurred the Islamic element of political identities. Yet, just below the elite level of state authority or antiimperial movements, religion retained its old vitality. New popular religious associations, neither outgrowths of established sufi orders nor led by the trained scholars of the 'ulama, sprouted across French-controlled Syria in the 1930s.[29] Although none became as famous as the Muslim Brotherhood, they resembled that movement, founded in 1928 as one of several popular religious organizations in Egypt.

Hasan al-Banna founded the Muslim Brotherhood as a vehicle to spread among the nonelite the instruction in sound Islamic behavior that the Egyptian national regime, focused as it was on attainment of full independence from Britain, was failing to deliver. The Brotherhood may have been a natural product of the Ottoman era 'ulama debate over the immutable core of Islam that also fostered Arabism and salafi "fundamentalism," but Banna had little respect for the contemporary 'ulama of al-Azhar, seen practically as parochial government functionaries by this time. Like the salafis, he also had little use for the sufism that dominated religious life in Egypt's villages and seemed steeped in error, but the Brotherhood nevertheless fit in the sufi tradition, albeit stressing the orthodoxy and orthopraxy of its founding shaikh. For some years the Brotherhood remained focused exclusively upon such "religious" concerns as education and providing the other elements of social care mandated by Islam, which encouraged its rapid growth. When the Brotherhood finally entered formally the political ring, running on platforms emphasizing social service, the mass appeal of a movement attuned to nonelite identities and concerns posed a powerful challenge to other political groups.

---

[28] Tripp, *History of Iraq*, 33–4, 40–5.

[29] Khoury, *Syria and the French Mandate*, 607–12; Itzchak Weismann, "The Politics of Popular Religion: Sufis, Salafis, and Muslim Brothers in Twentieth-Century Hamah," *IJMES* 37 (2005), 45–50.

The Brotherhood inevitably became a target of political violence and repression, which would lead to its radicalization, reaching a peak in the 1950s–1960s.[30]

By the time that the formal structures of European control over key elements of state authority weakened significantly or ended after the Second World War, the post-Ottoman countries of the Middle East may be said to have achieved a robust state of political activism, but there was no matured, unifying vision of political identity other than the conviction that European imperial control was undesirable. Until such control ended, no state had the ability or interest to force the population under its partial authority to conform to a more stable or durable identity. As a result of missing the opportunity to create workable nation-states, this weakness of state and political authority would continue into the era of independence, when the two forces uncontrollable by any state, Arabism and Islam, would assert their political influence.

[30] Donald Reid, "Political Assassination in Egypt, 1910–1954," *International Journal of African Historical Studies* 15 (1982), 625–51.

PART III

CONTEMPORARY POST-OTTOMAN STATES

Viewed from a certain dimly lit perspective, the fall of the Berlin Wall and the ensuing collapse of communism in eastern Europe marked "the end of history," but events after 1989 showed, if anything, rather the return of history and, indeed, of politics in post-Ottoman lands. In the Middle East, the Iraqi invasion of Kuwait and the lopsided war for Kuwait's liberation, which was made feasible by the collapse of Iraq's Soviet supporter, seemed to mark the death not of socialism but of Arab solidarity, leaving a void into which Islamism grew. In Turkey, the collapse of the neighboring superpower lessened the military-dominated Kemalist state's immunity from questioning, similarly aiding the rise to prominence of religiously minded political parties. In the Balkans, the discrediting of communism had a more immediate effect by removing the ideological basis for the established order and encouraging freer consideration of identities other than class-consciousness. There the fall of the wall also raised a question that many found unnerving: if ideological foundations could crumble so quickly, would borders achieved through the revanchist programs of the post-Ottoman era also be subject to collapse? This trend took its most destructive form in the most unnatural country, Yugoslavia, where questions of the nation and religious identity blended together to bloody effect, but such questions revived elsewhere as well, showing that they had survived in suspended animation during the communist decades not only in Yugoslavia's constituent republics but in neighboring states as well.

Such rapidity of fundamental shifts, and the fear created by their speed, suggested the enduring weakness of post-Ottoman states. Most of the recent disturbing patterns of politics across former imperial lands result from failures of states that act as if strong but find that their legitimacy among their populations has withered to the point where political protest cannot be contained by state power. In some cases the nature of protest has depended upon the legitimating identity espoused by the regime now subjected to criticism. Despite their weaknesses, the nationalisms developed after independence from the empire have provided some avenues of protest in the Balkans following the eclipse of the ideology of socialism and its reinterpretations of nationalism. Yugoslavia, which stressed in combination with socialism the idea of Yugoslav supranational (or neonational) solidarity, thus saw the resumption of the earlier nationalisms of constituent Yugoslav republics as a vehicle of both protest and vengeance on a discredited system. Where those early post-Ottoman authoritarian, state-strengthening nationalisms survived intact after 1945, however, political protest had to find another ideology for righting wrongs.

Religion has proven a viable channel of opposition, most obviously in Muslim countries of Turkey and the Arab region, but also in the Balkans, where nationalism in all countries but Albania reacknowledged the tie to its original close partner and rival, the church. That this happened in Yugoslavia has been widely recognized, but religion has surged in the society and politics of neighboring countries as well. The revival of religion indicates that almost all of the post-Ottoman nations have largely failed to separate themselves from the religious props created to instill the national ideal, thus undercutting any emergence of truly secular states.

To illustrate this trend to drawing religion into politics across the region, consider Avram Iancu Square in the center of Cluj, the ethnically mixed capital of Transylvania, Romania (Image 2). Transylvania passed in 1699 from Ottoman to Habsburg hands, where it was to remain until the collapse of the Austro-Hungarian empire. The region was a main objective of post-Ottoman Romania's version of nation-building revanchism, and in the Anglo-French reconfiguration of central Europe after 1918, it was awarded to Bucharest.

The new municipality installed by the Romanian regime provided the site on the plaza for the Orthodox cathedral, whose mass was intended to state the immovable Romanian identity of the city and region. This message was revived after 1992, when the city elected a nationalist mayor, Gheorghe Funar. Under Funar, the municipality restored the plaza and reinforced it as a nationalist statement, adding a heroic statue and plentiful Romanian flags to frame the tableau. Funar gained greater notoriety for his other urban development projects, which included painting

IMAGE 2 Dormition of the Theotokos Orthodox Cathedral, Avram Iancu Square, Cluj, Romania.

municipal property (trams, park benches, even rubbish bins) in Romania's national colors, but his attachment to Orthodoxy as a key ingredient in national identity should not be overlooked. After he finally lost the mayoralty in 2004, he became one of the Great Romania Party's members of parliament, where one of his more memorable proposals was to distribute Romanian bibles to every citizen.[1]

That religion revived in politics, either in conjunction with or in opposition to nationalism, was no surprise, because across the post-Ottoman region recent nationalist regimes failed at several levels, and sufficiently spectacularly that their flaws could not be overlooked. Populations lost faith in national leaders, and religion, as ever, seemed the obvious source of new faith. Almost all the established regimes showed no interest or

---

[1] On Cluj, see Rogers Brubaker et al., *Nationalist Politics and Everyday Ethnicity in a Transylvanian Town* (Princeton: Princeton University Press, 2006), which examines the Hungarian minority. Its virtue lies in its stress upon the situational nature of national identity and nationalism, but it ignores the glaringly obvious role of the majority, and of the municipal government elected by that majority, in creating situations triggering "national" reactions among the minority.

ability to move significantly beyond the state-as-an-end-in-itself principle implicit in the forms of nationalism developed in the early independence period. For some decades communism in the Balkans offered a program that, while as illiberal and autocratic as the preceding right-wing nationalist regimes', did at least include more sectors of society in its plans for development. Arab socialism offered a similar promise in the Middle East, particularly in the case of Egypt's 'Abd al-Nasir, who gained genuine popular support and admiration. With time, however, rulers increasingly used state resources to buy acquiescence to the continuation of regimes' ultimately self-serving control. The most important sectors to which leaders paid court were the military and the assorted secret police organizations, which across much of the post-Ottoman region remained the most powerful institutions. These Praetorian Guards protected regimes that grew ever more corrupt through longevity in power – as everyone knows, power corrupts, absolute power corrupts absolutely, and seemingly open-ended power confers the illusion of permanent immunity. The early disregard for the peasant majority thus not only resumed but expanded to include the rural-to-urban migrant underclass that grew spectacularly after 1945.

Use of such questionable methods made the control exercised by the state brittle, and the fragility of authoritarianism without legitimacy showed itself surprisingly quickly. The fall of the Berlin Wall took practically everyone by surprise, including the highest authorities on both sides of the Iron Curtain, and the suddenness of events rattled the establishment everywhere. Nicolae Ceaușescu might have been the only chief of a Balkan secret-police regime to be shot, but no leadership across the peninsula felt that anything could be taken for granted. The collapse of governments, and sometimes the redrawing of borders, did happen, with Greece being the most recent to succumb to the internal weaknesses of brittle political legitimacy. In Turkey, the end of the Soviet threat relaxed the ban on questioning the authoritarian state, but if a trigger for the sudden acceleration of the Kemalist establishment's loss of respectability must be chosen, then the Susurluk incident of 1996 stands out. The occupants and contents of a crashed car showed the tight connections among the establishment, the criminal underworld, and the "deep state," or the networks that executed numerous extralegal and violent political acts over preceding decades. The failure of the state and of the military to respond adequately to succeeding challenges, exemplified by the slack response to a terrible earthquake in 1999, deepened disgust with the Kemalist establishment's evidently pointless authoritarianism. In

Arab countries, the Arab Spring that began in 2010 was triggered by the routine and mindless oppression inflicted by the states' military-security complexes, whose members enjoyed immunity under fundamentally corrupt, unjust systems. The compelling need for governmental accountability has given the Arab Spring its durability, just as it has already delivered government in Turkey into the hands of an "Islamic" party. Islamically tinged political programs, with their emphasis on law, and liberal calls for democracy have much in common: both express popular outrage against fundamentally unjust states.

9

The Contemporary Balkans

To some extent, the Second World War in the Balkans took the gloss off post-Ottoman visions of the nation, its destiny, and its historic home-lands. The right-wing nationalist regimes that had ruled in most of the post-Ottoman countries in almost-unbroken continuity since the achieve-ment of independence either crumbled before Axis invaders and made lit-tle effort to resist brutal occupation (Serb-dominated Yugoslavia, Greece) or joined the ultimately losing side, suffering yet again national pain and humiliation (Bulgaria).[1] The humbling of the nation eased the rise of the Left, in part because the left organized the only serious resistance to occupation (Greece, Yugoslavia, and Albania) and in part because social-ism offered an ideology directed to addressing the needs and interests of the majority of the population in all of the post-Ottoman Balkans who had been practically ignored by previous regimes, with a few excep-tions such as Bulgaria's Agrarian Union government of Stamboliski. In lands where the proletariat was too inconsequential to justify Marxist-Leninist rule, postwar regimes did not fight against established national identity (except in Yugoslavia) but rather sought to reshape it to meet regime needs for legitimacy. The peasant and working classes became the embodiment of the nation, and the nation became effectively limited to those classes contained within each country's borders. "Iron Curtains" separating the Warsaw Pact, NATO, Yugoslavia, and Albania made

---

[1] On the challenge of restoring the national state after the war in Greece, see Mark Mazower, "Introduction," in *After the War Was Over: Reconstructing the Family, Nation, and State in Greece, 1943–1960*, ed. Mark Mazower (Princeton: Princeton University Press, 2000), 3–14.

borders unchallengeable. The nation thus still existed in public life and the popular mind, keeping it ready to step into the vacuum created by collapse of the Soviet Union and its satellite system.

That collapse opened once again old questions from Balkan countries' early post-Ottoman existence: what kind of state each should have, what ideology should legitimate the state, and indeed what borders the country should recognize. That such questions reappeared in countries whose ruling institutions once again lost their avowed reason for being with the discrediting of communism perhaps should not have surprised anyone as much as it did. Communism had taken hold in post-Ottoman (and post-Habsburg) countries that had lived under nation-building regimes whose weak legitimacy had pushed them into autocracy, a pattern of politics that ensured regime survival but did little to create efficiency. Trains neither ran on time nor served most regions adequately. Was it likely that a successor system so roundly condemned as morally and economically bankrupt would have been able to fix the weaknesses? Yet as the notion of "the end of history" suggested, the fall of the Berlin Wall was taken as the sign of complete victory for liberal democracy and market capitalism – of modernity, in fact; the only resulting problems expected in the West lay in finding ways to hold back the waves of liberated peoples yearning to be free to enjoy the good life in the First World, and in declining politely but convincingly to pay for fixing the communists' broken economic legacy. Illiberal nationalist and antediluvian religious impulses had no place in this self-congratulatory vision of the future. The dissolution of Yugoslavia, which was so bloody that it could not be overlooked to the same extent that the collapse of Czechoslovakia was, could thus only be explained by "ancient hatreds" and the ill effects of Ottoman rule.[2]

Resurgent nationalism and religiously tinged conflict were not, of course, either evidence of ancient hatreds or direct legacies of the Ottoman period. The often-violent nationalism was inherited from the intense and only partially completed program of nation building adopted by each significant Balkan state after independence, and particularly from their

---

[2] Kaplan's *Balkan Ghosts* has been rightly criticized for spreading the idea of ancient hatreds as the cause of Yugoslavia's collapse. Books with more serious claims to rational analysis, however, also suggested both ancient hatreds and the malignant effects of Ottoman rule. See, for example, Gerolymatos, *Balkan Wars*; Dennis Hupchick, *The Balkans: From Constantinople to Communism* (New York: Palgrave, 2002); and George Kennan, "Introduction," in *The Other Balkan Wars: A 1913 Carnegie Endowment Inquiry in Retrospect* (Washington, DC: Carnegie Endowment for International Peace, 1993).

various versions of irredentism. In most cases this did not lead to active campaigns to seize new territory, as in the late Ottoman era, although both Serbs and Croats clearly did have designs on lands outside the borders of their respective republics. The Catholic Croats, tied to the Muslim Bosniaks by an uneasy alliance against Serbian offensives in Bosnia, were contented with their important role in Bosnian affairs and absorbed no territory directly. Serbia's territorial ambitions echoed the revanchist program of Garašanin's *Načertanije*, in that Belgrade hoped to retain all Serb-inhabited lands, but Serbia soon had to renounce any idea of recovering all of the territory of Yugoslavia, which in the interwar period had represented the real culmination of the *Načertanije* program. The actual legacy from the irredentism of early nation builders to the post-1989 generation was less territorial aggrandizement than fear of losing what had once been gained, a fear made credible by each nation's taught belief that it had always been victimized by others. The flash points of Balkan instability in the 1990s corresponded to the areas allotted to the post-Ottoman nation-states in the last phase of revanchism, 1912–18: Kosovo, Macedonia, Bosnia-Hercegovina, and Thrace. Perhaps because Serbia had come closest to achieving its post-Ottoman revanchist goals, its fear led to violence because it had the most to lose. It feared that it would lose Kosovo, taken in the First Balkan War in 1912 but inhabited predominantly by Albanians, and that Serbs in Croatia and Bosnia would be oppressed by the treacherous enemies recognized from history books, the Muslims and the Catholics. Yet Greece also worried that it would lose the part of Macedonia that it had seized in the Balkan Wars, or even its entire north including western Thrace, where the population included large minorities of "Turks" and "Slavophone Greeks."[3] Bulgaria, repeatedly balked and punished in the Balkan and World Wars for its efforts to take Macedonia, territory gained from Russian hands in 1878 but then taken away by the other powers in the Treaty of Berlin later that year, felt insecure even while part of the Warsaw Pact, and the insecurity only worsened with the loss of old allies. It worried about Turkish designs on its southern territories, but Macedonia's secession from Yugoslavia caused a brief surge of expectation that this target of long-standing irredentist hopes might finally fall under Sofia's sway, if not control. The sense of insecurity, however, led to uncertainty about how, or whether, to revive any claim to land or people. Macedonia, in turn, worried that its

---

[3] Romania was equally worried about ex-Habsburg Transylvania, which it gained by Franco-British decision after the First World War.

neighbors might revive their designs upon its territory and treated all of them with marked prickliness.

Given the early intertwining of religious identity with the building of Balkan nations, religion and religious institutions perhaps inevitably revived in accompaniment to the surge in nationalism and national insecurities. Much like their young post-Ottoman predecessors, post-1989 regimes consciously renewed state identification with religion as a means of legitimacy building.[4] Churches proved eager to seize opportunities for new relevance after the extended decline in influence that they had suffered since 1945. None had fallen further than the religious institutions of Albania, which had banned religion since the late 1960s, but in other countries where persecution was less relentless, the ties that post-Ottoman regimes had created to bind religious authorities to the state and nation remained tight, but to the point that many churches and mosques (most Jews having died in the Holocaust) functioned as much as regime intelligence-gathering outposts as spiritual shelters. The established churches' revival was limited somewhat by the taint lingering from their forced association with the failed order, although there was a natural proclivity among people to "rediscover" religious identities ridiculed by now-discredited regimes when the legitimating ideology of communism was proven wrong. Sects that experienced the most striking growth were those without much hierarchy or recent historical baggage, especially evangelical Protestantism, Pentecostalism, and Mormonism. Established churches consequently hastened to reconfirm their original ties to the nation-building project as nationalism strengthened.

As in Chapter 6, the Balkans thus serve well as an introduction to the recent history of the relationships among the state, faith, and nationalism, ties that date from the transition from the Ottoman to the post-Ottoman eras. The intimate linkage between Orthodox Christianity and the nation established in the immediate post-Ottoman period continues, and the sudden political changes seen since the 1980s gave the linkage renewed importance. More significantly new, however, is the revival of religion in identity and politics of predominantly Muslim areas, including Albania and Bosnia. The resurrection of Muslim identity in the Balkans may also have boosted religious sensibilities in Turkey, where Islamic-tinged parties performed well in elections and entered government in

---

[4] Lavinia Stan and Lucian Turcescu, *Religion and Politics in Post-Communist Romania* (Oxford: Oxford University Press, 2007); Vjekoslav Perica, *Balkan Idols: Religion and Nationalism in Yugoslav States* (Oxford: Oxford University Press, 2002).

the 1990s. Rather than marking the spread of "Islamic fundamentalism" to Asia Minor and Europe, however, such growth in Muslim religious identity merely brings these countries closer to the standard set by the Orthodox Christian lands of the Balkans. It was Orthodox Serbia, after all, that gave Yugoslavia the strongest push into the abyss, in which the revival of nationalism and religion achieved greatest prominence.

YUGOSLAVIA

It has grown into a truism that some conflicts pitting adversaries identified primarily by religious labels really have nothing to do with religion. The decades-long struggle between Catholics and Protestants in Northern Ireland is often cited in this regard. In an important sense, this is true: the Northern Irish struggle was triggered much more by political, social, and economic discrimination against Catholics than by disputes over the doctrinal authority of the papacy. In another sense, however, it is impossible to deny that religion indeed lay at the root of the conflict, because the entrenched structure of discrimination originated in exactly such differing views of the papacy, with the political, social, and economic order of Northern Ireland having been established by British authority at a time when the Anglican Church still reigned supreme and Catholics were distrusted. Such a dichotomy, of worldly proximate causes and more intransigent, deeply rooted religious antagonisms, characterized the breakup of Yugoslavia.

Yugoslavia's violent dissolution took place in the full glare of worldwide media attention, but a brief recapitulation of its major phases will serve as a reminder of its course. Slobodan Milošević rose to the presidency of the Serbian League of Communists in 1987, following his well-publicized speech in Kosovo defending Serbian rights in the province, and in 1989 solidified his new reputation as a nationalist with a fiery oration to a huge crowd commemorating the six hundredth anniversary of the Battle of Kosovo Polje. Milošević rose to dominance in the federal presidency, in which the six Yugoslav republics (Serbia, Croatia, Slovenia, Bosnia-Hercegovina, Montenegro, and Macedonia) and two autonomous provinces (Kosovo and Vojvodina) had equal voting rights, triggering secession movements in first Slovenia and then Croatia. The predominately Serb-officered Yugoslav army withdrew from Slovenia after a brief conflict in 1991 but fought tenaciously in Croatia, keeping large parts of the secessionist republic under Serbian control. Belgrade's rolling campaign to prevent Serb-inhabited lands from falling under non-Orthodox control moved to Bosnia-Hercegovina in 1992. As in Croatia, the conflict was brutal and marked by atrocities against civilians; "ethnic cleansing," or the purposeful murder or expulsion of "national enemy" populations, became the best-known phrase of the war. After the Dayton Peace Accord of 1995 brought fighting to an end, the conflict returned to Kosovo, where a guerrilla campaign waged by Kosovar Albanians triggered the threat of further ethnic cleansing by Serbian forces, which in turn prompted a NATO air campaign against Serbia in 1999 that lasted until Belgrade agreed to withdraw from the province. Macedonia had left Yugoslavia without a struggle in 1992, and in 2006 Montenegro also seceded, leaving Serbia isolated and thus bringing Yugoslavia to an end.

Numerous observers and authorities, both established and overnight, sought to explain the proximate causes of the dissolution of Yugoslavia without reaching consensus, and the task of demonstrating conclusively the main responsibility of one or two factors is probably unachievable.[5] Certainly economic pressures brought on by Yugoslavia's heavy foreign-currency debts played a significant role, as did the loss of leadership and political coherence that occurred with the death in 1980 of Tito, the state's founder. Tito's death was perhaps the more important event, because the iconic creator of the republic of Yugoslavia had managed to control many of the tensions between regions that had bedeviled it, just as they had tormented the interwar kingdom, and he also had been careful to prevent any potential successor to his leadership from emerging. A growing Serbian belief that Tito had ruled in an essentially anti-Serbian manner was not wholly unfounded: of Croat-Slovenian heritage, Tito was well aware of the antagonism felt toward the Karadjordjević dictatorship of interwar Yugoslavia outside Orthodox regions, and Tito's partisans during the Second World War had had to fight not only Axis occupiers and their local collaborators but also Serbian royalist Četniks. Tito took increasingly strong steps toward limiting Serbian influence in Socialist Yugoslavia, including giving autonomy to the formerly Serbian-dominated multiethnic provinces of Kosovo and Vojvodina. Following his death, the state came under a system of control by committee, the federal presidency, with committee membership divided among constituent republics and provinces that had greater or lesser ethnic identities, a system likely to promote a sense of vacuum at the center, sclerotic decision making, and ethnic regionalism. Yugoslav identity had been

5 On analyses that appeared by 1995, see Gale Stokes et al., "Instant History: Understanding the Wars of Yugoslav Succession," *Slavic Review* 55 (1996), 136–60.

stronger than most commentary on the country's dissolution suggested, but disillusionment with the system started a shift toward regionalism/nationalism, and key to this was the issue of Kosovo.

Kosovo, a small province, played a surprisingly large role in the dissolution of Yugoslavia, because first Serbian ethnic agitation and then unilateral actions there by the republic of Serbia's political leadership raised the specter of Serbian assertiveness in the other constituent republics of Yugoslavia. Milošević, a theretofore unremarkable member of the Communist Party hierarchy in the republic, recognized the possibility of riding the surge of Serbian ethnic anxiety over Kosovo to control of the republic, in the course of which he ousted the patron who had secured for him every position he had held until 1987. In 1988 Milošević's Serbia unilaterally asserted direct control over the two provinces granted autonomy in the Tito era Yugoslav constitution of 1974, Kosovo and Vojvodina, thereby gaining control over their votes in the federal presidency; when he engineered the rise of a protégé to the leadership of Montenegro, Milošević had four of the eight votes in the presidency. It was the leadership of Slovenia, the smallest after Montenegro but richest republic and the one with the smallest Serbian population, that simply walked out of the last Yugoslav federal party congress in 1990, leaving the other three republics not controlled by Milošević (Croatia, Bosnia-Hercegovina, and Macedonia) incapable of defeating the Serbian leader's stated desire to centralize all authority in Belgrade; the leaders of those republics therefore felt that they had little choice but to follow the Slovenian example. Slovenia had come to resent ever more deeply Belgrade's economic demands and its control over the Yugoslav army, which became the main means used by Belgrade to exercise its authority in the republic, but the spectacle of Serbian assertiveness in Kosovo was also very alarming. Kosovo was small and had only a small Serbian population (like Slovenia), and it was the poorest part of Yugoslavia (meaning that its occupation would have to be funded by wealthier republics like Slovenia). The reason why the impoverished and overwhelmingly Albanian province of Kosovo was deemed worthy of Belgrade's insistence on control lay in its popular identification as the heartland of the Serbs, an idea promoted as part of the nation-building effort in Serbian education since the nineteenth century, and not coincidentally also as the heartland of the Serbian Orthodox Church.

Kosovo's status as an Orthodox center ensured the continuation of an overt religious coloring in the Serbian nationalism that revived in the atheistic Yugoslav state, and the religious undertones of Serbian anxieties were then echoed in the assertion of religious awareness among other nations, including the Catholic Croatians and Muslim Bosnians. The most significant Orthodox monasteries in pre-Ottoman Serbia lay in Kosovo, as did the seat of the Patriarchate of Peć, notionally the preserver of Serbian national identity during the dark centuries of Ottoman oppression; the national-millenarian myth of the Battle of Kosovo Polje also tied both church and national identity to the province.[6] Twenty-one priests in the province first called the plight of the dwindling Serbian Orthodox minority in Kosovo to public attention through an open letter to the patriarchate published in the church's newspaper in 1982, calling for action to prevent the "extinction" of the Serbs in Kosovo. The driving figures of the escalating religious-nationalist protests that Muslim Albanians were committing genocide against the Orthodox Serbs were three young bishops teaching at the theological seminary in Belgrade; all had received their doctoral degrees in theology in Athens and may well have acquired there an openness to political activism greater than much of the older Serbian church hierarchy had displayed.[7] That hierarchy followed its younger members' lead, however, with the patriarch German starting to talk of genocide against the Serbs in 1987. The church further boosted nationalist emotion by removing the bones of Prince Lazar, lauded as the martyred Serbian leader of the Battle of Kosovo Polje, from their Second World War era tomb in Belgrade for ceremonial reinterment in a monastery in Kosovo, taking them on a lengthy, publicized tour of Orthodox sites around the country. The church welcomed the turn to nationalism in Serbia's government, which had by the middle of the 1980s already gained the patriarchate permission to resume building a massive church in central Belgrade that had been started before the Second World War, and it supported Milošević in his campaign to reassert Belgrade's hold on Kosovo.

Milošević accepted such support, and the republic's warming relationship with the church encouraged a revival of religiosity among Serbs that previous communist era regimes would have viewed with alarm. Milošević himself apparently felt little but disdain for the church and its hierarchy, but their support suited his designs for a time. After he consolidated his

---

[6] On the place of Kosovo in national myth and church ideology, see Anscombe, "Ottoman Empire in Politics – II."

[7] Jasna Dragović-Soso, *"Saviours of the Nation": Serbia's Intellectual Opposition and the Revival of Nationalism* (London: Hurst, 2002), 125; Radmila Radić, "The Church and the 'Serbian Question,'" in *The Road to War in Serbia: Trauma and Catharsis*, ed. Nebojša Popov (Budapest: Central European University Press, 2000), 248.

power in Serbia and the dissolution of Yugoslavia gathered speed, clerical support for Milošević waned, and the church became a fixed part of the opposition to his rule within the republic throughout the 1990s. Loyalty to the church thus once again became an avenue of dissent against an authoritarian state that, until 2000, allowed no serious threats to its power to emerge. Yet like much of the opposition (whose most noteworthy figure for much of the decade was Vuk Drašković, whose novel *Nož* [The Knife, published in 1983] did much to stir the virulently anti-Muslim attitude reemerging among Serbs in the 1980s), the church objected primarily to Milošević's tactics and the continuation of communist (repackaged as socialist) rule, not to the nationalism of his purpose.[8] The Serbian Orthodox Church remained a firm and close ally of Radovan Karadžić, the political leader of the non-Communist Bosnian Serbs, in part because he was much more devout than Milošević ever attempted to seem, and in part because even the patriarch believed that all Serbs should be able to live in one state.[9]

Bosnia provided the arena in which religiously inspired nationalism could most clearly thrive, because the combatants were separated not by language or, arguably, culture, as they were in Kosovo, but only by national differences dependent upon religious affiliation. Bosnian Muslims were Bosniaks, who were, in their enemies' view, "Turks" (like all Muslims across the peninsula). Bosnian Catholics were Croats, who were, to their enemies, "Ustaše" (followers of the Fascist-supported Croatian state of the Second World War that persecuted Serbs, associated immediately in the public eye with Cardinal Alojzije Stepinac, archbishop of Zagreb in the Ustaša period, who was posthumously rehabilitated by the post-1991 Croatian government and canonized by the pope in 1998). Bosnian Orthodox were Serbs, who were, in others' terms, "Četniks" (paramilitaries who committed widespread abuses in Bosnia at the end of the First World War, as well as guerrilla supporters of the Serbian monarchy and church during the Second World War). All sides made a conscious effort to destroy the churches or mosques of their enemies, but the Serbs executed this campaign most effectively and determinedly, especially in targeting Muslim buildings, including not only mosques but centers of "Turkish" culture such as the National Library in Sarajevo. In

---

[8] On Drašković's novel, see Andrew Wachtel, *Making a Nation, Breaking a Nation: Literature and Cultural Politics in Yugoslavia* (Stanford, CA: Stanford University Press, 1998), 205–9.

[9] Lenard Cohen, *Serpent in the Bosom: The Rise and Fall of Slobodan Milošević* (Boulder, CO: Westview Press, 2001), 151–5.

the Serbian view, Muslims were really Serbs who had betrayed the nation by "turning Turk," and destruction of the symbols of that treasonous turn would restore the Serbianness of Bosnia.[10] Croats saw Bosniaks as renegade Croats but put the urge to destroy symbols of treason into effect less assiduously, except in western Hercegovina, a stronghold of the Ustaša in the Second World War and the arena for the worst Croat-inflicted abuses of Muslims and Orthodox Christians.[11] Under such pressure, it is no surprise that Bosniaks reacted with the swift resurrection of a specifically Muslim identity and a sense of being besieged by Christian enemies.

It seems ironic that this welter of historically formulated nationalisms grew in Bosnia, because the territory had been a stronghold of hardline communism and antiparticularist Yugoslavism in the Tito period.[12] Muslims there had experienced isolation and pressure from both Catholic and Orthodox Christians during the period under Habsburg rule, but the pressure worsened after Bosnia's inclusion in the Kingdom of Serbs, Croats, and Slovenes (1918–29), whose very name denied the existence of Bosnian (or Macedonian, Albanian, Montenegrin) identity, and under the Belgrade-centered monarchical dictatorship of the Kingdom of Yugoslavia (1929–41). In the interwar period Muslims became stalwarts of Yugoslavism, which helped to ward off pressure to identify themselves as Muslims of either Serb or Croat origins. This situation continued after Tito established the Yugoslav republic in 1945, and it was only for the 1971 census that the federal authorities created the category "Muslim in the sense of nationality." They did this primarily as a means of undercutting a recent rise in expressions of Croatian and Serbian national

[10] See, for example, Ivo Banac, *The National Question in Yugoslavia: Origins, History, Politics* (Ithaca, NY: Cornell University Press, 1984), 377. The idea that Muslims of Bosnia were descended from Serbs is also pushed in Drašković's *Nož*.

[11] Michael Sells, "Crosses of Blood: Sacred Space, Religion, and Violence in Bosnia-Hercegovina," *Sociology of Religion* 64 (2003), 309–31; Andras Riedlmayer, "Erasing the Past: The Destruction of Libraries and Archives in Bosnia-Herzegovina," *Middle East Studies Association Bulletin* 29 (July 1995), 7–11; Mitja Velikonja, "In Hoc Signo Vinces: Religious Symbolism in the Balkan Wars 1991–1995," *International Journal of Politics, Culture, and Society* 17 (2003), 25–40.

[12] On Bosnia-Hercegovina in the Yugoslav periods, see Noel Malcolm, *Bosnia: A Short History* (New York: New York University Press, 1996), 156–213; Fikret Adanır, "The Formation of a 'Muslim' Nation in Bosnia-Hercegovina: A Historiographic Discussion," in Adanır and Faroqhi (eds.), *Ottomans and the Balkans*, 267–83; Ivo Banac, "Bosnia Muslims: From Religious Community to Socialist Nationhood and Post-Communist Statehood," in *The Muslims of Bosnia-Herzegovina: Their Historic Development from the Middle Ages to the Dissolution of Yugoslavia*, ed. Mark Pinson (Cambridge, MA: Harvard University Press, 1993), 129–53.

particularism, and the importance of preventing Bosnia from becoming a flash point of national rivalries was demonstrated by the care taken to ensure that the republic was run by a staunchly communist (and thoroughly atheistic), determinedly Yugoslav, hierarchy. Tito was also pleased to keep the office of Yugoslav prime minister out of either Serb or Croat hands, having a Bosniak, Džemal Bijedić, serve as prime minister of Yugoslavia from 1971 until Bijedić died in a plane crash in 1977. Of the three major nationalities present in Bosnia, the Muslims clung most tenaciously to Yugoslavism and the ideal of a "multiethnic" republic, but with the discrediting of communism across eastern Europe and the collapse of the Yugoslav state as the result of conflicts among Serbs, Slovenes, and Croats, the established position became untenable. Thus was a bastion of Yugoslavism transformed into a nationalist battleground. The Serbs tried to rescue the core gains won in implementing the *Načertanije* in Bosnia, a land they viewed as originally Serbian and inhabited by Serbs, Serbs who had betrayed the nation by turning Turk, and Croat interlopers implanted by the Habsburgs (and the fascists and the Yugoslav communists); the Croats tried to regain lands in Bosnia-Hercegovina once included in the greater Croatia of the Ustaša, and inhabited by Croats, Croats who had betrayed the nation by turning Turk, and Serb interlopers settled by the monarchy; and the Muslims had to rediscover as quickly as possible the old "siege" identity, plausibly traceable back to the 1820s, to provide once again a defense against annexation by either neighbor after the death of Yugoslavism and communism.

BOSNIA

Bosnia, and the formation of a Bosnian Muslim national identity, followed an unusual trajectory among post-Ottoman states. With the exception of the occupied territories of Palestine, it was the last distinct Ottoman provincial territory to achieve independence without an extensive intermediate period of dissolution and absorption into another state (Bosnia was carved into separate banates in the period of Serbian royal dictatorship or autocracy, 1929–41, and was then absorbed into Ustaša Croatia after Yugoslavia fell to the Axis powers; these interludes of absorption were shorter than those experienced by Macedonia or Kosovo). It was also the only territory in which specifically Muslim identity had been at least cautiously encouraged as the path of post-Ottoman group solidarity. Austria-Hungary occupied Bosnia in 1878, moving inland from its Croatian/Dalmatian territories in order to defend against expansion by either the Great Bulgaria created by Russia at San Stefano or Serbia, which, also alarmed by the new Bulgaria, would inevitably seek to expand in Ottoman lands after only modest gains in 1878. With both Orthodox and suspect Catholic populations in its new defensive bulwark, the Austro-Hungarian administration was happy to have Muslims retain their religious identity, rather than joining either potentially troublesome Christian group; the new administration simply took the same precautions as the new states of the Balkans did, creating a specifically Bosnian Islamic institution, headed by a chief mufti, that was under Austro-Hungarian control rather than responsible to the shaikh al-islam in Istanbul.[13] The Austro-Hungarian period thus confirmed both Bosniak Muslim identity and the community's sense of isolation amid Christians, features seen already in the reign of Sultan Mahmud II. It was this model of specifically religious communal identity that revived after 1990, following a lengthy eclipse by Yugoslavism, and continues today.

Rediscovery of a meaningfully Islamic identity proved a difficult process, however, because of the mundane ideologies and atheism that flourished under Yugoslav political conditions. Religious institutions survived the period, and faith certainly did not die, but most of the religious authorities trained and practicing in the Yugoslav period had neither widely recognized moral rights to political authority in post-Yugoslav Bosnia nor the clear, aggressive, "Churchillian" leadership desired in the crisis immediately engulfing the new country.[14] Established religious figures held views of the relationship between Islam and the state that were within the range of orthodox tradition, particularly as it had developed since 1878. They tended to view Islam as a primarily personal matter, since the first concern of a Muslim should be ensuring one's own proper practice, or as a personal and communal system of beliefs and practices that derives from interpretation of scripture in accordance with lived conditions, which meant in Bosnia's case acceptance of the established reality of multiconfessional community regardless of the challenges emanating from neighboring republics' nationalists.[15] The popular choice for

---

[13] It was not the Croats' Catholicism that preoccupied Vienna but their Slavic ethnicity, which did not fit neatly into the ethnically divided dual monarchy of Austria-Hungary.

[14] For a glimpse of communist-era Bosnian religion, see Hamid Algar, "Some Notes on the Naqshbandi Tariqat in Bosnia," *Die Welt des Islams* 13 (1971), 168–203.

[15] On Fikret Karčić and Enes Karić, representative figures advocating such views, see Xavier Bougarel, "Trois définitions de l'islam en Bosnie-Herzégovine," *Archives de sciences sociales des religions* 115 (July–September 2001), 183–92. The third figure profiled by Bougarel, Adnan Jahić, had studied philosophy rather than any branch of Islamic thought in the Yugoslav period; his views after he turned to writing on Islamic politics

leadership therefore became Alija Izetbegović, who had the rare qualities of having been imprisoned by the discredited regime for his writings on Islam and of supposedly advocating an Islamic state in Bosnia.

Izetbegović, an employee of the Bosnian railway who had studied agronomy and law at university, was arrested for counterrevolutionary agitation in 1983 and sentenced to fourteen years' imprisonment because of his pamphlet *Islamic Declaration*, written in the late 1960s. This was a factually ill-grounded charge – as Izetbegović noted in his own defense, the tract made no reference to Yugoslavia or Bosnia – and he was released from prison in 1988, but the accusation and his imprisonment made for him a reputation that would appeal to many Bosniaks after 1990. His pamphlet was actually a rather general rumination upon Islam's place in society and the shortsightedness of states, such as Turkey, that were Muslim-majority but had consciously turned away from the established mores that upheld society and social cohesion. Such regimes copied instead the Western practice of attempting to control society through issuing rafts of prescriptive legal mandates. It would be better for the state in a Muslim-majority country to accept that shari'a could regulate society, essentially without state interference, allowing the state to concentrate its energies on modernization and development. Izetbegović upheld Japan as an example of a country whose state did not waste its energy fighting against accepted social mores but rather focused on development, a course that explained why it had advanced much further than Kemalist Turkey had. Some elements of Izetbegović's ruminations echo ideas of the Muslim Brotherhood, including an emphasis upon Muslims' building a stable society by improving and policing themselves rather than depending upon the state to uphold shari'a, but the *Islamic Declaration* hardly qualifies as a radical, let alone fundamentalist, tract. Its discussion of Muslim-majority countries, however, made Izetbegović a natural leader for the movement to prevent Bosniaks from being absorbed into greater Serbia or greater Croatia, and the party he founded, the Democratic Action Party (SDA), has consistently maintained a consciously Muslim identity and the goal of Bosniak independence. Also true to Izetbegović's ideas, however, it has not tried to institute a state system of shari'a, reinforcing the character of Bosnia as a Muslim-majority country whose society is shaped by Islam, rather than one governed by an "Islamic" state.[16]

---

following the collapse of the old order and outbreak of intercommunal war were attuned to those of Alija Izetbegović, who also had no formal religious training.

[16] See Bougarel, "Trois définitions de l'islam," 193–200, for his discussion of Jahić, a leading figure of the SDA.

Islam and Bosnian national identity have once again become effectively inseparable, recalling the situation that developed in the late Ottoman period and was consolidated in the Habsburg era. This resulted from the sudden, radical changes introduced by the breakdown of the established order and the revival of religiously influenced nationalism among Bosnia's near neighbors during a period of great insecurity about past gains and future losses. Bosniak nationalism thus shares with its Serb and Croat neighbors a linkage between religious and national identity, but even more clearly than in its neighbors' cases it has a fundamentally defensive nature. This Islam of national identity is specifically focused upon Bosnia and places no emphasis upon either proselytism or struggle on behalf of other Muslims abroad (it is noteworthy that Bosnian Muslims have shown little affinity for the mainly Muslim Kosovar Albanians, despite facing a common opponent in Serbian nationalism), and there is little scope for irredentism, except in reclaiming the parts of Bosnia still held by the Serbs. There seems little reason to fear that the establishment of a Muslim nation-state in Europe (should the current situation of suspended animation ever lead to creation of a practicable, functioning state) created a "threat of Islamic fundamentalism" to the continent.

MACEDONIA

Macedonia's secession from Yugoslavia in 1992 threatened to spread the conflicts ensuing from the federation's disintegration farther to the south and east than they had yet appeared. Macedonia had formed a prominent target of Serbian territorial ambitions from at least 1878 until Belgrade absorbed much of the area into Serbia as a result of the Balkan Wars of 1912–13, and Kosovo, Bosnia, and Croatia all provided clear examples of Milošević's readiness to fight for other lands considered to be rightfully part of greater Serbia. Belgrade governments had insisted upon calling Macedonia "South Serbia" until the Second World War ended the monarchy and introduced the communist regime, but Tito accorded official recognition to Macedonia as a national republic in Yugoslavia. Serbs in Yugoslavia showed real reluctance to accept the validity of Tito's creation of a separate Macedonian nationality and republic, but as Yugoslavia broke apart, Milošević's regime was unwilling to spread its resources further by adventuring in Macedonia while Bosnia, Kosovo, and Croatia were not yet secured. Macedonia thus managed to secede peacefully and entered the United Nations under the ungainly name *Former Yugoslav Republic of Macedonia* (FYROM), a process of establishing an internationally recognized nation-state that, ironically, opened a new "Macedonian Question" that jolted national sensibilities' around the Balkans.

Unlike Ottoman Macedonia after 1878, FYROM has not faced a serious threat of military conquest by any of its neighbors, and this marks a crucial difference between the old and new Macedonian Questions. It also hints at the continuing weakness of the states in surrounding countries. The reality of a modest region with a small, mixed population establishing itself as an independent country generated fears about other Balkan states' ability to retain territories won in the same way that Serbia gained Macedonia – seizure, with never a chance given to enacting the daily (or even a one-off) plebiscite that embodies national identity – and to hold on to populations still lacking the uniform "national consciousness" advertised by governing regimes.[17]

Actual and would-be leaders of FYROM certainly contributed to this rise in national insecurities by their statements in the period immediately preceding and succeeding secession from Yugoslavia.[18] The greatest threat to independence perceived by Macedonians in this period was from Serbia (at FYROM's request, UN peacekeeping troops were deployed along its border with Serbia from 1993 to 1999, when they were replaced by NATO forces) and, in order to repel any claim to land by Belgrade (or other neighbors), the republic's government redefined Macedonia as the nation-state of Macedonians, eliminating mention of minorities that had been included in the Yugoslav concept of the republic. Adapting rapidly to its self-image as a national homeland, moreover, the republic adopted a constitution that asserted its right to look after the interests of Macedonians in neighboring countries and others living abroad.

Achievement of autocephaly for the Macedonian Orthodox Church was the other high-profile issue of asserting nationhood taken up by the government shortly after secession from Yugoslavia. The church in the republic was effectively dominated by the Serbian Orthodox patriarchate, despite federal Yugoslavia's blessing to creation of a separate church

---

[17] Ernest Renan famously noted in a lecture of 1882, later published as "Qu'est-ce qu'une nation?" that the nation is a daily plebiscite. According to the most recent reliable census, in 1981, Macedonia's population was just below two million, of whom approximately two-thirds were Orthodox Slav and most of the remainder Muslims, of whom the greatest number were Albanians but also included Turkish, Macedonian, and Serbo-Croatian speakers.

[18] For a summary of key developments from 1989 to 1999, see Hugh Poulton, *Who Are the Macedonians?* 2nd ed. (Bloomington: Indiana University Press, 2000), 172–218.

in 1967. This struggle remains essentially unresolved, with the Serbian church (backed by the Belgrade regime) unwilling to grant more than autonomy, and the Macedonian church (backed by Skopje) unwilling to accept less than autocephaly. Given the historical pattern of establishing national churches seen throughout the Balkans, Macedonian insistence upon autocephaly was only to be expected. The status of the church as flag bearer for the nation was indeed already evident in 1993, when the main nationalist party proposed Metropolitan Mihail of Skopje as president of the republic.[19]

All of these moves toward building a new state and identifying it with the Macedonian nation helped to trigger strong reactions. Domestically, Albanians alarmed at finding their country explicitly identified as the homeland of a Slavic Orthodox nation, launched a brief insurgency in 2000. Internationally, responses also arose from Greece, worried about its northern territories, and Bulgaria, whose southwest was the only part of Macedonia it was able to retain after the First Balkan War of 1912. As far-fetched as it might seem, given that Macedonia lacked any credible military forces for years after achieving independence, there appeared to be a mirror image of the original Macedonian Question developing, with Macedonia coveting its neighbors' lands and people rather than being subjected to those neighbors' designs. Only Serbia, which had more pressing strategic concerns than the minimal threat to its control over disputed "Macedonian" territory in its south, and Albania, which was absorbed in severe domestic problems, spared little heed to the new Macedonia.

GREECE

While the rise of volatile, intertwined nationalist and religious emotions unleashed by the disintegration of Yugoslavia has been widely discussed, Greece experienced a less-publicized surge of religious-nationalist political strife. As in Serbia, the engine propelling the wave of what might be described as paranoia was fear of loss of national gains once considered safely consolidated. Of the two issues that have repeatedly drawn international attention to Greece since 1989, Macedonia and Cyprus, Macedonia has had the more electrifying effect upon domestic Greek public attitudes because of its perceived relevance to the territorial integrity

---

[19] Poulton, *Who Are the Macedonians?* 182.

of the Greece built through the Megali Idea.[20] It also is the subject on which the Orthodox Church of Greece has taken the most active stand, galvanizing the Greek overreaction to the secession of FYROM from Yugoslavia. The FYROM issue demonstrated that the church's close connection to Greek identity and its influence over public opinion continue to be strong more than 150 years after King Othon's regime established the national church.

Of all Balkan countries, Greece has seen the greatest continuity in linkages among Orthodox faith, national identity, and state politics since 1945. At the beginning of this period, the status of the church, or at least some of its leading figures, was indicated by the choice of Archbishop Damaskinos of Athens as regent pending a referendum on the return to rule of King George, who had avoided the brutal Nazi occupation in the war years by going into exile. Damaskinos was tolerable to most sides involved in the gathering dispute over liberated Greece's political future, because he acted with greater propriety and social conscience during the occupation and its aftermath than almost all politicians, and indeed many on the Left viewed the church as the most important symbol of Greek endurance through tribulations.[21] The church was no monolith in support for the rightist/nationalist side of the Greek civil war (1944–9), but its institutional history tied it more to the aims of the Right than those of the internationalist Left. Had the Left succeeded in seizing power, moreover, the church would have faced severe restrictions. With the victory of the Right in the civil war and its dominance until the downfall of the military junta (1974), the identification of the church and faith with the state and nation remained very close, a linkage raised to its most oft-cited form by the officers who staged a coup in 1967 and established the "colonels' junta." They justified the coup by asserting that they were defending "Helleno-Christian civilization" against assorted leftist and secularist threats.[22] The junta collapsed in 1974, however, following brutal repression of internal dissent and organization of a disastrous coup in Cyprus

[20] The recent financial collapse, by contrast, speaks to the long-enduring weakness of the nation-state, which from the nineteenth century has sought to buy legitimacy by clientelism and hiring the educated.

[21] John Sakkas, "The Civil War in Evrytania," in Mazower (ed.), *After the War Was Over*, 192, and Mark Mazower, *Inside Hitler's Greece: The Experience of Occupation, 1941–44* (New Haven, CT: Yale University Press, 1993), 95–6, 233 and 259.

[22] Richard Clogg, *A Concise History of Greece*, 2nd ed. (Cambridge: Cambridge University Press, 1992), 160; John Koliopoulos and Thanos Veremis, *Greece: The Modern Sequel, from 1831 to the Present* (New York: New York University Press, 2002), 149–50.

to engineer union of the island with Greece, which instead triggered the Turkish invasion to protect the Turkish Cypriot minority.

Stability returned to Greece under a civilian mainstream rightist government after 1974, and while nationalism maintained its vitality under both Right and Left, the influence of the church declined as a result of its identification, willing or unwilling, with the colonels' junta. The speed of this retreat accelerated after 1981, when Greece entered the European Economic Community and gained its most left-wing government with the electoral victory of the socialist PASOK party of Andreas Papandreou. Entry into the EEC opened the country to more pressure to moderate some of its tradition-bound laws, and the fact that it was the only Orthodox country in the EEC/EU until Bulgaria and Romania joined in 2007 heightened the sense of "brotherless" vulnerability.[23] Prime Minister Papandreou pushed for parliamentary approval of other controversial changes resisted strongly by the church and the weakened Right, including the removal of religious denomination from state identity cards, the introduction of civil marriage and divorce by consent, and the decriminalization of adultery.[24] Later in the decade, moreover, his government raised the possibility of nationalizing some church property.[25] It was against this background of opening to the Catholic/Protestant West and slow secularization of national life that church authorities sought to recapture the initiative as defenders of the nation in the 1990s.

Yugoslavia's disintegration gave the church multiple opportunities to reassert its importance to the nation, most strikingly in the "problem" of the Republic of Macedonia, which continues unresolved two decades later. The conservative Greek government in the early 1990s, preoccupied by matters such as handling the economic mess inherited from PASOK's decade in office, was taking a relaxed attitude toward Macedonia until the church began a concerted drive to alert the nation to the dangers of Macedonian irredentism and helped to organize a string of rallies, the largest of which attracted some 1.3 million protesters in December

---

[23] The idea of Greeks as a "brotherless nation" spread in the 1980s, with the phrase appearing even in the presidential address of 1985. Özkırımlı and Sofos, *Tormented by History*, 122.

[24] While the idea of adultery as a crime punishable by the state may now seem either quaint or outrageous, Greece lagged behind its fellow entrant into the EEC, Spain, by only a few years in decriminalizing the act. Like Greece, Spain had also just emerged from a military dictatorship that had sought to marry the church's authority to the state's.

[25] Charles Stewart, "Who Owns the Rotonda? Church vs. State in Greece," *Anthropology Today* 14/5 (October 1998), 7.

1992.[26] Macedonian views certainly seemed suspect, whether practical or not, given rumors of revanchist slogans such as "We fight for a united Macedonia" and "Salonica is ours" being sprayed on walls or shouted by fans at football matches in Skopje. Like the chants of Skopje Vardar supporters, however, Athenian football fans' habit of jeering visiting players from Salonica as "Bulgarians" says more about the mentality of football fans than about state policies, but the Athenian taunts do illustrate the still-lively awareness that Aegean Macedonia remains not quite surely and purely "Greek." The unrealistic specter of Macedonia seizing northern Greece and the country's second city, Salonica, draws on memories of the struggles to acculturate the large Slav population (be they defined as Macedonians or Bulgarians) in the region of Aegean Macedonia taken in 1912–13 and the ethnic strains of the civil war, in which the Left's fighting forces became ever more identified with the "Slavophone Greeks" of the north and the socialist countries of Bulgaria and especially Yugoslavia. In a noted incident of 1996, the emotions involved in this feeling of Greek insecurity caused an academic press to cancel publication of an anthropological study that documented the Slavic roots of villagers in Aegean Macedonia, as the result of concerns for the safety of its employees in Athens.[27]

These memories were not the only themes stressed by the church, however, as leading figures trumpeted warnings against the similarly improbable idea of (majority Orthodox Slavic) Macedonia forming the key link in an Islamic corridor designed to choke the Greek mainland. This supposed cordon, organized by Turkey, linked Turkey to Albania via Macedonia and the (oppressed, mostly peasant) Turkish and Pomak Muslim minorities of western Thrace (northeastern Greece) and the Rhodopi Mountains of southern Bulgaria.[28] Such themes caught public attention and stirred deep

[26] Özkırımlı and Sofos, *Tormented by History*, 122. For more on the church's leading role in pushing the nationalist view of foreign affairs, see Takis Michas, *Unholy Alliance: Greece and Milošević's Serbia* (College Station: Texas A&M University Press, 2002).

[27] Sarah Lyall, "Publisher Drops Book on Greece, Stirring Protests," *New York Times*, 17 February 1996. The author of the study subsequently found another publisher: Anastasia Karakasidou, *Fields of Wheat, Hills of Blood: Passages to Nationhood in Greek Macedonia, 1870–1990* (Chicago: University of Chicago Press, 1997).

[28] Özkırımlı and Sofos, *Tormented by History*, 122, and Clogg, *History of Greece*, 207–8. Early in my teaching career in southwestern Bulgaria, I and two American colleagues were "exposed" by a Greek newspaper as Turkish agents working to establish this Islamic confederation, on the basis of nothing more than the facts that after driving to Istanbul for a midwinter visit and having almost crashed the car in a snowstorm in Bulgaria, we took the southerly return route to Blagoevgrad via Greece, and that I am an Ottomanist (i.e., a Turkish nationalist, in the common Balkan Christian view). My colleagues, who

concerns. With the state reminded of the influence of the church within the nation and PASOK returned to power, in early 1994 Papandreou imposed a trade embargo on FYROM that closed the border to all goods but humanitarian supplies of food and medicine.[29]

Church leaders have succeeded in keeping the religion and its institutions integral parts of Greek politics and public life.[30] They have used rumors of special rights or concessions being extended to Muslims within Greece to demonstrate the continuing importance of Orthodox Christianity to national identity and state affairs, countering some of the pressure to secularize, or desacralize, sensed to be emanating from the EU. In 2006 the archbishop of Athens and All Greece, for example, called PASOK's nomination of a Muslim woman candidate in a provincial election an affront to "our civilization and our history."[31] Politicians acknowledge the importance of Orthodoxy by displays of church attendance that become more visible in times of political delicacy or tension.[32] The Greek parliament has voted several times to permit the building of the first mosque in Athens, the last EU capital to have one; a proposal to build one under the flight path to Athens airport in time for the 2004 Olympics (the archbishop of Greece had said, "The people are not ready to see a minaret in downtown Athens"), to be financed by Saudi Arabia, died under opposition from nearby residents, who then erected a chapel

later ventured again to Turkey via Greece, were then placed on a restricted-entry list by the Greek government. The story in the Greek newspaper was picked up by a Bulgarian newspaper, *Duma* (30 May 1995, citing the Greek newspaper *Tipos tis Kiriakis*), with details added about my supposed activity in Macedonia. The reports in both papers clearly drew on government sources (see note 29).

29 This embargo provided a windfall for many involved in smuggling through Bulgaria, as I discovered through an interminable wait at the border crossing in the recently sleepy Bulgarian town of Petrich in August 1994, the time of my only (and university-sponsored) visit to Macedonia. The *Duma* article showed its link to a state source by mentioning as evidence of my subversive activity not this trip but my later visit to the Bulgarian-Macedonian border. Like most of my expatriate colleagues, I waited many months for a residence permit and had to leave the country regularly to renew my tourist visa. On one occasion a colleague drove me to a nearby quiet border crossing in the hills; there, I "exited" Bulgaria, walked around to the "entry" side of the guard booth, was readmitted with a new visa, and then got back into my colleague's car. I thus never left Bulgarian territory, a fact presumably known by *Duma*'s source, as was the fact that my "subversive" activities on the far side of the border post lasted about a minute.

30 Yannis Stavrakakis, "Politics and Religion: On the 'Politicization' of Greek Religious Discourse," *JMGS* 21 (2003), 153–81.

31 Özkırımlı and Sofos, *Tormented by History*, 159–61. For an earlier striking example of the church's muscular role in politics, see Stewart, "Who Owns the Rotonda?" 3–9.

32 Galia Valtchinova, "Orthodoxie et communisme dans les Balkans: Réflexions sur le cas bulgare," *Archives des sciences sociales des religions* 119 (July 2002), 85–6.

on the site to commemorate their victory. Following a new authorization bill passed in 2006, a site for a mosque was announced in 2010, and, when built, the mosque will have room for five hundred people (for a current Muslim population of approximately 200,000) and no minaret and be under state control.[33] Slow though this pace of change in matters concerning Muslims (and the wider non-Orthodox population – proselytism that could woo any Greek away from Orthodoxy is tightly controlled) is, it is nevertheless remarkable, given the influence in public affairs exercised by the church and indeed by Greeks' strong Orthodox identity.

These factors, including sensitivity to the perceived spread of threatening Muslim influence, opened another path for the church to show leadership in rallying Greek opinion in the early 1990s: support for the Serbs in the breakup of Yugoslavia. The ecumenical patriarch, in fact, declared while visiting Belgrade that it was the duty of all Orthodox Christians to support Serbia, and certainly public opinion in Greece sided firmly with the Orthodox faction. Echoes of this support continued after the conclusion of not only the conflict in Bosnia but also the NATO bombing of Serbia in support of Kosovo's Albanians, as the comment of a leader of the fight against the Saudi-financed mosque of Athens showed: "We don't want another Kosovo here close to Athens. Kosovo used to be a center for the Orthodox faith, and today it is nothing."[34] Sensitive to public opinion, successive governments argued in support of Serbia within the important international organizations to which Greece belongs (NATO and the EU) and did not participate in military strikes in either the Bosnian or Kosovar campaigns; it has also been strongly suggested, for example in a report by the Dutch government regarding the Srebrenica massacre, that Greece supplied weapons and NATO planning information to the Serbs. Greek companies were suspected of violating the United Nations' embargo on Serbia. There was a "Greek Volunteer Brigade" of about one hundred men that fought alongside the Serbs (and Russian and Ukrainian volunteers) in campaigns including Srebrenica and may have taken part in the massacres executed after the city's fall. The Greek Orthodox Church formed part of the Serbian support network, seconding priests to the Bosnian Serb frontline forces, and in 1993 the archbishop

[33] Daniel Howden, "Muslims in Athens: In Search of a Place to Pray," *Christian Science Monitor* 14 October 2003, at http://www.csmonitor.com/2003/1014/p07s02-woeu.html; Andrew Burroughs, "Athens Muslims to Get a Mosque," *BBC News* 18 July 2006, at http://news.bbc.co.uk/1/hi/5190256.stm; "In Votaniko, the Mosque!" *Espresso* 2 May 2010, at http://www.greeksrethink.com/tag/comittee-of-islamic-mosque-in-athens/.
[34] Clogg, *History of Greece*, 209; Burroughs, "Athens Muslims."

of Athens invited the Bosnian Serb leader Radovan Karadžić to visit the Greek capital as an honored guest. There Karadžić told a mass rally, "We have only God and the Greeks on our side."[35] Although such signs of close interest in the Serbian plight seen among Greeks did not herald the rise of fundamentalist Orthodoxy (a claim rarely if ever heard, unlike the allegation of a fundamentalist Islamic threat posed by armed Muslims in Bosnia), it does indicate the vitality of religious identity in the public life of the contemporary post-Ottoman Christian world.

BULGARIA

Like several Yugoslav republics and Greece, Bulgaria reacted to the collapse of the Soviet-communist system in a manner harking back to the early nation-building era of its post-Ottoman existence, tempered by the experiences of the intervening decades. Concern for the solidarity and well-being of the nation, both the redeemed and the unredeemed parts, showed continuous strength, as did the reestablished ties between the nation and its origins in Orthodoxy. The cumulative effects of the recognized catastrophes that irredentist ventures in the Balkan and world wars proved to be and the disastrous policies of domestic cleansing of the nation in the communist period robbed Bulgarian nationalism of much of its old sense of direction. There also was no one behind whom the nation could rally: much as in the Ottoman period, there was no significant "resistance" movement in the communist era that could produce a notable figure with a clear basis for legitimacy as a post–Cold War national leader. Elections since 1991 have thus raised briefly then discarded a series of governments, with no party but the (ex-communist) Socialists showing any durability or credible ideology; the reprise of the post-Ottoman pattern became almost comic with the election of the expatriate, ex-Spanish-businessman, ex-King Simeon Sakskoburgotski (Saxe-Coburg-Gotha) to the prime ministry in 2001. The Saxe-Coburg-Gotha line was thus twice imported to provide Bulgaria with leadership, without great success. With a chronically weak state and no clear direction in domestic matters, it is unsurprising that Bulgaria has not adopted any

---

[35] Helena Smith, "Greece Faces Shame of Role in Serb Massacre," *Observer* 5 January 2003, at http://www.guardian.co.uk/world/2003/jan/05/balkans.warcrimes; Daniel Howden, "Greek Role in Srebrenica Massacre Investigated," *Independent* 29 June 2005, at http://www.independent.co.uk/news/world/europe/greek-role-in-srebrenica-massacre-investigated-496960.html. The most detailed discussion of Greek support for the Serbs is in Michas, *Unholy Alliance*.

adventurous policies in international affairs, other than to seek stability, and credibility, through voluntary renunciation of elements of state sovereignty to supranational institutions (an International Monetary Fund–organized currency board to manage state fiscal affairs since 1997) and alliances (NATO [Partnership for Peace since 1994, member since 2004], and the EU [associated since 1994, member since 2007]).

Unlike in neighboring countries where events produced a more aggressive nationalism, the church in Bulgaria failed to provide ideological guidance or national leadership. This did not result from lack of opportunity: as soon as the communist regime of Todor Zhivkov collapsed, all figures hoping to play significant future roles in politics, both communists and noncommunists, flocked to make highly publicized appearances in major churches and monasteries.[36] The Bulgarian Orthodox Church, however, split into rival camps, with a faction disputing the legitimacy of the patriarch, Maksim, because he had been selected by the atheist regime rather than chosen by the church in 1971. This split was legitimated by the socialists' main opponent in the early postcommunist period, the Union of Democratic Forces, which sought to pry the church from the ideological successors to the old regime.[37] Embroiled until 2010 in a schism concerning hierarchical authority and control over the church's physical property, it had neither the freedom from self-absorption nor the unified voice needed to influence politics in the name of the nation that it had been created to support. If it has contributed anything to Bulgarian politics since the end of the communist era, the church only fostered the sense of aimlessness by providing a dispute that rival political parties could exploit for electoral advantage.

Bulgaria's post-Zhivkov lack of direction also shows the impact of communist-era attempts to force the country's Muslim and ethnic Turkish minorities to assimilate into the Orthodox-Bulgarian model of the nation.[38] The most ambitious and well-publicized phase of this program commenced in the mid-1980s and targeted Bulgaria's Turks. The regime banned public use of Turkish, closed or destroyed mosques, and compelled Turks to rediscover their supposed Bulgarian origins by taking Christian-Bulgarian names – the most famous example being the Olympic

---

[36] Valtchinova, "Orthodoxie et communisme," 86

[37] Todorova, *Bones of Contention*, 359–71.

[38] On the Bulgarian Turks in the communist era, see Wolfgang Höpken, "From Religious Identity to Ethnic Mobilisation: The Turks of Bulgaria before, under and since Communism," in *Muslim Identity and the Balkan State*, ed. Hugh Poulton and Suha Taji-Farouki (New York: New York University Press, 1997), 54–81.

weight lifter Naim Süleymanoğlu, who became Naum Shalamanov until he defected to Turkey. This campaign, termed the "Revival Process," was enforced by the police and the army, with tanks used to cow obstreperous villagers. The regime justified its coercion by stressing a nineteenth-century myth that the local Turks were descendants of Bulgarians forcibly converted by the Ottomans in the seventeenth century, which was a story retold in a much-publicized movie, *A Time of Violence*, released in 1988 and submitted by the government as its candidate for the Academy Award (Oscar) in the Best Foreign Film category. The main results achieved by the Revival Process were the reinforcement of ethnic Turkish and Muslim identity (foreshadowing a similar process in Bosnia triggered by the primarily Serbian assaults on Muslims), the alienation of the Turks from the regime (and a strengthening of anti-Turkish prejudice among Bulgarians),[39] a mass exodus of Turks when the communist regime opened the border with Turkey to "let off steam" for several weeks in 1989, serious damage to the already rickety economy by disrupting a key part of the population working in cash crops such as tobacco and roses, and the creation of an essentially Muslim, largely Turkish political party as soon as the communist regime collapsed. This party, the Movement for Rights and Freedoms, has taken part in government regularly since the collapse of communism, simply by virtue of garnering the votes of Turks, Pomaks (Bulgarian-speaking Muslims), and Roma who have been thoroughly alienated from Bulgarian national(ist) parties, be they nominally liberal or socialist.[40]

This experience of the unintended consequences of paranoid nationalist persecution effectively inoculated Bulgarians against any inclination to react to the collapse of the old regime by attacking traditional enemies of the nation who had become "comrades" by decree of the communist state. Bulgarian sentiment may well have favored the Serbs over Muslims in Bosnia and Kosovo, but neither state nor people showed any serious interest in emulating the Serbs' campaigns of ethnic cleansing. Aggressively paranoid nationalism had been sufficiently discredited to drain energy from any urge to adopt a belligerent approach to either foreign affairs, as Greece did, or domestic matters, as Macedonia (where Macedonian nationalism, and the turmoil in Kosovo promoted discontent

---

[39] Höpken, "Religious Identity," 76–8; Mary McIntosh et al., "Minority Rights and Majority Rule: Ethnic Tolerance in Romania and Bulgaria," *Social Forces* 73 (1995), 943–6.
[40] On the strengthening of Muslim identity in recent years, see Kristen Ghodsee, *Muslim Lives in Eastern Europe: Gender, Ethnicity and the Transformation of Islam in Postsocialist Bulgaria* (Princeton: Princeton University Press, 2009).

among the large Albanian minority that led to a short armed conflict between state security forces and militants [helpfully labeled "terrorists" in Macedonian and Bulgarian media] in 2001) and Romania (where the Greater Romania Party did well out of simplistic nationalism, focusing particularly on repressing the Hungarian minority and, less realistically, regaining Bukovina and Bessarabia from Ukraine and Moldova) did.[41]

Macedonia nevertheless became a focus of Bulgarian attention, if not action, as Yugoslavia crumbled. Bulgaria's was the first state to recognize the new country after its secession from the Serbian-dominated rump Yugoslavia – although Turkey, almost as interested in seeing Macedonia's liberation from Serbia as was Bulgaria, was the first to have an ambassador accredited to Skopje. Bulgarian-Macedonian bilateral relations were extremely difficult to establish on a formal basis because of the states' failure to agree on whether Macedonian was a separate language or merely a cosmetically modified version of Bulgarian, a problem successfully bypassed (not solved) by artful treaty wording only in 1999. In the meantime, however, Bulgaria served as the economic lifeline for Macedonia while the Greek embargo was in force and Serbia was under international embargo, and it also became a crucial supplier of weaponry to Macedonia's nascent military. Since Bulgaria joined the EU, it has tried to portray itself as Macedonia's gateway into the union; thousands have taken advantage of Bulgaria's offer of easy (dual) citizenship to any Macedonian declaring Bulgarian ethnicity, presumably in order to gain an EU passport, just as Macedonians have also taken advantage of easily accessed subsidized study at Bulgarian universities. Despite Macedonian nationalists' fears that such soft policies have been intended to establish Bulgaria's dominant influence in the republic, Sofia has had two more obvious goals: preserving Macedonia's independence from Serbian and Greek threats and territorial integrity against Albanian separatism, and more importantly forestalling separatism in the remaining Bulgarian slice of Macedonia, Pirin Macedonia, which was absorbed in the Balkan Wars of 1912–13. Bulgaria's artful language allowing Macedonian and Bulgarian versions of agreements without acknowledging that Macedonian is a separate language gained in return an affirmation from Skopje that it would not interfere in Bulgaria's domestic affairs, that is, not encourage

---

[41] The head of the party, Corneliu Vadim Tudor, who was a panegyrist for Nicolae Ceauşescu until the communist dictator was shot, held a seat in the Romanian Senate from 1992 to 2008. He finished second in the Romanian presidential election of 2000 after running on a platform with little content beyond nationalism. After Romania joined the EU, he was elected a member of the European Parliament in 2008.

separatism in Pirin Macedonia.[42] NATO accession has also provided a degree of reassurance to Bulgarians about the territorial integrity of the state by once again providing a multipower protective umbrella, which lessens the dangers created by the weakness of the state that is at its most obvious in Pirin Macedonia and, especially, in the Turkish-populated regions of the south and northeast.

In the international arena Bulgaria's lack of prickliness and unpredictability has given it a reputation for political strength and stability that eased its entry into the EU, but in fact the placidity results more from the state's recognition of its own weakness than from strength. Much of the population puts little faith in the state to improve the lot of the average citizen – a lack of hope fully justified by successive regimes' apparent inability to control crime and corruption and to promote sustainable economic development. There has been much emigration by the young, and of the population remaining, little more than half bother to vote in parliamentary elections. The parlous condition of national public life helps to explain the Socialist Party's proven ability to rebound from multiple setbacks, from the collapse of communism to periodic electoral defeats suffered by sitting governments. No matter how discredited socialism was by the collapse of communism, no other political group has developed a reputation for standing for anything with ideological substance: as threadbare as socialism may be, it is the only political creed that might tempt people to believe. Simeon Sakskoburgotski won the election in 2001 with almost 43 percent of the vote largely on a promise of significantly increasing per capita income in eight hundred days, a target unsupported by any clearly outlined route to achievement but rather by his cachet as a monarch opposed by the communists of the recently imploded regime and by his reputation as a wealthy businessman in Spain. By the 2009 election, his party's share of the vote had collapsed to 3 percent. The Socialists rebounded, because theirs is the only party to show any interest in pensioners, the underserved countryside, and the urban poor. The weak state created after independence from the Ottoman empire remains weak, because it still has not found a credible means of boosting its legitimacy. Nationalism remains strong – and the vigorous showing by the Far Right Ataka Party in the 2009 election demonstrates the potential for political gain from nationalist themes. Until a party develops something

---

[42] Anton Kojouharov, "Bulgarian 'Macedonian' Nationalism: A Conceptual Overview," *Online Journal of Peace and Conflict Resolution* 6 (2004), 282, available at http://web.archive.org/web/20090227084311/http://www.trinstitute.org/ojpcr/6_1kojou.pdf.

more ideologically substantial than xenophobia or racism, however, nationalism will not strengthen the state.

ALBANIA

Albania's experience since the collapse of communism only confirms the weakness of crude and rude post-Ottoman nationalisms as political ideologies when unalloyed by practical substance, and it certainly illustrates also the weakness of states that have hoped to legitimate their existence through nation-building programs. Under the communist regime of Enver Hoxha, whose version of Stalinism-Marxism was as crude as the Albanian nationalism that he pushed, the state achieved its only period of dominance over the post-Ottoman country, but as soon as his murderously warped rule ended in 1985, the slackening of ruthlessness permitted the collapse of his Potemkin state.

Hoxha's legacy was that practically nothing still functioned on the social, political, or economic level by the time the communist monopoly on authority crumbled in 1990–1. In society, his main purpose had been to break any focus of loyalty or identity apart from Albania and socialism, both of which ultimately in his view meant himself. He killed or imprisoned landowning notables, clan leaders, and religious figures, and the pervasive security services worked assiduously to subvert family loyalty by stressing the duty of children to denounce reactionary parents. Religion was banned in 1967: most mosques and churches were destroyed, although a few were turned to other uses (the cathedral of Shkodra, the largest Catholic church in the Balkans, became a volleyball court) or made into cultural museums, and the remaining priests, imams, and Bektashi shaikhs were shot or imprisoned.[43] Parents could no longer give children names with religious or foreign origins (such as Enver [after Enver Pasha; Ar. Anwar] and Nexhmije [Ar. Najmiyya], the name of Hoxha's wife) but rather had to choose from a list of ideologically sound options; Albanians with now-common names such as *Ilir* and *Dardan* were almost invariably born after 1967.[44] In politics, however, the tradition of strong family identity continued, with the relations of the many communists purged by Hoxha suffering the same fate (shot

---

[43] On the lasting effects of this repression, see Frances Trix, "The Resurfacing of Islam in Albania," *EEQ* 28 (1995), 533–49.

[44] Such names derive from nationalist history, which asserts that the Albanians are descendents of the Illyrians and Dardanians and thus heirs of the oldest settlers of the Balkans.

or imprisoned – or, in especially surreal instances, "shot and deprived of electoral rights for five years") as those in disgrace, with the places of the once-influential purged taken by the relatives of Hoxha and his closest associates, almost all of whom were, like him, Tosks of southern Albania. As a result of successive bloody purges and promotions by connections, the party became practically as inept as the state. This ineptness manifested itself clearly in development of the country, which in Stalinist fashion started with forceful collectivization of agriculture before turning increasingly to industrialization (not just for economic purposes, but also to create an urban proletariat where practically none had previously existed), little of which was sensibly designed or efficiently implemented. The most lasting development concerned physical infrastructure and the draining of swampland, much of the labor for which was provided by the plentiful political prisoners.

When Hoxha's successor, Ramiz Alia, showed a lighter touch in controlling the country and began to tinker with the dysfunctional economic system, the party, the state, and the country began to fall apart, and none has really reconstituted itself as a coherent whole. Decades of heavy-handed instruction in Albanian nationalism, reinforced by the extreme xenophobia represented most famously by the hundreds of thousands of military pillboxes scattered across the country to allow the people to fight against the expected invading Yugoslavs, Soviets, Americans, and British, created a deeply rooted consciousness of being Albanian, but this national identity is practically meaningless, trapped in the tautology of "The faith of Albanians is Albanianism!" Irredentism holds no attraction: there is no clear push for a Greater Albania because the Albanians of Albania (stereotyped by the others as backward and insular), Kosovo (stereotyped as flashy and untrustworthy), and Macedonia (seen as rural and conservative) have only limited affinity for each other, as they have followed different trajectories since 1912. Neighbors' irredentism also presents little real focus for nationalism, since no state has shown clear interest in taking Albanian territory, despite some Greek Orthodox Church attempts to stimulate Greek interest in seizing the southern half of Albania, and Skopje's stated interest in the small Macedonian population in the east of the country.[45] Within Albania, all of the interregional distrust that was simultaneously repressed and exacerbated by Hoxha's regime resumed

[45] On Greek church irredentism toward "Northern Epirus," see Miranda Vickers and James Pettifer, *Albania: From Anarchy to a Balkan Identity* (New York: New York University Press, 1997), 111–2. In questioning me, the Greek border guard who started the story of my being a Turkish spy mentioned an improbably-high figure for the Greek minority

in full force: the Gheg north is the stronghold of the Democratic Party (PD), the Tosk south continues to back the (ex-communist) Socialists, and these main parties show little inclination to agree on anything. The lack of practical meaning in Albanian national identity was displayed in 1997, when the country dissolved, not quite into civil war, but at least into well-armed anarchy following the collapse of various pyramid investment schemes, for which the ruling PD was partially blamed. Although a lasting form of stability has returned to the country, the division between north and south continues, and it is difficult to see any real likelihood of Albania's joining the EU as long as such internal divides exist.

As this chapter shows, however, the recurring problems besetting Albania are hardly uncharacteristic of the post-Ottoman Balkans. Most states of the region remain weak, being representative of only restricted segments (ethnic, urban, regional, or state-employed) of society and distrustful of, if not hostile to, the significant parts of society not included in governing parties' sphere of allegiance. The enduringly brittle nature of such weak political systems, developed hastily under adverse conditions in each post-Ottoman country, has been once again demonstrated by Greece's inability to manage state affairs and finances, even after three decades in the EU. For countries not yet part of the EU or more recently inducted, political and economic conditions have been even less suited to the task of strengthening state legitimacy.

For most post-Ottoman Balkan countries, the nationalism developed soon after independence remains a tool that still holds some attraction as a source of at least a veneer of legitimacy. Little content has been added to the message of the nation, however, and questions of control over land and population, and of injuries to the nation inflicted by outside powers, remain sensitive enough to generate an emotive response. The extension of NATO membership, in particular, and either membership or the prospect of entry into the EU have reduced the worst fears about possible loss of territory gained through post-Ottoman revanchism, thus reducing also the likelihood of conflict. Neither supranational organization has proven capable of quelling the destabilizing influence on weak states

---

in Albania and then asked whether I had any interest in them. I assured him, truthfully, that I did not and resisted the impulse to add, equally truthfully, that if he wanted to consider the entire Balkan Peninsula as Greek, I couldn't care less. Given the widespread dislike of Albanians (and Turks, Slavs, etc.) in Greece, it is clear that the government was interested in that minority only as long as it stayed in Albania; if reunification with the mother nation were to happen, it would have to bring the territory of Albania in which the minority lived along with them.

exercised by the nationalism of the aggrieved, however, either within the region (Greece and Turkey have come close to conflict over borders on several occasions) or without (numerous examples elsewhere in postimperial Europe, but also in Western countries such as Belgium, could be cited). In the Balkans, religious institutions hold some promise of providing both "pastoral care" and "social glue" for societies ill served by such states, but, given the roots of most religious institutions in the nation-building programs of early post-Ottoman regimes, they too can succumb to the distractions of national politics. Religion has thus shown revived strength, but, as long as churches remain tied to nationalism's mundane pursuits, they will continue to fail to realize their potential influence in a region beset by doubt and anomie in public life.

10

Contemporary Turkey

Just as the resurgence of nationalism, religion, and conflict in the Balkans revived Western interest in the Ottoman period of control over that peninsula and sparked speculation about the empire's legacy there, so the course of Turkish politics since the 1980s has reopened the old question of where "Turkey" (first the Ottoman empire and now the Republic of Turkey) belongs. Is it part of Europe, deserving of admission into the European Union? Or does the revival of Islam in public life, which gives another twist to the idea of "neo-Ottomanism," undermine all that Atatürk achieved and mark Turkey as enduringly "oriental"?[1] The repeated successes of political parties deemed "Islamic" has provided ammunition for opponents of Turkey's entry into the EU, to whose arsenal of antiadmission rationales centered on objection to Turkey's "denial of the Armenian genocide" are now added warnings over letting "Islamic fundamentalism" disrupt the union. Such warnings seem comic in comparison to the question of genocide, not only because the Islam in Turkish politics bears little resemblance to that of countries such as Saudi Arabia that are usually called to mind by the term "fundamentalism," but also because Brussels would find Turkey's secular nationalists no easier to manage or manipulate. The EU in its original form bound together six countries that welcomed an institutional brake to nationalism following the experiences of the world wars, but as it has expanded into areas that feel little link or responsibility for the wars (other than as victims), the communal sense

---

[1] Neo-Ottomanism is an elastic term that can refer to foreign affairs, with Turkey acting as a mediator in formerly Ottoman areas; to domestic politics, with the idea of decentralization to give groups such as the Kurds millalike status in managing some of their own affairs; or to arts and culture.

of disapproval of overtly nationalist regimes has weakened. Kemalist Turkey would add another member to the growing "awkward squad" of the EU, made up of countries with strong characteristics of prickly state nationalism, including Greece and the former Warsaw Pact countries of Eastern Europe. Turkey has a clear record as part of NATO since 1952, however, proving a consistent, reliable member under both Kemalist and "Islamic" party regimes, despite earning a reputation as a tough bargainer within the alliance.[2]

Rather than criticizing Turkey for potentially introducing Islam as a disturbing element into the (Christian) European club, EU members might more usefully focus upon what the rise of Islamic politics indicates about the flaws apparent in the Kemalist state.[3] What should catch attention is not the fact that the Islamically oriented Justice and Development (Adalet ve Kalkınma or AK [Tr. white]) Party gained 46.66 percent of the votes cast in the elections of 2007 and thereby a clear majority in parliament (the more explicitly philoislamic Felicity Party polled 2.34 percent), but rather that so many Turks who did not describe themselves as religious chose to vote AKP, continuing a trend building since the 1990s.[4]

Islam in Turkish public affairs, like the rest of politics in overwhelmingly Muslim Turkey, is consistently focused upon domestic concerns, does not challenge in any notable manner the country and the nation as they have developed since the Atatürk period, and is not driven by any perceived need to campaign, violently or nonviolently, against non-Muslims abroad or at home. It draws its strength from its recognized, long-established role as the glue holding society together, and from its message of ensuring fairness and justice to responsible members of the Islamic community. The first part of the AKP's name appeals directly to this time-honored message: *Adalet* ('adala) is the Ottoman-Arabic, and Islamic, word for justice.

---

[2] The leader of the Welfare (Refah) Party, Necmettin Erbakan, favored withdrawal from NATO, but the idea was dropped after his party entered government in 1996. Military cooperation with Israel, however, has been more difficult for "Islamic" parties to accept.

[3] On the Christian ideals underpinning the EU's original embodiment, the European Coal and Steel Community, see Wolfram Kaiser, *Christian Democracy and the Origins of European Union* (Cambridge: Cambridge University Press, 2007).

[4] Joseph Szyliowicz, "Religion, Politics and Democracy in Turkey," in *The Secular and the Sacred: Nation, Religion and Politics* ed. William Safran (London: Frank Cass, 2003), 208, notes that the clear majority of voters who supported Refah in the 1994 election were not guided by any religious motivation.

THE RESTORATION OF RELIGION IN POLITICS

Such a message had demonstrated that it could appeal to much of the Turkish population half a century before the AKP was founded. The authoritarianism of the Atatürk regime had continued under his successor, İsmet İnönü, and became particularly onerous during the Second World War, when the country adopted armed neutrality in its efforts to resist both alliances' pressure to enter the conflict. It is possible to trace an echo of the Ottoman experience under Mahmud II (or indeed any of the absolutist monarchies of eighteenth-century Christian Europe). The state felt a compelling need to boost its armed strength, but in fact the military forces fought no foreign enemy, merely burdened Turkey's public life and finances. Turkey found itself hard pressed to sustain the expenditure, especially under the wartime-induced international economic disruptions that it confronted. Inflation rose markedly. The large firms that grew through the RPP's patronage under Kemalism's principle of statism were cushioned from that inflation by government contracts; the national economy, however, survived the war largely through the dynamism of the growing private sector, which felt more directly the effects of inflation. The private sector also found the wealth tax levied during the war very alarming because of the principle of confiscation that it represented, and it pushed for a lightening of the state's hand afterward. One partial solution to the state's financial woes after the war's end was to accept American money offered under the "Truman Doctrine"; domestically the regime eased its tight command over the taxpaying public, and especially the economic private sector, which chafed under the many government-issued restrictions and requirements. It was to İnönü's credit as a pragmatist that he recognized these pressures and chose to loosen the RPP state's control, rejecting the demands of hard-liners such as Recep Peker, the prime minister in 1946–7.

Pressure to change prompted İnönü and the ruling Republican People's Party to experiment again with permitting the development of new parties headed by ideologically "safe" people, meaning, in this instance, leaders of factions within the RPP who proposed alternative strategies to development. The most notable new political force was the Democrat Party (DP), which was founded early in 1946 and wished to loosen the state's command over economic affairs. As with Atatürk's short-lived initiative to create the Free Republican Party as a token alternative to the RPP in 1930, the DP proved surprisingly attractive to the public but, rather than dissolving it as Atatürk had with the FRP, İnönü accepted that the RPP needed to woo voters, and the dynamics of party competition accelerated. One of the major themes of change promised or instituted by both DP and RPP was the easing of restrictions on religious affairs, including the resumption on a limited basis of religious education in schools and the training of 'ulama. The government started in 1948 to permit limited numbers of Turks to perform the Hajj, with some nine thousand undertaking the journey in 1950 despite continuing currency restrictions, and in 1949 İnönü reshuffled the cabinet to appoint as prime minister a man known for his Islamic sensibilities.[5] In this competition the DP won, however, because the regime's moves were too little, too late to gain acceptance as genuine reforms. The aggressively "secularist" record of the RPP, and its reputation for authoritarianism, helped to limit the number of seats it held in the first freely elected parliament to 69, compared to the DP's 408.

Reaction to the easing of restrictions showed that Kemalist suppression of Islam in public life had not undermined the religious allegiances of much of the country. Religious training and sufi practice had been driven underground, not eradicated, by Atatürk's closure of medreses and abolition of brotherhoods. Sufi shaikhs took advantage of the more permissive atmosphere to appear again in public, although a number of them were promptly taken to court by the RPP regime before the 1950 election and the DP government after it took office. The most noted prosecution tried Kemal Pilavoğlu, a shaikh of the Tijani order who claimed forty thousand followers, some of whom were apparently waging a campaign against the personality cult of Atatürk by vandalizing the omnipresent statues and busts of his visage. Pilavoğlu was sentenced to fifteen years imprisonment, and the DP regime subsequently passed a law criminalizing anti-Atatürk acts.[6] As the DP's actions suggest, it never showed any sign of wanting to dismantle the main framework of the state and nation created under Atatürk's guidance (the leaders of the DP all originated in the RPP), and indeed, after winning the election of 1950, the party leadership ensured that steps proposed by some members to rescind key Kemalist measures, such as lifting the ban on wearing the fez and reversing the substitution of Latin for Arabic-Ottoman script, were never given room

[5] Lewis, Emergence of Modern Turkey, 420; M. Hakan Yavuz, Islamic Political Identity in Turkey (Oxford: Oxford University Press, 2003), 60; Feroz Ahmad, "Politics and Political Parties in Republican Turkey," in CHT4, 234.

[6] On the continuation of surreptitious religious instruction in the republic, and for an excellent description of the continuing force of Islam in orienting society in the provinces, see Meeker, Nation of Empire. On the sufi revival, see Lewis, Emergence of Modern Turkey, 420–4; Zürcher, Turkey, 244–5; and Yavuz, Islamic Political Identity, 62.

for consideration.[7] The DP nevertheless recognized that modernization did not depend upon Kemalism's erasure of Islam from public view, and that the efforts to eradicate it from public life ultimately hindered the working of the state by arousing resentment or disdain among much of the population. During its decade in power, therefore, the DP became increasingly identified with religious symbols and some of the sufi movement, seeking to maintain its popularity as the government's missteps in economic affairs and increasingly autocratic style of rule alienated some of its original supporters among Turkey's liberals and entrepreneurs. The DP did remain the most popular party until 1960, when its methods of rule, including its identification with religion, triggered a military coup.

Many of the DP's actions that appealed to Muslim sensibilities now seem almost symbolic, such as revoking the Atatürk era mandate that the call to prayer be given in Turkish (and every mosque reverted immediately to the Arabic call), but the nature of such measures indicates one of the main reasons for the revival of "political" Islam at the time: resentment of state actions that seemed to have little purpose other than interfering with the population's customs and rhythms of life. The Kemalist project of maximizing state authority sought to throttle all sources and venues of thought and discussion that were independent of state control. Imams were tolerated only in the mosque, and only if they followed the directives of state authorities, and because the state had stopped training new religious authorities, there developed a real need for guidance on important social and family matters, from leading prayers to proper performance of marriages and burial of the dead. State guidance carried little or no weight in such basic considerations of social life. Yet the Kemalist state not only regulated mosque life, it barred the independent dissemination of texts on religious subjects and in 1932 created instead a system of "reading rooms," the *halk evleri* or, in villages, *halk odaları* (people's houses/rooms), where Turks could read or listen to suitably instructive material on the nation and how it should pursue development. For a time, the state even tried to suppress or regulate the second-most-established institution of social life (after the mosque), the tea/coffeehouse, in order to neutralize the other significant route for evasion of the people's houses/rooms' dominance of approved social life.[8] This heavy hand made the

---

[7] Poulton, *Top Hat*, 171.

[8] For examples of methods used to tighten state control over social life, see M. Asım Karaömerlioğlu, "The Village Institutes Experience in Turkey," *BriJMES* 25 (1998), 47–73, and Serdar Öztürk, "Efforts to Modernize Chapbooks during the Initial Years of the Turkish Republic," *European History Quarterly* 40 (2010), 7–34.

DP's modest but sensible easing of restraints welcome. The DP abolished the people's house system, broadened the scope of religious education, and permitted publication and distribution of texts giving spiritual guidance such as Said Nursi's (1876–1960) *Risale-i Nur* (Epistles of Light), the main body of writings by the guiding figure of the influential "Nurcu" sufi movement – despite keeping Nursi himself under close observation, and in effect internal exile, until his death.[9] As noted, the controls placed on Nursi only confirm that the DP regime in its last days in power still had no intention of undoing the control of religion and the principle of the supreme power of the state that had been key concerns in the Kemalist period.

Although the coup of 1960 swept away the DP – and prompted political trials that resulted in execution of some of its leading figures, including the ousted prime minister, Adnan Menderes – no truly significant party, including the military, ignored the lessons about the oppressive state and Islam taught by the DP in government. The officer corps has recognized since 1960 that the ultimate goal of Kemalism, the creation of a state whose power is both unchallenged and unchallengeable, will always be defended; for this purpose the military has been ready to act against "Islamization" of the state where this implies either diversion of the state's power to any purpose other than command and control over Turkey's territory and population or the weakening of the state's power by making it subservient to any other authority, including religious law and its interpreters. Yet the military, and indeed most Kemalists, have also recognized the shortsightedness of the repressive state between 1925 and 1945. They have come to argue not against religious observance, but against the idea that to be a good Muslim requires more than individual performance of the five core duties of Islam (attestation of faith, prayer, fasting, almsgiving, and pilgrimage), that is, against the notion that the good Muslim must follow shari'a where it might impinge on the wide purview of the state's legal system.[10] The state of 1925–45 had interfered too much in Muslims' ability to perform even the five core duties, stoking needless disaffection and leading to the ouster of the RPP as soon as it allowed free elections. The military thus did not attempt to recreate the cleansing of religion from politics that had characterized the RPP period,

---

[9] Nursi had been one of the leaders of the Society of Muslim Union, the group held responsible for organizing the "counterrevolution" against CUP dominance in 1909, making him permanently suspect in the view of successive regimes descended from the CUP. Farhi, "Şeriat as a Political Slogan," 285.

[10] David Shankland, *Islam and Society in Turkey* (Huntingdon, UK: Eothen Press, 1999), 6.

allowing all post-1960 parties to adopt positions on religion similar to that which had worked effectively for the DP.

Such pragmatism in officers involved in the overthrow of the elected government and the staging of show trials in the aftermath may seem surprising, but the fact that the more radically authoritarian-nationalist men who drove the coup plot were themselves ousted from positions of influence over the reconstruction of state and politics by more moderate, more senior officers helps to explain the permanent change in the relationship between politics and religion. The most noted of the radical officers, the quasi-fascist Colonel Alparslan Türkeş, entered politics as a civilian in the mid-1960s and maintained his extreme nationalist stance (supported by a paramilitary organization, the Grey Wolves), but even he saw the wisdom of not trying to repress religion as completely as the RPP had done, beginning to highlight Islam as an integral part of Turkish heritage before the national election of 1969. Türkeş's party and paramilitary would play a large role in the 1970s, both taking advantage of and fomenting further the violent political chaos of that decade. Partly as a result of that turmoil, the 1970s also saw the first serious calls for introduction of shari'a. Both the campaigning for religious law and the political turmoil resulted mainly from the military coup of 1971, which undid some of the amelioration of state authoritarianism introduced following the 1960 coup.

Although the overthrow of the DP government and especially the executions of party leaders had generated popular resentment and ensured the continued relegation of the RPP to minority status in the 1960s, the military regime installed by the coup had made significant changes to Turkey's constitutional order, most of which were welcomed as a loosening of governing parties' grip on the state and population. The republic had functioned practically as a one-party state not only in the Atatürk-İnönü era but also, much to the regret of the RPP, under the DP in the 1950s, and the military regime of 1960 had commissioned revisions of the constitution to create checks and balances to limit the freedom of action of any party that might win office. Governing parties in the 1960s had lost much of their power to manipulate the judiciary, the media, and the universities, and perhaps most significantly had had to attend to the military high command, which had gained for the first time a recognized advisory role. The creation of a constitutional court that was empowered to (and frequently did) strike down laws passed by parliament formed an important part of the new checks-and-balances system – but also one that more subtly policed the supremacy of the Kemalist vision. The constitutional court, whose self-perpetuating order was dominated for decades after its creation by graduates of the strongly secularist-nationalist legal training system established in the Kemalist period, has until recently zealously attacked any party suspected of either pro-Kurdish or Islamic leanings.[11] The new constitutional order in the 1960s nevertheless did permit a wider range of political organizations, including notably class-based leftist parties.

All of these gains dispersing power from the ruling-party hands in which it had been concentrated were revoked or disrupted after the second military coup, in 1971, except that the military's constitutional advisory role was strengthened; it may have been the example of the Greek military junta, which had seized power a few years earlier only to win widespread international condemnation, that made the military leadership hesitate to take power directly. The coup had been precipitated by growing economic and political paralysis seen in many countries in the late 1960s (as elsewhere, Turkey's politics featured a struggle between leftists and a mainstream Right), but the military's intervention failed to give the needed sense of direction and only encouraged growing viciousness in the struggle among civilian parties to gain the power needed to push their own views. The violence, and the overall sordidness of politics, created an opening for a "clean" political platform, which Islam has the potential to provide.

Necmettin Erbakan became the leader of a sustained push to translate Islam, and especially the principles of justice and fairness for all believers, from a force recognized as an integral part of society by parties such as the DP and its "successor" the Justice Party (JP) into the core message of a political organization. Erbakan resembled the leader of the JP, Süleyman Demirel, in having a small-town background, a career as an engineer, a blunt and unpolished style of speaking that resonated with provincial voters, and even membership in the JP for most of the 1960s. Unlike Demirel, however, he identified relatively openly with sufism. He fell out with Demirel over the JP's reluctance to attack the influence of big business and especially foreign banks in Turkey; after winning an assembly seat representing the pious voters of conservative Konya in 1969, he formed a religious party with two other representatives. The military dissolved it after the 1971 coup, but the party

[11] Ceren Belge, "Friends of the Court: The Republican Alliance and the Selective Activism of the Constitutional Court of Turkey," *Law and Society* 40 (2006), 653–92.

soon revived under a new name. Campaigning on a rather unrefined platform, castigating capitalism and calling for boosting Islamic morals and solidarity, greater state activism in reorienting the national economy away from big business to smaller industrial firms, and resistance to "Zionist" banks and Western countries, Erbakan's party won a modest but, because of the overall political paralysis, influential share of votes in elections through the decade. In practical terms it accomplished practically nothing, however, despite entering government three times as junior partner in coalition with first the RPP (by this time a center-Left party) and then the JP.

POLITICS, THE MILITARY, AND ISLAM AFTER 1980

Chaos and rising violence by both leftists and rightists became the main theme of politics in the late 1970s, and in 1980 the military again acted to stop what it viewed as the most troubling trends. Political violence had led to the deaths of more than one thousand people, including not just activists of Left and Right but also more mainstream political and non-political figures. The government appeared incapable of controlling the situation or of handling a worsening economic crisis, and for the military the final straw was a mass rally in Konya, during which marchers called for the return of shari'a to restore order. The military intervened to arrest, expel, or kill suspected activists, particularly leftists; it dissolved political parties and banned their leading figures from participation in politics for ten years (shortened to seven years by a referendum in 1987 after the restoration of narrowly circumscribed democratic government).

Again the military had dissolved Erbakan's party and barred him from politics, but after the referendum overturned the ban on pre-1980 politicians, he once more resurrected the Islamic cause through the Refah (Welfare or Prosperity) Party (WP). The military had again altered the constitution, in order to reduce the likelihood of political gridlock, requiring parties now to receive at least 10 percent of the vote to gain representation in the National Assembly. The WP failed to clear that hurdle until 1991, when it entered an electoral coalition with the Far Right party founded by Türkeş and one of its offshoots. The main policy statement of Erbakan and the WP, *The Just Economic Order*, railed against banks and the capitalist West and preached for family and communal solidarity, with the state acting as the facilitator of an economic system in which work yields just rewards, rather than a system that acts as a conduit for siphoning most of the average person's pay into the pockets of bankers and corrupt bureaucrats.[12] Much of this program coincided with views of the Far Right, whose wholehearted embrace of the "Sèvres complex" bred distrust of the West as deep as Erbakan's, but the WP's appeal to "family values," applicable to not only the literal family but also local and national communities, invoked at multiple levels a more textured concept of solidarity based upon religion than the ideal preached by the hard-line nationalists. The message also gave the WP a critical advantage in appealing to Kurds, who after the 1980 coup grew ever more disenchanted with the mainstream parties, all of which worked in alliance with the military to repress signs of Kurdish identity. Another theme developed by the WP, a harkening back to the glories of the Ottoman past and the reasons for the Ottomans' success, also offered more to the Kurds than other Turkish parties did. A vague "neo-Ottoman" idea of reconstituting a milla system to ease tensions between the state and communities that chafed under the government's tight control held obvious appeal to Kurds, by far the largest group in such a situation.[13] All of the parties that claimed to speak for the disadvantaged, including the reconstituted RPP, did well in the early 1990s, but in the 1994 municipal elections, which capped a long period of economic turmoil that featured high inflation and a series of corruption scandals, the WP made the most noticeable gains, showing the efficacy of its strong grassroots network in capturing control of Ankara, Istanbul, and other municipalities.

Building upon its electoral successes in 1994 and its evident capabilities in managing often messy municipal affairs, the WP won the largest share of the national vote in 1995's assembly election and soon entered government, again in coalition. The period from the election until 1997, when the military forced the resignation of the government led by Erbakan and the subsequent dissolution of the WP, was one in which practically all significant parties demonstrated woefully low standards of ethical rectitude and political judgment. In the case of Erbakan and the WP, this meant that he gained the prime ministry by striking a deal with Tansu Çiller,

---

[12] A selection from this booklet appears in Shankland, *Islam and Society*, 210–14.

[13] On Ottomanism as it was perceived to have worked in the nineteenth century, see Yavuz, *Islamic Political Identity*, 41–2; on the continuing facination with neo-Ottomanism and Ottoman Islamic practice, see Yael Navaro-Yashin, *Faces of the State: Secularism and Public Life in Turkey* (Princeton: Princeton University Press, 2002). The idea of a "milla system" also appealed to Alevis, Turkey's largest religious minority, made up of both Kurds and Turks. Without a system granting them some form of communal protection, the Alevis would hardly gain from the rise to power of a strictly Sunni party.

the leader of a center-Right party, agreeing to halt investigations into corruption charges against her in return for her party's support in the assembly. The Foreign Affairs ministry remained in Çiller's hands, safeguarding Turkey's international relations from some of Erbakan's previously stated wishes to reject the Christian-"Zionist" West and turn to the Muslim East, but the prime minister still managed to alarm Kemalists, NATO, and the EU by visiting Iran and concluding there a trade deal, and by traveling to Libya. The latter trip damaged Erbakan's standing in Turkey, because Libya's dictator, Mu'ammar Qadhdhafi, publicly rebuked him for Turkey's oppression of its Kurdish population. At home he created alarm by making the son of Hasan al-Banna, the founder of the Muslim Brotherhood, a guest at his first meeting as prime minister (leading the Egyptian president, Husni Mubarak, to warn him against meddling in Egyptian affairs) and by hosting in his official residence numerous sufi and other religious authorities at a sundown breaking of the fast during Ramadan.

Erbakan's injection of Islamic undertones into government inevitably sparked a reaction from the military officers on the National Security Council that supervised the state under the constitution issued following the 1980 coup. The prospect of the open revival of brotherhoods beyond state control, the outright rejection of a major innovation introduced by Mustafa Kemal that such a development would entail, and the rise of shari'a to compete with the state's legal authority was abhorrent to the military defenders of the strong state. When a WP mayor of a small town near Ankara staged a "Jerusalem Liberation Day," at which the Iranian ambassador spoke and went beyond the anodyne platitudes of cautious diplomacy, the army sent a column of tanks through the town. The military followed this by forcing a package of anti-Islamist reforms on the government, and the WP's days not only in government but in legal existence were clearly drawing to an end. Members founded the Virtue Party even before the WP was formally banned, but the poor record of Erbakan's brief regime cost the successor party more than a quarter of the WP's previous share of the electorate by 1999, when the next national election was held. The Kemalist judiciary dissolved the Virtue Party in 2001; thereafter the "Islamic" politicians split into two factions, of which the Erbakan-dominated Felicity Party faded into irrelevance. It was the more "moderate," or practical, faction that formed the AKP of Recep Tayyıp Erdoğan and Abdullah Gül and took advantage of the continued sharp deterioration of established parties' legitimacy in the 1997–2002 period.

Given Erbakan's actions while in power, it was hardly surprising that the military acted to preserve the strong Kemalist state, but the burst of nationalist-secularist vigor unleashed by the armed forces' assertiveness proved brief. The security forces' capture of Abdullah Öcalan, leader of the leftist Kurdish paramilitary liberation organization the PKK, boosted the nationalists' cause, giving them the greatest percentage of the votes in the National Assembly election of 1999 and allowing them to form a coalition government, but its performance in office was again awful, not only in failing to root out corruption but in managing severe economic problems that culminated in a Turkish stock market collapse in 2001. Ultimately as damaging was the military's declaration in 1997 that Islamism posed a graver threat to the state and nation than Kurdish separatism did, a step that undermined its campaign to preserve a strong state under the high command's influence, if not outright control. The military's supremacy was justified by the Sèvres complex and by the greatest threat to Turkey's territory and unity, the deep dissatisfaction felt among much of the country's Kurdish population, not by religion. The military would find that some of its previous widespread public support had been alienated when next it threatened to dissolve a governing "Islamic" party, the AKP.

Other damaging blows to the reputations of the security services and the military occurred in the momentous closing years of the century, in which the economic disaster also brought nationalist parties so much blame. The most sensational event was the Susurluk scandal of November 1996, in which the occupants and contents of a car that crashed indicated close links among the security services, the criminal underworld, and violent political extremists. As the investigation into the accident progressed, the public gained a glimpse of the "deep state," or the illegal organizations and practices established and protected by successive governments as means of "solving problems," including liquidating targets ranging from Armenian assassins of Turkish diplomats abroad to Kurdish paramilitaries and leftist demonstrators in Turkey.[14] The deep state had roots in the CUP era, notably in the Teşkilat-i Mahsusa, but had grown since the 1970s, when political violence escalated and Alparslan Türkeş's party used its periods of participation in coalition governments to promote

---

[14] On the deep state, its recent growth, and its late Ottoman origins, see Ryan Gingeras, "Last Rites for a 'Pure Bandit': Clandestine Service, Historiography and the Origins of the Turkish 'Deep State,'" *P&P* 206 (February 2010), 151–74, and especially "In the Hunt for the 'Sultans of Smack': Dope, Gangsters and the Construction of the Turkish Deep State," *Middle East Journal* 65 (2011), 426–41.

right-wing personnel in the security services. The 1970s also saw the Turkish military intervention in Cyprus that put the northern part of the island under effective Turkish control but not formal responsibility, and northern Cyprus became an important base for the deep state's recruitment and planning operations. The murkiness surrounding the deep state was briefly lifted by Susurluk, and much of the Turkish public was disgusted by the view. Susurluk was still fresh in the public mind when a terrible earthquake struck northwestern Anatolia three years later. The shoddy construction of housing never tested for compliance with building codes showed graphically the effect of years of corrupt relations between politicians and the construction industry, and the army was criticized for being much quicker to look after its own assets than to help devastated civilian areas.

Elections in 2002 showed the extent to which much of Turkish society had come to feel alienated from the almighty state and its Kemalist elite defenders. Only two parties gained at least 10 percent of the votes cast, making them the only parties represented in the assembly. The RPP had not cleared the 10 percent barrier in 1999 but saw its popularity soar after Kemal Derviş, the technocrat who had implemented a recovery program upon becoming minister of economic affairs and the treasury following the stock-market crash of 2001, joined the party before the election. The other party in parliament was the AKP. The AKP and its figurehead and real leaders, Gül and Erdoğan, retained the support of people who had once backed the WP because of its reputation for honesty, justice, and equality but also won the backing of many economic and political liberals who wished to see reduced the dominance of the state and the privileged groups dependent on it. Erdoğan did not invoke Erbakan as his role model but rather Adnan Menderes, the Democrat Party prime minister who was executed after the 1960 coup, and Turgut Özal, the politician who most influenced Turkey's economic and political liberalization after the military permitted a resumption of electoral politics following the 1980 coup.[15] And there was Erdoğan's record of competent administration of Istanbul, where he had been mayor from 1994 until being imprisoned in 1998 for "inciting religious hatred" – for reading a poem by Ziya Gökalp, the early nationalist who became an honored figure in Atatürk's era. That experience of prosecution, imprisonment, and subsequent ban from politics bestowed upon Erdoğan the credential of persecution by the Kemalist establishment, which only added to his electoral attractiveness,

[15] Yavuz, *Islamic Political Identity*, 222, 256–9.

an attractiveness subsequently magnified by the military-judicial heart of that establishment's continued efforts to dissolve the AKP or break its hold on the assembly since 2002.

THE POLITICS OF "ISLAMIC REVIVAL" SINCE 2002

Since 2002 the AKP has established a record of relatively competent and clean government. Despite close scrutiny by many within and outside Turkey worried by the idea of political Islam, the AKP in government has not tried overtly to remake administration in an "Islamic" form. It has undoubtedly promoted candidates within the bureaucracy who are sympathetic to the party, which may be deplorable as a setback for the principle of the supremacy of objective qualifications over political ideology – but the bureaucracy since the CUP and Kemalist periods has been ever shaped thus. Just as the RPP found the party-dominated system of government that it had developed to be flawed only after it passed into the hands of the DP in 1950, so complaints over staffing changes wrought in the heretofore staunchly Kemalist bureaucracy seem like crocodile tears. The bureaucracy should be an issue of real interest or concern only when it does not serve its primary purpose, moreover, which is to execute policies devised at the top level. And at that top, elected level, AKP government has acted relatively responsibly by holding to positions it staked out in electoral campaigns, and the power to rule alone given it by its sweeping electoral victories has not yet persuaded it to attempt to implement overt Islamization of government or public life.

Skepticism over charges of Islamization should not suggest, however, that the AKP in government has not attempted real change: the target of its most significant policy initiatives has been the aggressive, devoutly "secularist" guardians of the Kemalist state: the military, the judiciary, and by inference the "deep state." The AKP has been a strong proponent of Turkish entry into the EU, not only because of the economic opportunities that this might open for the commercial middle class that supports the party, but also because of the EU's precept that Turkey's military must submit to civilian control and stay out of politics. This pressure helped the AKP government in 2004 to reduce the authority of the National Security Council to that of an advisory, rather than supervisory, body. In the same year the Turkish government helped to persuade the Turkish population of northern Cyprus to vote to accept the plan proposed by Kofi Annan to reunify the island, an issue on which the military by contrast had always taken a hard-line view. A solution to the Cyprus problem would not only ease relations with the EU but also open an important base of the deep state to closer scrutiny. Greek Cypriot rejection of Annan's plan, however, prevented resolution.

Most significant by far, however, has been the AKP government's push for constitutional reform. The constitution issued by the military officers who staged the 1980 coup was authoritarian; in venerable CUP-Kemalist style, it placed the state in a position of unchallengeable authority, and it tried to ensure that the nature of that state would remain Kemalist. The military and the judiciary were not made answerable to any elected government. Members of the military could not be tried by civilian courts, regardless of the nature of the crime or complaint lodged against them. Any hint of belonging to a sufi brotherhood resulted in dismissal of officers, and they had no right to appeal to any authority outside the military. The civilian court system was similarly outside government control, because the judges of the constitutional court at the top of the judicial hierarchy were appointed by the president upon recommendation by the sitting judges of the court, a staunchly Kemalist institution since its founding. The AKP government proposed amendments overturning such constitutional limits, and elements within the military high command who viewed with alarm the undoing of the legacy of 1980 made clear their displeasure with the direction of the proposals, effectively turning the referendum on the amendments into one on the AKP government. When the government's proposals were approved by referendum in 2010, it was thus the military (and the judiciary, which in 2009 had launched an attempt to have the AKP dissolved on the dubious grounds that it was trying to introduce shari'a law) that had to retreat.

Such a hotly contested battle for votes on change to the constitution made clear that the Islamic character of the AKP under Tayyıp Erdoğan is not the crucial element to the party's rise and cannot be seen as a critical weakness that will trigger its collapse. The AKP has survived in government, and indeed has strengthened the powers and responsibilities of that government, as a result of two prime factors: its record of relative administrative competence in the face of opposition from an entrenched Kemalist establishment, and widening senses of popular disillusionment with that military and civilian Kemalist old guard. There is no guarantee that the AKP will maintain its pattern of effectiveness, or that the often irascible Erdoğan will not attempt to turn authority into authoritarianism, but if Christian Europe were to rebuff Turkish aspirations to membership in the EU as a result of concern over Islam in government, it would appear thoroughly hypocritical unless it were also to declare openly its Christian identity. A decade of government by a thrice-elected "Islamic" party has made Turkey a more democratic and more mature polity.

11

Contemporary Arab Countries

Unlike the Balkans, the Arab lands in the years after 1989 saw no ideological revolution to rival the collapse of communism in Eastern Europe; unlike Turkey, they experienced little experimentation with any semblance of politics that could produce unexpected electoral results or a change in government. Rather the opposite: frustration built over the immovability of governing orders that seemed to abide by no meaningful ideology at all, revolutionary or conservative. This frustration led eventually to the largely uncoordinated popular explosions that began the Arab Spring in 2010; long before then, however, discontent had spurred a search for alternatives, of which Islam has been the most durable. Islam's promise, as ever, lies in its moral content and its message of justice prevailing when God-given principles of right action are followed. In a region of authoritarian, single-party states that make their own rules for society but are selective in how they apply law, the dream of a legal system impervious to the whims of amoral plutocrats exerts a powerful call. Such states tried to emulate their European and Turkish models in establishing tight control over the institutions of religion, but Sunni Islam's lack of a priesthood or hierarchy made such control harder to enforce than in the Balkans. That Islam remained a live factor throughout the period since 1918, including in the heyday of Arab socialism and seemingly secular nationalism, is suggested by the experience of a neighboring country with a better record of democratic politics since 1945. Turkey's (grudging) acceptance of parliamentary, and governing, parties popularly seen as attuned to Islamic principles only acknowledged the durability of religious influences in politics since the loosening of one-party control after 1945. It should have been as readily apparent that Islam would retain its vitality as a mode of political expression in Arab lands that experienced even more autocratic rule.

POLITICS, ARAB NATIONALISM, AND MILITARY AUTOCRACY

Arab nationalism shaped the Middle East in the 1950s and 1960s, but the height to which Arabism rose was surprising, even accidental. It became the potent force of this time because it attached itself to an Egyptian leader, Jamal 'Abd al-Nasir (Nasser), who stumbled into the role of Arab leader without having looked for it. Once he accepted the part, Arabism controlled him more than he led it, and the flaws within Arab nationalism as a practical ideology almost destroyed him. Arabism's political toxicity weakened its attractiveness to other leaders, but by the time of 'Abd al-Nasir's death in 1970, most regimes and populations in the region had evolved to an open identification with it, making a full-scale renunciation difficult. Without a realistic ideology or program of national development, and lacking any credible source of legitimacy, regimes relied upon simple repression to stay in power. Arab nationalism's most enduring achievement has been the creation of a military-security services network that has stunted any hope of political, social, or economic development in the region.

That the military autocracy of Arab nationalism began in Egypt is ironic, because Egypt was the post-Ottoman country to embrace most fully its historical geographic or regional identity as the basis of the nation-state. For the apostle of Arabism, Sati' al-Husri, Egypt's disinterest in Arabism was an infuriating weakness in the movement, but for Egyptians at both elite and popular levels, whatever bonds of identity linked them to peoples in the Fertile Crescent and Arabia were based on religion rather than ethnicity – "the Arabs" were the natives of the Arabian Peninsula. As Egyptian nationalist governments gradually reduced Britain's power over their country, they developed a secondary interest in tracking the ambitions of the Hashimite monarchs of Iraq and Jordan, who were regarded as agents of continued British influence in the Middle East; insofar as Egypt began to espouse interest in "Arab affairs," it grew out of concern to block Iraqi and Jordanian plans for aggrandizement and to maintain pressure on Britain.[1] This explains why the Muslim Brotherhood was the only Egyptian organization to render practical support to the Palestinian

[1] Michael Doran, *Pan-Arabism before Nasser: Egyptian Power Politics and the Palestine Question* (Oxford: Oxford University Press, 1999).

revolt of 1936–9 but also why the Egyptian government sent forces into Palestine in the 1948 conflict over Israel's creation. The army's assignment there was to monitor the Jordanians as much as fight the Zionists. As members of the expeditionary force that was humiliated directly by the Zionists and indirectly by the better-prepared Jordanians, 'Abd al-Nasir and other junior officers later banded together to execute a coup against the self-serving elite that had mishandled the war.

'Abd al-Nasir and his fellow "Free Officers" involved in the 1952 coup thought and acted as Egyptians. After the 1936 Anglo-Egyptian agreement that lessened British control over Egyptian defense and other key affairs, the Egyptian military grew rapidly, and in 1938 'Abd al-Nasir was among the first nonelite (rather than the Ottoman-era "Turco-Circassian" land-owning elite) graduates from the military academy. One of his classmates and later fellow conspirators was Anwar Sadat; 'Abd al-Nasir was the son of a postal clerk, and Sadat was also the son of a minor bureaucrat in a poor village. The Free Officers certainly had no love for the British, but the Wafd had managed to reduce Britain's control by 1952; as 'Abd al-Nasir later claimed to have realized during the Palestine war, the real battleground was Egypt itself. By this the Free Officers saw the monarchy and the Turco-Circassian pashas as the cause of Egypt's real problems hindering socioeconomic development: they had used the nationalist platform of driving out the British as a cover for using governmental authority to further the interests of their class. The early actions of the officers after they took power showed the direction of their concerns, insofar as they had managed to decide them. They abolished the titles and privileges of the pashas, exiled the king and then dissolved the monarchy, and carried out a significant redistribution of land. The latter move was momentous: for the first time, those in authority did something meaningful in the interest of the poor mass of the long-championed Egyptian nation. This move gave them a significant if rather inchoate constituency that helped to gain them time in which to suppress potential rivals and then decide what else needed to be done for the people.

As tempting as it might be to dismiss this concern for the underclass as simply a pose as meaningless as the propaganda of most post-Ottoman nation builders, the social and economic reformism of the Free Officers was real and addressed the most significant challenge that confronted every government in the region after 1950: rapidly accelerating population growth that produced tremendous pressure for social services (education, housing, health care, etc.) and jobs, and urbanization, as the young and landless left the villages to find work in the cities. From 1950 to 1960 in Egypt, the population grew from 20.4 million to 25.33 million, and the percentage of the population living in urban areas rose from 31.9 percent to 45 percent.[2] The old political notables of Egypt and other countries, made up largely of major landowners, proved incapable of managing the social pressure and need for rapid economic development, creating situations favorable to sudden, system-breaking political change. Labeling the coups or revolutions that happened in Egypt, Syria, and Iraq in the 1950s as "Arab nationalist" movements should not obscure the domestic social and economic substance driving unrest.

In the new republic of Egypt the Arab cause played little role until 1955–6. Several issues of those years drew the regime into Arab affairs, even though its interests in Arabism were still decidedly Egyptian. First was the pressing need to strengthen the army, not only to build the force needed to secure the coup domestically but to defend Egypt's one vulnerable land border: Palestine, where Israel now stood as an aggressively hostile power. In February 1955 Israel launched a raid in force into Ghaza, which had been under Egyptian control since the 1948 war. Israeli raiders killed thirty-seven Egyptian soldiers and wounded thirty-one more, then retired practically untouched into Israel. 'Abd al-Nasir's response, after failing to win Western approval of arms sales, was to get weaponry from Czechoslovakia. The arms were significant, but more electrifying was the symbolic slap delivered to the old colonial powers, now enmeshed in the histrionics of the Cold War. 'Abd al-Nasir gained thereby the admiration not just of Egyptians but of all Middle Eastern populations still antagonistic toward the colonial powers and disgusted by the inability or unwillingness of their own regime leaders to break with the "imperialists."

This led in turn to the miscalculated Anglo-French-Israeli plot to seize the Suez Canal. The Egyptian regime had had some hope of gaining Western agreement to arms sales because relations with Britain and other powers had not been bad after 1952; indeed, 'Abd al-Nasir's regime successfully negotiated an agreement with Britain in 1954 concerning withdrawal of British forces from the canal zone. This belief that business could be conducted with Western powers on a basis of equality led 'Abd al-Nasir to approach Britain, the United States, and the World Bank for funding for his next grand project to aid the poor rural and urban sectors of the Egyptian nation: the construction of a huge dam on the Nile at Aswan. Control of the Nile and associated irrigation works would

---

[2] L. Carl Brown, *Religion and State: the Muslim Approach to Politics* (New York: Columbia University Press, 2000), 126.

reclaim land for agricultural use, and the hydroelectric power generated could boost industrial development. 'Abd al-Nasir thought that he had a funding package arranged with these multiple lenders, only to have the Americans suddenly renege in 1956, essentially in retaliation for the Czech arms deal. 'Abd al-Nasir's solution was to nationalize the Suez Canal, still owned primarily by British shareholders and the only significant cash-generating asset in Egyptian territory not yet under Egyptian control. This move prompted Britain, France, and Israel, each of which worried about 'Abd al-Nasir's subversive intentions in regional and Cold War affairs, to devise a cunning plan: Israel would attack Egypt, legitimating an Anglo-French intervention to secure the canal zone in the interests of global trade.

While the Egyptian military won no victory in the 1956 conflict, the regime nevertheless reaped a tremendous political boost when pressure from the United States made Britain withdraw from the canal zone, causing the scheme to collapse. 'Abd al-Nasir became the hero of the Middle East – to the surprise of Egyptians, who realized that the continued links between other postmandate regimes and the former colonial powers did not mirror the sentiments of the populations placed under their control. To what degree shared satisfaction over humiliation of Britain, France, and Israel constituted a coherent ideology of "Arab nationalism" is, of course, difficult to determine.

This two-year period nevertheless both consolidated 'Abd al-Nasir's hold over Egypt and turned him into the idol of much of the population in other former mandate territories, and his rise to fame made the role of "champion of the Arabs" an attractive model for aspiring politicians – and especially military officers – in other countries to emulate. 'Abd al-Nasir indirectly secured Syria for the Ba'th Party, for example. In 1958 the Ba'th was in a weak position as part of a fractious government coalition but had a stronger following among a similarly splintered army officer corps; out of a politics of survival, and with decisive action by supportive officers, the Ba'th triggered an invitation to unite delivered to Egypt. 'Abd al-Nasir, having won the role of Arab hero, did not refuse, although his acceptance was conditional upon Egypt's controlling the new United Arab Republic (UAR). In the immediate term this bolstered the Ba'th by briefly making them (junior) partners of the popular 'Abd al-Nasir, thus ending the confusion in Damascene politics, and giving them a taste of the success that military intervention in politics could yield. They also perversely benefited later from Egypt's having essentially turned Syria into a colony: Egypt dissolved Syria's parties, including the

Ba'th, but rivals with greater standing within Syria had more to lose from suppression. Egyptian rule soon lost its popularity with the Syrian military, (ex-)politicians, and wider public, so that when Syrian officers staged another coup in 1961, eliminated the Nasirists, and declared that Syria had seceded from the union, 'Abd al-Nasir had to accept it. Parties' forced hibernation during the Egyptian interlude meant that from that point political coherence took time to rebuild, leaving the government elected at the end of 1961 vulnerable to another coup, which Ba'thist officers duly staged in 1963. From then until the Arab Spring broke there in 2011, the Ba'th controlled Syria.[3]

Ba'thist supremacy over Syria depended upon continued control of the military and the establishment of multiple security services willing and able to destroy political alternatives. The Ba'th never accomplished as much as Egypt's Free Officers did in easing socioeconomic pressures: the Egyptian-dominated UAR introduced to Syria the same land reform program that had been instituted in Egypt, but the results were disappointing, because the limits on holdings and size of redistributed plots in Egypt's Nile-watered conditions were not adjusted adequately to the rainfall-dependent agriculture of Syria. Unlike Egypt, moreover, Syria had neither the large domestic market nor the natural energy sources to support much industrial development. Too much of what Syrian regimes have collected as revenue has gone into the military preparedness demanded by the Arab nationalists' requirement of resolute rejection of its neighbor, Israel. Ba'thist ideology has always proclaimed a goal of equality of opportunity for all members of the nation, but in Syria this has meant little more than creating government and military jobs for graduates and closing opportunities for the previously privileged. It is a weak record on which to build a strong case for legitimacy to rule.

In Iraq the Ba'th, which also took power through a series of (bloodier) coups, similarly failed to build legitimacy, despite having a larger domestic market than Syria; river-fed irrigated agriculture, as in Egypt; and far more abundant energy than either of its "Arab nationalist" rivals. The Hashimite monarchy was overthrown in 1958, with much of the royal family and the leading cadres of government obliterated. The revolutionary regime soon introduced land reform, and the leftist army officer who became the republic's new leader significantly raised expenditures

---

[3] See Patrick Seale: *The Struggle for Syria: a Study of Post-War Arab Politics, 1945–1958* (New Haven, CT: Yale University Press, 1987), and *Asad: The Struggle for the Middle East* (Berkeley: University of California Press, 1988).

on social services in the cities. As this suggested, the model of initial action was again 'Abd al-Nasir's Egypt, riding high in popular opinion across the region after not only Suez but now "union" with Syria, but neither the leftists nor the Ba'thists who executed later coups in 1963 and 1968 saw any pressing need to follow Syria's lead in political self-abnegation by seeking union with Egypt. They had the money to continue to spend on social services, especially after full nationalization of the Iraq Petroleum Company in 1972, and they sought to boost or defend themselves ideologically by deriding 'Abd al-Nasir's credibility as an Arab nationalist, a pastime in which Syria after 1961 and, as ever, the remaining Hashimite monarchy in Jordan were also willing to indulge. Cairo, of course, responded in kind.[4]

This extended period of interstate but intranational bickering highlighted the disadvantage of Arabism compared to even the crude nationalisms of the Balkans. Balkan regimes never had to care much about their neighbors, and indeed reveled in reviling them as occupiers of their nations' "rightful" territories; Arab nationalist leaders had to beware the comments of political critics outside lands they controlled because of the stoutly asserted bonds between peoples divided only by artificial borders. Criticism, in turn, had to concentrate upon leaders, not "the Syrians," "the Jordanians," or "the Egyptians," both boosting the insecurity of such regimes and making them extremely reluctant to make concessions in any issue requiring negotiation, knowing that deviation from "national principle" would gain them a torrent of abuse addressed directly to the fraction of the nation under their control.

Interstate vitriol thus formed a poor basis for policy, pushing leaders into projects that, as is usually the case in foreign affairs, either were beyond their ability to control or indeed belied the pan-Arab ideology that they championed. 'Abd al-Nasir in particular allowed himself to be goaded into shortsighted tactical maneuvers that undercut any real chance of continuing to advance Egypt's interests. The "progressive" Arab socialist measures championed by the Ba'th pushed Egypt deeper into state management of the economy through nationalization of most companies and corporations, increased emphasis on worker rights, and state investment in industrial development. Oil wealth allowed Iraq to do this, but Egypt could not afford such policies for long, and Anwar Sadat rescinded much of the Arab socialist program after 'Abd al-Nasir's

---

[4] Malcolm Kerr, *The Arab Cold War: Gamal 'Abd al-Nasir and His Rivals, 1958–1970* (Oxford: Oxford University Press, 1971).

death. Also damaging to Egyptian interests after Syria's secession from the UAR was 'Abd al-Nasir's decision to commit troops to support a coup in North Yemen, where the new republican regime offered repairs to Cairo's claim to Arab leadership by agreeing union with Egypt. From 1963 through 1967 Egypt's military became ever more bogged down in a Yemeni civil war, as the supporters of the ousted ruler, the Zaydi Shi'i Imam Badr, fought back (with Saudi support). Suspicion of Iraq convinced 'Abd al-Nasir to send troops also to Kuwait in 1961 to protect it from the Baghdad regime – an embarrassing example of cooperation with the British, who had first dispatched units when Iraq started to threaten invasion immediately after Britain had declared Kuwait independent.

Criticism from rival regimes over Egyptian pusillanimity against Israel led 'Abd al-Nasir to create the Palestine Liberation Organization and Palestine Liberation Army in 1963, intending thereby to create an Egyptian-controlled simulacrum of activism that could deflect criticism from Cairo. The ploy failed to meet its goal, because continued barbs from Damascus, Baghdad, and 'Amman drove 'Abd al-Nasir to adopt a more threatening posture toward Israel in 1967, triggering the almost-certainly undesired and probably unexpected Six-Day War, in which the Egyptian, Syrian, and Jordanian militaries were crushed with embarrassing speed. Iraq was also humiliated, its modest contribution of forces mauled by the Israeli air force without ever reaching the Jordanian front. The Arab nationalist militants against Israel failed because no leader or capital could be in charge of planning, coordinating, or executing any project, but all regimes that had claimed the role of Arab leadership had to bear responsibility for the obvious failure. 'Abd al-Nasir resigned after the debacle but returned to office after possibly genuine demonstrations in the streets of Egypt's cities. The regime in Baghdad soon fell to coup plotters, King Husayn had to fight the no-longer-Egyptian-controlled PLO (backed by a Syrian armored column) to retain control over Jordan in "Black September" 1970, and the Damascus regime also then changed, with the radical Ba'th leadership toppled after two serious political-military miscalculations (1967 and Black September) by the more methodical Hafiz Asad.

Subsequent regimes heeded the lesson of 1967. Most still espouse Arab nationalism publicly, and the sense of nationality at popular level certainly still lives, but as a practical ideology of state it has been moribund since the 1970s. Each regime has taken care of its own interests and generally avoided entanglement with fellow nationalists. Partial exceptions have occurred where the handful of states involved have each had specific, attainable goals that serve their own interests. Egypt and Syria, for example, launched a well-planned attack on Israel in 1973 that had nothing to do with aiding the Palestinians or even destroying "the Zionist Entity" but was designed rather to break their political-military stalemates with Israel following the Six-Day War.[5] Other Arab states belatedly scrambled to show their support, mainly through the oil boycott organized by most of the Arab members of the Organization of Petroleum Exporting Countries (OPEC), who sought to punish the governments most blamed for rushing armaments to Israel after the initial Egyptian-Syrian successes. The "Arab nationalist" OPEC member Iraq, however, not only ignored the boycott to profit from the spiraling oil price but actually increased production.[6] Iraq nevertheless gained crucial support from other Arab states during its 1980–8 war with Iran, at least after the war that it had started for purely Iraqi reasons turned against it. As in the case of the oil boycott, it was indicative of the parlous state of Arab nationalism as an ideological influence upon policy makers that the leading roles in providing assistance were played by the monarchical regimes of the Gulf, which had always been least associated with the socioeconomic revolutionism that Arab nationalism had implied in the 1950s and 1960s and that Saddam Husayn had excoriated as American puppets in "justifying" Iraq's breaking of the 1973 oil boycott.

Egypt perhaps inevitably was the country to show most openly that Arab nationalism would no longer be allowed to determine the direction of major state policies. Mindful of the social pressures engendered by population growth, Sadat in the 1970s not only revoked 'Abd al-Nasir's socialist measures but turned explicitly to capitalism, welcoming foreign investment for the first time since the 1950s. When that failed to resolve Egypt's socioeconomic problems, he sought cuts in government expenditure by making peace with Israel. As long as the most powerful state in the region remained hostile, Egypt had to devote massive resources to military preparedness. The Camp David Accords (1978) and subsequent peace treaty with Israel eased the pressure to waste scarce revenue on the armed forces, both by reducing the need for a high state of military readiness and by winning billions of dollars in ongoing American military

[5] The Arab summit in Khartoum in August–September 1967 had decided, in effect, to limit the effort to regain Palestine to politics and diplomacy, and the abdication of initiative on the issue was completed by 1974, when the Rabat summit acknowledged Palestinian responsibility for finding a solution.

[6] Daniel Yergin, *The Prize: The Epic Quest for Oil, Money and Power* (New York: Touchstone Books, 1992), 614.

assistance.[7] Egypt's long-lived sense of geographic identity made such an open break with Arab solidarity possible, although of course the move carried risks.

Sadat's assassination in 1981 warned other regimes against doing anything bold in international affairs, even though the peace with Israel was not the sole cause of the killing of the Egyptian ruler. Almost no ruler has had the legitimacy that Sadat, principal architect of the 1973 war, to some extent had; nor has any really built a latent regional-national community like Egypt's to which a daring leader could appeal. After Asad came to power in Syria, he redirected regime focus to Lebanon but never renounced the Arab nationalist pose, in part because of rivalry with the Ba'th in Iraq. Saddam Husayn in Iraq tried for a time to build Iraqi identity by stressing pre-Islamic Mesopotamian history, but, because the first several decades of Iraq's existence had been shaped by the Hashimites' Sunni Arab nationalism, the best opportunity for building real resonance for "Iraq for the Iraqis" to rival "Egypt for the Egyptians" had been missed. Saddam never showed enough consistency in the messages about identity that he pushed to make much impression on Iraqis' extant views, as his role in ignoring the oil boycott and his (un-Ba'thist) visible adoption of religion after his defeat in Kuwait suggests. He never had to care whether "the Iraqi people" looked to his regime as its representative, as the massive wealth derived from oil income made a motivational ideology unnecessary, since there was no need to persuade the population to pay significant taxes. The pervasive secret police apparatus funded by that oil wealth ensured whatever cooperation from the general population was deemed necessary.

Lacking any persuasive ideological basis, most regimes in the Middle East now have little with which to build their claim to legitimacy other than good government and management of their growing populations' needs. While it is important to recognize the great difficulties involved in meeting needs in a relatively resource-poor region, most regimes have proved strikingly incapable of fulfilling the requirements for legitimacy. In the megacities of the region, rural immigrants construct shantytowns officially unattached to the creaky infrastructure of public services; in the urban sprawl of a city such as metropolitan Cairo (population in 2010

---

[7] Although Egypt now spends a much lower percentage of GDP on its military than most other Arab countries, the reductions expected after Camp David were slow to materialize, because Arab regimes' ostracism of Egypt gave a credible rationale for increasing defense expenditure.

estimated to approach twenty million), the physical and noise pollution, the impossibility of transit through jammed streets, and the shortage even of potable municipal water make life trying. For those lucky enough to take full advantage of the overcrowded education system, few jobs await after graduation. The hotel doorman and the taxi driver who hold doctorates are legion. Under 'Abd al-Nasir, the state became the default employer, promising graduates a job after university, a program that Sadat loosened but no regime has abolished for fear of unrest; by 2000 the waiting time between graduation and entry into the massive, sclerotic, poorly paid, corrupt, and ultimately pointless bureaucracy was more than six years.[8] In marked contrast to the majority's daily struggle to survive Cairo's stresses, the top political and military figures of the Husni Mubarak regime amassed staggering fortunes under the protection of their Praetorian Guard. Repression became the constant under the Egyptian and other regimes that have been in power for decades and faced little systemic check on their sense of prerogative. It is this situation that has once again heightened the importance of Islam, as a source of identity and as a source of morality in public – national – life.

THE ENDURANCE OF ISLAM IN SOCIETY AND POLITICS

Islam had never disappeared from public life and supralocal identity, although the intense concentration upon the hopes and travails of Arab nationalism after 1952 often overshadowed that fact. The very nature of Arabism made it impossible for any but the most devout atheist to cleanse Islam from the national ideology: the immutable and eternal nature of God's revelation, delivered in Arabic, was the preservative for a medieval liturgical language that nobody had spoken for centuries.[9] State repression helped to obscure religion's durability by driving Muslim groups

---

[8] Khalid Ikram, *The Egyptian Economy, 1952–2000: Performance, Policies, and Issues* (Abingdon: Routledge, 2006), 296.

[9] The parallel with Hebrew, revived by (largely nonobservant) Jews who wanted to create a national out of a religious community, is difficult to ignore. The vibrancy of religious parties in Israel over recent decades also mirrors the Arab experience. In both areas, the 1967–73 period provided a boost to the religious vote. The 1967 war legitimated Zionism for many Orthodox Jews by delivering Judea and Samaria in a stunning fashion that seemed God-blessed; the near-disaster of the 1973 war, in turn, damaged the credibility of the established secular Zionist elite. For Arabs, the convincing victory of the country defined by religion, Israel, stripped the gloss from the secularist-socialist Arab nationalist regimes; the "moral victory" of 1973 did not directly aid religious revival but rather confirmed that states fighting for their local interests could achieve more than those hobbled by Arabism.

underground. 'Abd al-Nasir banned the Muslim Brotherhood in 1954 as part of his assertion of political control, not only because of the brotherhood's popularity but because of the links between it and the figurehead leader of the 1952 revolution, General Muhammad Najib, who became president upon dissolution of the monarchy. 'Abd al-Nasir maneuvered to oust Najib from the presidency and then to purge his supporters, and as part of this campaign the brotherhood had to be broken.[10] Thereafter functionaries or officers in unions or other state-controlled organizations who displayed any inclination toward Islamism found themselves sidelined. In Syria during the UAR period all political parties were dissolved, but the brotherhood rebounded in the first post-UAR election to win ten seats in the reconstituted parliament; following the next military-Ba'thist coup in 1963, it was banned.

In Syria, Egypt, and other countries the repression of the brotherhood, combined with the tight control established over formal institutions of Islamic learning such as al-Azhar in Cairo, encouraged the further decentralization of Islamic authority. Building on the late Ottoman streak of religious reformism, which emphasized renewed study of the core and immutable texts, lay interpretation of matters pertaining to shari'a became abnormally unmoored from the interpretive norms of any of the schools of jurisprudence. This has led in the worst circumstances to an approach that is literalist but unlettered: focused upon absolute imperatives and restrictions distilled from textual references but without much reasoned consideration given to the meanings of the terms or the contexts in which they appear. A woman might don a headscarf in accord with the Qur'anic injunction to dress modestly; donning a full burqa might reflect the rigidity of lay interpretation of what modesty requires. Activists who demand death for adulterers on grounds far short of the evidence required by scholarly shari'a – or who deem it right to fly passenger jets into crowded buildings – are guilty of the worst excesses of unlettered literalism. Fortunately they are few among the many who have displayed more profound commitment to religion not only in private but in public life as well since the 1950s.

---

[10] Following its proscription, the brotherhood was accused of launching an assassination attempt on 'Abd al-Nasir, providing the pretext for removing Najib. Someone emptied a pistol in the direction of 'Abd al-Nasir during a speech in October 1954 but failed to hit anyone, and the speaker's promptness in switching to an oration about his willingness to sacrifice himself for Egypt raises some doubt about an opportune plot. On the assassination attempt see, for example, Joel Gordon, *Nasser's Blessed Movement: Egypt's Free Officers and the July Revolution* (Oxford: Oxford University Press, 1992), 179–84.

"Islam is the solution" is a well-known slogan used by the Muslim Brotherhood to good effect where the organization is at least tolerated, tapping into that popular regard for religion. For anyone not convinced by the simplicity of the phrase, of course, the slogan is problematic. It seems unnervingly close to the American game of Jeopardy, but with much more at stake: if Islam is the answer, what is the question? To a meaningful extent the public identification with faith reflects the lack of anything else in which to believe. Experience shows that political ideologies of nation, class, or even liberal parliamentarism have all been long on slogans and short on meaningful content for the bulk of the population not among those privileged by connections to regime authorities. At root, however, the most powerful message for Muslims in many countries is the moral force of the religion. In countries where there is no institutional check upon the power of the state, where law is created and applied *by* the state but not *to* the state, the limit upon what the politically powerful can do depends upon their own sense of moral shame.[11] Islam, with its emphasis upon responsibility to and for fellow believers, its duty to charitable action toward others, its code of legality designed to prevent or repair grievances within the community, is powerfully attractive. The most relentlessly stressed idea among proponents of Islamic values in politics is justice – justice not only in truly caring for the socioeconomic well-being of citizens but of tying the pervasive power of the state to the principle of doing what is right, not what is in the self-interest of those with might. A great part of Islam's appeal lies in its promise of law and legality sanctioned by God: there is indeed a higher legal authority than the army officer and his clique who seized power long ago and have abused it ever since. The revival of religion in political affairs carries a strong echo of the Ottoman public reaction against the harsh, unpredictable rule of Sultan Mahmud II, who ignored law in waging his campaigns to "restore civilization."

Every regime that came to power by extraordinary, illegal means has abridged, suborned, and misapplied law, putting a premium upon protecting "the revolution" (and itself). Every monarchical regime threatened

---

[11] This weakness in the legitimacy of Arab nationalist republican regimes in particular was already evident in the 1970s. An authority on politics of the time, and one hardly unsympathetic to Arabism, identified political legitimacy as the central problem of government and the stunted development of "legality" as the core of the legitimacy problem. Michael Hudson, *Arab Politics: The Search for Legitimacy* (New Haven, CT: Yale University Press, 1977), 2, 17. Those same regimes survived more than three decades after Hudson wrote, until the unrest of the Arab Spring shook and, in some cases, damaged or toppled them.

by revolution has followed the same tactic to some degree. As in so much else, 'Abd al-Nasir's Egypt established the model that others copied elsewhere. Within five months of the 1952 coup, the Free Officer regime set up a "Treason Court" that was clearly a political tool: it had a wide remit, loose procedural guidelines, judges with little judicial background, and an evident task of humiliating those on trial. This was followed later in 1953 by two military courts, one to try "communists" and the other, the "Court of the Revolution," to try any other "political crimes"; neither cared much for procedure or indeed law. In 1954 "People's Courts" were established to prosecute (or persecute) Muslim Brothers. All of these courts were eventually wound down after draining the pools of their likely targets, although the Court of the Revolution was revived following the defeat in the Six-Day War and again when Sadat was eliminating rivals after his succession to 'Abd al-Nasir. In the meantime, all others suspected of politically sensitive errors were dispatched to the standing system of military courts.[12]

All of this was "legal": such measures had been used on a more limited scale by the occupying power and by the khedival regime during the period of British control over Egypt; nor were they banned under Egypt's constitution of 1923, which allowed the declaration of martial law in emergency situations. The constitutionalists did not foresee the practically permanent state of emergency that the defenders of the revolution saw fit to perpetuate – but 'Abd al-Nasir's regime rewrote the constitution repeatedly to ensure that it was modernized in line with the revolution's needs. Power was concentrated in the hands of the president–military governor of the country, who could issue laws by decree. The parliament was retained but, since only 'Abd al-Nasir's Arab Socialist Union Party was permitted, it was yet another regime tool. For most of the 'Abd al-Nasir period, the civil judiciary was the only institution that retained some element of autonomy, at least in legal matters lacking direct political interest; this, too, changed in 1969, when it was placed under tighter regime control following a (metaphorical) "massacre of the judiciary."[13] Sadat reversed this throttling of the nonpolitical judicial system in the 1970s but only on terms that did not threaten the concentration of power in regime hands, and with the military court system retained as a permanent feature of political repression. Where nonmilitary courts in the post–'Abd al-Nasir period have returned decisions that had political ramifications,

[12] Brown, *Rule of Law*, 76–83.
[13] Brown, *Rule of Law*, 88–92.

the regime's security apparatus has often simply found other, extralegal ways of achieving its goal of stifling political dissent.[14]

Much like the AKP government in Turkey, the post-Mubarak administration of President Muhammad Mursi, a Muslim Brother, placed priority upon constitutional reform to break the repressive powers lingering from the old regime. One of the key stipulations of the revised constitution of 2012 barred military courts from trying civilians except for crimes damaging the armed forces. Echoing the AKP's distrust of the old regime's judiciary, Mursi suspended the constitutional court's authority in November 2012. He thought the move necessary because the court had dissolved the first constituent assembly elected in spring 2012 and appeared likely to void the next incarnation of the constitution-writing convention before it could finish its task; for a movement that gained popularity from its appeal to the power of law, however, suspension of the court was politically foolish. Mursi's decree, so reminiscent of previous regimes' circumventions of law, triggered protests, which caused him to reverse most of it in December. His reward was victory in the referendum on the draft constitution later that month.

Countries such as Iraq and Syria, but also others ruled by authoritarians who seized power by coup such as Libya, Tunisia, and Algeria, made the Egyptian system under Sadat and Mubarak seem liberal. The 1973 constitution of the Syrian Arab Republic declared the supremacy of law, prohibited torture, held all suspected of criminal acts to be innocent until proven guilty, and safeguarded the private home against entry or search except when justified by law. These guarantees were nominal, since the state of emergency declared after the 1963 coup continued until the Arab Spring unrest of 2011. The constitution certainly did not stop house-to-house searches in Aleppo in 1980 to root out Muslim Brotherhood members and sympathizers, some eight thousand of whom were seized; when the brotherhood subsequently tried to assassinate Asad, security forces machine-gunned hundreds of the imprisoned Islamists in their cells. The regime's campaign against the brotherhood peaked in 1982, when the military attacked the Brethren's next stronghold, the city of Hama, and killed at least ten thousand people.[15] Saddam's treatment of the Kurds was similarly infamous, not just in the notorious chemical-weapons attack at

---

[14] For an example, see Mona el-Ghobashy, "The Metamorphosis of the Egyptian Muslim Brothers," *IJMES* 37 (2005), 373.

[15] Rogan, *Arabs*, 405–9 recounts the regime-Islamist struggle in some detail but imputes to the brotherhood little more than anti-'Alawi sentiment; the repression of the pre-Asad Ba'th gets no mention.

Halabja but in the murderous Anfal campaign waged in 1991–2. Iraq's Shiʻa suffered tremendously under Saddam as well, but the almost routine brutality everywhere, including among Sunnis and at high levels of government and the military, ultimately distinguished his regime from his authoritarian neighbors'.[16] A Shiʻi man in 2002, for example, asked too many questions about the fate of several uncles detained more than a decade previously, leading to an argument with security paramilitaries, during which he cursed Saddam. After several tortured months in prison, he was taken out for a show. In that show, he lost part of his tongue to two paramilitaries, one armed with pliers and the other with box cutters, who told his assembled neighbors and remaining family (his mother forced to carry a portrait of the president) that this is what happens to anyone who insults the leader.[17]

Mapping the progress of the Arab Spring gives a good picture of the places where brutality, corruption, and oppression became most routine. In Tunisia, it was ordinary mistreatment that first sparked the Arab Spring. Muhammad Bu ʻAzizi, a young fruit seller, felt humiliated by a policewoman's slapping him in front of many witnesses. She slapped him because he objected to her stealing more than usual of his fruit. He tried to lodge a protest with local government; when he could not, he set himself on fire in front of the municipal headquarters. The endemic corruption and misrule of the regime run by Zayn al- ʻAbidin Bin ʻAli, a former security chief who in 1987 had ousted Habib Bu Ruqayba (Bourguiba), the man who had led Tunisia to independence, created a responsive audience for a video of Bu ʻAzizi's friends and family protesting his mistreatment that was posted on Facebook. In Egypt the protests that led to the confrontations in Tahrir Square and the ouster of Husni Mubarak also fed off Internet outrage over oppression. A young Alexandrian, Khalid Saʻid, posted online a video of police pocketing the proceeds of a drug raid; when police found him during an identity sweep through an Internet café, they took him outside and beat him to death. The photo of

---

[16] Baʻth leaders, led by Saddam, purged the military officer corps repeatedly from 1968 to the outbreak of war with Iran, with annually at least 100 officers thought to have been killed or imprisoned from 1973 to 1978 (Anthony Cordesman, *The Gulf and the Search for Strategic Stability: Saudi Arabia, the Military Balance in the Gulf, and Trends in the Arab-Israeli Military Balance* [Boulder, CO: Westview Press, 1984], 741–3). Executions continued during the war; for views of Saddam from high-ranking military officers, see Kevin Woods et al., *Saddam's Generals: Perspectives of the Iran-Iraq War* (Alexandria: Institute for Defense Analysis, 2011).

[17] Craig Smith, "Aftereffects: Hussein's Rule; Iraqis Tell of a Reign of Torture," *New York Times*, 24 April 2003.

his battered face posted online sparked protests that tapped the anger of the non-Internet-savvy population as well. The endemic brutality of the Qadhdhafi and Asad regimes triggered the much bloodier civil wars in Libya and Syria, while the pervasive repression of the Shi'i majority in Bahrain and the alienation of much of Yemen's population by the corrupt and authoritarian 'Ali 'Abdallah Salih raised protests in those countries. In all instances, wherever violence has characterized the Arab Spring, the regimes inflicted the first, most frequent, and heaviest blows.

Islamists did not plan or lead the eruption of the Arab Spring, but they and their views stepped into the leadership and ideological vacuums that emerged, giving unusual relevance to the question of what Islam-as-politics might mean. If "Islam is the solution" to state ruthlessness as well as to the widespread inequalities and unfairness in the society under such tyranny, then this suggests (re-)introduction of shari'a, and indeed all discussion of Islam in public life soon centers on the issue. The question for anyone doubtful about Islamic law is, Whose shari'a is to be supreme, the unlettered literalists', like that of the Taliban in Afghanistan, or that of "modernists" who embrace the knowledgeable interpretation that shari'a has always required to be functional?[18] In Egypt, the answer that emerged from the post-Mubarak Muslim Brotherhood–led government was moderately reassuring: one of the clauses in the 2012 constitution tightened the application of the article in the Sadat era constitution that identified shari'a as the main source of law by requiring that jurisprudents of al-Azhar be consulted on shari'a issues. Despite Hasan al-Banna's low opinion of the 'ulama, the Muslim Brothers in 2012 tied law to the classically trained jurisprudents to guard against fallacious interpretation. In Muslim Brotherhood opinion, Sadat and Mubarak era legal authorities had interpreted the shari'a-basis requirement too loosely, but the reference to al-Azhar inserted into the 2012 constitution also limits the scope for damage by the growing numbers of salafi literalists.[19]

In Egypt and other countries the answer to the question of "Whose shari'a?" depends in part upon the nature of the regime that proponents

---

[18] Noah Feldman highlights the problem of whose interpretation should rule in *The Fall and Rise of the Islamic State* (Princeton: Princeton University Press, 2008), chap. 3. On several streams in Islamic "modernism" eschewing uninterpreted literalism, see Daniel Brown, *Rethinking Tradition in Modern Islamic Thought* (Cambridge: Cambridge University Press, 1996), chap. 6, and Raymond Baker, *Islam Without Fear: Egypt and the New Islamists* (Cambridge, MA: Harvard University Press, 2003).

[19] William Shepard, "Muhammad Said al-Ashmawy and the Application of Sharia in Egypt," *IJMES* 28 (1996), 39–58.

of Islam oppose. The harsher the oppression, the greater the militancy of those calling for a loosening of militarism, authoritarianism, and cronyism. The best-known and most influential example was that of Sayyid Qutb, an employee of the prerevolutionary Egyptian Ministry of Education; growing disillusioned with the Western-style culture that he had admired, he joined the Muslim Brotherhood in 1951. In line with the trend to lay interpretation and the return to basic texts, he wrote a detailed commentary on the Qur'an. Lengthy and painful imprisonment by the revolutionary regime in the 1950s radicalized him, however, and his most famous publication, *Signposts on the Road*, legitimated the use of violence to overthrow the despotic regime. From its founding in 1928, the brotherhood had focused upon improving its members, and from there society, by restoring Islamic principles to, and correcting errors in, the way in which people lived. A reformed, Islamic society would lead to a state imbued with those same values. Having been imprisoned under brutal conditions by a regime that showed no interest in the values of society, and one that moreover seemed determined to prevent those who wished to live by God-given principles from being able to do so, Qutb saw no alternative to breaking the despotic, "Pharaonic" regime. Qutb was executed (mainly for writing *Signposts on the Road*) in 1966, but his ideas resonated with the generation of Islamists who suffered similar trauma in 'Abd al-Nasir's prisons or those of other authoritarians.

Sadat, who had been linked to the Muslim Brotherhood before 1952 (as was indeed 'Abd al-Nasir for several years) and styled himself "the Believer President," reprieved the Islamists and other regime opponents in the 1970s, thus beginning the reintegration of religion into public life and politics. In large part because of their strong grassroots organization resulting from their long-standing educational and social welfare programs, the brotherhood was by far the most resilient and effective opposition party under the regime's pseudodemocratic rule since the 1970s, and the organization became steadily more sophisticated, and moderate, in its politics.[20] Sadat was not assassinated by a Muslim Brother but by one of the small extremist groups influenced by Qutb.[21] In other countries, this pattern has held as well: where the brotherhood

[20] On the brotherhood's flexibility and evolution, see el-Ghobashy, "Metamorphosis," and Nathan Brown, *When Victory Is Not an Option: Islamist Movements in Arab Politics* (Ithaca, NY: Cornell University Press, 2012), 66–71, 86–94.
[21] Saad Eddin Ibrahim, "Anatomy of Egypt's Militant Islamic Groups: Methodological Note and Preliminary Findings" *IJMES* 12 (1980), 423–453.

or other groups have been most ready to take up violence has been in countries where repression has been most severe (Syria, Algeria),[22] where there has been radicalization through competition for the role of most determined opponent of an immovable oppressor (Algeria, Palestine), or where oppression has been heavy and identified with the old enemy: foreign, non-Muslim powers (Palestine in particular, but also Iraq and Lebanon under circumstances combining sectarianism with Anglo-American occupation in the former and Israeli in the latter). Jordan, by contrast, has handled champions of Islamic politics such as the brotherhood with some sophistication, mixing repression with elements of co-optation and opportunities to share local authority (and thereby also responsibility).[23]

For anyone worried about "Islamic" government, Jordan's example may show the safest way forward. There might be nothing as effective as direct experience of the challenges involved in managing the tremendous socioeconomic pressures present in most Arab countries to force the vocal champions of Islam to add pragmatic detail to the slogan "Islam is the solution." It could also happen that an elected "Islamic" government improves conditions within some countries, as arguably it has in Turkey. God knows, after all, that some fresh ideas to challenge the nationalist, socialist, and indeed capitalist slogans of the past half-century might just be a good thing.[24]

---

[22] The scholar François Burgat asserted (Vicki Langohr, "Of Islamists and Ballot Boxes: Rethinking the Relationship between Islamisms and Electoral Politics," *IJMES* 33 [2001], 591) that any Western political party subjected to the repression visited upon the Islamic Salvation Front, which became the main antiregime group in Algeria's civil war after 1992, would have been similarly radicalized, as the American reaction to 11 September 2001 suggests. Although President Bush told Congress that America's first duty was to remain true to its values, attacks that obeyed no rules legitimated suspension of rules in response. A declaration of war on terrorism, a foe so vaguely defined that no one could be identified as a friend, led to dilution of civil liberties at home (the Patriot Act), suspension of the due process of law (Guantanamo Bay), invasion and occupation of a country uninvolved in 9/11 (Iraq), and a long-running program of remote-controlled assassination of suspected terrorists and assorted innocents (Afghanistan, Pakistan, Yemen, etc.).

[23] Quintan Wiktorowicz, *The Management of Islamic Activism: Salafis, the Muslim Brotherhood, and State Power in Jordan* (Albany: State University of New York Press, 2001); Brown, *Victory Is Not an Option.*

[24] Sadat not only revoked much of the socialist program in Egypt, he adopted a form of capitalism to encourage foreign investment and job creation. It was only partially successful, because the mammoth bureaucracy that he inherited could not be removed from investment decision making. John Waterbury, *The Egypt of Nasser and Sadat: The Political Economy of Two Regimes* (Princeton: Princeton University Press, 1983).

CONCLUSION

It is impossible to predict the future course of Islamic and secular political programs in the Middle East, but it will undoubtedly take a long time for significant change in the internal conditions of countries of the region to take root. The still-extant regimes, especially the military-republican autocracies but also the monarchies, inevitably resist change that would threaten their position and perquisites of power, and their suppression of nonregime organizations and parties has blocked the development of viable alternatives. Islam has the current advantage in offering a different vision, due to factors ranging from its emphasis upon justice and the moral imperative to act for the good, to its very nature as a nonhierarchical religion, and to the impossibility of trying to delegitimate it that nationalist regimes have recognized; were the suffocating security services of the current regimes restrained, however, reform programs in other guise would develop.[25] "Secular" thought has been as stunted by regime repression as has "radical Islam."[26] Where new governments assume power, they will need to learn through experience the practical basics of politics. In Egypt, the "secularists" opposed to Mursi have shown through their efforts to subvert a political system much freer than the one most of them enjoyed in the Mubarak era that opposition parties will need to learn the same lessons. New regimes will also need time to make much progress in overcoming socioeconomic challenges, not least in fostering job creation in a region relatively poor in natural resources and educational opportunities (in relation to the size of the school-age population). One point that should be clear, however, is that military autocracy and Arab nationalism have nothing to offer.[27]

[25] On liberalism lurking below the surface of nationalist thought, see Christoph Schumann, "The 'Failure' of Radical Nationalism and the 'Silence' of Liberal Thought in the Arab World," *Comparative Studies of South Asia, Africa and the Middle East* 28 (2008), 404–15.

[26] Ibrahim Abu-Rabi', *Contemporary Arab Thought: Studies in Post-1967 Arab Intellectual History* (London: Pluto Press, 2004), chap. 3.

[27] The military coup that overthrew Muhammad Mursi on 3 July 2013 occurred after this book entered production, but events in Egypt only extend the military's calamitous record of involvement in politics. The justifications cited by defenders of the coup ranged from flimsy to spurious. The portrayal of the janissaries used to legitimate their destruction in 1826 fits the Egyptian military and security forces: in their six decades of control over Egypt, they built a rich array of political, economic, and social privileges that they could not bear to see subjected to even the modest restrictions attempted by the Mursi regime. It is clear that neither they nor the state institutions that they had shaped over those decades would willingly execute an elected Muslim Brotherhood government's directives. The coup has prompted commentary about the blow to political Islam struck

Generals make bad politicians; captains, majors, and colonels are even worse. The time of the military man in the Middle East is past: with a few exceptions consisting primarily of small countries with large and aggressive neighbors (Lebanon, Kuwait, and the other small Gulf emirates), no state needs the disproportionately large defense establishments that the autocracies have developed. Israel won the struggle over Palestine in 1967 and sealed its victory by making peace with its most threatening foe, Egypt; all of the Arab regimes know the struggle is over. They pose no real existential threat to Israel and, although the reverse is not quite true, Israel has never overthrown a regime, despite its military superiority. Among Israel's significant military advantages is not just better weaponry but greater professionalism: every Arab military force is officered by men judged according to political reliability, not just by professional competence, as the dearth of coups since the early 1970s indicates.[28] The standards of political reliability were set, moreover, by an assortment of immature officers (Lieutenant-Colonel 'Abd al-Nasir, Major Sadat, Captain Asad, Captain Qadhdhafi, et al.) who were fired not only by legitimate class resentments but also by a romantic ideal of the nation and the illusion that military efficiency was all that was needed to achieve progress. The example of Atatürk impressed those active in the 1950s – but their record resembled more closely that of the leaders of the CUP from 1908 to 1918.

For those who became enamored of the Arab national ideal and embraced Arab nationalism, failure was practically inevitable. Arab nationalism as it developed in the interwar period set just two goals: expulsion of European imperial powers and erasure of the European-drawn borders. The first was almost achieved by the time 'Abd al-Nasir inaugurated the golden age of Arabism in the mid-1950s. The second will never be achieved except through an implausible voluntary confederation even tighter than today's European Union (a project that after more than six decades still has not achieved integration). For all the effort that nationalist education programs have invested in building a sense of unity

---

by the Brotherhood's "failure" to govern, but the "new" military regime's rapid reconstruction of the Mubarak-era security state promises continuation of the conditions that have promoted religion in politics. It is worth noting that a decade after the Turkish military toppled the "Islamist" government of Erbakan and abolished the Welfare Party, the AKP under Erdoğan was poised to break the military's domination of political affairs.

[28] Politicization of the officer corps helped to explain why Syrian forces performed so badly in 1967 compared to even the puny army in the 1948 war with Israel. Eliezer Be'eri, *Army Officers in Arab Politics and Society* (London: Pall Mall Press, 1970), 170.

across the huge territory stretching from Morocco and Mauritania to Iraq and Oman, there are huge problems involved in inculcating acceptance of a supralocal identity that is so far removed from the local focus of the strongest personal allegiances. The experience of the UAR is all too replicable: Syrians' practical interests and those of Egyptians were far from identical, and decisions made in Cairo alienated those who had initiated the union project. It is commonly thought that the Palestinian Arabs suffered in the 1918–48 period because they could not rally behind an agreed candidate among the local notables, and that pattern of competing leadership has been replicated on the Arab plane. The most damaging effects of asserting the importance of Arab identity without any means of choosing a motor for unity or a leader for the project have been internal. There can be no strong political legitimacy for any "national" regime that identifies its interests with a population largely outside its country's borders. As Serbia might attest, stoking pointless fear about neighboring peoples does harm to a country's interests – but a sense of normality of difference from those neighboring peoples is nevertheless important in building popular cohesion and a plausible sense of social, economic, and political mission for any government. Identities that are more closely matched to the now-long-established borders have grown over the decades, and governments should embrace that trend unequivocally.

Whatever national identity becomes dominant, regimes and foreign powers should adjust to elements of Islam in public life as both normal and likely to endure for the foreseeable future. Of all the political "ideologies" that have influenced the region, it is the only one that is truly "authentic" and not directly or indirectly imported from Europe, and it cannot be excised from society. As ever, where "Islamic politics" seems a frighteningly militant project, the key to understanding its nature lies in the politics, not the religion. A movement that stresses the primacy of law should be welcomed, not vilified as an antidemocratic force. After all, as one champion of Islam quipped, "Islamists have been subjected to higher moral standards, ... as if they were the only authoritarians among an assembly of tried and true democrats."[29]

---

[29] El-Ghobashy, "Metamorphosis," 381.

Conclusion

State, Faith, and Nation

Politics is reactive. Throughout the turbulent history of Ottoman and post-Ottoman lands over the past 250 years, violence and disorder have resulted from regimes' perceptions of their own weakness when facing a threat to their own existence. Government actions in response to such weakness have, in turn, triggered occasionally strong reactions from the populations over which they have had nominal or acknowledged authority. The nature of such reactions has been influenced by the perception of communal life dominant within each society, and the degree of violence in the reaction has tended to grow as the ideas framing such perceptions have themselves appeared threatened. That this pattern will continue over the next few years or decades seems all too probable.

Within this pattern of turbulence, the transition from Ottoman to post-Ottoman states generated a significant change in the nature of the perils facing regimes and in the popular responses to governmental actions. In the Ottoman period both the state and the majority of society perceived an urgent, existential threat to the empire because of its status as "The Abode of Islam"; in this sense, the sultanate and its most important subjects benefited from basic consensus on the nature of the threat, which proved a great advantage in comparison to the plight of most post-Ottoman countries, where new states lacked any point of real agreement with "the people." For the Ottomans, consensus meant that the main story line of political development in the empire's last century was one of balancing the regime's need to strengthen itself to ward off Christian Europe with maintenance of the limits upon its domestic freedom of action placed by identification with Islam. As long as the imperial authorities could be seen to uphold religiously grounded principles of law and justice, they did not have to divert extraordinary resources to coercing loyalty. For post-Ottoman countries, the story line of historical development has expanded to include not only the search for strength against possible foreign foes but also the struggle against domestic threats, of which the lack of meaningful connection to the population has been the most serious and enduring. Of these threats, there is little doubt about which was the most serious: as creations of the great powers, none faced any real threat of attack. Of all the wars fought by post-Ottoman states, only one was purely defensive and wholly unprovoked: Bulgaria's brief struggle to repel the Serbian invasion of 1885. The very practice of using their armed forces as nation-building tools suggests that the states have always recognized the lack of immediate external threats, as the attention to educating soldiers in ideological citizenship has undermined preparedness to fight. Much of the violence inflicted by post-Ottoman states has occurred within their countries' borders and has targeted civilians resistant to regime ideology.

From their inception, post-Ottoman states lacked the legitimacy that Ottoman rule had had, and nationalism proved a necessary but flawed instrument with which to try to build it afresh. Nationalism is morally neutral: it is simply an aspiration to a goal (an independent country governed by and for members of the nation). Its aim was obviously attractive to post-Ottoman politicians because it legitimated their rise to power – a point marking, in another sense, "the end of history." Two potential dangers deriving from nationalism, however, became manifest quickly. The first is its emphasis on a goal, implying a lack of safeguards against the principle that "the end justifies the means." States that have succumbed to the temptation to put this principle into practice in their pursuit of power have soon discovered that much of the strength "gained" has to be diverted to coercing obedience from the people in whose name the regimes have acted. This occurred in the Ottoman empire as well, notably in the reign of Mahmud II. The second potential danger in nationalism is its short-termism: what comes after achievement of the nation-state? All of the region's nations were purpose-built by young post-Ottoman regimes that needed them to justify their own existence, but the states so legitimated already represented the goal of nationalism.

Perhaps because of the time needed to teach or coerce populations into considering themselves bound together into nations, regimes never devoted enough attention to developing an answer to the inevitable question of "What next?" – encouraging them to create crises in order to keep "the end of history" just out of reach. For a time one of the means used by Balkan regimes to build the nation, irredentism, offered a simplistic answer: as long as part of "the nation" remained enslaved abroad, nationalism's goal remained unachieved. Turkey never formulated any clear answer to the question, necessitating continued teaching of the Sèvres complex and harassment of internal recalcitrants, especially the Kurds. When Arab nationalist regimes rose to power, the main target of their ideology, the European imperial powers, had largely withdrawn from the region; Israel, the last "imperialist settler colony," therefore became the focus, but after Israel won the struggle for Palestine, the regimes' inability to develop a "postnationalism" ideology became ever clearer. For several decades Arab nationalists offered hope of a meaningful purpose in improving the lot of their countries' large and growing underclass, but in this too they have failed. The step that no post-Ottoman regime has taken has been to restore explicitly moral content – be it of religion or of some other powerful idea that can shape social life – to the national program, recognizing that the means to any goal are indeed of utmost importance, and that principled governance can serve as the natural "postnationalist" program legitimating the state.

So, what does the future hold? Whether the decades since the end of the Cold War will prove a regional turning point as important as the shift from Ottoman to post-Ottoman eras remains to be seen, of course. Historians have enough difficulty in seeing the past; they cannot see the future. There are certainly grounds for worry, but also some for cautious optimism.

State weakness is not new across the region but is to be feared more than ever in the contemporary period, because the long history of foreign and domestic insecurities has driven the rapid growth in size of states across the region since the nineteenth century. The institutions of state are huge, and the scared elephant is often more destructive than the secure. Ottoman bureaucracy grew with recognition of the need for organization capable of improving extraction of resources from the population to repel the European threat. The growth in size of states accelerated in the post-Ottoman period, with the need to extract resources now combining with the need to coerce popular allegiance while new regimes taught their populations that new bases for state-society relations were necessary and rightful. The military and in the twentieth century the more secretive security and intelligence services became cornerstone institutions of the state, with claims upon budgets and "national" resources to match. While popular acceptance of new regimes and their legitimacy was under construction, moreover, the temptation to buy loyalty – or at least toleration of the regime – led to use of the state as a spoils system, distributing jobs to co-opt anyone who had the potential to ruffle the still-fragile state-society relationship. This pattern repeats across the region, from Greece throughout its existence as an independent country to Egypt from 'Abd al-Nasir until today, with its policies of state as employer of last resort.

Yet from the CUP period until today, domestically insecure states have rarely achieved competence in self-defense, despite spending so freely on their military branches. The need to vet officers for ideological sound-ness saps command capability, and the desire to use compulsory military service to teach conscripts loyalty to the nation and to the ideology of the rulers of the day similarly carries costs in combat preparedness. Post-Ottoman states, all but Turkey created by the European powers, have thus always felt vulnerable to foreign pressure, regardless of how unwel-come such pressure might be to the populations that regimes nominally represent. Membership in, or association with, multilateral defense orga-nizations such as NATO has relieved post-Ottoman states in the Balkans and Turkey of some of their externally generated insecurity. Arab states, by contrast, have had no such recourse to reassurance since the demise of the Baghdad Pact in the 1950s – although it could be argued that regimes expertly parlayed the Cold War superpower rivalry in the Middle East into practical guarantees of survival.

Removal of security guarantees contributed to the turmoil of recent years. The collapse of the Soviet Union and the Warsaw Pact destabilized the Balkans, and Arab regimes have been deeply shaken by American actions following the end of the Cold War. The wars against Iraq over the invasion of Kuwait in 1991 and for no clearly valid reason in 2003 drove home the reality of the region's military weakness, but perhaps more wor-rying for some regimes was the American reluctance in the Arab Spring to prop up strongmen in Egypt and Tunisia who were once considered protégés of the West. Given the authoritarian, oppressive nature of most post-Ottoman regimes, any pressure on their inherent insecurities holds promise of rapid change. Whether such change is destructive (as it was in Yugoslavia and is proving to be in Syria) or constructive (as it might prove to be in other Arab countries) will surely take years to determine.

Even a note of optimism as cautious as this seems may strike many observers as utterly naïve. Instability for stability is rarely a good trade, and the fall of old leaders promises to give rise to Islamic fundamentalist regimes that will prove dictatorial and repressive. Plus ça change, plus c'est la même chose. The trade is actually instability for instability, pre-cisely because regimes across the post-Ottoman region have relied heavily upon armed repression to keep themselves in power. The longer that such regimes stifle all elements of public life outside their direct control, the greater the building of pressure that could explode. Insofar as Islam is a political force, it is due to its stress upon justice through law, and it is the oppressive nature of the state that makes Islamic morality such an appealing prospect. This pattern has repeated through the nineteenth century until today, from Mahmud II's empire to Bashar Asad's Syria. The strength of religion in shaping communal senses of morality is no monopoly of Islam, of course, but despite Christianity's signs of revival, the state's capture of its institutional power has hobbled faith's ability to play a similar role in the Balkans. In a sense the Christian-majority Balkans form a more "secular" zone than Muslim-majority post-Ottoman lands, because secularism (strict separation of church and state) is a distinctively Christian idea: it focuses on barring the influence of the *institutions* of religion and mundane governance on each other. The Balkan states are not truly secular, because they influence church affairs, hobbling Christianity's potential to rally opposition. In comparison to Christianity, Sunni Islam has no "church" institution to be joined to, or separated from, the state. In Turkey and Arab countries, where states control only much-less-developed institutions of religion, therefore, the principles of belief – of faith – have perennial independent power to rally opposition.

Whether religiously inspired political leaders will prove more lastingly moral and law-abiding, or indeed in any other sense more conscious of the reciprocal responsibilities characteristic of stable state-society relations, than were their predecessors is impossible to predict. Now-long-entrenched traditions of authoritarian rule will be hard to break quickly: the Democrat Party in Turkey, after all, found it difficult to renounce the advantages of the authoritarian state devised by the RPP in the preceding decades of single-party rule. Recognition of the importance of respect for law, however, is certainly the first step to the remaking of state power on a more sustainable basis.

Bibliography

Archival Sources

Başbakanlık Osmanlı Arşivi, Istanbul

Cevdet Dahiliye
Hatt-i Hümayun

National Archives, London

Foreign Office

Published Sources

Abou-el-Hadj, Rif'at Ali. *The 1703 Rebellion and the Structure of Ottoman Politics*. Istanbul: Nederlands Historisch-Archaeologisch Institut, 1984.
   "The Ottoman Vezir and Pasha Households 1683–1703: A Preliminary Report." *Journal of the American Oriental Society* 94 (1974), 438–47.
   "The Social Uses of the Past: Recent Arab Historiography of Ottoman Rule." *International Journal of Middle East Studies* 14 (1982), 185–201.
Abu Manneh, Butrus. "Sultan Abdulhamid II and Shaikh Abulhuda al-Sayyadi." *Middle Eastern Studies* 15 (1979), 131–53.
Abu-Rabi', Ibrahim. *Contemporary Arab Thought: Studies in Post-1967 Arab Intellectual History*. London: Pluto Press, 2004.
Adanır, Fikret. "Semi-Autonomous Forces in the Balkans and Anatolia." In *Cambridge History of Turkey* 3, ed. S. Faroqhi, 157–85.
   "The Formation of a 'Muslim' Nation in Bosnia-Hercegovina: A Historiographic Discussion." In *Ottomans and the Balkans*, ed. Adanır and Faroqhi, 267–83.
Adanır, Fikret and Suraiya Faroqhi, eds. *The Ottomans and the Balkans: A Discussion of Historiography*. Leiden: Brill, 2002.

Ahmad, Feroz. "Politics and Political Parties in Republican Turkey." In *Cambridge History of Turkey* 4, ed. Kasaba, 226–65.

Akarlı, Engin. "Law in the Marketplace: Istanbul, 1730–1840." In *Dispensing Justice*, ed. Masud, Peters and Powers, 245–70.

"The Problems of External Pressures, Power Struggles, and Budgetary Deficits in Ottoman Politics under Abdülhamid II (1876–1909)." PhD dissertation, Princeton University, 1976.

Aksakal, Mustafa. *The Ottoman Road to War in 1914: The Ottoman Empire and the First World War.* Cambridge: Cambridge University Press, 2008.

Aksan, Virginia. "Military Recruitment Strategies in the Late Eighteenth Century." In *Arming the State: Military Conscription in the Middle East and Central Asia, 1775–1925*, ed. Erik Zürcher, 21–40. London, I. B. Tauris. 1999.

"Ottoman Political Writing, 1768–1808." *International Journal of Middle East Studies* 25 (1993), 53–69.

"The One-Eyed Fighting the Blind: Mobilization, Supply, and Command in the Russo-Turkish War of 1768–1774." *International History Review* 15 (1993), 221–38.

Ottoman Wars 1700–1870: An Empire Besieged. Harlow: Pearson Education, 2007.

Akyıldız, Ali and M. Şükrü Hanioğlu. "Negotiating the Power of the Sultan: The Ottoman Sened-i İttifak (Deed of Agreement), 1808." In *The Modern Middle East: A Sourcebook for History*, ed. Camron Amin, Benjamin Fortna, and Elizabeth Frierson, 24–30. Oxford: Oxford University Press, 2006.

Algar, Hamid. "Some Notes on the Naqshbandi Tariqat in Bosnia." *Die Welt des Islams* 13 (1971), 168–203.

Alon, Yoav. *The Making of Jordan: Tribes, Colonialism and the Modern State.* London: I. B. Tauris, 2007.

Anastasopoulos, Antonis. "Crisis and State Intervention in Late Eighteenth-Century Karaferye (mod. Veroia)." In *Ottoman Balkans*, ed. Anscombe, 11–34.

"Lighting the Flame of Disorder: Ayan Infighting and State Intervention in Ottoman Karaferye, 1758–59." In *Mutiny and Rebellion*, ed. Hathaway, 73–88.

Anderson, M. S. *The Eastern Question, 1774–1923: A Study in International Relations.* London: Macmillan, 1966.

The Rise of Modern Diplomacy 1450–1919. London: Longman, 1993.

Anscombe, F. J. "Graphs in Statistical Analysis." *American Statistician* 27, no. 1 (1973), 17–21.

Anscombe, Frederick. "Albanians and 'Mountain Bandits.'" In *Ottoman Balkans*, ed. Anscombe, 87–114.

"The Balkan Revolutionary Age." *The Journal of Modern History* 84 (2012), 572–606.

"Continuities in Ottoman Centre-Periphery Relations, 1787–1915." In *Frontiers of the Ottoman State*, ed. Andrew Peacock, 235–52. Oxford: Oxford University Press, 2009.

"Islam and the Age of Ottoman Reform." *Past and Present* 208 (August 2010), 159–89.

"On the Road Back from Berlin." In *War and Diplomacy*, ed. Yavuz and Sluglett, 535–60.

"The Ottoman Empire in Recent International Politics. I: The Case of Kuwait." *International History Review* 28 (2006), 537–45.

"The Ottoman Empire in Recent Politics. II: The Case of Kosovo." *International History Review* 28 (2006), 758–93.

The Ottoman Gulf: The Creation of Kuwait, Saudi Arabia, and Qatar. New York: Columbia University Press, 1997.

Anscombe, Frederick, ed. *The Ottoman Balkans, 1750–1830*. Princeton: Markus Wiener, 2006.

Antonius, George. *The Arab Awakening: The Story of the Arab National Movement*. London: Hamish Hamilton, 1938.

Baer, Marc. *Honored by the Glory of Islam: Conversion and Conquest in Ottoman Europe*. Oxford: Oxford University Press, 2008.

Baker, Raymond. *Islam without Fear: Egypt and the New Islamists*. Cambridge, MA: Harvard University Press, 2003.

Banac, Ivo. "Bosnia Muslims: From Religious Community to Socialist Nationhood and Post-Communist Statehood." In *Muslims of Bosnia-Herzegovina*, ed. Pinson, 129–53.

The National Question in Yugoslavia: Origins, History, Politics. Ithaca, NY: Cornell University Press, 1984.

Barkey, Karen. *Empire of Difference: The Ottomans in Comparative Perspective*. Cambridge: Cambridge University Press, 2008.

Belge, Ceren. "Friends of the Court: The Republican Alliance and the Selective Activism of the Constitutional Court of Turkey." *Law and Society* 40 (2006), 653–92.

Belge, Murat. "*Genç Kalemler* and Turkish Nationalism." In *Turkey's Engagement with Modernity: Conflict and Change in the Twentieth Century*, ed. Celia Kerslake, Kerem Öktem, and Phillip Robins, 27–37. Basingstoke: Palgrave Macmillan, 2010.

Bell, John. *Peasants in Power: Alexander Stamboliski and the Bulgarian Agrarian National Union, 1899–1923*. Princeton: Princeton University Press, 1977.

Berkes, Niyazi. *The Development of Secularism in Turkey*. New York: Routledge, 1998.

Bilge, Mustafa. "Mustafa Pasha, Buşatlı." *İslam Ansiklopedisi*, 31/345. Istanbul: Türkiye Diyanet Vakfı, 2006.

Birtek, Faruk and Thalia Dragonas, eds. *Citizenship and the Nation-State in Greece and Turkey*. Abingdon: Routledge, 2005.

Black, Cyril. *The Establishment of Constitutional Government in Bulgaria*. Princeton: Princeton University Press, 1943.

Blinkhorn, Martin and Thanos Veremis, eds. *Modern Greece: Nationalism and Nationality*. Athens: ELIAMEP, 1990.

Bojanić-Lukač, Dušanka and Tatjana Katić, eds. *Maglajski Sidžili 1816–1840*. Sarajevo: Bošnjački Institut Fondacija Adila Zulfikarpašića, 2005.

Börekçi, Mehmet. *Osmanlı İmparatorluğu'nda Sırp Meselesi*. Istanbul: Kutup Yıldızı, 2001.

Bougarel, Xavier. "Trois définitions de l'islam en Bosnie-Herzégovine." *Archives des sciences sociales des religions* 115 (July–September 2001), 183–92.

Brockett, Gavin. "Collective Action and the Turkish Revolution: Towards a Framework for the Social History of the Atatürk Era, 1923–38." *Middle Eastern Studies* 34 (1998), 44–66.

Brown, Daniel. *Rethinking Tradition in Modern Islamic Thought*. Cambridge: Cambridge University Press, 1996.

Brown, L. Carl. *Religion and State: The Muslim Approach to Politics*. New York: Columbia University Press, 2000.

Brown, Nathan. *The Rule of Law in the Arab World: Courts in Egypt and the Gulf*. Cambridge: Cambridge University Press, 1997.

    When Victory Is Not an Option: Islamist Movements in Arab Politics. Ithaca, NY: Cornell University Press, 2012.

Brubaker, Rogers, Margit Feischmidt, Jon Fox, and Liana Grancea. *Nationalist Politics and Everyday Ethnicity in a Transylvanian Town*. Princeton: Princeton University Press, 2006.

Castellan, Georges. *Histoire des Balkans (XIVe–XXe siècle)*. Paris: Fayard, 1991.

Cevdet, Abdullah. *Tezâkir 1–12*. Ankara: Türk Tarih Kurumu, 1986.

Cezar, Yavuz. *Osmanlı Maliyesinde Bunalım ve Değişim Dönemi*. Istanbul: Alan Yayıncılık, 1986.

Cleveland, William. *Islam against the West: Shakib Arslan and the Campaign for Islamic Nationalism*. Austin: University of Texas Press, 1985.

    The Making of an Arab Nationalist: Ottomanism and Arabism in the Life and Thought of Sati' al-Husri. Princeton: Princeton University Press, 1971.

Clewing, Konrad and Oliver Jens Schmitt, eds. *Geschichte Südosteuropas vom Mittelalter bis zur Gegenwart*. Regensburg: Verlag Friedrich Pustet, 2011.

Clogg, Richard. "Aspects of the Movement for Greek Independence." In *The Struggle For Greek Independence: Essays to Mark the 150th Anniversary of the Greek War of Independence*, ed. Richard Clogg, 1–40. Hamden, CT: Archon, 1973.

    A Concise History of Greece (2nd edition). Cambridge: Cambridge University Press, 1992.

    "The Greek Millet in the Ottoman Empire." In *Christians and Jews in the Ottoman Empire: The Functioning of a Plural Society*, 2 vols., ed. Bernard Lewis and Benjamin Braude, i/185–207. New York: Holmes and Meier, 1982.

Cohen, Amnon. "The Army in Palestine in the Eighteenth Century – Sources of Its Weakness and Strength." *Bulletin of the School of Oriental and African Studies, University of London* 34 (1971), 36–55.

Cohen, Lenard. *Serpent in the Bosom: The Rise and Fall of Slobodan Milošević*. Boulder, CO: Westview Press, 2001.

Commins, David. *Islamic Reform: Politics and Social Change in Late Ottoman Syria*. Oxford: Oxford University Press, 1990.

Cordesman, Anthony. *The Gulf and the Search for Strategic Stability: Saudi Arabia, the Military Balance in the Gulf, and Trends in the Arab-Israeli Military Balance*. Boulder, CO: Westview Press, 1984.

Couderc, Anna. "Religion et identité nationale en Grèce pendant la révolution d'indépendence (1821–1832): le creuset ottoman et l'influence occidentale." In *La Perception de l'Héritage Ottoman dans les Balkans*, ed. Sylvie Gangloff, 21–41. Paris: l'Harmattan, 2005.

Darden, Keith and Anna Grzymala-Busse. "The Great Divide: Literacy, Nationalism, and the Communist Collapse." *World Politics* 59 (2006), 83–115.

Daskalov, Roumen. "Modern Bulgarian Society and Culture through the Mirror of Bai Ganio." *Slavic Review* 60 (2001), 530–49.

Davison, Roderic. *Reform in the Ottoman Empire*. Princeton: Princeton University Press, 1963.

Dawn, C. Ernest. "The Formation of Pan-Arab Ideology in the Interwar Years." *International Journal of Middle East Studies* 20 (1988), 67–91.

  "The Origins of Arab Nationalism." In *Origins of Arab Nationalism*, ed. Khalidi, Anderson, Muslih, and Simon, 3–30.

  From Ottomanism to Arabism: Essays on the Origins of Arab Nationalism. Urbana: University of Illinois Press, 1973.

Deringil, Selim. "'The Armenian Question Is Finally Solved': Mass Conversions of Armenians in Anatolia during the Hamidian Massacres of 1895–1897." *Comparative Studies in Society and History* 51 (2009), 344–71.

  "'There Is No Compulsion in Religion': On Conversion and Apostasy in the Late Ottoman Empire, 1839–1856." *Comparative Studies in Society and History* 42 (2000), 547–75.

  The Well-Protected Domains: Ideology and the Legitimation of Power in the Ottoman Empire, 1876–1909. London: I. B. Tauris, 1998.

Devereux, Robert. "Süleyman Pasha's 'The Feeling of the Revolution.'" *Middle Eastern Studies* 15 (1979), 3–35.

Dodd, C. H. "The Development of Turkish Democracy." *British Journal of Middle Eastern Studies* 19 (1992), 16–30.

Doran, Michael. *Pan-Arabism before Nasser: Egyptian Power Politics and the Palestine Question*. Oxford: Oxford University Press, 1999.

Douwes, Dick. *The Ottomans in Syria: A History of Justice and Oppression*. London: I. B. Tauris, 2000.

Dragostinova, Theodora. *Between Two Motherlands: Nationality and Emigration among the Greeks of Bulgaria, 1900–1949*. Ithaca, NY: Cornell University Press, 2011.

Dragović-Soso, Jasna. *"Saviours of the Nation": Serbia's Intellectual Opposition and the Revival of Nationalism*. London: Hurst, 2002.

Duijzings, Ger. "Religion and the Politics of 'Albanianism': Naim Frashëri's Bektashi Writings." In *Albanian Identities*, ed. Schwandner-Sievers and Fischer, 60–9.

Dumont, Paul. "La revolution impossible: Les courants d'opposition en Anatolie 1920–1921." *Cahiers du Monde russe et soviétique* 19 (1978), 143–74.

Eldem, Edhem. "Capitulations and Western Trade." In *Cambridge History of Turkey 3*, ed. Faroqhi, 283–335.

El-Ghobashy, Mona. "The Metamorphosis of the Egyptian Muslim Brothers." *International Journal of Middle East Studies* 37 (2005), 373–95.

Erdem, Hakan. "'Do Not Think of the Greeks as Agricultural Labourers': Ottoman Responses to the Greek War of Independence." In *Citizenship and the Nation-State*, ed. Birtek and Dragonas, 67–84.

"'Perfidious Albanians' and 'Zealous Governors': Ottomans, Albanians, and Turks in the Greek War of Independence.' In *Ottoman Rule in the Balkans, 1760–1850: Conflict, Transformation, Adaptation*, ed. Antonis Anastasopoulos and Elias Kolovos, 213–40. Rethymno: University of Crete, 2007.

"Recruitment for the 'Victorious Soldiers of Muhammad' in the Arab Provinces, 1826–1828." In *Histories of the Modern Middle East: New Directions*, ed. Israel Gershoni, Hakan Erdem, and Ursula Woköck, 189–206. London: Lynne Rienner, 2002.

Eren, Ahmet. *Mahmud II. Zamanında Bosna-Hersek*. Istanbul: Nurgök Matbaası, 1965.

Ergene, Boğaç. "On Ottoman Justice: Interpretations in Conflict (1600–1800)." *Islamic Law and Society* 8 (2001), 52–87.

Ersanlı, Büşra. "The Ottoman Empire in the Historiography of the Kemalist Era: A Theory of Fatal Decline." In *Ottomans and the Balkans*, ed. Adanır and Faroqhi, 115–54.

Esmer, Tolga. "A Culture of Rebellion: Networks of Violence and Competing Discourses of Justice in the Ottoman Empire, 1790–1808." PhD dissertation, University of Chicago, 2009.

Fahmy, Khaled. *All the Pasha's Men: Mehmed Ali, His Army and the Making of Modern Egypt*. Cambridge: Cambridge University Press, 1997.

"Mutiny in Mehmed Ali's New Nizami Army, April–May 1824." In *Mutiny and Rebellion*, ed. Hathaway, 129–38.

Farhi, David. "The Şeriat as a Political Slogan: Or 'the Incident of the 31st Mart.'" *Middle Eastern Studies* 7 (1971), 175–99.

Faroqhi, Suraiya, ed. *The Cambridge History of Turkey, vol. 3: The Later Ottoman Empire, 1603–1839*. Cambridge: Cambridge University Press, 2006.

Feldman, Noah. *The Fall and Rise of the Islamic State*. Princeton: Princeton University Press, 2008.

Findley, Carter. *Bureaucratic Reform in the Ottoman Empire: The Sublime Porte 1789–1922*. Princeton: Princeton University Press, 1980.

"The Tanzimat." In *Cambridge History of Turkey* 4, ed. Kasaba, 11–37.

Turkey, Islam, Nationalism, and Modernity. New Haven, CT: Yale University Press, 2010.

Finkel, Caroline. *Osman's Dream: The Story of the Ottoman Empire 1300–1923*. London: John Murray, 2005.

Firkatian, Mari. *The Forest Traveler: Georgi Stoikov Rakovski and Bulgarian Nationalism*. London: Peter Lang, 1996.

Fischer, Bernd, ed. *Balkan Strongmen: Dictators and Authoritarian Rulers of Southeastern Europe*. London: Hurst, 2007.

Fromkin, David. *A Peace to End All Peace: Creating the Modern Middle East, 1914–1922*. London: Deutsch, 1989.

G. "Textes historiques sur le reveil arabe au Hedjaz." *Revue du Monde Musulman* 46 (1921), 1–22.

Gammer, Moshe. "The Imam and the Pasha: A Note on Shamil and Muhammad Ali." *Middle Eastern Studies* 32 (1996), 336–42.

Gerber, Haim. "'Palestine' and Other Territorial Concepts in the 17th Century." *International Journal of Middle East Studies* 30 (1998), 563–72.

Gerolymatos, Andre. *The Balkan Wars: Myth, Reality, and the Eternal Conflict.* Toronto: Stoddart, 2001.

Gesink, Indira. "'Chaos on the Earth': Subjective Truths versus Communal Unity in Islamic Law and the Rise of Militant Islam." *American Historical Review* 108 (2003), 710–33.

Ghodsee, Kristen. *Muslim Lives in Eastern Europe: Gender, Ethnicity and the Transformation of Islam in Postsocialist Bulgaria.* Princeton: Princeton University Press, 2009.

Gingeras, Ryan. "In the Hunt for the 'Sultans of Smack': Dope, Gangsters and the Construction of the Turkish Deep State." *Middle East Journal* 65 (2011), 426–41.

"Last Rites for a 'Pure Bandit': Clandestine Service, Historiography and the Origins of the Turkish 'Deep State.'" *Past and Present* 206 (February 2010), 151–74.

Sorrowful Shores: Violence, Ethnicity, and the End of the Ottoman Empire, 1912–1923. Oxford: Oxford University Press, 2009.

Ginio, Eyal. "Paving the Way for Ethnic Cleansing: Eastern Thrace during the Balkan Wars (1912–1913) and Their Aftermath." In *Shatterzone of Empires: Coexistence and Violence in the German, Habsburg, Russian, and Ottoman Borderlands,* ed. Omer Bartov and Eric Weitz, 283–97. Bloomington: Indiana University Press, 2013.

Göçek, Fatma. "Ottoman Provincial Transformation in the Distribution of Power: The Tribulations of the Governor of Sivas in 1804." *Scripta Hierolosymitana* 35 (1994), 31–41.

Gordon, Joel. *Nasser's Blessed Movement: Egypt's Free Officers and the July Revolution.* Oxford: Oxford University Press, 1992.

Gould, Andrew. "Lords or Bandits? The Derebeys of Cilicia." *International Journal of Middle East Studies* 7 (1976), 485–506.

Gradeva, Rossitsa. "Osman Pazvantoğlu of Vidin: Between Old and New." In *Ottoman Balkans,* ed. Anscombe, 115–61.

Grandits, Hannes. "Violent Social Disintegration: A Nation-Building Strategy in Late Ottoman Hercegovina." In *Conflicting Loyalties in the Balkans: The Great Powers, the Ottoman Empire and Nation-Building,* ed. Hannes Grandits, Nathalie Clayer, and Robert Pichler, 110–34. London: I. B. Tauris, 2011.

Greene, Molly. "An Islamic Experiment: Ottoman Land Policy on Crete." *Mediterranean Historical Review* 11 (1996), 60–78.

Guilmartin, John. "Ideology and Conflict: The Wars of the Ottoman Empire, 1453–1606." *Journal of Interdisciplinary History* 18 (1988), 721–47.

Haddad, Mahmoud. "Iraq before World War I: A Case of Anti-European Arab Ottomanism." In *Origins of Arab Nationalism,* ed. Khalidi, Anderson, Muslih, and Simon, 120–50.

Halaçoğlu, Yusuf. "Bağdat – Osmanlı Dönemi." *İslam Ansiklopedisi*, 4/435. Istanbul: Türkiye Diyanet Vakfı, 2006.

Hanioğlu, M. Şükrü. "Blueprints for a Future Society: Late Ottoman Materialists on Science, Religion and Art." In *Late Ottoman Society*, ed. Özdalga, 28–116.

A *Brief History of the Late Ottoman Empire*. Princeton: Princeton University Press, 2008.

"The Second Constitutional Period, 1908–1918." In *Cambridge History of Turkey* 4, ed. Kasaba, 62–111.

Hathaway, Jane. "Ottoman Responses to Çerkes Mehmed Bey's Rebellion in Egypt, 1730." In *Mutiny and Rebellion*, ed. Hathaway, 105–13.

Hathaway, Jane, ed. *Mutiny and Rebellion in the Ottoman Empire*. Madison: University of Wisconsin Press, 2002.

Heath, Roy. *The Establishment of the Bulgarian Ministry of Public Instruction and Its Role in the Development of Modern Bulgaria, 1878–1885*. New York: Garland, 1987.

Hering, Gunnar. "Die Osmanenzeit im Selbstverständnis der Völker Südosteuropas." In *Die Staaten Südosteuropas und die Osmanen*, ed. Hans Georg Majer, 355–80. Munich: Südosteuropa-Gesellschaft, 1989.

Herman, Didi. *An Unfortunate Coincidence: Jews, Jewishness, and English Law*. Oxford: Oxford University Press, 2011.

Heyd, Uriel. "The Ottoman 'Ulema and Westernization in the Time of Selim III and Mahmud II." *Scripta Hierosolymitana* 9 (1961), 69–77.

Heywood, Colin and Colin Imber, eds. *Studies in Ottoman History in Honour of Professor V. L. Ménage*. Istanbul: Isis, 1994.

Hickok, Michael. *Ottoman Military Administration in Eighteenth-Century Bosnia*. Leiden: Brill, 1997.

Höpken, Wolfgang. "From Religious Identity to Ethnic Mobilisation: The Turks of Bulgaria before, under and since Communism." In *Muslim Identity and the Balkan State*, ed. Hugh Poulton and Suha Taji-Farouki, 54–81. New York: New York University Press, 1997.

Horowitz, Richard. "International Law and State Transformation in China, Siam, and the Ottoman Empire during the Nineteenth Century." *Journal of World History* 15 (2004), 445–86.

Hourani, Albert. *Arabic Thought in the Liberal Age*. Cambridge: Cambridge University Press, 1983.

A *History of the Arab Peoples*. Cambridge, MA: Belknap Press, 1991.

Hudson, Michael. *Arab Politics: The Search for Legitimacy*. New Haven, CT: Yale University Press, 1977.

Hupchick, Dennis. *The Balkans: From Constantinople to Communism*. New York: Palgrave, 2002.

Hurewitz, J. C., ed. *Diplomacy in the Near and Middle East: A Documentary Record, 1535–1914*. Princeton: Princeton University Press, 1956.

Ibrahim, Saad Eddin. "Anatomy of Egypt's Militant Islamic Groups: Methodological Note and Preliminary Findings." *International Journal of Middle East Studies* 12 (1980), 423–453.

Ikram, Khalid. *The Egyptian Economy, 1952–2000: Performance, Policies, and Issues*. Abingdon: Routledge, 2006.

Imber, Colin. "Ibrahim Peçevi on War: A Note on the 'European Military Revolution.'" In *Frontiers*, ed. Imber, Kiyotaki, and Murphey, ii, 7–22.

Imber, Colin, Keiko Kiyotaki, and Rhoads Murphey, eds. *Frontiers of Ottoman Studies: State, Province and the West*. 2 vols. London: I. B. Tauris, 2005.

İnalcık, Halil. "State, Sovereignty and Law during the Reign of Süleyman." In *Süleyman the Second and His Time*, ed. Halil İnalcık and Cemal Kafadar, 59–92. Istanbul: ISIS Press, 1993.

İnalcık, Halil, Suraiya Faroqhi, Bruce McGowan, and Donald Quataert. *An Economic and Social History of the Ottoman Empire*. Cambridge: Cambridge University Press, 1997.

Ismail, F. "The Making of the Treaty of Bucharest, 1811–1812." *Middle Eastern Studies* 15 (1979), 163–92.

Itzkowitz, Norman and Vamik Volkan. *The Immortal Atatürk: A Psychobiography*. Chicago: University of Chicago Press, 1984.

Itzkowitz, Norman. "Eighteenth Century Ottoman Realities." *Studia Islamica* 16 (1962), 73–94.

Ottoman Empire and Islamic Tradition. Chicago: University of Chicago Press, 1972.

Jelavich, Barbara. *History of the Balkans*. 2 vols. Cambridge: Cambridge University Press, 1983.

Jelavich, Charles. *South Slav Nationalisms: Textbooks and Yugoslav Union before 1914*. Columbus: Ohio State University, 1990.

Kadıoğlu, Ayşe. "The Paradox of Turkish Nationalism and the Construction of Official Identity." *Middle Eastern Studies* 32 (1996), 177–93.

Kaiser, Wolfram. *Christian Democracy and the Origins of European Union*. Cambridge: Cambridge University Press, 2007.

Kaplan, Robert. *Balkan Ghosts: A Journey through History*. New York: Vintage, 1994.

Kara, İsmail. "Turban and Fez: Ulema as Opposition." In *Late Ottoman Society*, ed. Özdalga, 162–200.

Karakasidou, Anastasia. *Fields of Wheat, Hills of Blood: Passages to Nationhood in Greek Macedonia, 1870–1990*. Chicago: University of Chicago Press, 1997.

Karal, Enver Ziya, ed. *Selim III.ün Hatt-ı Humayunları*. Ankara: Türk Tarih Kurumu Basımevi, 1942.

Karaman, K. Kıvanç and Şevket Pamuk. "Ottoman State Finances in European Perspective, 1500–1914." *Journal of Economic History* 70 (2010), 593–629.

Karaömerlioğlu, M. Asım. "The Village Institutes Experience in Turkey." *British Journal of Middle Eastern Studies* 25 (1998), 47–73.

Karpat, Kemal. "Ifta and Kaza: The Ilmiye State and Modernism in Turkey, 1820–1960." In *Frontiers*, ed. Imber, Kiyotaki, and Murphey, i, 25–42.

Karsh, Efraim. *Islamic Imperialism: A History*. New Haven, CT: Yale University Press, 2007.

Kasaba, Reşat, ed. *The Cambridge History of Turkey, vol. 4: Turkey in the Modern World*. Cambridge: Cambridge University Press, 2008.

Kayalı, Hasan. "The Struggle for Independence." In *Cambridge History of Turkey* 4, ed. Kasaba, 112–46.

    Arabs and Young Turks: Ottomanism, Arabism, and Islamism in the Ottoman Empire, 1908–1918. Berkeley: University of California Press, 1997.

Kennan, George. "Introduction." In *The Other Balkan Wars: A 1913 Carnegie Endowment Inquiry in Retrospect.* Washington, DC: Carnegie Endowment for International Peace, 1993, 3–16.

Kerr, Malcolm. *The Arab Cold War: Gamal 'Abd al-Nasir and His Rivals, 1958–1970.* Oxford: Oxford University Press, 1971.

Khalidi, Rashid, Lisa Anderson, Muhammad Muslih, and Reeva Simon, eds. *The Origins of Arab Nationalism.* New York: Columbia University Press, 1991.

Khoury, Dina. *State and Provincial Society in the Ottoman Empire, Mosul 1540–1834.* Cambridge: Cambridge University Press, 1997.

Khoury, Philip. *Syria and the French Mandate: the Politics of Arab Nationalism, 1920–1945.* Princeton: Princeton University Press, 1987.

Kiel, Machiel. *Art and Society in Bulgaria in the Turkish Period.* Assen: van Gorcum, 1985.

Kitromilides, Paschalis. "'Imagined Communities' and the Origins of the National Question in the Balkans." In *Modern Greece*, ed. Blinkhorn and Veremis, 23–66.

    "The Orthodox Church in Modern State Formation in South-East Europe." In *Ottomans into Europeans: State and Institution-Building in South-East Europe*, ed. Alina Mungiu-Pippidi and Wim van Meurs, 31–50. London: Hurst, 2010.

    "Orthodox Culture and Collective Identity in the Ottoman Balkans during the Eighteenth Century." *Oriente Moderno* 18 (1999), 131–45.

Kiyotaki, Keiko. "The Practice of Tax Farming in the Province of Baghdad in the 1830s." In *Frontiers*, ed. Imber, Kiyotaki, and Murphey, i/91–107.

Kojouharov, Anton. "Bulgarian 'Macedonian' Nationalism: A Conceptual Overview." *Online Journal of Peace and Conflict Resolution* 6 (2004) 282–295. http://web.archive.org/web/20090227084311/http://www.trinstitute.org/ojpcr/6_1kojou.pdf.

Koliopoulos, John and Thanos Veremis. *Greece: The Modern Sequel, from 1831 to the Present.* New York: New York University Press, 2002.

Koliopoulos, John. "Brigandage and Irredentism in Nineteenth-Century Greece." In *Modern Greece*, ed. Blinkhorn and Veremis, 67–102.

Konortas, Paraskevas. "Nationalisms vs Millets: Building Collective Identities in Ottoman Thrace." In *Spatial Conceptions of the Nation: Modernizing Geographies in Greece and Turkey*, ed. Nikiforos Diamandouros, Thalia Dragonas, and Çağlar Keyder, 161–80. London: I. B. Tauris, 2010.

Kunt, İ Metin. "The Waqf as an Instrument of Public Policy: Notes on the Köprülü Family Endowments." *Studies in Ottoman History*, ed. Heywood and Imber, 189–98.

Kushner, David. "Ali Ekrem Bey, Governor of Jerusalem, 1906–1908." *International Journal of Middle East Studies* 28 (1996), 349–62.

Landis, Joshua. "Nationalism and the Politics of Za'ama: The Collapse of Republican Syria, 1945–1949." PhD dissertation, Princeton University, 1997.

Levy, Avigdor. *The Jews of the Ottoman Empire*. Princeton: Darwin Press, 1994.

"The Officer Corps in Sultan Mahmud II's New Ottoman Army, 1826–39." *International Journal of Middle East Studies* 2 (1971), 21–39.

Lewis, Bernard. *The Crisis of Islam: Holy War and Unholy Terror*. London: Phoenix, 2004.

The Emergence of Modern Turkey (2nd edition). Oxford: Oxford University Press, 1968.

"Freedom and Justice in the Modern Middle East." *Foreign Affairs* 84/3 (May–June 2005), 36–51.

"Ottoman Observers of Ottoman Decline." *Islamic Studies* 1 (1962), 71–87.

Libson, Gideon. "On the Development of Custom as a Source of Law in Islamic Law." *Islamic Law and Society* 4 (1997), 131–55.

Lockwood, W. B. "Language and the Rise of Nations." *Science and Society* 18 (1954), 245–52.

Lutfi, Ahmed. *Tarih-i Lutfi*. Istanbul: Matbaa-i Amire, 1873.

Makdisi, Ussama. *Artillery of Heaven: American Missionaries and the Failed Conversion of the Middle East*. Ithaca, NY: Cornell University Press, 2008.

Malcolm, Noel. *Bosnia: A Short History*. New York: New York University Press, 1996.

"Myths of Albanian National Identity: Some Key Elements, as Expressed in the Works of Albanian Writers in America in the Early Twentieth Century." In *Albanian Identities*, ed. Schwandner-Sievers and Fischer, 70–87.

Mango, Andrew. "Atatürk." In *Cambridge History of Turkey* 4, ed. Kasaba, 147–72.

Mardin, Şerif. *The Genesis of Young Ottoman Thought: A Study in the Modernization of Turkish Political Ideas*. Syracuse, NY: Syracuse University Press, 2000.

"Ideology and Religion in the Turkish Revolution." *International Journal of Middle East Studies* 2 (1971), 197–211.

Masters, Bruce. *Christians and Jews in the Ottoman Arab World: The Roots of Sectarianism*. Cambridge: Cambridge University Press, 2004.

Masud, Muhammad, Rudolph Peters, and David Powers. "Qadis and Their Courts: An Historical Survey." In *Dispensing Justice*, ed. Masud, Peters, and Powers, 1–44.

Masud, Muhammad, Rudolph Peters, and David Powers, eds. *Dispensing Justice in Islam: Qadis and Their Judgments*. Leiden: Brill, 2006.

Maxwell, Alexander. "Krsté Misirkov's 1903 Call for Macedonian Autocephaly: Religious Nationalism as Instrumental Political Tactic." *Studia Theologica* 5 (2007), 147–76.

Mazower, Mark. *The Balkans: A Short History*. New York: Modern Library, 2000.

Inside Hitler's Greece: The Experience of Occupation, 1941–44. New Haven, CT: Yale University Press, 1993.

"Introduction." In *After the War Was Over*, ed. Mazower, 3–14.

"The Messiah and the Bourgeoisie: Venizelos and Politics in Greece, 1909–1912." *Historical Journal* 35 (1992), 885–904.

Mazower, Mark, ed. *After the War Was Over: Reconstructing the Family, Nation, and State in Greece, 1943–1960*. Princeton: Princeton University Press, 2000.

McCarthy, Justin. *Death and Exile: The Ethnic Cleansing of Ottoman Muslims, 1821–1922*. Princeton: Darwin Press, 1995.

McIntosh, Mary, Martha Abele Mac Ivor, Daniel Abele, and David Nolle. "Minority Rights and Majority Rule: Ethnic Tolerance in Romania and Bulgaria." *Social Forces* 73 (1995), 939–67.

Meeker, Michael. *A Nation of Empire: The Ottoman Legacy of Turkish Modernity*. Berkeley: University of California Press, 2002.

Ménage, Victor. "Some Notes on the 'Devshirme.'" *Bulletin of the School of Oriental and African Studies* 29 (1966), 64–78.

Michas, Takis. *Unholy Alliance: Greece and Milošević's Serbia*. College Station: Texas A&M University Press, 2002.

Millas, Hercules. "History Textbooks in Greece and Turkey." *History Workshop* 31 (1991), 21–33.

———. "Non-Muslim Minorities in the Historiography of Republican Turkey: The Greek Case." In *Ottomans and the Balkans*, ed. Adanır and Faroqhi, 155–92.

Miller, Ruth. *Legislating Authority: Sin and Crime in the Ottoman Empire and Turkey*. New York: Routledge, 2005.

Miller, William. "The Changing Role of the Orthodox Church." *Foreign Affairs* 8 (1930), 274–81.

Millman, Richard. *Britain and the Eastern Question, 1875–1878*. Oxford: Clarendon Press, 1979.

———. "The Bulgarian Massacres Reconsidered." *Slavonic and East European Review* 58 (1980), 218–31.

Mufti, Malik. *Sovereign Creations: Pan-Arabism and Political Order in Syria and Iraq*. Ithaca, NY: Cornell University Press, 1996.

Nagata, Yuzo. *Tarihte Ayanlar: Karaosmanoğulları Üzerinde bir İnceleme*. Ankara: Türk Tarih Kurumu, 1997.

Navaro-Yashin, Yael. *Faces of the State: Secularism and Public Life in Turkey*. Princeton: Princeton University Press, 2002.

Ochsenwald, William. "Ironic Origins: Arab Nationalism in the Hijaz, 1882–1914." In *Origins of Arab Nationalism*, ed. Khalidi, Anderson, Muslih, and Simon, 189–203.

———. *Religion, Society, and the State in Arabia: The Hijaz under Ottoman Control, 1840–1908*. Columbus: Ohio State University Press, 1984.

Ortaylı, İlber. *İmparatorluğun En Uzun Yüzyılı*. Istanbul: Hil Yayın, 1987.

Özcan, Abdülkadir, ed. *Anonim Osmanlı Tarihi*. Ankara: Türk Tarih Kurumu Basımevi, 2000.

———. *Defterdar Sarı Mehmed Paşa: Zübde-i Vekayiat*. Ankara: Türk Tarih Kurumu Basımevi, 1995.

Özdalga, Elisabeth, ed. *Late Ottoman Society: The Intellectual Legacy*. London: Routledge, 2005.

Özkaya, Yücel. *Osmanlı İmparatorluğunda Dağlı İsyanları*. Ankara: Dil ve Tarih Fakültesi Basımevi, 1983.

XVIII. Yüzyılda Osmanlı Kurumları ve Osmanlı Toplum Yaşantısı. Ankara: Kültür ve Turizm Bakanlığı, 1985.

Özkırımlı, Umut and Spyros Sofos. *Tormented by History: Nationalism in Greece and Turkey.* London: Hurst, 2008.

Öztürk, Serdar. "Efforts to Modernize Chapbooks during the Initial Years of the Turkish Republic." *European History Quarterly* 40 (2010), 7–34.

Öztürkmen, Arzu. "Folklore on Trial: Pertev Naili Boratav and the Denationalization of Turkish Folklore." *Journal of Folklore Research* 42 (2005), 185–216.

Palairet, Michael. *The Balkan Economies, c. 1800–1914.* Cambridge: Cambridge University Press, 1997.

Pavlowitch, Stevan. *A History of the Balkans 1804–1945.* London: Longman, 1999.

Paxton, Roger. "Nationalism and Revolution: A Re-Examination of the Origins of the First Serbian Insurrection 1804–1807." *East European Quarterly* 6 (1972), 337–62.

Perica, Vjekoslav. *Balkan Idols: Religion and Nationalism in Yugoslav States.* Oxford: Oxford University Press, 2002.

Peters, Rudolf. *Crime and Punishment in Islamic Law: Theory and Practice from the Sixteenth to the Twenty-First Century.* Cambridge: Cambridge University Press, 2005.

Petmezas, Socrates. "From Privileged Outcasts to Power Players: the 'Romantic' Redefinition of the Hellenic Nation in the Mid-Nineteenth Century." In *The Making of Modern Greece: Nationalism, Romanticism, and the Uses of the Past (1797–1896),* ed. Roderick Beaton and David Ricks, 123–35. Farnham: Ashgate, 2009.

Philliou, Christine. *Biography of an Empire: Practicing Ottoman Governance in the Age of Revolutions.* Berkeley: University of California Press, 2011.

Pinson, Mark, ed. *The Muslims of Bosnia-Herzegovina: Their Historic Development from the Middle Ages to the Dissolution of Yugoslavia.* Cambridge, MA: Harvard University Press, 1993.

Pinto, Vivian. "Bulgarian." In *The Slavic Literary Languages: Formation and Development,* ed. Alexander Schenker and Edward Stankiewicz, 37–51. Columbus, OH: Slavica, 1980.

Pipes, Daniel. *Greater Syria: The History of an Ambition.* Oxford: Oxford University Press, 1990.

Poroy, Ibrahim. "Expansion of Opium Production in Turkey and the State Monopoly of 1828–1839." *The International Journal of Middle East Studies* 13 (1981), 191–211.

Poulton, Hugh. *Top Hat, Grey Wolf and Crescent: Turkish Nationalism and the Turkish Republic.* London: Hurst, 1997.

Who Are the Macedonians? Bloomington: Indiana University Press, 2000.

Quataert, Donald. "Clothing Laws, State and Society in the Ottoman Empire, 1720–1829." *International Journal of Middle East Studies* 29 (1997), 403–25.

"Ottoman History Writing and Changing Attitudes towards the Notion of 'Decline.'" *History Compass* 1 (2003) ME 038, 1–9.

The Ottoman Empire 1700–1922. Cambridge: Cambridge University Press, 2005.

Radić, Radmila. "The Church and the 'Serbian Question.'" In *The Road to War in Serbia: Trauma and Catharsis*, ed. Nebojša Popov, 247–73. Budapest: Central European University Press, 2000.

Reid, Donald. "Political Assassination in Egypt, 1910–1954." *The International Journal of African Historical Studies* 15 (1982), 625–51.

Reynolds, Michael. "Buffers, Not Brethren: Young Turk Military Policy in the First World War and the Myth of Panturanism." *Past and Present* 203 (2009), 137–79.

Shattering Empires: The Clash and Collapse of the Ottoman and Russian Empires, 1908–1918. Cambridge: Cambridge University Press, 2011.

Riedlmayer, András. "Erasing the Past: The Destruction of Libraries and Archives in Bosnia-Herzegovina." *Middle East Studies Association Bulletin* 29 (July 1995), 7–11.

Rodogno, Davide. *Against Massacre: Humanitarian Interventions in the Ottoman Empire 1815–1914*. Princeton: Princeton University Press, 2012.

Rodrigue, Aron. *French Jews, Turkish Jews: The Alliance Israélite Universelle and the Politics of Jewish Schooling in Turkey, 1860–1925*. Bloomington: Indiana University Press, 1990.

Rogan, Eugene. *The Arabs: A History*. London: Allen Lane, 2009.

Römer, Claudia. "On Some Hass-Estates Illegally Claimed by Arslan Paša, Beglerbegi of Buda 1565–1566." In *Studies in Ottoman History*, ed. Heywood and Imber, 297–318.

Rood, Judith. "Mehmed Ali as Mutinous Khedive: The Roots of Rebellion." In *Mutiny and Rebellion*, ed. Hathaway, 115–28.

Rosen, Lawrence. *The Anthropology of Justice*. Cambridge: Cambridge University Press, 1989.

Rosenthal, Steven. "Foreigners and Municipal Reform in Ottoman Istanbul: 1855–1865." *International Journal of Middle East Studies* 11 (1980), 227–45.

Roudometof, Victor. "Invented Traditions, Symbolic Boundaries, and National Identity in Southeastern Europe: Greece and Serbia in Comparative Historical Perspective (1830–1880)." *East European Quarterly* 32 (1998), 429–68.

"The Social Origins of Balkan Politics: Nationalism, Underdevelopment, and the Nation-State in Greece, Serbia, and Bulgaria, 1880–1920." *Mediterranean Quarterly* 11 (2000), 144–63.

Rustum, Asad. "Idara al-Sham: Ruhuha wa Haykaluha wa Atharuha." *Dhikra al-Batal al-Fatih Ibrahim Basha, 1848–1948*. Cairo: Matba'a Dar al-Kutub al-Misriyya, 1948.

Sadat, Deena. "Ayan and Ağa: The Transformation of the Bektashi Corps in the 18th Century." *Muslim World* 63 (1973), 206–19.

"Rumeli Ayanlari: The Eighteenth Century." *Journal of Modern History* 44 (1972), 346–63.

Sahara, Tetsuya. "Two Different Images: Bulgarian and English Sources on the Batak Massacre." In *War and Diplomacy*, ed. Yavuz and Sluglett, 479–510.

Said Pasha, Küçük. *Said Paşa'nın Hatıratı.* 2 vols. Istanbul: Sabah Matbaası, 1328.

Sakaoğlu, Necdet. *Anadolu Derebeyi Ocaklarından Köse Paşa Hanedanı.* Istanbul: Tarih Vakfı Yurt Yayınları, 1998.

Sakkas, John. "The Civil War in Evrytania." In *After the War,* ed. Mazower, 184–209.

Salzmann, Ariel. *Tocqueville in the Ottoman Empire: Rival Paths to the Modern State.* Leiden: Brill, 2004.

Saul, Norman. *Russia and the Mediterranean, 1797–1804.* Chicago: University of Chicago Press, 1970.

Schumann, Christoph. "The 'Failure' of Radical Nationalism and the 'Silence' of Liberal Thought in the Arab World." *Comparative Studies of South Asia, Africa and the Middle East* 28 (2008), 404–15.

Schwandner-Sievers, Stephanie and Bernd Fischer, eds. *Albanian Identities: Myth and History.* Bloomington: Indiana University Press, 2002.

Seale, Patrick. *Asad: The Struggle for the Middle East.* Berkeley: University of California Press, 1988.

The Struggle for Syria: A Study of Post-War Arab Politics, 1945–1958. New Haven, CT: Yale University Press, 1987.

Sells, Michael. "Crosses of Blood: Sacred Space, Religion, and Violence in Bosnia-Hercegovina." *Sociology of Religion* 64 (2003), 309–31.

Şevket, Mahmut. *Sadrazam ve Harbiye Nazırı Mahmut Şevket Paşa'nın Günlüğü.* Istanbul: ARBA, 1988.

Shankland, David. *Islam and Society in Turkey.* Huntingdon, UK: Eothen, 1999.

Shaw, Stanford and Ezer Kural Shaw. *History of the Ottoman Empire and Modern Turkey: The Rise of Modern Turkey, 1808–1975.* Cambridge: Cambridge University Press, 1977.

Shepard, William. "Muhammad Said al-Ashmawy and the Application of Sharia in Egypt." *International Journal of Middle East Studies* 28 (1996), 39–58.

Shields, Sarah. *Fezzes in the River: Identity Politics and European Diplomacy in the Middle East on the Eve of World War II.* Oxford: Oxford University Press, 2011.

Shissler, A. Holly. *Between Two Empires: Ahmet Ağaoğlu and the New Turkey.* London: I. B. Tauris, 2003.

Shpuza, Gazmend. *Kryengritja fshatarësisë së Shqipërisë së Mesme dhe udhëhequr nga Haxhi Qamili.* Tirana: Shtëpia Botuese 8 Nëntori, 1979.

Skiotis, Dennis. "From Bandit to Pasha: First Steps in the Rise to Power of Ali of Tepelen, 1750–1784." *International Journal of Middle East Studies* 2 (1971), 219–44.

"The Greek Revolution: Ali Pasha's Last Gamble." In *Hellenism and the First Greek War of Liberation (1821–1830): Continuity and Change,* ed. Nikiforos Diamandouros, John Anton, John Petropoulos, and Peter Topping, 97–109. Thessaloniki: Institute for Balkan Studies, 1976.

"The Lion and the Phoenix: Ali Pasha and the Greek Revolution." PhD dissertation, Harvard University, 1971.

"Mountain Warriors and the Greek Revolution." In *War, Technology and Society in the Middle East*, ed. V. J. Parry and M. E. Yapp, 308–29. London: Oxford University Press, 1975.

Sluglett, Peter. "The Mandate System: High Ideals, Illiberal Practices." In *Liberal Thought in the Eastern Mediterranean: Late 19th Century until the 1960s*, ed. Christoph Schumann, 29–49. Leiden: Brill, 2008.

Stan, Lavinia and Lucian Turcescu. *Religion and Politics in Post-Communist Romania*. Oxford: Oxford University Press, 2007.

Stavrakakis, Yannis. "Politics and Religion: On the 'Politicization' of Greek Religious Discourse." *Journal of Modern Greek Studies* 21 (2003), 153–81.

Stavrianos, Leften. *The Balkans since 1453*. New York: New York University Press, 2000.

Stewart, Charles. "Who Owns the Rotonda? Church vs. State in Greece." *Anthropology Today* 14/5 (October 1998), 3–9.

Stokes, Gale, John Lampe, Dennison Rusinow, and Julie Mostov. "Instant History: Understanding the Wars of Yugoslav Succession." *Slavic Review* 55 (1996), 136–60.

Stokes, Gale. "The Absence of Nationalism in Serbian Politics before 1840." *Canadian Review of Studies in Nationalism* 4 (1975), 77–90.

Politics as Development: The Emergence of Political Parties in Nineteenth-Century Serbia. Durham, NC: Duke University Press, 1990.

Storrs, Christopher, ed. *The Fiscal-Military State in Eighteenth-Century Europe: Essays in Honour of P. G. M. Dickson*. Farnham, UK: Ashgate, 2009.

Sumner, B. H. *Russia and the Balkans, 1870–1880*. Oxford: Clarendon Press, 1937.

Szyliowicz, Joseph. "Religion, Politics and Democracy in Turkey." In *The Secular and the Sacred: Nation, Religion and Politics*, ed. William Safran, 188–216. London: Frank Cass, 2003.

Tabakoğlu, Ahmet. *Gerileme Dönemine Girerken Osmanlı Maliyesi*. Istanbul: Dergah Yayınları, 1985.

Tachau, Frank. "Language and Politics: Turkish Language Reform." *The Review of Politics* 26 (1964), 191–204.

Tell, Tariq. "Guns, Gold, and Grain: War and Food Supply in the Making of Transjordan." In *War, Institutions, and Social Change in the Middle East*, ed. Steven Heydemann, 33–58. Berkeley: University of California Press, 2000.

Todorova, Maria. *Bones of Contention: The Living Archive of Vasil Levski and the Making of Bulgaria's National Hero*. Budapest: Central European University Press, 2009.

Imagining the Balkans. Oxford: Oxford University Press, 1997.

Tripp, Charles. *A History of Iraq*. Cambridge: Cambridge University Press, 2000.

Trix, Frances. "The Resurfacing of Islam in Albania." *East European Quarterly* 28 (1995), 533–49.

Tzanelli, Rodanthi. "Haunted by the 'Enemy' Within: Brigandage, Vlachian/Albanian 'Greekness,' Turkish 'Contamination,' and Narratives of Greek Nationhood in the Dilessi/Marathon Affair (1870)." *Journal of Modern Greek Studies* 20 (2002), 47–74.

Üngör, Uğur. *The Making of Modern Turkey: Nation and State in Eastern Anatolia, 1913–1950*. Oxford: Oxford University Press, 2011.

Ursinus, Michael. "Die osmanische Balkanprovinzen 1830–1840: Steuerreform als Modernisierungsinstrument." *Südost-Forschungen* 55 (1996), 129–60.

Uzunçarşılı, İsmail. *Meşhur Rumeli Ayanından Tirsinikli İsmail, Yılık Oğlu Suleyman Ağalar ve Alemdar Mustafa Paşa*. Istanbul: Maarif Matbaası, 1942.

Valtchinova, Galia. "Orthodoxie et communisme dans les Balkans: Réflexions sur le cas bulgare." *Archives des sciences sociales des religions* 119 (July 2002), 79–97.

van den Boogert, Maurits. *The Capitulations and the Ottoman Legal System: Qadis, Consuls and Beratlıs in the 18th Century*. Leiden: Brill, 2005.

Velikonja, Mitja. "In Hoc Signo Vinces: Religious Symbolism in the Balkan Wars 1991–1995." *International Journal of Politics, Culture, and Society* 17 (2003), 25–40.

Veremis, Thanos. "From the National State to the Stateless Nation 1821–1910." In *Modern Greece*, ed. Blinkhorn and Veremis, 9–22.

The Military in Greek Politics: From Independence to Democracy. London: C. Hurst, 1997.

Vickers, Miranda and James Pettifer. *Albania: From Anarchy to a Balkan Identity*. New York: New York University Press, 1997.

Wachtel, Andrew. *Making a Nation, Breaking a Nation: Literature and Cultural Politics in Yugoslavia*. Stanford, CA: Stanford University Press, 1998.

Wasti, Syed Tanvir. "Feylosof Riza." *Middle Eastern Studies* 38 (2002), 83–100.

Watenpaugh, Keith. *Being Modern in the Middle East: Revolution, Nationalism, Colonialism and the Arab Middle East*. Princeton: Princeton University Press, 2006.

"'Creating Phantoms': Zaki al-Arsuzi, the Alexandretta Crisis, and the Formation of Modern Arab Nationalism in Syria." *International Journal of Middle East Studies* 28 (1996), 363–89.

Waterbury, John. *The Egypt of Nasser and Sadat: The Political Economy of Two Regimes*. Princeton: Princeton University Press, 1983.

Weismann, Itzchak. "The Politics of Popular Religion: Sufis, Salafis, and Muslim Brothers in Twentieth-Century Hamah." *International Journal of Middle East Studies* 37 (2005), 39–58.

Taste of Modernity: Sufism, Salafiyya, and Arabism in Late Ottoman Damascus. Leiden: Brill, 2001.

Wiktorowicz, Quintan. *The Management of Islamic Activism: Salafis, the Muslim Brotherhood, and State Power in Jordan*. Albany: State University of New York Press, 2001.

Wilson, Mary. "The Hashemites, the Arab Revolt, and Arab Nationalism." In *Origins of Arab Nationalism*, ed. Khalidi, Anderson, Muslih, and Simon, 204–21.

Woods, Kevin, Williamson Murray, Elizabeth Nathan, Laila Sabara, Ana Venegas. *Saddam's Generals: Perspectives of the Iran-Iraq War*. Alexandria: Institute for Defense Analysis, 2011.

Yasamee, Feroze. "European Equilibrium or Asiatic Balance of Power? The Ottoman Search for Security in the Aftermath of the Treaty of Berlin." In *War and Diplomacy*, ed. Yavuz and Sluglett, 56–78.

Yavuz, M. Hakan. *Islamic Political Identity in Turkey*. Oxford: Oxford University Press, 2003.

Yavuz, M. Hakan with Peter Sluglett, eds. *War and Diplomacy: The Russo-Turkish War of 1877–1878 and the Treaty of Berlin*. Salt Lake City: University of Utah Press, 2011

Yergin, Daniel. *The Prize: The Epic Quest for Oil, Money and Power*. New York: Touchstone Books, 1992.

Yılmazer, Ziya, ed. *Vak'a-nüvis Es'ad Efendi Tarihi (Bâhir Efendi'nin Zeyl ve İlaveleriyle) 1237–1241/1821–1826*. Istanbul: Osmanlı Araştırmaları Vakfı, 2000.

Yosmaoğlu, İpek. "Counting Bodies, Shaping Souls: The 1903 Census and National Identity in Ottoman Macedonia." *International Journal of Middle East Studies* 38 (2006), 55–77.

Zilfi, Madeline. *The Politics of Piety: The Ottoman Ulema in the Postclassical Age (1600–1800)*. Minneapolis: Bibliotheca Islamica, 1988.

Zürcher, Erik. "The Ottoman Legacy of the Turkish Republic: An Attempt at a New Periodization." *Die Welt des Islams* 32 (1992), 237–53.

 Turkey: A Modern History. London: I. B. Tauris, 1994.

 The Young Turk Legacy and Nation Building: From the Ottoman Empire to Atatürk's Turkey. London: I. B. Tauris, 2010.

Index